MORALITY, MORTALITY

Volume I

OXFORD ETHICS SERIES
Series Editor: Derek Parfit, All Souls College, Oxford

THE LIMITS OF MORALITY
Shelly Kagan

PERFECTIONISM
Thomas Hurka

INEQUALITY
Larry S. Temkin

MORALITY, MORTALITY, Volume I
Death and Whom to Save from It
F. M. Kamm

MORALITY, MORTALITY

VOLUME I

Death and Whom to Save from It

F. M. Kamm

New York   Oxford
OXFORD UNIVERSITY PRESS
1993

Oxford University Press

Oxford   New York   Toronto
Delhi   Bombay   Calcutta   Madras   Karachi
Kuala Lumpur   Singapore   Hong Kong   Tokyo
Nairobi   Dar es Salaam   Cape Town
Melbourne   Auckland   Madrid

and associated companies in
Berlin   Ibadan

Copyright © 1993 by F. M. Kamm

Published by Oxford University Press, Inc.
200 Madison Avenue, New York, New York 10016

Library of Congress Cataloging-in-Publication Data
Kamm, Frances Myrna.
Morality, Mortality / F.M. Kamm.
p. cm. — (Oxford ethics series)
Contents: v. 1. Death and whom to save from it.
ISBN 0-19-507789-X
1. Terminal care—Moral and ethical aspects. 2. Death.
I. Title. II. Series. R726.K35 1993
174′.24—dc20   92-9496

2 4 6 8 10 9 7 5 3 1

Printed in the United States of America
on acid-free paper

Preface

This book is concerned with death, with certain theoretical issues in the distribution of scarce resources, and with the practical problem of the acquisition and distribution of organs for transplantation. Chapters 1 through 4 on death derive from material written as far back as 1982, and an article "Why Is Death Bad and Worse Than PreNatal Nonexistence," in *Pacific Philosophical Quarterly,* June 1988. On various drafts, I received helpful comments from Thomas Nagel, Derek Parfit, Raziel Abelson, and Lawrence Sager. The appendix on inclines and declines benefited from presentation at the New Jersey Regional Philosophy Association meeting in which I commented on work by Michael Slote. Chapters 5 through 7 developed from an article, "Equal Treatment and Equal Chances," in *Philosophy and Public Affairs,* Spring 1985. I was first prompted to write on the topic by Sharon Slovick and have been the beneficiary of helpful discussions with Thomas Nagel, Derek Parfit, John Taurek, William Wilcox, Lawrence Sager, Louis Kornhauser, and David Wasserman. My views were presented at a New York Philosophy and Public Affairs meeting, at a Central Division meeting of the American Philosophical Association, at Drew University, and at a meeting of the Society for Ethical and Legal Philosophy. The audience discussions were very helpful. The material in chapters 8 to 10 derive from my article "The Choice between People, Commonsense Morality, and Doctors," in *Bioethics,* Summer 1987. On these related topics I received helpful comments from Derek Parfit, Shelly Kagan, Ronald Dworkin, Lawrence Sager, and Louis Kornhauser. I also benefited from comments when the material was presented at the Society for Ethical and Legal Philosophy, the Colloquium on Law, Philosophy, and Social Theory at the New York University Law School in Fall 1989, and the Philosophy Department Colloquia of the University of California (Berkeley) and the University of Chicago in 1991. The material in chapters 11 through 15 is related to my article "The Report of the U.S. Task Force on Organ Transplantation: Criticisms and Alternatives" in *The Mt. Sinai Journal of Medicine,* June 1989. I have received helpful comments from Derek Parfit, Thomas Scanlon, Thomas Nagel, Louis Kornhauser, Drs. Linda Emmanuel and Joel Zinberg, and Seana Shiffrin. I first discussed the issue of organ transplantation at the invitation of Rosamund Rhodes at the Conference on Justice and Medicine, Mt. Sinai Medical School in 1987, and am indebted to many people at Mt. Sinai, including Dr. Dan Moros. I presented on the topic again at an Ethics Luncheon in the series organized by Dr. Arthur Zitrin, New York University School of Medicine, at a Faculty Colloquium, New York University Law School (organized by Prof. Samuel Estreicher), at the Ethics Colloquium Series, Harvard Medical School, at meetings of the Society for Ethical and Legal Philosophy and the New York Society for Philosophy and Public Affairs, at a working group of the Program in Ethics and the Professions at Harvard University, in a DeCamp Lecture in Bioethics at Princeton University, at an Ethics Grand Rounds at Harvard Medical School, at the University of Pittsburgh Medical Center, and at a New York University Medical School Conference on Transplantation. The comments of these audiences were very helpful, as were conversations with Dr. Thomas Starzl and Richard Weil. I thank the editors of the journals in which the articles appeared for permission to reprint sections.

My work on this book has been financially supported by a grant from the American Council of Learned Societies, a New York University Presidential Fellowship and Research Challenge Fund Grant, an American Association of University Women Fellowship, a Silver Fellowship in Law, Science and Technology at Columbia University Law School, a Fellowship in Ethics and the Professions, Harvard University, and a fellowship at the Center for Human Values, Princeton University. Over the years, I have also benefited from the support of Dean Ann Burton at New York University who provided funds for typing and other related services. For all this help I am very grateful.

I am grateful to the typists who went through so many drafts, Nerssa Miller, Marie Palumbo, Helen Snively, and Lynne Gay, to Leigh Cauman for her editorial advice, and to Lynne Gay for help in creating the index. Stephanie Collings helped a great deal with proofreading.

At Oxford University Press my greatest debts are to Angela Blackburn and the editorial and production staff. They have been extraordinarily patient and helpful.

While writing the material in this book, I have received support and encouragement from Mala Kamm, Samuel Kamm, Mara Alexander, Jane Cohen, Norman Daniels, Jeffrey Gorden, and Janet Radcliffe Richards.

Most of the material in this volume developed post-Ph.D. thesis. As such it could never have appeared in this form if Barbara Herman, Joshua Cohen, Baruch Brody, Gerald Dworkin (when at M.I.T.), and various friends at the Columbia University Department of Philosophy had not helped me in completing my Ph.D. thesis at M.I.T. (This is a debt that should have been acknowledged in *Creation and Abortion,* for that book had its origins in that thesis.)

Many of the topics in this book are also very much the product of my years at New York University, its Department of Philosophy, its School of Law, and to some degree, its School of Medicine. NYU and New York have been wonderful places in which to work.

I am especially grateful to Thomas Nagel for his support and the example of his intellect. On this project, in particular, my biggest debt over the years is to Derek Parfit, for encouragement, discussion, and wonderfully detailed comments. (Even he could not, however, save me from my many mistakes, which are my responsibility alone.) This book is dedicated to these two philosophers.

New York, New York   F.M.K.
October 1992

Contents

Contents

III. SCARCE RESOURCES: THEORETICAL ISSUES, SPECIFIC
RECOMMENDATIONS, AND ORGAN TRANSPLANTS

MORALITY, MORTALITY
VOLUME I

Introduction

Topics

Morality, Mortality, as a whole, deals with certain aspects of ethical theory and with moral problems that arise primarily in contexts involving life-and-death decisions. The importance of the theoretical issues is not limited to their relevance to these decisions, however. They are, rather, issues at the heart of basic moral and political theory.

The first volume comprises three parts. We begin with four chapters (and an appendix) discussing death and why it is bad for the person who dies. Part II explores a cluster of problems that arise in giving aid. The general question raised is whether we should always in aiding act so as to save the greater number of lives or to produce the greatest amount of good. The practical problems of organ transplantation are discussed in the third part.

Chapter 1 examines the question of why death is bad; chapter 2 examines this question further but also discusses whether death is worse than prenatal nonexistence (the asymmetry thesis). Chapter 3 offers a final proposal on these two questions. Chapter 4 considers how one should deal with death, given what makes it bad and worse than prenatal nonexistence. An appendix examines the general significance of inclines versus declines in life—a possible factor in making death worse than prenatal nonexistence. (One topic that is not discussed in these chapters, but is discussed in chapter 11, is the scientific criteria for the presence of death [e.g., whole-brain death, higher-brain death, cardiopulmonary collapse, etc.].)

Part II, which is composed of chapters 5 through 10, is concerned with problems in the morality of saving lives. In chapter 5, we consider arguments for the following radical claim: the fact that we could save a greater number of lives is not a reason to save some people rather than others when we cannot save everyone. Against this view, we present an argument which claims to prove that it is worse if more die than if fewer do, but we then counterargue that considerations of justice and fairness might stand in the way of preventing this worse state of affairs, requiring us to give to a group with the greater number of people and to a group with the smaller number equal chances to be saved. This means there would be a conflict between considerations of the Right (e.g., justice, fairness) and considerations of the Good (e.g., maximizing lives saved).

In chapter 6, we try to argue against the existence of this conflict in two ways. The modest way is to show that considerations of the Right do not demand equal chances; the strong way is to show that considerations of the Right require us to count numbers of lives in order to save the greater number and to engage in substitution of lives that are equivalents from a certain perspective. In discussing the modest approach, we consider what makes a policy unfair and the significance of the distinction between direct and indirect need for aid. In chapter 7 we examine two other procedures besides straightforwardly saving the greater number, which, however, still consider the number of people one can save: proportional chances and what I call the Ideal Procedure, which can only be used when there is some chance of saving everyone. Finally we consider the difference which present versus future need may make.

In chapter 8 we examine cases in which the choice we face is not between different numbers of lives but between equal numbers of lives when saving one group but not the other would be accompanied by some additional lesser good. Our aim is to investigate whether and under what conditions substitution of equivalents and aggregation are incorrect and, accordingly, under what conditions additional utilities (goods) should be irrelevant to our choice. We distinguish between direct and indirect need for aid and between extra utility that would come to persons whose lives are at stake, and extra utilities that would come to persons whose lives are not at stake. Furthermore, we distinguish between different types of irrelevance, one type based on different spheres of interest and considerations of fairness, the other on relative insignificance of effect. Five principles for the second type of irrelevance, describing which extra utilities should be irrelevant and why, are examined in Chapters 8, 9, and 10. We deal not only with cases in which each person has a right to have his life preserved, but also with cases in which we merely take an interest in each person's special interest in his own survival. Under the rubric of what I call Sobjectivity we describe in detail how subjective and objective, personal and impersonal, partial and impartial perspectives interrelate when decisions are being made as to which extra utilities to count and which not to count. In these chapters we also reexamine the justification for counting numbers of lives.

In chapter 10 we contrast the permissibility of aggregating certain extra utilities as costs that inhibit the saving of lives with the impermissibility of aggregating these extra utilities as equivalents to and so substitutable for lives. We apply our results on irrelevant utilities to the paradox of group beneficence, and consider further the distinction between extra utility that is distributed over many people whose lives are not at stake and extra utility that is concentrated on the person whose life is at stake. In conclusion, we briefly compare Sobjectivity with contractualist moral reasoning.

Part III, which consists of five chapters, deals with the problem of the acquisition and distribution of organs for transplantation and allows us to apply our theoretical discussion of saving lives and relevant/irrelevant utilities. However, the discussion can be understood independently of the first two parts, and the conceptual issues and procedures on which it focuses are relevant to dealing with any scarce resource, including money and time which are needed to use other plentiful resources. In chapter 11, as an aid to dealing with categories that are of current concern to the medical community, we first summarize the recommendations of the U.S. Task Force on Organ Transplantation on acquisition and distribution of organs and discuss and criticize the total-brain-death criterion for death. We then discuss the role of informed consent of the original organ owner and his family in relation to the State in the task of acquiring organs, as well as the moral possibility of sale, trading, and taking of organs. Finally we consider the morality of more controversial proposals for acquiring organs: "donation" from fetuses, donation from live donors where there is significant risk to the donor, and (the most radical) killing some persons for the sake of acquiring organs for others. In chapter 12 we begin the discussion of distribution by analyzing factors that may be relevant in three situations: true scarcity of resources, temporary scarcity of resources, and uncertainty as to the type of scarcity. First we consider the different concepts of need and urgency and their relation to each other: what makes one person needier than another and why is greater need a factor which should give one person a stronger claim to resources? We present arguments for and against the view that the younger are needier than the older. We offer proposals concerned with a possible diminishing marginal utility of life, fairness, and the relation between helping the worst off and equality. We examine the concept of outcome with an eye to deciding what effects of a transplant and differential effects between potential recipients are morally relevant and irrelevant. The relation between the factors of need and outcome is considered, and several rationales for procedures which give outcome more weight relative to need—moving away from maximin—are considered. In chapter 13 we discuss the relative weight that should be assigned to urgency and outcome when need is constant, but the discussion also bears on the relation of need to outcome. In chapter 14, we consider whether and why, when need and urgency are held constant, greater outcome should be given weight in decisions. Here we examine various theories in more detail, including contractualist moral reasoning. Discussions of how much weight to give to waiting time, the role of ability to pay in distribution decisions, and problems in deriving the government's duty to pay complete the chapter. In chapter 15 we discuss procedures for the distribution of resources, critically examining one proposed procedure and another one actually used at a major transplant center. Finally, a new distribution procedure is described for application in conditions in which resources are scarce, using the particular example of organ transplants.

Methodologies

Some philosophers begin with a theory—composed of prominent concepts, and principles or procedures—whose correctness is either immediately clear to them or has been argued for; in either case, they accept the theory to be logically prior to its application to specific cases. If they are convinced of the theory's correctness, they will accept any implications it might have for particular cases. For example, they may believe that happiness maximized is the most important goal, no matter how it is achieved. Although such philosophers may sometimes feel uncomfortable with the results of their theory, they do not allow their intuitive responses to cases to overrule the theory. (They may, however, expect their theory to give an account of why they have such intuitive responses that diverge from the theory. This is like the scientist who must account for our seeing a stick in water as bent, though it is straight.)

A Second Method

Other philosophers may begin in the same way but are not so firmly committed to their initial theory. Instead, they examine its implications for various cases, and if the implications conflict with their pretheoretical judgments, they sometimes use this conflict as a reason for altering their theory. What is it about such judgments that enables them to sometimes overrule a theory? The same mind that initially accepted a theory as plausible also finds the implications of that theory to be implausible. That is, a pretheoretical response to the moral significance of general principles or ideas was necessary to accept a theory; the same type of response, only more than one, is called forth by cases.[1]

How a Theory May Change

How does a theory change? Consider a theorist who is committed to maximizing happiness. Suppose he is confronted with cases in which there are no actual harms (in the form of diminished utility) but he agrees nevertheless that there is wrongdoing. An example is someone who has been treated paternalistically. His utility may be enhanced but his will has been violated, and this is a wrong. The theorist, despite his theory, may agree that it is right that a person direct his own life, even if his utility is diminished.

Our theorist would here be conceiving of a case involving factors that he may never have thought of before, such as a case that distinguishes wrongs from harms. He then responds to this case in ways that imply that he is rejecting as a standard for evaluating its outcome the maximization of utility or the satisfaction of given desires. He may then shift to another standard for evaluating outcomes, for example, a Kantian one or a novel theory of goods.

No doubt, the theorist already holds some views that allow him to conceive of such new factors and also to respond to them in such a way that he will judge his utilitarian theory to be inadequate. These views which are used to judge the adequacy of his theory may not change. But a rather significantly deep principle—his principle of utility maximization—has been jettisoned or revised.

A Third Method

A third philosophical method (there may be others) begins with responses to cases—either detailed practical cases or hypothetical cases with just enough detail for philosophical purposes—rather than with a total or even a tentative commitment to a theory. This procedure is attractive because it permits recognition of new factors that may be morally relevant in certain cases, factors emphasized by no theory yet developed. Philosophers using this method try to unearth the reasons for particular responses to a case and to construct more general principles from these data. They then evaluate these principles in three ways: Do they fit the intuitive responses? Are their basic concepts coherent and distinct from one another? Are the principles or basic concepts in them morally plausible and significant, or even rationally demanded? The attempt to determine whether the concepts and the principles are morally significant and even required by reason is necessary in order to understand why the principles derived from cases should be endorsed.[2]

Thomas Nagel ("The Fragmentation of Value") says that despite differences over theoretical justifications, there is a wide area of moral agreement about policies and conduct. Nagel leaves it as something of a mystery why this is true. The missing step can be provided if we see the various theorists as beginning (in their theorizing) with "commonsense judgments" about conduct, which they then seek to justify. Non-radical consequentialist theorists, who do not overturn such ordinary judgments about conduct and policy, will find themselves trying to generate from their theories the ordinary judgments that are more deontological than consequentialist. All this is not to say that differences in theories are not important, even when they do not lead to different policies or conduct. For some understandings of why we should do what we may all agree we should do can be right and other understandings can be wrong, first in whether they can, in fact, account for the agreed-upon judgments, and second, in the different self-conceptions with which they provide us.

The Method Used or Presupposed in This Book

The method used or presupposed in this book is closer to the third method than to the first two. We present hypothetical cases for consideration and seek judgments about what may and may not be done in them. The fact that these cases are hypothetical and often fantastic distinguishes this enterprise from straightforward applied ethics, in which the primary aim is to give definite answers to real-life dilemmas. Real-life cases often do not contain the relevant—or solely the relevant—characteristics to help in our search for principles. If our aim is to discover the relative weight of, say, two factors, we should consider cases that involve only these two factors, perhaps artificially, rather than distract ourselves with other factors and options. For example, if we wish to consider the importance of property rights relative to that of saving a life, we should not consider cases in which we have the option to avoid violating a property right in order to save a life.

Some people have difficulty considering cases in which the factors and alternatives are purposely limited and thus are different from those of the real world in which other alternatives are possible. This tendency may simply reflect the fear of having to make hard decisions; therefore, to test this hypothesis, one must find out whether such people are afraid to make decisions in real life cases in which the alternatives are limited. Furthermore, the tendency in itself to introduce other options into a hypothetical case reveals something about a person's judgment concerning the relative weight of the original alternatives. For example, it is possible that it is only because someone believes that it would be wrong to violate a property right in order to save a life that he feels the need to consider ways of saving the life without violating this right.

If cases are very unlike real ones, can we have responses to them? Or do our responses reflect carryover from real-life cases that are similar but also crucially different, with the crucial differences present only in real life being responsible for our responses? I believe we are capable of explicitly excluding certain real-life factors and conceiving of and responding to cases with only the factors we wish to attend to at the time.

Some people may claim that they have no strong, pretheoretical responses to at least some of the cases I present. This does not matter, I think, so long as enough people have definite responses. What are these responses, and why does it not matter if only a few people have them? Often in other discussions they are described in the language of vision: one is supposed to "see" something immediately. The term "intuition" is used, suggesting something mysterious.

The responses to the cases with which I am concerned are not emotional responses but are judgments about the permissibility or impermissibility of certain acts. These judgments are not guaranteed to be correct, and one must give one's reasons for making them. These reasons, in turn, are not personal emotional responses to the acts but are the properties of the acts themselves.

Even though these judgments are not guaranteed to be correct, if they are, they should fall into the realm of a priori truths. They are not like the racist judgments that one race is superior to another. The reason is that the racist is claiming to have "intuitions" about empirical matters and that this is as inappropriate as having intuitions about the number of planets or the chemical structure of water. Intuitions are appropriate to ethics because ours is an a priori, not an empirical, investigation.

Responding definitively to a case does not necessarily mean responding quickly. But the fact that a response takes time to make does not mean that it is being deliberately constructed. Having responses to complex and unfamiliar cases requires that one see a whole complex landscape at once, rather than piecemeal. This often requires deep concentration. Only a few people may be able to respond to a complex case with a firm response. If "Goldilocks" is the fairy tale best associated with Aristotle's doctrine of the mean, then the "Princess and the Pea" is the fairy tale best associated with the method I describe: it tells of someone, despite much interference, who cannot ignore a slight difference that others may never sense. Because even slight differences can make a moral difference, it may be necessary to consider a large variety of cases with only slight differences among them. This approach involves thoroughly working over a small area with the result of greater depth. Sometimes, however, a detail interesting in its own right is omitted for the sake of better exhibiting the final result.

Those who have definite responses are the natural sources of data from which we can isolate the reasons and principles underlying their responses. The idea here is that the responses come from and reveal some underlying psychologically real structure, a structure that was always (unconsciously) part of the thought processes of some people. Such people embody the reasoning and principles (which may be thought of as an internal program) that generate these responses. The point is to make the reasons and principles explicit. Because we do not begin with an awareness of the principles, it is less likely that the responses to cases are the results of a *conscious* application of principles to which one is already committed. In this connection, one advantage of considering somewhat bizarre cases is that our responses to them are less likely to be merely the application of principles we have been taught, and the novelty of the principles we derive from them suggests that our investigation is going beyond the conventional.[3] An alternative model is that certain concepts that people have always worked with (even consciously) commit them—without their having realized it, consciously or unconsciously—to other concepts. The responses to cases reveal that one set of concepts and principles commit us to others, and these other concepts and principles can then be added on to the description of the underlying structure of the responses, but the structure was not always psychologically real.

We are not arguing that such principles are correct simply because they generate responses in some people. Rather, to be plausible, such principles must be related to morally significant ideas. It would be ideal if we could show that the concepts and principles that generate or account for the responses in cases are required by reason. Furthermore, it is not assumed that the role of principles, if they are discovered, is to help us decide cases to which our responses are not clear. It is quite possible for some people to have clear, pretheoretical judgments about every case, without being able to articulate principles. (Indeed, because the principles to be discovered are likely to be correctly formulated only if they are derived from all the types of data, using a principle based on only one type of case in order to decide another type of case may lead to the wrong answer regarding the latter case.) Still the principles may help some who lack certain intuitions.

What would be the purpose of making principles clear and explicit if we did not need them to settle cases about which we are uncertain? Perhaps it is simply to attain a greater understanding of what underlies our responses; perhaps it is to help us organize our moral thinking. Having our principles in hand may also make it easier for us to point out crucial factors in cases to those people who do not share our responses. Furthermore, it is possible to acquire a deeper understanding of our pretheoretical judgments by way of principles or theories that explain them, even though we are less certain of those principles and theories than we are of the judgments themselves. That is, our certainty about our pretheoretical judgments is different from, and not necessarily increased by, a deeper understanding of them.

Finally, we should not expect such principles to be simple or singular. They may be complex, in the attempt to capture results, in many cases, and many of their components may prove to be irreducibly important. We may expect, however, a continuity in content between the factors we point to in certain cases and the components of the most general principles derived from those cases. In moving from cases to principles, one is less likely to find the same discontinuity in content that marks a two-level theory whose principles are essentially utilitarian but that commends deontological responses to cases as a way of maximizing utility in the long view.

NOTES

1. In a recent article, "Causing and Preventing Serious Harm," in *Philosophical Studies* (65 1992:227–255) Peter Unger has argued that our intuitions about cases are more likely to lead us astray and to be inconsistent than our intuitions about fundamental principles. He claims to have shown this by confronting us with cases that involve multiple options rather than just two, and by arguing that we will find it permissible to perform an act when it is one of several options even if we would not find it permissible to perform this act if it were one of two options. This, he thinks, should unsettle our confidence in our intuitions about the

permissibility of acts. After considering Unger's cases, my own sense is, first, that my intuitions about the permissibility of an act do not alter in the varying contexts he presents and, second, that if others' responses do change as he claims, this may be through too great self-concern, e.g., if they will already perform an act judged permissible which causes harm, they may incorrectly be tempted to simply do any act that reduces the harm they produce.

2. For more discussion of ways of relating ethical theories and judgments of cases, see my "Ethics, Applied Ethics, and Applying Applied Ethics," in D. Rosenthal and F. Shehade (eds.), *Applied Ethics and Ethical Theory,* pp. 162–187 (Salt Lake City: University of Utah Press).

3. Derek Parfit emphasized this point.

I

DEATH: FROM BAD TO WORSE

1

Why Is Death Bad?

At death, you break up; the bits that were you
Start speeding away from each other forever
With no one to see. It's only oblivion, true:
We had it before, but then it was going to end,
And was all the time merging with a unique endeavor
To bring to bloom the million-petalled flower
Of being here. Next time you can't pretend
There'll be anything else.

Philip Larkin

This chapter is concerned with the question, Is death *bad* for the person who dies, and, if so, why?[1] (What our scientific criteria should be for the occurrence of death is a different question, dealt with later.)

The Badness of Death

Many people think that death is bad because it is associated with a painful process of dying, because it suggests the possibility of a bad afterlife,[2] because it may come too early, or because it deprives those who live on of people they care for. Some people say they mind their own death because things will go on without them; if all other people died also, death would not be so bad.

Let us set aside these issues, however. Let us assume that death is painless, not "untimely," and involves no afterlife or return to life, only posthumous nonexistence.[3] Let us also assume that we are concerned with why death is bad for the person who dies rather than with why it is bad for people who remain alive after his death and that, even if everyone died at once, something worse has happened to each person than would have happened if he and *everyone else* had lived instead.[4]

Epicurus's Question

Epicurus asked, How can death be bad for someone at all?[5] Epicurus's skeptical query reflects a view that has two slightly different components. First, something is bad for someone if and only if it involves a bad *experience* for him; but, if we are not present when death is (because death involves our nonexistence), it cannot

13

involve a bad experience for us. Second, for something to be bad for someone, there must be someone for whom this is bad; but if we do not exist once we are dead, there will not be anyone for whom this is bad.

Nagel's Answer

Thomas Nagel answers Epicurus's question by saying that death is bad for the person who dies because it causes him to have had fewer of the goods of life than he might otherwise have had.[6] (These goods may include simply being an experiencing subject.) We do not look for a bad experience that someone has either in being dead or in the approach of death. Rather we locate the evil of death in the comparison between the life the person actually has if he dies now and the life he would have had if he had lived longer. Once someone comes into existence we begin something like an accounting of how many goods his entry contains. As a result of his death he may have fewer such goods than he would otherwise have had. For the same reason, being in a coma is bad even if it involves no bad experiences. Since (we shall assume) it involves no consciousness or sensation,[7] it is another way, *not* involving nonexistence, of losing out on all the goods of life. We can refer to Nagel's view as the *Deprivation Account*.

On Nagel's view, therefore, death need not be an experienced event in order to deprive us of the goods of life and so be bad. We need not even be present (as the person in a coma is) to suffer the evil of death. It is *worse for us* to die than to get more goods of life, even if we will not *be in a worse state* than life when we die.

In fact there are two comparisons being made in Nagel's argument: The first is between the actual and possible lengths of life, one being better than the other. The other is between a period after the person dies, which involves nonexistence, and the possible period of additional goods of life that might have been substituted for it. A period of goods is better than a period of nothing in itself and insofar as it contributes to the total good a person accumulates in his life. (The first comparison depends on the second.)

On Nagel's type of account, the nothingness of death is bad not because it is an intrinsic evil, bad in itself, like pain, but because it is a comparative evil: it prevents the existence of greater good. Given their views on death, Epicureans are committed to rejecting this point. This seems to suggest that they cannot accept the further view that there are comparative evils *within life*. That is, they cannot agree that a pleasurable experience, good in itself, may become a comparative evil if it stands in the way of even greater pleasures. Of course, in such comparisons the experiencing person continues to exist, though he is having less pleasure than he might have had, whereas, in death there is no longer a person; but it is Nagel's point to deny that this really makes a difference to the comparative judgment on which the claim that death is bad depends.

Sometimes death may be good or indifferent if it ends a bad enough or indifferent enough life (or, more precisely, if its alternative would be a bad or indifferent stretch of life to come). But then in such cases the things that have made or will make the life bad (pain, for example) or indifferent (being in a coma, for example) can be seen as themselves bad, either intrinsically (like pain) or only comparatively (like coma). They prevent more goods of life. (The coma is in itself indifferent, and may be comparatively good if the alternative is pain.)[8] Therefore, a death that comes either after a "natural life span" or when everyone else also dies may not be even comparatively bad because the natural decline of faculties that is to come or the absence of other people has already ruined prospects for the goods of life. The important point is that it is always, in itself, a bad thing for a person to lose out on more good life, whether through death or otherwise. (It may, of course, be instrumentally good that one lose out on goods.)

One important factor that distinguishes death from lived states that contain no goods (like coma) is that death is (by definition) permanent, whereas a lived state may end. It is because killing someone who is living in an indifferent lived state might prevent recovery that killing someone in a coma differs morally from unplugging a brain-dead person from a life-support machine.

The fact that death can be bad need not, of course, mean that it is appropriate to spend much time worrying about it. (The same is true of pain.)

Criticisms: The Impossibility of Comparisons?

Nagel's type of account contains a good deal of truth but also seems to fail in several important ways. One criticism that has been made of it,[9] however, also fails. It has been argued that death's depriving someone of goods of life can be bad for the person only if he *is* then worse off than he would otherwise have been; but if he is dead (and, therefore, *is not*), this comparison cannot be made. Being able to say that he could have been better off if he had not died is said to depend on being able to say that he could have been better off than he *is* when dead, and this cannot be done.

This criticism is incorrect because some things, like death, can be bad for us without making us be in a worse state than we would have been in. It is simply worse for someone to have a short rather than a long life (assuming adequate content of the life). One could also say that his life did not go as well as it might have gone. One could say that nothing is not as good as something good, and if the person in question had not died and had nothing further added to his life, he could have had something good added to it. We say these things on the basis of comparing something in the past, that is, the life someone actually led, ending when it did, with the life he might have led had he lived on.

Suppose this is an explanation of the claim that someone would have been better off living longer than dying when he did. This helps explain why we often benefit someone in saving his life even if he suffers some pain as a result of this. This is also a comparative statement. If it were not bad for someone to lose out on further goods of life—even if he is not then in a worse state than he could have been in—then it would not be worth suffering even a small amount of pain for the sake of remaining alive. An explanation of the claim that it would have been better to live on than die also helps explain why it is better for someone to die than to live on in misery. This is another comparative statement. Thus life can sometimes be worse for a person than the alternative of nonexistence, even though nonexistence is not a better state of being. These views make sense if we compare the life the person would have if he lived (including the state of misery) with the life he would have had if his life had ended before the misery began.[10]

Criticisms: Unexperienced Harms

Nagel's view on why death is bad is intimately connected with the *general* thesis that someone can be harmed without experiencing anything bad. This thesis is certainly relevant to a Nagel-inspired attack on Epicurus since what makes death bad in Nagel's view is not something we experience. (One might say rather that it is what we *do not* experience—more goods—that makes death bad.) This general thesis seems to be true; yet there are important reservations we should have about it.

The Solace of the Unexperienced

First, Nagel fails to appreciate the peculiar solace—occasionally enough to make us heroic rather than cowardly—afforded by the prospect of death, in contrast with the prospect of some experienced misfortune. So, for some loss *x,* which is less than death, the fact that consciousness of *x* is sure to accompany it may make death preferable. That is, we may prefer to suffer a *greater loss* (that death involves) that is *easier to bear* than a smaller loss that is more difficult to bear (because experienced). There is then a deviant sense in which death is "unbearable": it is not something we must bear.

In general, it may be that the intrinsic evils (such as pain) are harder to bear than nonintrinsic, comparative evils (such as not having more goods of life), even though the former constitute lesser losses than the latter.[11] (This also suggests that one cannot decide whether it is irrational not to do something merely by seeing whether the losses involved are smaller than the eventual benefits. A painful procedure may be too much to bear even for a very great eventual gain. The fact that it is not irrational to refuse the lesser pain for the greater benefit does not mean it would be irrational to do so.)[12]

Benefits of Experience and Action

Second, Nagel's focusing on the thesis that someone can be harmed without experiencing anything bad, especially by employing certain particular examples to support it, makes it hard to see which deprivations in particular make death so bad. Consider, for example, a particular case that Nagel employs in which one's reputation is ruined by false beliefs had by others after one's death. Nagel argues (correctly I think) that one is harmed by this, even if one never finds out about it, never experientially suffers the consequences of it, and does not even exist when it occurs. (Some may find this case unconvincing because they believe that it is unimportant what others think of us. Nagel's point can be made in other ways. For example, if I destroy all of Rembrandt's paintings after his death, I harm him. I should refrain from doing this for *his* sake.)

Some might be tempted to claim, contrariwise, that such things are bad only because discovery of them would be bad (because painful), and hence, one cannot be harmed if one never finds out. This claim makes two errors. First, it neglects the fact that finding out would be painful only because it would be discovery of something that is bad independent of discovery. (Nagel makes this point.) Second, it neglects the possibility that finding out might actually be an improvement, if one views knowledge of what is done to one as a good in itself.[13] For example, finding out that one has been cheated means that at least one has not been made a fool of totally.

However, using the case of posthumous false beliefs to support the claim that death too is an unexperienced harm has several problems. First, it fails to highlight the particular sort of goods whose elimination by death primarily makes death bad for us. That is, the good that corresponds to the evil of a ruined reputation after death is that the reputation is not ruined after death. The obtaining of this good, however, is totally consistent with our experience remaining exactly as it would have been if the harm had occurred; we will never experience the difference. This benefit to us of not having been harmed by false beliefs after our death is an *unexperienced good*. However, this is not the sort of benefit whose loss arouses our main concern with death.[14] What makes us most concerned about death is that it deprives us of the *goods of experience and action*.

Posthumous nonexistence is among the unexperienced harms whose correction usually involves experienced goods.[15] It may be that a life whose only goods are unexperienced and nonactive ones (for example, the good of being a source of stimulation to others) is worth living. But, presumably, if we are concerned with the person whose life it is, we would wish for him different sorts of goods as well, goods that do not make him only a means to the good lives of others. Indeed, an idea that Nagel emphasizes elsewhere[16]—what it is like to be someone from the inside—is relevant here. Goods of experience at least are known from the inside, even if *their* total value is often not given by the inside component alone, but requires something else to be going on. (Robert Nozick's example of the Experience Machine[17] illustrates this point: We can be harmed if our inner life has all the qualities of someone who is being loved, or someone who is proving a theory, but in fact, we are not really being loved or proving a theory. The "feel" is there, but not the reality of anything beyond the feel.) The goods of activity, though usually experienced, need not be experienced in order to be goods; that is, we might really do something without being aware of it.

Hedonism

In attacking the view that all goods and evils are experienced by the person whose goods and evils they are we are attacking a basis for hedonism. But the claim that death is bad is consistent with a hedonistic theory of the goods of life. Limiting the goods of experience to happiness, a hedonist can simply say that death is bad because it deprives us of more happy experiences. Suppose one rejects the view that happiness alone counts and accepts the view that experiences besides happiness are goods as well. Or suppose one believes that experience is only part of every good, i.e. there must be real achievement for there to be a good, but no achievement can be a good without experience of it. One can still accept the view that all goods are experienced goods and that the only unexperienced evil is the prevention of more experienced goods. It will follow that death is bad because it prevents more experienced goods. A theory of value focusing on experienced goods is, in many ways, more in line with the major concern most of us have about the deprivations of death than is the theory of unexperienced goods. (It does, however, leave out goods of activity, possibly unexperienced. It will also fail to deal with the problems raised by Nozick's Experience Machine, unless it is the variant that claims that experiencing is a necessary though not a sufficient condition for all goods.)

Nonexperienced, Nonactive Benefits

There is a particular irony in Nagel's use of the posthumous-false-belief case, given his theory of why death is bad: If someone can be harmed by a ruined reputation after death, he can also be benefited by promotion of his reputation after death. If he can be benefited after his death, then death does not deprive him of all future benefits. If this benefit he can receive after death is one he could have received in life, then death does not deprive him of all the goods of life. We might, therefore, for all we know, receive more benefits and goods of life posthumously than while alive. This considerably weakens Nagel's claim that death is bad because it deprives us of the goods of life. It is a problem we avoid if we focus on the goods of activity and experience that death prevents.[18]

What needs to be emphasized within the scope of a view like Nagel's, therefore, is that death is bad primarily because it deprives us of more of the goods of experience and action. Death is bad, though not experienced, and life is good *because* experienced and acted in. It is goods such as these that I should be taken to be referring to in the following pages when I discuss the goods of which death deprives us.

Focusing on these goods may, furthermore, make it easier for some to accept the thesis that death is bad for the person who dies. Some who think that one cannot in fact be harmed by such things as posthumous rumors may believe this because they think one cannot be benefited by their opposites, of which one has no experience. However, they may accept the view that death is bad, though not experienced, if the alternative to it is experienced goods or action. So one can accept a much more limited view of unexperienced *evils* than Nagel thinks is necessary (as well as a more limited view of what can be goods) and still hold the view that death is bad.

SUMMARY

That death is bad for the person who dies has been explained so far by its involving curtailment of the experiential and active goods of life, where such goods can include simply being a conscious self. The point has also been made that some of those goods of life whose loss makes death so bad can be lost without death, making life without them no better than death. Consciousness (including sensation) seems a prime candidate for a good for whose loss death is not necessary and whose permanent loss is as bad as death. In discussing why death is bad and, in what follows, whether it is worse than prenatal nonexistence, I do not exclude the possibility that no consciousness and no activity, which death and prenatal nonexistence share but which may also be present *in* life, are what make death bad. The person's nonexistence that death causes can be taken as the sufficient, but perhaps not necessary, condition for these other factors of no consciousness and no activity.

Criticisms: Being All Over versus Not Having More Goods

The points presented so far still represent only revisions of Nagel's basic thesis. A third criticism would, if correct, more substantially revise that thesis. Nagel's view implies that the nothingness of death derives its badness from the goodness of what it prevents. But perhaps the nothingness of death has, as the existentialists emphasize, its own negative value for us, simply as nothingness.

If this were so, staying alive could be good not because it involves things that are intrinsically good (and by comparison with which nothingness is bad), but because it compares favorably with the intrinsic (noncomparative), albeit nonexperiential, badness of the nothingness of death. People may want to stay alive only because the alternative is posthumous nothingness. It may be that something—even without any intrinsically positive features—is preferable to post-something nothingness, and yet, if something has intrinsically negative features (such as torture), these can override the negative of nothingness.[19]

I believe a basic criticism of the Deprivation Account of why death is bad lies buried in the "nothingness" thesis, insofar as it implies that death is bad because it means everything for oneself is *all over*. Since we could prefer to postpone things being all over, even if this did not increase the total amount of goods we had in our life, we must be trying to avoid something about death other than that it diminishes the amount of goods of life we have. That is, Nagel's view is tied to a quantitative notion—death's interference with there being *more* goods. However, the condition that things not be all over for us is not necessarily connected with our having *more* goods than we would otherwise have if we died. For example, someone might prefer putting off a fixed quantity of goods of life by going into a coma and returning to consciousness at a later point to have them. Such a person (call him the *Limbo Man*) would be concerned with his not being all over, in a way that was independent of wanting *more* goods of life. (He would also not be concerned with any subjective experience of living longer since he would feel the same whether he went into coma for one year or twenty thousand years. Whenever he wakes up, it will seem to him that he woke up just as soon.) Furthermore, an extreme version of his attitude could help explain the "nothingness" proponent's claim that life is good only relative to the badness of nothingness: this person could care little for the goods of life per se and could see living as a means of avoiding his being "all over." As evidence for this, he would not object to living completely in an unconscious state, so long as this was a coma from which it would be possible for him to return to life. I shall discuss the Limbo Man in detail below (pp. 49–54).

Criticism: Never Having Existed

It seems that the idea of never having existed is not so terrifying as the idea of death. If this is true, it might seem to be the basis for a fourth type of criticism of Nagel's thesis: From the point of view of having goods of life, never existing is surely worse than dying. *If* death is bad *because* it prevents *more* goods of life, wanting to avoid it could be *no* reason at all for giving up *all* the goods of life by not existing. So how can the badness of death be fully captured by the idea that it reduces the quantity of the goods of life, if I do not care more about what reduces the quantity even further (i.e., my never having existed) than about death?

A way out of this seeming difficulty is to emphasize that the loss of more goods of life must be some *subject's* loss, and total nonexistence would mean that there had been no subject. Therefore, we would not have a negative attitude to it, even though it *is* the loss of goods to a subject due to death that we worry about. We can consider it a loss to someone that he never have existed only by, at one and the same time, imagining him to have existed as a subject and not to have existed as a subject. (A less successful way out of this criticism is to emphasize that we are concerned only about what can still happen, and once we exist, total nonexistence cannot happen to us. But this characteristic of our concerns does not mean the loss of total nonexistence is not greater and worse in itself. We might just not be as concerned with this worse event.)[20]

Criticism: The Morality of Killing

A fifth criticism of a Nagel-type answer to why death is bad turns on the morality of killing. It begins by noting that Nagel's answer would present difficulties *if* we wanted to defend the view that killing someone is equally wrong whether the victim would otherwise have had many or few goods of life—at least *if* wrongness depends on how bad an outcome we produce. (Nagel himself would not agree that wrongness depends in this way on badness.) That is, if death is bad because we lose goods of life, it is worse the more goods we lose. If killing is wrong because it produces a death that is bad, it would be more wrong the more goods it deprives someone of. It would be a greater wrong to deprive someone of more goods. (Nagel might respond that *everyone* feels that he loses out on an infinite future. Realistically, though, one couldn't have more than a hundred years of life and so some lose more than others in being killed. Should not the realistic prospects determine how bad death itself is and, if wrongness depends on badness, how wrong killing is?)

If wrongness depended on badness, Nagel's view might also raise problems if we wanted to distinguish between the wrongness of two acts that cause equal loss of the goods of life. Suppose, for example, we put someone into a coma for one year, and after that year, the person awakens for more of a normal life. Our offense would not be considered as serious as killing someone. But suppose that someone else, if not interfered with, would have only one more year of life and then die of natural causes. If we kill him (given no legitimate excuse or justification), we will be treated very harshly by the criminal system. Yet we will have deprived the person of only one year of the goods of life, as in the coma case.

In the killing case, we have taken from the person "everything he would have had." In the coma case we have not since the person returns to conscious life. Is this redescription of what we have done in each case a factor of crucial moral significance, so that it distinguishes the killing from inducing a one-year coma? Suppose we put someone into a coma, knowing that he will never recover from it, though the cause of his dying while in the coma is not related to our coma-inducing act or to the coma itself. We would then have taken from the person everything of significance he would have had, though this is so only because something else (the cause of death) has determined how much there is to take. In such a case, we would not, I believe, be treated as harshly as if we had killed someone. However, if *our act* were the cause of death, we would be charged with the more serious offense of killing. Furthermore, this may be so even if, in taking everything from the person that he would have had, we took essentially nothing since he would have died anyway very soon after.

The point of these objections is that it is *not* only because we think life could be good that we think killing a person is wrong. The fact that one person determines the nonexistence of another against his will, even in his own interest (as in involuntary euthanasia), is a factor in making killing wrong. Some would even say that a person's determining his own nonexistence is wrong. We could accept Nagel's view of the badness of death, consistent with all this, if we just hold that what makes killing wrong is to some degree independent of what makes death bad. Wrongness is not derivable from badness of outcome.

Perhaps, however, wrongs *should* be categorized strictly according to how much harm is done. On this measure, killing someone who would die *very* shortly anyway should not be as serious an offense as killing someone who would have lived a long life. A different account than Nagel's of why death is bad might make it possible to account for the wrongness of killing (even when someone kills himself) *without* conceding that killing is wrong in accord with the harm it does. Nagel's account emphasizes that the person loses future goods that do not yet exist. But a commitment to the equal wrongness of killings that cause many or few goods to be lost may lead us to emphasize instead *what already exists, the person,* independent of what he will come to have if not killed. Then anything, whether occurring naturally or by human intervention, that stops the process maintaining the person already present might be bad. Here what is bad is not that no more goods occur, but interfering with the life process of a certain type of being. Like attacking a beautiful work of art that would disintegrate soon anyway, or acting disrespectfully to someone who will be a high official for only a moment longer, it may be offensive for people or even for nature to stand in the relation of causing death to a person. This sort of badness of death, however, seems different from how bad death is for the person who exists.

SUMMARY

The following criticisms of Nagel's Deprivation Account which have been suggested so far seem significant: His view results in overemphasizing the significance of unexperienced goods; it ignores the possibility that nothingness in itself is bad, insofar as this means that things being all over is bad; it does not consider that our attitudes toward death are connected to the significance of the destruction of a certain type of entity or interference with a certain process, per se, rather than with the loss of more goods. We shall consider additional objections in the next chapter.

NOTES

1. This and the following three chapters deal with philosophical issues about why death is bad. For those interested in a philosophical discussion of what our scientific criterion of death should be, see Chapter 11.

2. It is incorrect to say that it is fear of the unknown per se that is involved in fear of death; it is rather fear that the unknown will be bad.

3. Accepting that people are finite does not imply they should live as though they are. That is, it might be recommended that people live as close to the life they would have lived if they were immortal. This is primarily because some think that the projects and ideals of immortal beings must be more significant ultimately than those projects and ideals that cater to a flawed (mortal) form of life. So, for example, it is better on this view to engage in work requiring for its completion more than a single life span. One can do this without wasting one's time because there are other human beings and future generations who will take up where a single person leaves off. A life lived in this way may, however, not have in it certain distinctively human projects.

4. If everyone else's dying made one's own death less bad, it would still make the world much worse and should not be wished for. That others *have* died (especially loved ones) may, however, make it easier in another sense for us to die: If they had to go through it, why shouldn't we?

5. In the "Letter to Menoeceus" in *Letters, Principal Doctrines and Vatican Sayings,* G. Russell, trans. (New York: Macmillan, 1964).

6. In "Death," reprinted in *Mortal Questions* (Cambridge: Cambridge University Press, 1979). This is the answer he emphasizes. He suggests others, reduction and the *prospect* of future permanent nothingness, but does not develop these notions fully.

7. If this is in fact not true, imagine a lived state, coma*, of which it is true.

8. Could we conclude that one would be better off dead than living a life of pain if we agreed that it would be better to be unconscious than to experience any given moment of pain, and that continuing unconsciousness would be equal in value to death? The conclusion would not follow from the premises. For it might be that one would rather be dead than live through many moments of pain, but one would still prefer to live even if all one's conscious experiences were painful. That is, *continuous* pain may simply be unbearable, but pain interrupted by unconsciousness, which allows one to recuperate (albeit unconsciously) and is followed by more pain, may instead be *bearable*. This could be so even though the consciousness of pain would not seem discontinuous to us. If it were *bearable,* then we might prefer to remain alive even though there was no content to life but pain, simply in order to continue to be experiencing, conscious subjects. This would show that Nagel is correct when he claims that simply experiencing is a good. (A weaker claim could also be argued for: that simply experiencing is a good that adds to good contents of experience, but is *overridden* by bad contents. Then even if we rejected a life of interrupted consciousness that was only consciousness of pain, this rejection would not show that experiencing in itself was not a good.)

9. H. Silverstein, "The Evil of Death," in *The Journal of Philosophy* 77 (1980):401–423.

10. It is possible that, at any given time, someone would be worse off if he were alive

than if he were nonexistent, even though staying alive would make his life better overall in comparison with a shorter life, because of later events. We here need an idea of how temporary nonexistence could be comparatively beneficial. Here the miserable part of the longer life is an intrinsic evil, but also an instrumental good since it leads to later goods.

11. The fact that intrinsic and more comparative evils fall into the more-and-less-diffi-cult-to-bear categories was suggested to me by Derek Parfit.

12. This conclusion may have application to a case like that of the Texas Burn Victim. This person claims that a painful lifesaving procedure was not warranted for the sake of the disfigured and handicapped life he has now, though he agrees that his life is worth living. This may just be the claim that the costs were greater than the benefit. But it might also imply that some experiences are so hard to bear that even a benefit agreed to be greater than the cost cannot justify others in requiring one to go through that experience. Here the judgment is made by considering the perspective of someone in the midst of living life, with pain and benefit both in the future.

13. I owe this point to Eric Wefald.

14. Sometimes, of course, we may be concerned about death because it will prevent unexperienced goods. For example, someone might be concerned that if he dies early he will not do anything in life that will make future generations admire him. The admiration is an unexperienced good.

15. Someone having less of an experienced intellectual insight than he might have had, without his knowing his loss, is also having an unexperienced harm whose correction is experienced.

16. See his "What It Is Like to Be a Bat," in *Mortal Questions,* pp. 165–180.

17. *Anarchy, State and Utopia* (New York: Basic Books, 1974).

18. We also need not agree with all the particular examples of unexperienced evils that Nagel presents. For instance, to illustrate the fact that something bad is happening to a person if he wastes his life, even if he experiences great pleasure in doing what wastes his life, Nagel presents the case of a man who searches for a method of communicating with asparagus plants. But, we may counterargue, although this man's life may not be a good one *because* of the pleasure he has, it may also not be an example of a wasted life. The aim of the project, or the world view that motivates it, may rescue it from that fate. Indeed it is interesting to see that the nature writer Annie Dillard describes a case very similar to Nagel's and believes it involves a very worthwhile life. In her essay "Teaching a Stone to Talk," in *Teaching a Stone to Talk* (New York: Harper & Row, 1982, pp. 67–76), she describes a "man in his thirties who lives alone with a stone he is trying to teach to talk. Wisecracks on this topic abound . . . but they are made as it were perfunctorily, and mostly by the young. For in fact, almost everyone here respects what Larry is doing, as do I." (On the other hand, among the wisecracking dissents to Dillard's line of thought is Garrison Keillor's: "Stones and trees speak slowly and may take a week to get out a single sentence, and there are few men, unfortunately, with the patience to wait for an oak to finish a thought," from "The Lowliest Bush a Purple Sage Would Be," in *Happy to Be Here* (New York: Penguin Books, 1983, pp. 224–227.) This example also reminds us that success should not be necessary to make a life worthwhile. That is, if one spends one's life on a project and turns out to have been wrong in one's conclusions, this may diminish the value of one's life but not make one's efforts worthless. The problem is to distinguish why many think the man who spends his life trying to teach a stone to talk has wasted his life, but do not think the scientist who develops the wrong theory has. Presumably, the distinction has something to do with its having been reasonable for the scientist, at the time he worked, to think the theory was true, and his work's really having played a part in our coming to know the true theory. The stone-teacher's project lacks these characteristics. A second problem is present in a case Nagel uses to

illustrate comparative evils: In discussing a person who declines from adult to infant mentality, he argues that the baby-like state the adult is in is not in itself bad since we do not feel sorry for any actual babies who occupy it. Rather, it is the relation of his infantile state to the adult state he once was in and would otherwise have been in that makes us think a misfortune has befallen him. My analysis of this case is somewhat different. First, I agree that the infantile state that follows adulthood *is* worse than the continuation of adulthood. But, if this is so, then infancy lasting as long as it *naturally* does in real babies may also be worse than adulthood beginning earlier. The fact that we don't feel sorry for babies may only reflect our acceptance of the inevitable course of species development. It may also reflect the fact that real infancy, unlike the adult's incapacity, will end, and the fact there is no *decline* to the infantile. If science ever makes it possible to bypass infancy, we may feel sorry for those who go through it. So the infantile state *can* be bad relative to better prospects in *both* a real baby and an afflicted adult. These comments on the infantile have their analogues in the evaluation of prenatal nonexistence, as we shall see.

19. Unamuno, however, seemed to think that there were no evils that could override nothingness; he was willing to burn forever rather than die.

20. Contemplating our never having existed also involves contemplating not being a self we in fact now care for. But, of course, if we had not existed, the nonexistence of ourselves would not have been the nonexistence of a cared-for self since we would not have existed to care for ourselves. So it is a noncared-for self that would be nonexistent, rather than a cared-for self. This makes total nonexistence less bad.

If we did think it would have been a harm to a person who exists that he not have existed, it seems that we also would have to consider it a harm to a particular *possible* person never to have come into existence. For example, suppose I am contemplating creating someone I will call Susan and have organized her genetic material so that I know exactly what she will be like. I then decide not to create her. How could there be a harm to her if there will never have been an actual person and, therefore, no one who loses out on all the goods of life? If we act out of concern for the person who loses goods, we should resurrect someone rather than create someone totally new, even if we could give the resurrected person fewer additional goods than the totally new person would have. This is not to deny that when we create a new person we are doing something *like* benefiting him in creating him, if he will have a good life. (See my *Creation and Abortion,* New York: Oxford University Press, 1992, for more on this.) But it remains true that it is not exactly like benefiting someone already in existence or who once was in existence. (Of course, if we are simply interested in producing the grandest possible life, it makes no difference whether we create anew or resurrect.)

There is a line of argument, however, that might differentiate what the above discussion has tried to assimilate: the nonexistence of a possible person and the contemplated nonexistence of an actual person. It is possible that the thought that what actually is might not have been is disturbing to some people. For these people the remedy is to think that there is a requirement that all things that actually exist, exist necessarily.

2

The Asymmetry Problem: Death and Prenatal Nonexistence

This chapter is concerned with the question, Is death *worse* for the person who dies than his nonexistence prior to his creation, and if so, why? Dealing with this question will also lead us to reconsider our first question, What makes death bad?

The Asymmetry Problem

Let us now move from Epicurus's question to Lucretius's question. Lucretius recognized[1] that we are not disturbed much about the fact of our nonexistence prior to our creation. If so, he asked, why are we so disturbed about our nonexistence after death? Nonexistence before life and nonexistence after life seem symmetrical; yet our attitudes toward the two seem asymmetrical.[2]

There are other possible asymmetrical attitudes and beliefs that are related to this one. For example, belief in an afterlife, when it is not accompanied by belief in a prelife, may be based on an asymmetrical attitude toward prenatal and posthumous nonexistence. Also, suppose that we are told that people alive *now* have longer lives than was originally thought. If we prefer to discover that the extra years come at the end rather than at the beginning, we shall again be exhibiting an asymmetrical attitude.[3] (Suppose we are told something similar about people already dead. Would we prefer to discover that they died later than we thought, rather than that they were created earlier? Would there be an asymmetrical attitude of the same type toward these options?) Again, would we prefer an infinitely long life that has no beginning, but ends, or an infinitely long life that begins but does not end, the lives having equivalent contents? If we prefer the latter, we exhibit the asymmetrical attitude.

I believe, the asymmetrical attitude is also exhibited if we would prefer to be told that we began living a life of *constant* length and content later in the future rather than earlier, and if we would prefer a life of constant content to end later in the future rather than earlier by interrupting it with periods of unconsciousness.

Lucretius points to the asymmetrical attitude in order to argue against its rationality: we ought to be no more concerned about death than about prenatal nonexistence. (Why not no less concerned about prenatal nonexistence than about death?) An account of why death is bad that supports a *symmetrical* attitude would, on

Lucretius's view, at least be on the road to rationality. But suppose we—contra Lucretius—think that an asymmetrical attitude with greater concern about death is in some sense justified or at least rationally understandable. Then an account of why death is bad that does not generate an asymmetry may be missing something. An explanation of the asymmetry may, therefore, be related to the correct account of the badness of death.

It should be emphasized that the asymmetrical attitude is consistent with bemoaning the loss of goods due to prenatal nonexistence. It just claims there is a further difference in warranted attitude toward prenatal and posthumous loss.

Nagel's Answer

What does Nagel say about Lucretius's question? At first, he argues that, unlike death, not being created earlier than we were in fact created does not deprive *us* of more of the goods of life. This is because whoever would have been created much earlier than we, in fact, were would not have been us. (For a different sperm and egg would have joined.) This, he suggests, accounts for our asymmetrical attitudes in a manner consistent with his thesis that death is bad because it deprives us of more goods of life.

Nagel, however, also considers an objection to this proposal raised by Robert Nozick. Suppose we originated from spores that contained our genetic code and that could have been triggered off much earlier than they in fact were. Then it would indeed have been *we* who enjoyed many extra years. Nagel agrees that we would still react to the discovery of this loss of past life differently from the way we react to our deaths. So the problem of accounting for the asymmetrical attitude reappears, given Nagel's explanation of why death is bad. If his account of why death is bad is complete, why is there an asymmetrical attitude?

Williams's Answer

A second possible approach to the asymmetry problem is based on the view, slightly different from Nagel's, that death is bad for the person who dies because it interferes with the achievement of his *categorical* plans, desires, and commitments. These *categorical* projects give one a reason to go on living; one wants to go on living in order to complete the projects.[4] Categorical projects are contrasted with *hypothetical* projects, which one undertakes *if* one does go on living; hypothetical projects cannot provide a reason *for* going on living.

Interference with categorical projects is certainly something bad about death. Those who think it cannot be bad for us to have our projects and desires interfered with by death because we will not be around to experience their frustration mistake what we want: we want completed projects, and fulfilled desires, not only to avoid unpleasant feelings from unfulfilled desires or knowledge of uncompleted projects. So death interferes with our getting the completed projects we want and is, therefore, bad for us. Unlike death, it is said, the failure to begin existence earlier cannot interfere with our desires and projects since there were none prior to our existence. This account of why death is bad, it is suggested, explains the asymmetry.

One problem with this argument, it seems to me, is that, once we are alive, we may indeed have "desires" *for* the past and may regret not having had earlier years in which to fulfill these desires. For example, not preexisting our actual creation can interfere with desires to have seen certain events that occurred before we existed. Furthermore, we may have commitments or plans for the future whose fulfillment requires our having been born earlier; a plan for my immediate future might be frustrated because I did not begin life earlier. Nonetheless, even if we have such frustrated plans, prenatal nonexistence seems different from death.

Most importantly, it seems that a person who has no desires or plans for the future with which death can interfere, can still have asymmetrical attitudes toward death and not being created earlier. Such a person can enjoy and appreciate goods that life brings, without desires or commitments, because life has things in it that are good and capable of being appreciated independent of whether they are objects of prior desires. They are not good because they are desired, but worthy of being desired because they are good. It is true that if he has the asymmetrical attitude he will have the desire to go on living. This is not the sort of desire that Williams has in mind when he speaks of categorical desires. Categorical desires make the desire to go on living instrumental and hypothetical relative to the desire to do something specific with one's life. Nevertheless, once we are alive we commonly do have the desire to go on living, and it is interfered with by death. But prenatal nonexistence can interfere with desires we have *now* for earlier life. If our desire to go on living is stronger than our desire for past life—and this is one basis for claiming there is an asymmetrical attitude—can we say that death is worse just because it interferes with a stronger desire? But we wish to know whether the stronger desire to avoid death as against prenatal nonexistence is justified because death is really worse than prenatal nonexistence. We cannot, therefore, show that the stronger desire is justified by showing that death is worse because it interferes with it. (I cannot show that it is correct to desire an apple more than an orange because it is worse to be without an apple than to be without an orange by showing that being without an apple interferes with a stronger desire I have for an apple.)

So, death can deprive people of goods they did not plan for, or think about getting, and so can prenatal nonexistence. If death is bad and seems worse than prenatal nonexistence, even when it does not interfere with categorical projects, then the fact that prenatal nonexistence did not interfere with categorical projects could not explain the asymmetrical attitudes.

Parfit's Answer

A third answer to the asymmetry problem is based on an insight of Derek Parfit's.[5] This insight is mentioned by Nagel and supports the answer he ultimately favors. Parfit observes that we seem to care less about what we *have* already suffered than about what we *will* suffer, quite generally. For example, he claims, if I wake up one morning and do not remember what day it is, I would prefer that it be the day after I underwent *very* painful surgery rather than the day before I am to undergo only moderately painful surgery (assuming there are no aftereffects of the very painful surgery) (Surgery Case). One extension of this view is that I may care less about the goods of life I have already had than about goods I am still to have. Here our preferences are determined by where we are on the time line, rather than by a view from the outside on our life as a whole and how much good or bad it will have in it as a whole.

Let us employ this point of Parfit's in connection with death and prenatal nonexistence.[6] Whenever I am born, the loss of life's goods I sustain by not having been created earlier is behind me. However, the loss of goods due to death is still to come. Or, from another point of view, the extra goods I could have had if I had been created earlier are goods that would have been behind me at the time I was actually created, and the point when I would consider the possibility of earlier creation. If I care less about past goods than about future goods, my having been created earlier will not mean much. The goods death deprives me of, on the other hand, are still to come. Not caring much about the absence of these earlier goods is the correlative of not caring much about their having existed.

If I care more about the loss of future goods than about the loss of past goods, what makes death bad is the absence of more future goods, not just the absence of more goods. It is only the latter characteristic—the absence of more goods—that it shares with prenatal nonexistence. Parfit is pointing to a basically asymmetrical attitude toward past and future; he explains our caring more about avoiding death than about prenatal nonexistence by noting that we care more about future losses than past ones.

But is it rational to care less for evils and goods that are behind us than for those to come? Does this asymmetry in caring hold only for goods and evils of experience and (experienced) action? (That is, do we also care less about past *un*experienced goods and evils than about future unexperienced goods and evils?) It cannot be merely that there is nothing we can do about the past that makes us care less about it. This becomes clear if we imagine that our future is totally determined, that the time of our death, as well as the fact of our death, is determined, and that we can do nothing about it. We would still be more disturbed about the loss that death will bring than about past nonexistence.

Presumably the preference for future over past experienced goods is related to the fact that a person in the present, though not now enjoying either past *or* future goods, is yet to experience the future because of time's passage; the past can no longer affect him experientially. This makes it often true that future goods are as acceptable to someone as present goods.

Whether there is a justification for our preferences, and whether they apply to unexperienced goods and evils, the Parfitian solution to the asymmetry problem presupposes that *what happened* in the past through prenatal nonexistence was just as bad for the person as what will happen because of his death in the future. We just care less about it from where we are now; it only *seems* not to be so bad because it is in the past. This explanation of our asymmetrical attitudes does not claim that death *is* worse than prenatal nonexistence because we care more about it. If we *do* care more about death, although it is *intrinsically* no worse than prenatal nonexistence, then we can only say that the idea of death has bad consequences—our concern— that the idea of prenatal nonexistence does not have. (I believe the Parfitian view is essentially related to asymmetrical *concerns*. If a creature cannot have concerns, the question is whether it would be justified for it to be more concerned with future than past.)

Objections: The Outside Point of View

This Parfitian proposal about our asymmetrical attitudes is based on sympathetic recognition of the point of view that someone has from *within his life* as he is living it. In particular, it recognizes the view he has *now* of things before his creation and ahead of him. However, we (and he) may also take a view of his life from the outside, surveying his life line as a whole.[7] This outside view, like the inside view, may incorporate the (controversial) view that a person's life moves in one direction: forward from the past into the future. This view is referred to as "time's passage." It employs not only the notions of before and after but also those of past, present, and future and of what are to be past and future at certain points. But it does not essentially employ the notions of past and future from the perspective of *now, within the life,* as does the view from within. The outside view of a life may be the view of some other person who is living at a certain point in time. Unlike other possible outside views, the one I discuss here is not atemporal or timeless: there is a *now* outside the life we are viewing.

If we take this type of outside view of the life line of someone who *will* exist (but does not yet exist), the loss of goods due to not existing earlier is not yet in the past. From the outside point of view, therefore, someone who *will* be a real person is now, and will be, losing out on more goods of life. Likewise, looked at from outside, painful surgery that *will* take place earlier in life cannot seem less bad than any done later because the surgery has already occurred, since it has *not* already occurred. In the case of future pains, we do not sense an asymmetry between the earlier and the later.

Nevertheless, I think, we can feel an asymmetry between prenatal and post-humous nonexistence even when we view a life from outside and both are in the future. That is, prenatal nonexistence still seems less bad than death. We do not feel the need to rush the person into existence to avoid as much prenatal nonexistence as we can when the total length of life will not be increased. If anything, we can still feel the desire to put off creating the person, so that his ending is as late as possible, even when the total length of life (and its content) will not change. Therefore, if we want to postpone the life of fixed length, how could the Parfitian answer to the asymmetry problem be correct?

A Defense of the Parfitian Proposal: Outside View Parasitic on Inside

Perhaps the following defense of the Parfitian proposal is available. From the outside view we may say of someone not yet born that, whenever he is born, he *will already* have suffered the loss of goods through prenatal nonexistence, and that he *will,* therefore, feel his past loss as less significant than his future loss. And if we delay, creating him, then he will not yet have to face his future loss. (We would then be basing *our* asymmetrical judgment as outside observers on a sympathetic identification with his [future] perspective; we would not be making a judgement from a totally outside view.) If this fact, parasitic on the past/future distinction of the internal view, accounts for the asymmetrical attitude in an outside observer toward a life not yet begun, then the Parfitian proposal would remain intact.[8] To test for this, we might see whether we feel any asymmetry when looking at the life line of someone who *has* already lived and died. That is, do we prefer that he have been created later rather than sooner given a life of constant length and content; do we prefer that extra years have been added to his life after his birth or that he have been created earlier.[9] For him, death has already occurred, the event which represents the loss is in the past though loss may be going on eternally. The event and all the loss were in the future *from his internal point of view while he was alive.* (The prenatal loss of someone yet to be created is happening now and is in the future, yet it *will be* in his past *from his point of view.*)

A Second Defense: The End to All Future Goods?

A second defense of the Parfitian view is that when loss of *prenatal* goods is still (at least in part) in the future, it represents the loss of some future goods, but not the loss of *all* future goods since some more are yet to come. It is only with death that we lose the possibility of all future goods. Likewise, so far as sensing an asymmetry in the life line of those already dead, it might be said that although their loss of prenatal and posthumous goods are both (in part) in the past, only the posthumous nonexistence implies that they *will* never *in the future* have goods. This could be the reason why we think there is still an asymmetry in their case. That is, even the death that occurred in the past is of greater concern to us than the prenatal nonexistence because it alone represented the loss of the possibility of *all* goods in the future; in this sense it was a worse event than late creation.

However, this defense of the Parfitian view seems to require us to alter the view somewhat. That is, it is not just that we care less about the loss of past goods than about the loss of future goods. What we care about is the end to *all* future goods, the end of the possibility of any more future goods, that death represents. This is essentially the concern discussed above (pp. 19–20) as "it's all over." Prenatal nonexistence does not represent the end of the possibility of future goods since existence follows it. Not caring much about the absence of goods in the past because that absence is over with—Parfit's proposal—is different from not caring about a past loss because it does not eliminate the possibility of more good things to come in the future, whereas future (posthumous) nonexistence does. By contrast, not caring much about past pain is due entirely to its being over with.

Of course, prenatal nonexistence (but not posthumous nonexistence) means there is no possibility of more goods in the past.[10] It is part of the asymmetrical attitude that we do not care about this loss of the *possibility of a past* (rather than merely past goods) as much as about the loss of the *possibility of a future* (rather than merely some future goods). This is the Parfitian point about greater concern for the future reappearing.

A fundamental alternative to the Parfitian proposal would exist if it could be argued that (1) what happens to someone because of his not existing earlier really *is* different from what happens to him because of death, as seen from a perspective outside the life, and (2) what happens because of prenatal nonexistence is less bad than what happens because of death. We shall continue the investigation of this issue in the next chapter.

Objections to a General View that the Future Matters More than the Past: Valuing Our Lives as Products

Let us put to one side Lucretius' question and consider a *more general view* that might be derived from Parfit's Surgery Case, a view Parfit himself does *not* accept. This view tells us to care less about *all types* of past goods and evils not just experiential goods or evils, than about future goods and evils, even when the past goods are better than those to come and the past evils are worse than those to come. For example, consider the following case (Case A) whose structure is similar to that of the Surgery Case. We ask various people which of two possible descriptions they would prefer to be true of the world: (1) that they already have many good years full of achievements and meaningful involvements behind them but will die shortly; (2) that they have just been created, but will have a few years ahead of them with a moderate amount of goods.

If we extrapolate from the response to Parfit's Surgery Case, we would expect people to prefer (2) to (1). But I do not think they do, and if they did it might well be the morally wrong preference to have. It would amount to being willing to give up having had a whole meaningful life, full of achievements, for the sake of even a few goods in the future.

Furthermore, any preference for (2) would exist only if the future goods were those of experience or action. For only the desire to experience or act could overcome the desire to *have* lived a good, meaningful life in the past. Future nonexperiential, nonactivity goods are too much like *having had* the goods of experience or action in the past to make one feel tempted to give up for their sake the many past goods that account for one's having lived a good life.

Why would the preference for (2) over (1) be morally wrong? I believe it is wrong to live so as to deny the value of experiences or actions once they are over (so that any amount of future action and experience is preferable to any amount or type of past ones). There is a stronger and a weaker version of this thesis. The weaker version claims that it is wrong to deny the value of past experiences and activities that amount to meaningful achievements apart from just being good experiences. The stronger version includes this, but adds that it is wrong to deny the value of past experiences simply as experiences. (For example, the weaker claim might say that we should not prefer a future life in which we do not solve an important philosophical problem to a past life in which we do. The stronger claim might say that we should not prefer a future life in which we experience a small physical pleasure to a past life in which we experienced a great physical pleasure. I believe that both stronger and weaker claims are true, the stronger being assimilable to the achievement model, which the weaker employs explicitly.) I will limit myself to the weaker claim for the present. Why is it true?

Let me say first that I believe it is wrong to live one's life acting on each occasion with the aim of making one's life have a certain structure or be of a certain type. In deciding what to do, one has one motivation too many if one thinks of the structure of one's life. One must decide how to act on the merit of the *acts* one is contemplating; then, as a byproduct, one's life will have the "structure" of, for example, sincerity or seriousness. It would be wrong not to engage in certain activities simply because one thinks they would disturb the so-called "narrative structure" of one's life.

Yet I also believe that it is wrong not to care when one looks back at one's life as it was lived, from the outside so to speak, that it amounted to something good, that one produced a life of a certain sort by living it in the right way, acting for the right reason on each occasion. Preferring any small amount of future good life to such a *product* does imply not caring about the product.[11]

Preferring a future life that consists entirely of a few good months to a long past of, for example, goodness and insight, may also seem wrong because of how we will feel when the few months are over. It is at that point of death that the product we have made in living will (or should) be of special importance to us. But, of course, it is to avoid the regrettable course of events, rather than the regret of them, that we should not exchange many past for a few future goods.

Good Experiences

One might argue that, if all one cared about was experiencing pleasure, it would be all right to exchange many past goods for a few future ones. This is because a person who cared only for experienced pleasure should, presumably, not care for the nonexperiential good of "having experienced much pleasure." Such a person does not care about producing anything; he cares only about experiencing pleasure, though he will produce a certain life as a byproduct. The stronger, rather than the weaker, claim denies that even a lover of pleasure should prefer a small amount of future pleasure to the achievement of a great amount of past pleasure, from a point of view inside his life.

It should be emphasized that, although we do not care *as much* about prenatal nonexistence as we do about death, we do (or should) care about the loss of goods in the achievement mode (including the achievement of pleasurable experiences) due to prenatal as well as to postnatal nonexistence.

Valuing the Actual over the Possible

Yet another case raises an additional objection to preferring any small amount of future good to any great amount of past good. In Case A we asked which description one would prefer to be true of one's own actual life. In Case B we ask the apparently senseless question, Should someone be willing to exchange his own *actually lived* long life of goods for a few future goods? Strictly speaking, of course, this is an impossible supposition, but grasping the sentiment behind the question is possible, I think. How much could someone care for the work he has done or the relationships to which he has given his life if he would will them not to have existed for the sake of some small amount of future good?

These two cases provide two different reasons for preferring past to future goods. Case A emphasizes valuing one's life as an achievement. Case B emphasizes caring for the particular things one has actually done. Interestingly, these two reasons may conflict. Suppose one were given the opportunity to exchange a short actual past life with some important particular goods in it for a long past life with *more* of the *same type* of goods. For example, one might be given the opportunity to exchange a short actual life with relationships to particular people for a long life with the same relationships to different people. The desire to have a good product may conflict with caring about the particular people with whom one had the relationships one did have. I think it would be wrong to turn one's back on one's actual life if it was a good one. (And if it were a bad one?)

To take a particular case, suppose that the idea of wiping out an actual past makes sense. Also, suppose that intense states of awareness or creativity were always preferable to relationships with other people, so that it would make sense to avoid the latter to achieve the former. Finally, suppose it is true that attachment to particulars matters only when it is a question of particular persons. That is, it would be all right to wipe out one's actual past and substitute a greater creative act for an actual, less important creative act. Its being wrong to wipe out one's actual personal relations to achieve a great creative act would then mean that a commitment to a person can have weight even when—by the first supposition of complete undoing of the past—there will be no person in distress if the commitment is not kept or even no commitment made at all. It would also mean that once a morally significant relationship with a particular person exists, undoing it is different (even on the first supposition) from avoiding the relationship to begin with in order to pursue creative acts. In short, even if a certain type of work dominates possible personal relations, actual personal relations could dominate possible work.[12]

What explains the appropriateness of commitment to the actual over pursuit of the better possible? It is tempting to say that such commitment is appropriate because it is a measure of how deep and, hence, worthwhile our actual relationships and activities are. That is, how much one is willing to sacrifice to keep them is a measure of their depth. This explanation, however, may be misleading if it gives the impression that one's actual activities and relations are better than the possible activities and relations. This is not what is intended. The idea is that once one is deeply involved with some ways of life, it would be a betrayal to pursue some other way of life, or even to regret *not* having pursued what one might have, had one not already made certain choices. There is a deontological flavor to all this.[13]

Reconciling Responses

Some way of reconciling the response to Parfit's Surgery Case with the response to cases like (A) and (B) must be provided. For Case A and Case B suggest that we should prefer, even from a point inside our life, the life of greater goods of achievement (A), or an actual life (B), even if it is in the past. This might seem to suggest that we should also prefer the life with less pain even if the pain is in the future. Yet I believe Parfit is right that from a point inside our life we would, and may permissibly, prefer greater pain in the past to less pain in the future.

Presumably the reconciliation has something to do with the fact that a life with less pain in it is not the sort of life a person, viewing his life from the outside, would care much to have produced; it is not a great achievement. Since he does not care about this product, he will not prefer that he suffer future pain to produce it. Of course, in the *process of living* he may care a great deal about having a life with as little pain as possible. The view from outside, which shows concern for the product but not with how much pain is in it, is an example of heroism at a distance. It is easier than real heroism, but nevertheless may show us what the heroic act would be.

The Formal versus the Experiential Properties of a Life

Building on this point, it might be suggested that the appropriate test for what is worthwhile in life is what we could care about when evaluating the life not only from the outside, but also after it has been lived. By this test, much of the qualia of life, which we care about while living, may drop out. A life full of achievements may not be considered worse for the pain that was in it, and the pleasures occurring independently of any meaningful projects may not add to the value of the life. That is, while we are living, our sensations matter to us. However, in retrospect, it is what might be called the *formal structure* of our life (the achievements)—independent of the *experiential properties* (e.g., pain/pleasure qualia)—that we primarily check in order to see to what our life has amounted. This view may seem to conflict with the idea (discussed on p. 32) that even a life of pleasure can be considered an achievement. But it denies only the correctness, not the possibility, of considering it an achievement. And there may be no conflict if non-experience-grounded achievements are dominant in evaluation.

An Alternative View

An alternative to this view is that a life with more pain in it *is* worse than one with less pain, other things being equal. From within the life, however, we are not willing to do the "heroic thing" and suffer in the future rather than have it be true that we suffered more in the past. (One heroic view says that pain doesn't matter. The other heroic view says, suffer some future pain to prevent a worse life with more past pain in it.) But even when the future pain is small and so undergoing it is not truly heroic, we would not choose to suffer it. How is this consistent with its being true that the life containing more pain is the worse life, other things being equal? Such a life may be worse, but if the pain is in the past, we just don't care, because its being a worse life in this way *does not reflect badly on us as persons.* So, from the view outside, we aim less at a good life than at a life that reflects well on us as persons.

Experienced versus Nonexperienced Goods and Evils

One way to describe the reconciliation of responses to Parfit's Surgery Case and cases like (A) and (B) is that asymmetrical attitudes toward past and future goods and evils apply only to goods and evils of experience (including experienced action). Furthermore, it applies to these goods and evils only when one is not concerned with them as marks of achievement that reflect well on us.

Two possible limitations on this way of describing the Reconciliation Thesis should be mentioned. First, experienced goods may not work in the same way as experienced evils. That is, one may not prefer discovering that one will have a few experienced goods in the future, and none in the past, to discovering that one will have no experienced goods in the future, and many in the past. This is a possibility if any acquaintance with the experiential goods (but not with the evils) of life winds up being treated like an achievement, if one really cares enough about these good experiences. (One can still prefer many past experiential evils to fewer overall and in the future, even if one doesn't prefer some experiential goods in the future over more in the past.)

Second (a point we shall elaborate on in the Appendix to Part I), there may be a residual preference for having a fixed amount of *nonexperienced* goods in the future rather than in the past because this means that a rising rather than a declining fate characterizes our product. Indeed, preference for future over past unexperienced goods just amounts to a preference for an incline over a decline, based presumably on the view that such an incline really is better.

Self and Others

Suppose our pain does not matter much to us from the outside view. Parfit thinks that we react with more concern toward *other* people's past pain than to our own, except when they are still alive and their greater pain is in the past.[14] For he thinks that if they are still alive, we identify with their perspective, which is to discredit past pain and to avoid future pain. My sense in this matter, however, is that we remain more concerned with the past pain even of a still-living person than with our own past pain. We can also note that we may react with more concern to the idea of their lives' being a painful product than to ours' being a painful product.

It might be suggested that this seeming greater protectiveness toward others than toward ourselves probably has two sources. First, there is a tendency to see ourselves as agents rather than as passive recipients of goods or harms, with the reverse for others. However, we do not take this view of our future pain, i.e., we protect ourselves from it. The second possibility is that we react as we do to others versus ourselves because there is no distinction in how we *feel* other people's past and future experiences (we literally feel neither). However, there is a distinction at a given point in time in our relation to our own past and future experiences. (The former will have been felt, the latter will be felt.)

Notice also that when we begin (mistakenly perhaps) to treat distant parts of our own lives as belonging to a person different from who we are now, we may sympathize with our own past pain in the way we sympathize with that of others. For example, suppose I think of the child I was and how she suffered. I am likely to wish that the pain could have been distributed more equally over that childhood and my present and future life. (On the one hand I treat the earlier stage as a different person, on the other hand because I recognize it still as me, I wish I now could take on part of the burden.) I would not think this way in Parfit's Surgery Case about a great pain I suffered yesterday.

Suppose we do, in some respects, take a more objective, temporally neutral view, one *not* parasitic on considering whether goods or evils are in the past or yet to come, when we consider other people's lives. (At least if they are already dead.) Do we also think their death was not worse for them than their prenatal nonexistence? If we retain more of an asymmetrical attitude toward their death and prenatal nonexistence than to other bads (and goods) in their life, how can a Parfitian approach alone account for the asymmetrical attitude toward death and prenatal nonexistence? It would seem that other factors, observable from a point outside the life, would have to be in play, since this seems to be the perspective from which we are judging their lives.

The Nagel/Parfit Proposal and Achievement

Parfit's insight can be used to modify Nagel's view about why death is bad in a way that helps explain why death at least seems worse than prenatal nonexistence. Call this the *Nagel/Parfit Proposal:* Death is bad because it prevents additional goods of life, and from the perspective within life, it *seems* worse than prenatal nonexistence because we do not care as much about past as about future goods. However, we have presented cases in which the loss of past goods would *not* matter less than the loss of future goods because we care about whether we have achieved something in our lives. Therefore, in order for the Nagel/Parfit Proposal to solve the asymmetry problem, it must be the case that there are goods we lose through prenatal and posthumous nonexistence that we care about less once they are over and more if they are still to come. So they must be unlike goods of achievement. It must also be true that we care *much* more for such goods than for goods not subject to this structure of concern, goods conceivable under the "achievement" or "product" mode that give our life its formal structure. We do not care more about these achievement goods if they are in the future rather than if they are in the past. Since we do not care much about our past nonexistence, and the Nagel/Parfit proposal explains this by reference to a greater concern for future goods that does not apply to nonexperiential goods, the proposal seems committed to our not caring very much about goods of achievement relative to experiential goods. Yet we obviously do care a great deal about goods of achievement. Why then do we care less about past nonexistence than about death?

Derek Parfit[15] has offered two possible responses to this question. First, he says, when we are considering Lucretius's question and are concerned with the badness of our own future nonexistence, we are thinking primarily about experiential goods. That is strongly suggested by the view I have emphasized that what is so terrible is the thought "ALL OVER," for that thought fails to apply to the goods of achievement. As far as those goods are concerned, death seems to matter very little. Death cannot touch those goods. That could be enough to explain why, when we are considering Lucretius's argument and considering the badness of past non-existence, it is experiential goods with which we are concerned.

But, we might ask, why do we focus on experiential goods in considering

Lucretius's question? Why not be concerned that more achievements are impossible in the future as well as not present in the past? "ALL OVER" *does* apply *at least to* more achievements that depend on our acts even if death cannot eliminate achievements already accomplished (or such goods as depend on others beliefs about us or their acts towards our achievements.) And if we are then focusing on achievements as well, why not past ones?

Second, Parfit says, to regret the fact that we did not start to exist earlier, we have to imagine something like Nozick's spore. More important, even if we do imagine this, we couldn't simply assume that, if we had been born earlier, we would have had all the same achievements AND MORE. We know that, if we had been born earlier, our lives would have gone very differently. I argue that we may have attachment to our ACTUAL achievements. If that's so, that could help to explain why we don't regret not having been born earlier. We know that the price of this would have been to undermine those particular achievements. However, this explanation could, perhaps, be thought away. We could be asked to imagine that, even if we had been born earlier, our actual achievements would have been the same: we would have had these, and more. The question would then be, if we imagine this, would we regret that we weren't born earlier? Some of us would. But suppose we wouldn't regret it as much as death. There might then be, Parfit agrees, a problem for the Nagel/Parfit proposal, based on the difference between goods of experience and goods of achievement (at least, if Parfit's first response was not adequate).

In addition to this concern about the Nagel/Parfit approach, I have argued that it is a significant revision of their proposal to say that posthumous nonexistence is worse than prenatal nonexistence because only posthumous nonexistence eliminates the *possibility* of any future goods, rather than its just limiting their number. (Here recall the Limbo Man.)

It has been noted that one way to criticize the Nagel/Parfit Proposal is to see whether what happens if we die is *really* worse than what happens because we did not exist earlier, not merely *seems* worse. It was suggested that we should look for factors visible from a perspective outside the life and not parasitic on the view from inside it, that would make death really worse than prenatal nonexistence. Then, for example, we could justify the asymmetrical attitude toward those already dead, thinking their deaths had been worse for them than their prenatal nonexistence, not merely because their death was in their future but prenatal nonexistence was always in their past. We will consider these issues further in the next chapter.

NOTES

1. In *De Rerum Natura,* 2nd ed. Cyril Bailey, ed. (Oxford: Oxford University Press, 1922).

2. One *could* imagine someone who was very disturbed that there was a time when he hadn't amounted to anything, but was satisfied knowing he had amounted to something though he would turn into nothing. This would be the reverse asymmetrical attitude.

3. It may seem that one can have asymmetrical attitudes toward death and prenatal nonexistence, but not have asymmetrical attitudes toward (1) losing out on having a *few* more

future years followed by death, and (2) losing out on having had a *few* more past years (rather than an infinite number of past years). After all, a few more years does not provide an escape from death. But, if one does not want one's life ever to end, shouldn't one want to put off its ending even by a few years? And, if one wants one's life not to end more than one wants to have always been in existence in the past, then shouldn't one care more about having a few more future years than about a few more past years?

4. Such a view is suggested by Mary Mothersill in her paper "Death," and by Bernard Williams (who introduces the notion of "categorical" projects) in his paper, "The Makropoulos Case, or the Tedium of Immortality," both in Rachels, ed., *Moral Problems,* 1st ed. (New York: Harper & Row, 1971).

5. Described most fully in *Reasons and Persons* (Oxford: Oxford University Press, 1985), pp. 170–186.

6. Since this material was originally written, A. Bruckner and J. Fischer have discussed the application of Parfit's point to death and prenatal nonexistence in their article, "Why Is Death Bad?" *Philosophical Studies* 50 (September 1986): 213–221, making similar use of Parfit's work to that which I make here and in "Why Is Death Bad and Worse than Prenatal Non-existence," in *Pacific Philosophical Quarterly* 69 (June 1988):161–164.

7. The case of the Texas Burn Victim (discussed earlier) was discussed as possibly another instance where we might resist making a decision about good and bad policies on the basis of a view outside the life. But in that case, from a point within his life even a *future* benefit might not override too great pain in the *sooner* future. (Parfit discusses those who can accept asymmetrical attitudes toward past and future and yet want to reject greater concern for pain in the nearer future than in the further future. This still differs from weighing nearer future pain more than a further greater good. It is the latter we considered in the Texas Burn Victim Case discussion.)

8. In the case of pains that *will* come earlier and later in life, we could not generate asymmetrical attitudes from the outside view in the same way, I think. This is because whenever the person comes into existence, the earlier pain is still ahead of him. So the outside view may mimic the tendency of the inside view to care more about pains closer to realization, wanting these to be put off into the future. (I believe this is the dominant tendency, though there is a recognized conflict between wanting the pain to be over with and wanting it to be further in the future. Both are motivated, in part, by the desire that the pain not be *now*.) There is no less concern about the pains that will come earlier in the future just because they will be in the past sooner.

9. In the second case I abstract from the idea that his life would have been totally different from what it was if he had started earlier but not if he had started later or gone on later. Suppose his life would have the same content, only with additions either way.

10. Fred Feldman emphasizes this in "F. M. Kamm and the Mirror of Time," *Pacific Philosophical Quarterly* 71 (March 1990): 23–27.

11. I use "product" loosely; there is no entity being produced, but rather something like a good performance.

12. If this is true, it provides one with some reason for avoiding relations that will generate commitments or perspectives that override greater goods.

13. Parfit has suggested to me that this idea is related to a view defended by Robert M. Adams in "Existence, Self-Interest, and the Problem of Evil," *Nous* 13 (1979). He argues that judging from a point outside one's life that things would have been better had they been different does not imply that one should regret that they are not different when one judges them from a perspective within one's actual life.

14. See *Reasons and Persons.*

15. In correspondence.

3

Accounting for Asymmetry?

This chapter is concerned with whether there are properties observable from a view *outside the life,* rather from within it, that help to explain why death is worse than prenatal nonexistence. These properties must make nonexistence-in-the-future different from nonexistence-in-the-past in ways other than just that it *is* in the future. I think several factors suggest themselves, though perhaps none are truly explanatory. This chapter is also concerned with what more we can say about the fact, or beliefs about the fact, that something exists in the future that will help illuminate the explanatory role of this fact. Many of the factors that may explain why death is really worse depend on asymmetries related to time: the (supposed) fact that causation has a *direction (forward),* so that the past affects the future, but the future does not affect the past; the (supposed) fact that there is a direction in time, *from past to future;* and the fact that there is a *before and after* in the passage of time. But some of these features may not be objective at all. Rather, they may be features of the subjective view of those who are observing another's life from the outside, comparable to the tendency of the person whose life it is to focus on his future from where he is now, which is a characteristic of his subjective view. If this were so, the asymmetrical features dependent on the asymmetries related to time and causation might explain the asymmetrical attitude, but they might not justify it.

The Destruction of the Person

Death involves destruction of the person, but prenatal nonexistence and coming to exist do not. Because of death, something of value that already existed is taken apart. It suffers a defeat. A person does not come to an end in the same way that a book does, intact. (This factor was first raised in Chapter 1 in connection with the morality of killing, see pp. 20–21.)

Death Happens to the Person

Death involves bad things *happening to* a person, such as his destruction and deprivation of future goods. Even if the person is not there when death is, death comes *to* the living person. Prenatal nonexistence does not include an event that involves nonexistence happening to a person, even though the fact that he did not come into existence earlier affects the person who will exist.[1]

If it were worse to have something happen to one than to be negatively affected by events that did not happen to one, it would be worse to be armless through (painless) loss of an arm (even before psychological habituation to having the arm) than to be armless through a genetic defect. This may seem dubious. Perhaps psychological habituation to what is lost is necessary for there to be a difference.

Taking Away What Was Ours

Despite the last point, the factor of "happening to a person" helps us to see the incompleteness of the description of death as bad because it deprives us of more of the future goods of life. There are at least two ways in which we think of goods we do not have. Some goods we never had, others have been taken from us. It is true that, if I do not get to keep my jewel, we might describe this as not getting some totally new thing, namely, having-my-jewel-at-$t(f)$ (where "$t[f]$" is "a time in the future"). We might also say that death cannot deprive me of what I already had because what I had was having-my-jewel-at-$t(p)$ (where "$t[p]$" is "a time in the past"), and that is already gone. But, in fact, we do not think in this way. We think of death as taking away what already was and would have continued to be but for death. The absence of more goods because of death, therefore, is not just the absence of more goods; it is the elimination of old ones. By contrast, prenatal nonexistence does not deprive us of what was ours already. (However, prenatal nonexistence can prevent achievements. Death cannot touch them, though it does prevent more of them.) Prenatal nonexistence does prevent our having what *will* be ours, making it impossible that what will be ours was always ours.[2] We may care less about the fact that prenatal nonexistence prevents what is ours always having been ours than that death takes away what is ours, in part because it does not happen to us while we exist. But even within life, we care less about not having always had an item that is ours now than about having it taken away once it is ours. This is so even though we were alive and yet without the item, and this might be enough to say that not having the item *happened* to us. The fact that we *care* differentially about what is taken rather than what is not given is *not* what makes things worse, however. We care differentially as a reflection of a worse-making property, namely something being taken away. Or at least this is the claim.

In general, there are three ways in which we can make it the case that something does not exist or someone does not have something. One is by taking something away, the other is by not giving or producing it, and the former is often worse. Even when there is no ownership involved. So it is less bad that the world is deprived of a painting because someone does not paint it, or does not paint it as soon as she might have, than that the painting is destroyed (even by natural causes) once it exists.

Vulnerability

The previous three factors bear on the existence of another factor that distinguishes death from prenatal nonexistence. The fact that a person can be destroyed and that an event that deprives him of goods he already had can happen to him indicates that he is weak and vulnerable. By contrast, the fact that someone does not come into existence earlier or is negatively affected by what goes on before he exists does not reflect negatively on *his* capacities. Neither he nor his nature can be said to have failed to resist forces that prevent the goods of life if he does not yet exist. (He *is* shown, however, to be a being of a lesser sort than, for example, an ever-existing God.) Death exposes the vulnerability of what exists.

Notice also that when someone is already alive, his failure to draw goods to himself, as well as his inability to resist the goods' being taken away, exposes his powerlessness. But if the person does not yet exist, there is no inability to draw existence to himself that exposes his powerlessness. (So the distinction between not getting something and having it taken away is even more pronounced in the contrast between prenatal versus posthumous nonexistence than in similar contrasts *within* a life.)

That Death Is a Decline

Suppose that losing out on more of the goods of life is bad for the person. Then the fact that his nonexistence came to an end with his creation can be seen, from the point of view of any person who actually exists, as a move from a bad to a good state of affairs for him. It can be represented as an *improving* course of events (see [a] in Figure 3-1). But, assuming that life is not too terrible, death can be represented as a *declining* course of events, a movement *to* the absence of goods (see [b] in Figure 3.1).

There is, I believe, a quite general preference for a rising over a declining course of events, expressing the view that one course of events is truly better. One reason we may think the incline is better is that it represents one correct relationship to the good, that is, heading to it or bringing it about. When life that once existed is over, we are heading away from the good, or bringing about what is not good. Of course, being with the good (i.e., alive) is another correct relationship to it, but if this is accomplished as well in combination with heading to or bringing about the good this is better than if it is in combination with heading away from it.[3]

On this ground we also believe different types of lives are better. For example, we think a career better that improves as the years go by as against one that starts off at the top and then declines (holding content constant).[4] Death constitutes a decline.

The difference between inclining and declining states of affairs is connected in at least two ways with Parfit's suggestion that we care more about future goods and evils than about past ones. First, if an inclining life is better than a declining one, we might refuse to sacrifice it just to obtain more goods in the future. That is, if we were asked whether we prefer (1) to have lived an incline and die now, or (2) to have lived a decline (with content the same) but with some more time to live, it might be right to prefer the incline.

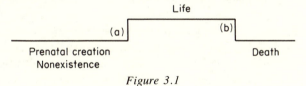

Figure 3.1

Second, we asked in Chapter 2 whether there was a preference for future *un*experienced goods and past *un*experienced evils as well as a preference for future experienced goods and past experienced evils, where the first preference is based on belief in the good-making properties of an incline. The first preference could be based on a preference for a life that inclines rather than declines, because having goods in the future, rather than the past, creates an incline. (Having goods far in the future rather than in the near future does the same.) This is a preference based on the judgment that inclines make things better, a judgment which we may make when looking at a life from the outside.[5]

The fact that death involves *destruction and decline that happens* to a person by *taking away what was his*—and the *vulnerability* that this signifies—may also help account for why some people would (mistakenly, I think) prefer total nonexistence to even a good mortal life. If we focused just on that aspect of death involving the absence of more of the goods of life, then it would be hard to understand how death could be a reason for preferring total nonexistence with no goods at all. But once we add such factors as destruction and decline happening to the person through the taking away of what was his, the case against creating someone at least is comprehensible. This is especially true given that there is no one who will miss out on anything if he is not created.

We may refer to the cluster of factors that exhibit a person's vulnerability, including destruction and decline happening to him, through taking away what is his, as the *Insult Factor*. It is important to emphasize that the insult can occur without anyone's being conscious of it. (This factor is to be contrasted with what we call the *Deprivation Factor,* which is the basis of Nagel's Deprivation Account of why death is bad.) The several factors represent insults to the person, rather than any further loss of time alive.[6] So the person who never had an arm and the person who has lost an arm live equally hard lives. A court may say one is no worse off than the other. But one has suffered an insult the other has not suffered, and in this sense, something worse has happened to him. (This may assume that the genetic defect that resulted in armlessness was not the result of someone/something altering genes that were once normal. In which case, even if nothing happened to *a person*—since he did not yet exist—there was a taking away of something.)

The Endlessness of the Nothingness of Death

For every person who ever exists, the absence of goods (and nothingness) prior to his birth comes to an end, but the absence of goods and nothingness caused by death is permanent. We take this as the endlessness of posthumous nonexistence. If we read the location of prenatal nonexistence behind an incline as one of its properties, then our prenatal nonexistence may seem better than the period of no life after life. This is because the former will lead to life. To use a more loaded phrase, it has the *potential* for life. All this depends on belief in time's passage from past to future.

The fact that death involves nonexistence in the future and that prenatal nonexistence involves nonexistence in the past for anyone in existence makes us think that prenatal and posthumous nonexistence are identical, only located differently, before and after life. But if nonexistence is in the future, it represents an *end* forever to life. Prenatal nonexistence, because it precedes life, is not an end forever to life. Being in the future turns nonexistence into a qualitatively different thing. By contrast, a pain's being in the future rather than in the past need not make the pain into a qualitatively different thing.[7] If we did not believe in the direction of time, however, the different *locations* of posthumous and prenatal nonexistence would not have this significance. This analysis depends on the idea of time's passage. (Is nothingness bounded, i.e., does it come to an end, in [a] of Figure 3-1 and is it unbounded in [b]? Even if we assume time's passage, nothingness in [a] is unbounded in the past, nothingness in [b] is bounded in the past.)

Emphasizing that prenatal nonexistence does not mean that the possibility of life is all over should not give the impression that what we care about is the possibility of life at some point. It is, rather, that we care about life's not ending, if it once starts. If we want it not to end, we want it not to be taken away without return, and so we want there to be no point in the future after which it is impossible for it to *continue* to be. So, we should rather say that prenatal nonexistence does not interfere with the possibility of life's *continuing,* but death does.

We object to the end of something that exists but not (as much) to its not having always existed, nor even to the possibility that it wouldn't have existed, nor to the impossibility of its existence. This implies that we are not as disturbed at our failure to be categorically necessary beings, as at our failure to be necessarily continuing beings.

However, prenatal nonexistence, but not future nonexistence, does signify the *impossibility* of existence in the further past for a life that began.[8] Why do we not care as much about this as about the impossibility of its future existence? Is the answer only the Parfitian one, that someone might say, "It is not in the future, and there just is the difference in concern?" Someone might say, "But if time has a direction, is it worse for there to be the impossibility of continuity of life in the direction in which time itself is headed, rather than in the direction away from which time is headed? If there is a point after which life's continuance is not possible but time is going beyond that point, this is worse than not to have been 'where time has been.' " But this still doesn't seem to mean anything more than that it is worse if the impossibility of life is in the future rather than if it is in the past, and the emphasis on the future is the Parfitian point reappearing.

That the evils of destruction, decline, vulnerability, and permanent cessation of goods once in existence could all happen to a person may also explain a preference for beginning a life of *constant quality and quantity* later rather than earlier in the future. That is, the desire to put off the existence of a good life stems from the desire that something good be over as late as possible. (It is not just that the period prior to a good is more acceptable because good will succeed it, but the period after a permanent end of good is bad because it is totally empty. For dislike of death need not involve dislike of total nonexistence.)

We can call the factor of a once-existing thing being permanently over the *Extinction Factor.* I believe the end of all possibilities of life for us in the direction of time, more than the Deprivation and Insult Factors, awakens terror in us. It is crucial to emphasize that I do not mean it is the *terror in us* that makes death bad; it is the factor of the possibility being all over of more of a life in the direction in which time moves that makes the death bad.

This factor is really what was emphasized in discussing the Limbo Man earlier—distinguishing not having more *possibility* of the goods of life from not having more goods of life. There it was held to make death bad; the question now is whether it also makes death worse than prenatal nonexistence, or is it only an unilluminating rephrasing of what death is, having its analogue in prenatal nonexistence and dependent for any role in explaining asymmetry on Parfit's point about concern for the future?

Death as the Determiner of Our Finitude

That death is the permanent end of life supports the further claim that, in coming after prenatal nonexistence, it *determines* our finitude. Call this the *decisiveness* of death. Likewise, it might be said, the last vote necessary to defeat a bill is in itself just like all the votes that went before it, but, given that those which came before did not determine the outcome, the last vote is crucial. The final vote can seem more significant than the others because one need worry only after it is cast. Yet, once in place, it makes all the votes that preceded it seem more effective since, if they had not been cast, *it* would not have been decisive. The decisiveness of death also produces the evil of *being a totally time-bound creature*. So long as only one end of our life (the beginning) is fixed, no definite boundaries can be drawn around our life. Once *both* ends are fixed, we can definitely be pinned down. We amount to so much and no more (or no less, in case a further future would have marred the whole). Though we can take seriously the existence of both boundaries, we dislike death more because we focus on the last boundary to be put in place. It is the boundary but for which the other would have been innocent enough. (This again assumes time's passage.)

The fact that death is decisive suggests that we *should* care more about prenatal nonexistence than we do (if not as much as about death). The fact that death sets one boundary gives the other boundary new importance. The fact that we do not care much about prenatal nonexistence, therefore, suggests that we may not really take seriously the fact that we will die. The aspect prenatal nonexistence shares with death—lessening the total of life's goods—would not matter if there were no death. Not ending would be adequate compensation for any losses in past existence.[9] It is only if we end that time lost through prenatal nonexistence becomes valuable. Similarly, it is usually only when we come to the end of a good activity that we regret its not having begun earlier. Failure to regret earlier losses may show that we do not take seriously the fact of the later one.

However, decisiveness would not play a part in accounting for the asymmetrical attitude if we retained that attitude though we would have no beginning (i.e., were not bounded in that direction) but would end. And it seems that we would.

The Significance of Living at Later Times

Another factor that might account for the asymmetrical attitude is the desirability of being alive at later, rather than earlier, times, apart from interest in putting off the end. Why is this true if the content of earlier times is not necessarily worse than the content of later times? We can imagine that someone has a choice whether to live a given content earlier or later. Even with the same content, the future is still seen as the *outcome and fulfillment* of more of the past. It may be that being around when the story is further along is seen as better, other things equal, than being around at its earlier stages because we then know more about what things *amount to*. By this I do *not* mean that if we are further along we can always obtain knowledge of the past we missed and, in addition, have knowledge firsthand of a later period. We might lack information about what precedes any time we came into existence; yet existing later might still be preferable because what we know is the story as it is further along.

What if we could have crystal balls that tell us the future but not the past? Why wouldn't it then be better to live earlier rather than later, or indifferent, since we will *know* the outcome of later times anyway? Perhaps because it is simply more valuable to *participate* in a later period, rather than just know about it.

Consequences of Living On

A final factor that may help to account for the asymmetry[10] is that the consequences of starting earlier may be worse than the consequences of going on longer. For example, if one had begun life earlier, one would be older at any given time than one would be otherwise. By contrast, if one begins as one actually did and goes on longer, one is not older than one would have been at any given time at which one would have existed. If being older at any given time is a bad consequence, one would have a preference for going on later versus having begun earlier. Hence, one would object more to not going on than to not having begun earlier.

However, if only our chronological age now were greater as a consequence of having started earlier, but not our psychological or physical age (deterioration), this factor would probably be unimportant.

Nagel/Parfit versus Other Factors

We have pointed to nine factors: (1) Destruction; (2) "Happens To"; (3) "Take Away What One Had"; (4) Vulnerability and Powerlessness; (5) Decline versus Incline; (6) Impossibility of Continuing Life; (7) Decisiveness of Death; (8) Not Being Around Later; and (9) Consequences of Beginning Earlier. I shall assume that (8) and (9) are not significant and that (7) is wrong since asymmetry would remain even if decisiveness were avoided by our having extended indefinitely into the past. How can we evaluate the relative importance of the Nagel/Parfit proposal and the remaining factors (so far as they do not depend on that proposal) in accounting for the asymmetry problem and for the badness of death?

Let us imagine various situations in which our creation and death occur somewhat differently than they actually do, so as to eliminate certain of these factors. We can then see whether eliminating some of these factors would alter our view about whether death is worse than prenatal nonexistence. If eliminating the factors does not significantly alter our asymmetrical view, then those factors cannot be very important in accounting for the asymmetry.

Death

Imagine that death does not destroy us physically. We enter instead into an unconscious, insensate state through the action of a force-field that inhibits organic function. Imagine, further, that we did *not* come into existence, but existed in this unconscious, insensate state forever in the past and were somehow triggered into consciousness. (Some might argue that there was no person until active consciousness began. But, I think, we could say that a completed physical organism was me even if my conscious life had not yet begun.) Then our prenatal nonexistence—really unconscious existence—like death, would happen to us and would show us to be too weak to overcome forces keeping us from the goods of life.

The differences between not giving a good and taking it away and between incline and decline cannot be altered in our conception of prenatal and posthumous nonexistence, I think. We can, however, eliminate the factor of permanent posthumous nonexistence from death. Imagine that it involves an unconscious, insensate state interrupted by miniscule periods of return to consciousness every trillion years.[11] Then our "nonexistence" continues to be temporary. For my purpose here, which is to eliminate only the factor of *permanent* nonexistence, we must also suppose that the total of miniscule periods of consciousness do not add up to what is experienced as a continuous and substantial period of consciousness. If this additional supposition is thought to be illegitimate, we can achieve my purpose in another way. Imagine that death involves an unconscious, insensate state that lasts a trillion years and is then interrupted for *one* miniscule period of consciousness followed by *permanent* nothingness. We then ask ourselves whether our *concern* with death in this latter case begins only after the trillion years (when nonexistence will be permanent) or even before (when unconscious insensate existence will be temporary)?

Figure 3-2 corresponds to the new descriptions of creation and death, with the understanding that *both* alternatives to permanent nonexistence discussed above are represented in the right-hand side of the figure. Instead of death, let us say that we are representing *death**.

Is death* any better than death, from the view outside the life? It does not seem to be. This suggests that the only remaining "outside" factors that could play significant roles in accounting for asymmetry are: (5) decline, (3) the taking away of significant life once had (given that the miniscule return is insignificant), and (4) the vulnerability of consciousness and/or sensation once in existence. Furthermore, *modified* outside factors are still available to play explanatory roles. These include (6) the impossibility of any *significant* amount of continuation of the goods of life (as opposed to having a miniscule period in a trillion years). Are any of these factors really important?

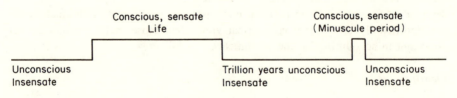

Conscious, sensate
Life

Conscious, sensate
(Minuscule period)

Unconscious
Insensate

Trillion years unconscious
Insensate

Unconscious
Insensate

Figure 3.2

Declines, Takings, and Vulnerability

Let us see whether decline, taking away of consciousness/sensation that has been, and vulnerability of these (rather than the Nagel/Parfit Proposal) help account for the asymmetry. First, imagine that these three factors occur in the past of a now-living person rather than in his future. (Alternatively, with respect to someone already dead, imagine that they occurred earlier in his life rather than at its end.) If they occur in the past they will, of course, signify only temporary cessation of a significant amount of the goods of life. That seems acceptable, since we wish to isolate their roles independent of permanent cessation of a significant amount of goods.[12] These factors are negatives even in the past, I believe. They would not, however, be a source of much misgiving, especially not now, to the person in whose past they occurred.

An Analogy

We might also consider an analogy. Suppose we compare (a) someone who began life sighted and after a few moments of sight went blind, with (b) someone who was born blind, was always blind, but who will have a few minutes of sight before he dies. (See Figure 3-3.) Does the fact that the second life involves an incline whereas the first involves a decline, vulnerability, and a taking away create a significant difference? (In both cases there is also *permanent* cessation of a significant amount of good.) Or is the total time spent blind most significant in evaluating the people's lives? The total time seems to me most significant.[13] It is only when we introduce identification with and habituation to sight and (the further separate facts) of memory of sightedness and problems of adjusting to blindness, that decline seems *much worse*.[14] Furthermore, the separate fact of destruction of the organs of sight, independent of the loss of sight, does not seem to add anything. So, the facts of decline and destruction per se do not count here, at least.

Notice that this example is specifically constructed so as to contain only a very brief period of sight relative to all the time of blindness, whether we incline to it or decline from it. The point of constructing the example in this way is to mimic the truth about the human life span in comparison to infinite time; even a life of one hundred years is like the minuscule period of sight. However, constructing the example in this way (as in [a] and [b]) may also be misleading for it is possible that decline is in some ways worse when the thing declined from is something substantial. The longer the human life span, the more substantial the entity declined from appears *from the human perspective*, even though, from the point of view of the universe, it is a minuscule period of time.

Likewise, an incline to sixty years of sight after ten years of blindness may seem better than a decline to ten years of blindness after sixty years of sight (as in [a'] and

Figure 3.3

[b′]). Something has to be pretty firmly "there" in order for incline or decline not to be swamped by the insignificance of what we incline to or decline from. (This may be one reason why the death of a newborn, even assuming it is a person, does not seem so serious, though the newborn loses out on more life than someone who dies at a later age.) It seems that we have to watch for the interaction effects between decline and what we decline from and to and between incline and what we incline to and from.

Still it is important to point out that, even when incline/decline matters, one might exchange the incline pattern for a decline pattern, in order to obtain a bit more actual time with a good such as sightedness.

Total Absence of Good

The worst life (with respect to vision) would be a constant state of blindness with no sight. Unlike a constant state of blindness, a constant state of nonexistence—a person never having come into existence at all—does not, I think, worry us. We should spend more to resurrect a dead person than to create someone who never existed, other things equal, *if* we act from concern for the particular individual who would or would not live. Even when we contemplate in the case of someone who now exists with definite properties, the possibility that he should never have existed, nothingness is not the threat it seems when it comes after something that already exists. This is a reason some might have for preferring never to have existed rather than to die.

This contrast between constant blindness (worse than decline to blindness) with constant nothingness (not necessarily worse than decline to nothingness) suggests that the individual's decline into nonexistence or unconsciousness/insensateness is more important than the individual's decline into blindness. But this need not be due to the relative importance of decline in comparison to the amount of time of nonexistence. It may be due to the significance of there ever having been a subject. There will not be a subject in matters of life and death unless nonexistence comes as a change from something, rather than as constant nothingness.

Conclusion

What shall we conclude about the significance of the factors of decline, of taking away, and of vulnerability? They are all negatives in comparison to their opposites, and their badness is greater as that to which we decline is worse and that from which we decline is better. They are, however, factors of "insult" rather than of deprivation, given that the goods lost are the same whether we failed to incline earlier or failed to decline later. This alone suggests that they cannot be as important in accounting for why death is bad as is the loss of more goods of life, at least when the loss of good is great (as it is). However, the Insult factors do have the virtue of being identifiable from outside someone's life as negatives of death not shared by prenatal nonexistence, unlike *future* (versus past) losses of goods of life evaluated from a point within life.

Death's Endlessness

Let us now turn to the factor of the endlessness of death. We have modified it to take account of a minuscule interruption to nothingness, so that we are concerned with it as the permanent end to *significant* periods of continuing life. (In this context, I shall think of a significant period as anything from several years to infinity. The idea of significance is context dependent.) We do not object to death simply because it is the permanent end; for if it were temporary with a minuscule reprieve, it would be equally bad. Why do we object to death's ending all significant periods of life? Suppose it were simply because there would be a smaller total of goods of life credited to our account. Then this problem could be remedied by our finding out that we had, after all, been living infinitely before the point we thought we had begun. This would amount to the claim that we had always been in existence but will come to an end. In general, for any loss of future significant goods, we can imagine the same amount added to our past.

If our greater worry about death in comparison to prenatal nonexistence still does not disappear as we add goods to the past, then it is *future* loss that is of concern to us. One way to explain this is by reference to the Parfitian point; we just are more concerned with future absence of goods. But insofar as only the *future* absence of goods also signifies that there has been a decline and that something that existed has been taken away and that we are vulnerable, these three factors may also be explanatory.

The Limbo Man

There is, however, a further alternative interpretation of the data presented so far. (It was first mentioned as a criticism of Nagel in Chapter 1.) Let us grant the significance of future losses, because they are in the future and also perhaps because they involve Insult factors. Still, there is more than one way in which to be concerned about future losses. The Nagel/Parfit view emphasizes loss of the *additional quantity* of the goods of life. A second way to be concerned about future losses focuses not on the quantity of what is lost, but on the fact that the goods and the person will be over forever. For example, someone may be concerned that death, *because* it eliminates significant future goods, *means* that any significant life for himself is all over; all potential for and possibility of himself living a significant period is eliminated. The loss of goods via prenatal existence does not do this since his life is still to come and prenatal nonexistence does not foreclose the possibility of the continuation of life once begun.[15]

A person who has this reason for his concern that there will be no more future goods if he dies might prefer to go instead into a living coma from which he could come back to consciousness for a significant but not infinite period of time. He might also be willing to extend the unconscious state further and further into the future, putting off actually living the significant but finite period. This is the *Limbo Man*. (See Figure 3-4). Insofar as the Limbo Man is concerned with the absence of the possibility of any significant future for himself (rather than with more and more

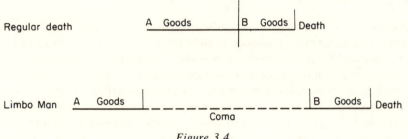

Figure 3.4

goods per se), the Insult Factors may also have more weight. This is because they weigh less relative to concern over *quantity* of goods.

Such a man chooses this "limbo" as against living the *same* finite conscious period sooner. That he prefers this arrangement suggests that postponement would diminish what causes him to think that death is bad. Therefore, something other than the loss of more and more future goods of life plays a role in his view of the badness of death. That is, since he does not choose to put off the lived experience for the sake of getting *additional* goods of life and since he is willing to go without experiencing goods just for the sake of having the possibility of experience always there, his concern that he and goods for him not be "all over" is not captured by the Nagel/Parfit Proposal. In sum, "no more goods" in the Nagel/Parfit Proposal signifies no additional goods (a quantitative notion). However, there is a different concern about "no more goods" that is signified by a fixed set of goods being all over.

There are really two types of Limbo Man, who may act on two types of reasons. He may truly care about the goods of life and want these not to be all over, even when this does not mean that their total will increase. Or he may want future life not so much for the sake of the goods within it as in order to avoid the fact of himself being all over. But eternal limbo would also mean he is not over, so why is the possibility of returning to goods important? He may care about future goods because they mean *he* will not be all over and a life worthy of him, i.e., with goods in it, will be possible. The second, *Radical,* of Limbo Man prefers putting off a future significant period of goods because he wants there to be a significant period of a good *future for him* as far into the future as possible. He wants there to be no time in the future when there is no significant good future time for him; he wants a significant good future for him not to be totally a thing of the past, permanently over. (These are all different ways of making the same point.) Things, therefore, can get better because goods are further in the future, since the potential for his living is present longer.

Either Limbo Man's response to the end of all possibility of (significant periods of) life, which we referred to as the Extinction Factor, is terror. The suggestion that a Limbo Man may live in order to avoid dying helps explain the view (described on p. 19) that life derives its positive value relative to the alternative of death as a negative factor involving a person being all over. In this sense, the idea that the nothingness of death is an intrinsic, albeit unexperienced, evil is not laughable.

Extending Oneself into the Past

A Limbo Man's reasons for extending his life into the future are not available for extending one's life into the past. Let us suppose that the Limbo Man is asked which of the following three states of affairs he would prefer: (1) that he began when he did, at $t1$; (2) that he was in existence infinitely in the past, in a coma state that ended at $t1$; (3) that he began consciousness later than $t1$, but for each period in which he thought he had been conscious yet turns out to have been alive and unconscious instead, his existence (albeit in an unconscious state) began that much earlier.

I do not believe that even a Limbo Man would prefer (2) or (3) to (1) because the desire not to have things be all over, the desire that the universe continue to hold the possibility of one's existence once one has already existed is *already* satisfied by *ordinary* prenatal nonexistence followed by life. We need not alter the past as we must alter the future in order to achieve what the Limbo Man desires.

On the other hand, moving the beginning of his existence backward, albeit in an unconscious state, *would* help someone whose concern was that he had not always existed and that there was a point before which it is impossible he existed, at least so long as the move was backward to a significant period of conscious goods. Such a person would not feel the asymmetrical attitude showing greater concern for death. That asymmetrical attitude is concerned with the future impossibility of one's life. But insofar as only the future impossibility of our life is associated with the Insult Factors, these as well as brute concern for *future* possibility may explain the asymmetry. Only the Insult Factors would point to differential factors observable from *outside* the life. The brute preference for the future is felt by someone from a point within his life.

Significant Returns

We have noted how minuscule "comebacks" would not improve matters over permanent nonexistence. Let us now consider a minimal comeback that would be an improvement (call it m).

Parfit has suggested (in conversation) that the plausibility of the Limbo Man example may depend on how long the significant return to consciousness is. He suggests that, if it is another seventy-year period, one might not take seriously that this period *will* end and so not prefer to put off having it. That is, if the life would last as long as this, our bias towards the near would make us unconcerned about its distant end. Parfit suggests that if we imagine instead only a few years of additional life, we avoid this problem.

If we pick an even smaller period, say three weeks, for m, we can acquire further evidence that concern about things' being all over is different from worry about no more goods of life in a quantitative sense. Accordingly, let us suppose that someone does not worry about his future nonexistence as the temporary period of limbo approaches, but postpones his concern until the three-week comeback period arrives. Since the three-week period does not in itself provide many additional goods of life, it is probably not because it represents more goods that worry is postponed. Rather, it is comforting because it serves as a *buffer zone* between one's life and one's life being all over.

These considerations may also help explain why the last days or moments of someone's life tend to have increasing significance, even as the amount of goods they represent decreases. Each additional day or moment is not (or not only) valued for the additional goods it brings, but rather because it puts off everything's being all over. "Everything's being all over" (as I have been trying to explain) does not reduce to there being fewer goods of life in the future than there might otherwise have been. This may be something to keep in mind when caring for the dying: what may be insignificant as an extension of real goods can be significant as a buffer.[16]

How Significant Is the Limbo Man?

How large a role does this concern for being in the future per se (rather than just continuing into the future consciously with more and more goods) play in our concern about death? An objection to its being very important is presented by the following test (based on a suggestion by Parfit): Suppose the Limbo Man is striking a bargain with God to go into the limbo state in order not to be all over, but another option is offered to him. Instead of going into limbo and coming back to get all and only the goods he would have gotten if he had gone straight along to his end, he is offered the option of going straight along to his end without limbo and getting some *additional* goods. Perhaps he would opt for a *slight* increase in future goods coming sooner over somewhat less coming later in the future. This would suggest that later-in-the-future-because-over-later serves only as a tie breaker; that is, not much is necessary to override its weight. If so, how can it be very important in accounting for our concern with death? (Note the following contrast: If Parfit is right, we would not give up some future goods for the sake of having had more goods in the past (when distinctive achievement or product is *not* an issue). Yet we would give up ending later, in order to get more goods earlier in the future. This is true, even though we can equally well say, "We must be all over sometime; so why pay in goods to avoid its happening sooner?" *and* "Future goods must stop sometime; so why pay in total good (including past good) to avoid there being no more goods now?") This suggests that not having more and more future goods of *life* is more important than being all over in accounting for why death is bad—and truly worse than prenatal nonexistence.

Choosing What We Fear More to Avoid What We Fear Less

Nevertheless, I strongly suspect that the *terror* of death stems from our awareness of the fact that we will be all over, the Extinction Factor. To prefer having a greater amount of earlier future goods to putting the end further off is a triumph of rationality over fear. That is, *one* reason death is bad is that it prevents additional future goods. Call this *R1*. Another reason is "being all over." Call this *R2*. We know we cannot avoid *R2* if we want actually to have the significant finite goods of life sometime. The alternative is putting them off forever to avoid *R2*. So we accept *R2* sooner rather than later for the sake of dealing to some degree with *R1*. It is also reasonable to come to life rather than not exist at all, for the sake of actually experiencing or acting. These are rational moves.

Indeed, if we are *really* rational, I believe, we will always resist the temptation to go into the limbo state. We will take goods of life as soon as we can. We will also prefer a world in which we have had greater past goods and do not go into limbo, to a world in which we had fewer and fewer past goods and do go into limbo. These rational moves do not show that *R2* is not more important in accounting for our distinctive concern with death than is *R1*. *It just shows that we care more about something else than we care about our distinctive concern with death*. This can be true even though the absence of the thing we care more about (more goods of life) is also one of the things that make death bad.

In this respect, what I have been claiming is that the distinctive evil of death— being all over in a sense that contrasts strongly with having quantitatively fewer goods—may behave like an intrinsic evil of experience. We tend to fear these intrinsic evils more than we fear the absence of great goods; yet we will undergo these evils in order to obtain these goods. For example, the idea of being boiled alive in oil holds a terror for us that total nonexistence does not, and yet we might prefer to have a good life rather than never exist even though we know we will be boiled in oil at its end. The amount of expected goods needed to overcome the terror of being boiled in oil is probably greater than the amount necessary to justify coming into existence and dying a normal death, or the amount necessary to justify becoming nonexistent sooner rather than putting off the end with an intervening limbo state. This is because being boiled in oil involves an *experienced* evil whereas being all over involves an *unexperienced* evil. In sum, I would not necessarily avoid that which causes me terror by choosing that which does not cause me terror (e.g., total nonexistence or quantitatively fewer goods).[17]

Eternal Limbo

Of course, putting off the significant goods further and further into the future is no total solution to the negative factor of life's being all over. For once one returns from the temporary limbo, one will be all over in a while. If one avoids this by never coming back, one will be as good as dead anyway. If conscious experience is a good, being as good as dead is bad, to put it mildly. The Radical Limbo Man, however, cares so little for actually living and so much for just still being unfinished combined with the eternal possibility of a good life worthy of him, that for him the subtle distinction between being all over, on the one hand, and *never* exercising a real capacity to return to good life, on the other hand, is significant. He would stay in limbo forever.

Consider stories in which someone exchanges his immortal soul for *eternal* life on earth. Some have said that such eternal life from which there was no escape would be terrible, even if life were not intrinsically bad. Having an escape route may not be a sufficient improvement, however; one might fear using it if it meant a permanent end. What Faust should really hold out for is the possibility of an eternal life of experience and action with the possibility of an escape that can be temporary, so that the potential for his future *infinite* return is never cut off.

SUMMARY

In trying to account for the badness of death we have now come to focus on three factors: the *Insult Factor*, that death happens to a person who has already existed and undoes him; the *Future Deprivation Factor*, that death deprives the person who dies of significant future goods (the Nagel/Parfit point); and the *Extinction Factor*, that death means that the possibility of anything significant for the person in the future is over. The second factor exhibits a brute concern for future over past loss; if it did not it would just be the Deprivation Factor and would be shared equally with prenatal nonexistence. The Deprivation Factor—independent of temporal location—does make both death and prenatal nonexistence bad as does concern with goods of achievement rather than with goods considered in a non-achievement mode. The third factor is meant to be distinguished from the Future Deprivation Factor in its concern with "being all over" rather than with not having more and more goods of life. If the third factor is dependent on a brute concern with the future impossibility of existence (rather than past impossibility), *this* aspect of it will not be asymmetrically observable from outside someone's life. The second and third factors may, however, be combined with those factors which make death an insult, and those factors do seem to be asymmetrically present in death as compared with prenatal nonexistence. Only the Insult Factor seems totally independent of brute concern for the future. (It is true that only a loss that at some point is in the future can take away what was or happen to what was. But it is not because there will be nothing in the future that we are insulted. It is because there will be nothing in the future of what was in the past. Furthermore, the insults are observable from outside a life that has already ended.)

NOTES

1. So in Nozick's Spore Case, even if the spore is not the person, but only gives rise to the person, *when* the spore is triggered may affect a person. That is, he does not live as long as he would have had he been triggered earlier. If *I* were identical with the spore, and did not merely arise from it, nonconscious existence would be happening to me.

2. Fred Feldman points this out in "F. M. Kamm and the Mirror of Time."

3. The idea of moving in the wrong direction relative to value is found in Nagel's discussion of the wrong of intending harm, in *The View from Nowhere* (New York: Oxford University Press, 1986).

4. Not all declines are permanent and the preference for an incline over a decline need not depend on the permanence of the decline. A life of alternating ups and downs may be worse than a life of steady improvements, given otherwise identical contents.

5. For further discussion of why inclines may make things better and declines make them worse, see the appendix following chapter 4.

6. I have attributed the Deprivation, rather than the Insult, Factor to Nagel. However, in "Death" he does also emphasize the way in which death (and certain other evils) involve processes of reduction from what the person once was. Nagel does not, however, note the way in which prenatal nonexistence lacks these characteristics.

7. This is on the supposition that the future pain is also followed by nonpainful life. Because of the special significance of the time period just before the end, pain that *ends* a life may also be a qualitatively different thing from other periods of pain. Our final time alive

may have such special significance because there is no time after it that can compensate for anything bad in it, and only good that happens later (not earlier) is seen as compensatory. This would be another example of the significance of future over past goods. We rely on this view in denying some good to the young because they will be compensated by having a future. We give the good to an old person because he has no future to compensate him for having no goods now. However, that he has no future means not only that there is no way to compensate for a bad final stage of life. It means that we want him to have a good last stage before disaster comes. But does this not suggest that past good *can* be compensatory for a future disaster? In helping the old, of course, we may be denying a young person something when there is no *certainty* he will have a future and giving something to an older person who has already had a full life. These factors raise moral problems.

8. It might seem that the fact that prenatal nonexistence comes to an end and posthumous nonexistence does not implies that the former is less bad because it has deprived us of less good time alive than death will. For if nonexistence comes to an end, must it not be finite rather than infinite? However, it does seem possible to talk of an *infinite* period prior to one's creation that nevertheless comes to an end. It might be thought that, even if the infinite period ended, any being *living through it* would never come to *its* end. This, too, appears to be incorrect. That is, a being could experience coming to the end of an infinite time period. We, in fact, began, and we *cannot* conclude from this that the universe does *not* extend back in time infinitely. Therefore it must be possible to pass through an infinite time period. I owe these points to Derek Parfit.

9. Though it could not make up for noneternal existence if eternal existence were crucial to the value of a being.

10. Mentioned in conversation by Mary Mothersill.

11. I owe this idea to Derek Parfit.

12. A methodological caution, however: We may be missing a significant interaction effect between two properties when we consider them separately rather than in combination. For example, it may be significant if we (a) decline into (b) permanent cessation of a significant amount of goods. However, we can consider some factors separately now and then combine them later.

13. This example was put to me by Derek Parfit.

14. The question can also be raised whether interfering with patterns of identification and habituation can be bad, independent of further adjustment problems or painful memories.

15. Nagel mentions in "Death" (footnote, p. 9) that "something about the future *prospect* of permanent nothingness is not captured by the analysis in terms of denied possibilities." However, his emphasis is on the *prospect* element (Parfit's suggestion), rather than on permanent nothingness.

16. However, I believe, it is the real-goods value of further life, not buffer value, that should be used in deciding whom to help avoid death when we cannot help everyone.

17. The tiebreaker argument also suggests a failure to take seriously what I have called the Principle of Contextual Interaction. That is, it seems to assume that if a factor (a) is unimportant relative to another factor (b), it is unimportant tout court. But factor (a) may still be important relative to factor (c).

4

Appropriate Attitudes
toward Nonexistence

If by Eternity is understood not endless temporal duration but timelessness, then he lives eternally who lives in the present.

Wittgenstein

Given the factors that we have suggested play a part in our asymmetrical attitude toward death and prenatal nonexistence, how should we evaluate that attitude?

Insult Factors

Let us begin by considering factors under the insult category.

Suppose we focus on deprivations happening to someone per se, considered apart from the absence of goods that death involves. This may indicate overconcern with insult rather than injury. Such concern with insults could lead one to prefer that a life, with whatever goods it holds, never have existed, merely so as to avoid its ending. Someone with such an attitude might be charged with being too proud and possessive and not caring enough about the goods of life.

Concern for the *vulnerability* exhibited when something is destroyed should be tempered by recognition of the fact that the vulnerability or invulnerability of a thing does not necessarily reflect on its intrinsic worth. Transient beauty is no less great because it lasts only a brief time.

The End of the Better

Indeed, it may actually be better that a more perfect rather than a less perfect thing be eliminated by death because of what this signifies. This will be true, for example, if the goods of life persist until death and are eliminated only by death. For this suggests that there is nothing internal to those goods that makes them end before death. In contrast, if a human relationship or interest becomes boring before death, this reflects negatively on that relationship or interest. The way in which something ends, rather than simply that it ends, shows us its worth. (These views are inconsistent with the belief that, in a sense, an end only comes when called for. That is, there is some dissatisfaction, some worm in the apple, which calls forth the cause that ends the seemingly good relationship, interest, or the like. To the extent that this belief is true, it suggests that there are imperfections inherent in all things that end.)

So it is often better that death destroy what is good, even though death is more harmful if that happens. For it is better that death deprive us of good relationships or pursuits than that it end a life that contains no such goods. For example, as we improve the lives of older people, so that their lives would have gone on well but for death, we make death worse for those people. Yet that is no reason not to improve their lives. It is better that life go on in a way that allows for something worse to happen. Sometimes *within a life* as well the continuation of the goods of life is not possible because of external causes, that is, causes that do not reflect negatively on the goods of life themselves. For example, an illness can end the goods of life before death. It is commonly preferred that death come during such an illness rather than by an accident in the midst of health. Yet its coming in illness could mean that there were fewer total goods in the life. This is because the alternative to the illness in life would have been the goods' continuing up to death. Although death *itself* deprives us of more when our good life would go on but for death, we lose as much (only earlier) if illness robs us of goods before death and then death finishes us off.[1]

The Good of Senseless Deaths

Therefore, it may be wrong to prefer that death itself *make sense* by ending a bad life rather than ending a life that could have continued on well—to prefer, for example, that death end a bad illness rather than that an accident end a happy life. We would then mistakenly approve of a world in which the time a person spends well and happy is shortened. As people's lives improve, therefore, we can look forward to more and more *senseless* deaths, deaths that end lives that would otherwise have continued to be good. Indeed, we should prefer that all deaths be senseless in this way. Of course, if terminal illness is unavoidable, death may be best when it occurs right at the point where a disease would put an end to the goods of life anyway, including even the good of dealing well with the illness. In such cases, death does not prevent future goods, and it does end what still is, if only momentarily, a good life. It only prevents oncoming misery.

If the fact that life ends does not reflect negatively on the good contents of life, it does reflect negatively on human life per se, insofar as it would be better to have further goods and insofar as finitude is an internal characteristic of human life. It also reflects badly on the world as it is that persons die if they are, in being mortal, not being treated properly, that is, not being treated as befits an individual who does not deserve to die. (I am here assuming that goods of life, which are present *only* because we are finite, do not outweigh goods we would have if not finite.) Those who find comfort in the fact that life's finitude puts an end to misery are left with the fact that human life is not as good as it could be: misery within the life has put an end to its goods before death occurs.

Inclines and Declines

The shape of events at the edges of life, as well as within it (*incline or decline*) is also an Insult Factor. How much concern with this factor is appropriate? Consider first the "within life" question. Does concern with incline or decline show a lack of appreciation for the goods themselves? It may be that proper involvement with what goods one has, at the moment one has them, makes comparative evaluations of these goods with other goods impossible. If one focuses on what one has at any given moment, one is less aware of how this experience compares with past or future experiences. So, to the extent that one does *not* attend to and make the best of each experience one is having, the shape of one's life will matter more, since awareness of shape—though not the shape itself—depends on relative evaluations. But surely it is better to attend to and make the best of, each experience than not to.

This is not to say, however, that comparative judgments would not be true and that decline will not be a defect. But if, from within a life, attention to the good one has when one has it prevents one from making actual comparisons, then *actual* concern about decline or incline is a sign of something gone wrong in living one's life.

A similar story could be told about incline and decline at the beginning and the end of life. If one should be most concerned with the non-shape goods of life, there should be more emphasis on prenatal *and* postnatal nonexistence as no-goods, rather than on whether there is an incline from or decline to them per se.

A More Empirical Point

It could be argued that living in a decline and so having greater goods earlier in life might be beneficial because it would increase the total amount of good. That is, the goods one has had are not merely over with; they help form the sort of person one is and will become in the future. The right sort of good may fortify us and allow us to get more out of the worse times than we would otherwise. (This is a counterargument to the claim that a decline contains fewer goods since one cannot appreciate lesser goods as much once one has had greater ones. If we allow knowledge of incline and decline to be present, an incline will also involve the good of having more to look forward to, but a decline will have the good of good memories).

Character

Good character and wisdom seem strong exceptions to any attempt to downgrade inclines, however. It seems to matter a lot whether we have good character and wisdom at first and then lose them within life (decline) or are without them at first and achieve them in life (incline). That is, we should care whether we are corrupted or saved. With respect to other goods, such as health, wealth, and talent, badness of the decline *is* minimized by involvement with whatever good *is* present, and the ability to master a decline gives rise to the good of strengthened character and resourcefulness. But when such good character traits are themselves involved in the decline—the very traits that one thinks should protect *themselves* against decline, can anything minimize the negative weight of decline?[2] These are the cases in which cutting off a life before it gets worse seems most tempting.

However, cutting off a life that is about to turn for the worse with respect to character may only prevent the full flowering of badness and its instantiation in acts and attributes. Such a cutting off may be preferred by someone with good character yet the fact that one has to die to avoid turning into a bad person means that one is *already* a person with the capacity for such bad change.

Further, if one's future has already been claimed by one's worsening character, escape by death is hardly a major victory. Something similar can be said about escape from pain and misery by suicide, which is often described as a victory. There is not much reason to feel that one is victorious in the face of pain simply because one can escape it by death: if it forces one to such lengths by taking over one's life it has already scored a big win. It has either wiped out all the goods of one's life or made it impossible to stay and enjoy those which remain. Analogously, it would be peculiar to think that one could show how weak the Mafia is by pointing out that one can escape it by leaving all one's belongings and moving, impoverished, to another country.

Other Factors

A major factor in accounting for the asymmetrical attitude, it was suggested above, is concern for the loss of future significant periods of the goods of life (the *Future Deprivation Factor*). Although a brute concern for *future* (versus past) losses, it was admitted, did not alone show that future losses were worse for one than past losses. In addition, there seems to be a separate concern about significant goods being "all over" (the Extinction Factor): a life could be made worse or better, without varying the total of future goods, by ending that life sooner or later in the future. (It was admitted that the impossibility of a future is matched by the impossibility of a past, as a result of prenatal nonexistence, and brute concern for the future does not mean the future impossibility is worse.) How should we deal with these factors?

Extinction Factor

Consider the Extinction Factor first. Putting off the goods of life further into the future in order to avoid their being over can take several forms. We have already described two such forms in discussing the Limbo Man and the Radical Limbo Man. A third form involves preferring that a life begin as late in the future as possible, even though the content and length of the later life will be the same as that of the earlier life. All these "strategies" seem to conflict with a proper appreciation of the goods of life. Given that total goods remain constant, someone who cares for the goods should, I think, want them sooner rather than later. If it is right to appreciate the goods of life, it seems we should master our desire to put off having them until a later future. This is because, if we put them off, we are resisting the pull of the good, even if we will eventually get these goods anyway. But the good should be *irresistible*. Therefore, concern with putting off goods, like concern with the shape of the order in which goods come, shows greater concern for *self* than for the goods themselves.

But what of the conflict between past and future goods? If we would prefer that a given set of goods come in the future rather than that they have come and gone in the past, does this preference show a greater or a lesser appreciation of the goods of life? Many might say that it shows greater appreciation of the goods of life. (This assumes that we are interested in the goods for their own sake, not just as a way to avoid being "all over.")

Could we possibly argue that preferring that the goods of life be past shows that one has greater appreciation of them? It has already been argued that it would be wrong to prefer a few years in the future, not amounting to much as a product, to having lived a good life in the past, considered as a product. But, holding products constant, could we not prefer the security of having experienced many goods, rather than risk not getting as much in the future?[3] Suppose we eliminate the element of risk from the future, as it is irrelevant to the question that concerns us here. Is it then revelatory of greater appreciation to prefer having goods in the past rather than in the future? I do not think so.

Suppose we allow that there would be *more* or better experienced goods in the past. Do we then show greater appreciation of goods by preferring that they be in the past?

In *some* ways I think this question is similar to the following: Who loves great art the most, the person who will give up being an artist for the sake of supporting others who will produce greater art than he can, or the person who will not sacrifice his own artistic work in this way?[4] I take supporting the work of others to be analogous to greater goods that *will not* be experienced by us, but *have been* in the past, and doing one's own work as analogous to our experiencing goods in the future. Perhaps all we can say is that there is more than one way of showing appreciation for the goods of life (and art). (The difference between the case of art and the case of life, of course, is that my past goods are goods I *have experienced*, whereas art that others produce is not art I *have produced*.) Yet, I have suggested that wanting a fixed quantity of goods in the near rather than further future does exhibit greater appreciation for them.

Certainly the more seriously we take our life as a product, the more we appreciate past goods. We may think (mistakenly) that what happened in the past is not real. But if we take seriously our lives as products and our experiences as achievements within our lives, then we will not question the reality of our own past.

Deprivation Factor

Throughout this discussion, I have been agreeing that not getting more goods of life (in the sense of more and more additional goods) is indeed bad. But it is time to point out how this may be less important than it seems and, hence, how a Deprivation Factor may be of less significance, whether it is deprivation of future or of past goods. This would be so if either (1) human life does not, in fact, contain the possibility of many goods, no matter how long one lives; or (2) the most important goods of life are not such that the more, the better—or, more precisely, are not such that the more time we have with them, the better.

With respect to the first point, it may seem that many of the activities and goods people involve themselves with have no *objective* value, so they are not desired because they are truly worthwhile. This means that it is not the case that we ought to desire the things we do desire if we did not. Suppose it were true that most people spend much of their lives valuing or merely pursuing the valueless, or, even worse, pursuing the objectively bad. Is it possible that valuing or pursuing the valueless or bad is itself an objectively valuable activity, perhaps if one is under an illusion as to the true worth of what one pursues. It seems hard to believe that it is. And, if it is not, perhaps a source of comfort in the face of death can lie in realizing that in losing these things one is not losing much. On the other hand, robbing much of life of its value is a high price to pay for such comfort.

When More Time Having Goods Is Not Better

Let us now consider certain true goods that are not such that more time having them is better. For example, the goods of fine character and wisdom—especially retaining a fine character once one attains wisdom—are supposed to make long life and the enjoyment of other goods better. In dying, a person who would have continued to have these goods of character and wisdom loses a better life, and hence something more valuable, than what is lost by a person who lacks fine character or wisdom. Yet the good person in losing life loses something that he needs less than another person does since he has already achieved something that is important in life. (Therefore, our despair at someone's being killed does not necessarily increase as his need for further life increases, given that we suffer less when the worse person is killed.)

If there are any other true goods in life, wisdom and fine character will make it possible to appreciate the value in a long life. Someone who is wise, therefore, will try to stay alive. He is not only less likely to risk losing his life for foolish reasons (true by definition, given wisdom), but given what he has, he may be less likely to want so much the less valuable things for which others risk their lives. But such a person values life and tries to stay alive more out of a capacity to enjoy and appreciate, and less out of need. Whether he stays alive or not depends on his biological capacity. Similarly, if one has achieved some insight while working, this insight may either spur one on to more work if one is not physically tired, or allow one to sleep more peacefully if one is physically tired.

Being versus Exercising

The view behind this analysis is that such things as fine character and wisdom are both the most important goods in life and to a large degree complete in themselves once one has them; the exercise of them is secondary. They are like the knowledge of a truth that one does not need to keep thinking about. Having a good character and having wisdom can be thought of as ways of *being* rather than as ways of acting or experiencing, though they involve the disposition to behave and experience in certain ways. In a sense, to achieve this type of being brings one closer to death than to life since one does not need the life in which to act out and experience one's character and wisdom. Such goods lead to a certain self-containment and detachment from life. At the same time, they heighten the ability to enjoy life and give one a stronger sense of being alive. (This could be taken to be a version of the Socratic view that philosophers prepare to die, in that they live a life that makes death of less consequence, if philosophers ever actually aimed at developing such a character.)

This may seem like a non-Aristotelian view, Aristotle having emphasized the exercise of virtue over a long life as constituting the good life. (Kant on the other hand de-emphasized duration of the good will and emphasized the value given by its intrinsic nature.) The view we are discussing does not deny that continued life can bring goods to the person who lives, both the goods of exercising virtues and other sorts of goods. Nor does it deny that if a person does stay alive, he will not be good and have a good life unless he exercises his virtues. It also does not conflict with the desire of the good person to remain alive for the sake of exercising virtues for the benefit of others. Therefore (to use Bernard Williams's distinction cited previously, p. 26), exercising virtues *can* be partially a categorical project, prompting one to go on living. It is not merely a hypothetical project, which one takes on *if* one remains alive. But all this is still different from saying that someone ought to go on living simply in order to keep the character he has achieved or to exercise it for its own sake. If someone really has a good character and it would remain with him if he lived, he already has the most important thing. Losing it through death is not the same as losing it *in life*. The latter is a loss revealed (as well as caused) by the failure to exercise the virtues *if* one goes on living.

The Threat That Death Presents to Different Goods

If this analysis were correct, we could draw the following additional conclusions: the goods of life that are truly most important may not be those with which we are emotionally most involved, or about which we feel most passionately. Death may be less of a threat to the most important goods than to the less important ones; yet people probably dislike the idea of death most intensely because of their great attachment to the less important goods. Many even *fear* a life that contains only what I have suggested are the more worthwhile goods. Such a life, full of wisdom and virtue, may seem close to death; one may even say that someone who has had these goods alone has never really "lived." It would turn out that the things that many people say make them feel "really alive" are not the greatest goods of life at all; indeed they may be its evils. Death, then, would be bad for the person who dies because it deprives him of what is *not* most deeply worthwhile.

The Goods of Action and Experience

The emphasis on character and wisdom, however, may leave out important goods to which death is a threat, for example, faithful love, of people or of projects, or aesthetic awareness. If they exist (and are what they seem to be), these goods of life would lie more completely within the realm of action and experience. Even here, however, once one has achieved the relationship or awareness, it will remain eternally true that one has achieved it, even if one dies. Although I oppose the view that wanting more of such goods is "greedy," nonetheless, to place more emphasis on having done or had such things than on actually doing or experiencing them does tend to make it matter less to us that these goods come to a permanent end.

This is not to deny that there remains an almost conceptual conflict between, on the one hand, valuing an achievement as action or experience and, on the other, caring more about that achievement's *having occurred* than about still-to-be-lived experiences and actions. Though this borders on paradox, I believe nevertheless that the past achievement of, say, great sensory awareness can stand as a replacement for future awareness and should not be exchanged for less great sensory awareness in the future. (Even when one can no longer remember the past experiences.)

It is a cliché to say that those who have experienced much and deeply are less threatened by death than others are. Such people have already achieved a great deal before death.[5] We are tempted to say that they are fulfilled, without implying, however, that they have had enough or would get nothing more out of future goods. (The problem here is to explain the idea of fulfillment without relying on the idea of being totally filled.) Those who are fulfilled and experience deeply may lose more when they lose further life (since that further life would be rich) than those who have had little in life and who experience only superficially. Yet these others need life more since they do not know it so well. In one sense it matters less that the better future is lost than that the worse one is, although we on the outside may despair more at loss of the former than of the latter.

Many of the acts and experiences we wish to have, however, are important not for the *occurrent* qualities of acting and experiencing, but for the sake of what they bring about and for the sake of our having brought about these outcomes; here there is no problem in valuing already past achievement.

Conclusion

I conclude that, both within life and at the beginning and end of life, one should not prefer putting off goods (if it does not increase the total amount of goods) or overly emphasize declines and endings (even while doing certain things to avoid them), at least when they do not reflect negatively on the goodness of that which ends. Above all, the more one can totally identify oneself with the goods one has achieved in life and the more it is really correct to do this, the luckier one is.

SUMMARY

In these chapters we have discussed why death, assumed to be total nonexistence, is bad for the person who dies and, related to this, why it is worse than prenatal nonexistence.

One answer, for which Thomas Nagel has argued, is that death deprives the person who dies of goods of life he would have had if he had lived (the *Deprivation Factor*). This is, I believe, part of the answer. Nagel, however, seems to misargue for it. That is, since death is bad though it involves no bad experiences, he argues that we can be harmed (or benefited) by what we do not experience, citing as an example the fact that one can be harmed by a ruined reputation after death. But one may disagree with this broad claim and still agree that death is bad for us (in part) because it deprives us of goods of life.

To see this, we noted that the good corresponding to the (supposed) harm of a posthumously ruined reputation is *no* ruined reputation after our death. If this is a good, it is an *unexperienced* good. However, it cannot be the absence of such goods as these that makes death bad for us, for we could continue to have such unexperienced goods after death. It is, rather, the fact that death deprives us of goods of experience and action that makes death bad for us.

One might even accept the (dubious) theory that all goods of life are experienced goods and still believe that death is bad because it deprives us of more such experiences. It could be true that death is bad, though not itself a bad experience, only because its alternative is goods of experience and action. All this would be consistent with its being true that no unexperienced occurrence whose alternative is *also* an unexperienced occurrence could be a harm. Therefore, we have modified the Deprivation Account of why death is bad so as to focus on loss of goods of experience and action.

Then we asked why death is worse for us than not beginning life earlier than we did, given that prenatal nonexistence also deprived us of more such goods of experience and action. One answer, suggested in the work of Derek Parfit, is that death is not worse than prenatal nonexistence, but only seems that way. This is because the loss brought about by our death lies in the future, but the loss through prenatal nonexistence is already in our past. We simply do not care as much about past experienced goods or ills as about those to come, even though they *are* in all other respects the same. This explanation implies that it is only from a perspective within a life that the asymmetrical attitude toward past and future loss of goods of life exists; if we look at a life from outside it we do not find this asymmetry. The *Future Deprivation Factor* combines Nagel's and Parfit's points.

I have suggested two different sorts of answer to the question of why death is bad and worse than prenatal nonexistence. They are intended to allow us to see that there are factors that make death bad, and worse than prenatal nonexistence, even if we view the life from outside it. In addition to the Deprivation Factor (shared with prenatal nonexistence) there are what I call the *Insult* and the *Extinction Factors,* both clusters of related factors. Neither of these is shared with prenatal nonexistence.

The Insult Factor arises because death involves a loss of goods happening to a person who already exists. Prenatal nonexistence deprives us of goods, but not by confronting us when we already exist and undoing what we already are. In confronting us when we already exist and undoing what we already are, death takes away what we think of as already ours and emphasizes our vulnerability. As part of this insult factor there is also the fact that death is seen as a *decline* from the good of life into nonexistence, assuming time's passage into the future. In contrast, our prenatal nonexistence is seen as ending with an *incline,* an improvement from nothing to the goods of life.

The Extinction Factor is that death ends permanently all significant periods of a person's life; there is no more possibility of significant periods of life. This property is not shared with prenatal nonexistence since that period holds the possibility of life to come. I believe that the end of all possibilities of life for us, in the order of time's passage, more than insult or deprivation, awakens terror in us. (It is the factor itself, however, that, supposedly, helps account for the badness of death not our terror in response to it.) The Extinction Factor has its analogue: the impossibility of existing earlier than we did in fact exist. Only if not being where "time is going" is worse than our not having been where time was, do we have a factor explaining an asymmetry that is visible from outside the life.

Is there evidence that this Extinction Factor is independently significant at least with respect to explaining why death is bad (even if it is not independent of Parfit's point in explaining the asymmetry)? Yes, if there is a general preference for putting off the end of life when this would do nothing to increase the total goods in a life. For example, we might prefer, as creators, to put off beginning someone else's life of fixed length and content in order to have it end later. We might also prefer interrupting our own life to enter into a limbo state and return later to complete our life, with no overall change in content, so that goods of life will not be over as soon. A Radical Limbo Man, who took the Extinction Factor to an extreme, might actually have no interest in the goods of life except as a vehicle for consciousness of himself, seeing his conscious life as a worthy means of avoiding permanent nonexistence. Such a person would take what is bad to be not loss of opportunity for the goods of life, but lack of possibility of conscious existing *per se*. The Radical Limbo Man might as willingly enter into a coma state that offered him the possibility of coming back to conscious life as he would undertake to live consciously, without even feeling the need to take advantage of the option to return to consciousness. That way he extends himself and has the eternal possibility of goods as well.

It is concern with the total absence of possibility of more conscious life for us, I believe, that lies behind the claim that the nothingness of death is bad in itself, not merely bad instrumentally. Death is bad because it is final. The limbo state, by contrast, is only relatively bad because there are no goods of life, including consciousness, in it. It lacks the badness of everything significant's being over once and for all.

But how important can this Extinction Factor be if one should rationally prefer not going into limbo and getting $n + 1$ goods to going into limbo and coming back for n goods? That our reason, which tells us to maximize goods, can triumph over the Extinction Factor does not show that being all over is not a source of terror at death. For, analogously, I may feel terror at the prospect of being boiled in oil at the end of my life and no terror at the idea of never coming to existence, and yet prefer to come to life for the sake of its goods rather than avoid being boiled in oil by never existing.

Though the Insult and Extinction Factors as described are not shared with prenatal nonexistence, prenatal nonexistence has properties not shared with death. It makes impossible, as posthumous nonexistence does not, existence prior to one's actual beginning. And it prevents us from having always had what we will have. If we care about these properties less than about those of posthumous nonexistence because of a brute concern for the future, we shall not have used them to justify the claim that death is worse than prenatal nonexistence. But if taking away what we have already had is an insult in a way that not having something (when we do not even yet exist) is not, and if not being where "time is going" is worse (as judged from a point outside life) than not having been where it was, then the two factors help account for the asymmetry. If there were something better about being where time is going, this need not, however, mean that we should sacrifice greater past goods for fewer goods in the future.

Finally, we dealt with how a good person might cope with the three identified reasons for death's being bad: Deprivation, Insult, and Extinction. First, such a person would minimize his concern with the Deprivation Factor if the most important goods of life are such that having more and more time alive does not increase the amount of good we have had. And, indeed, it seems to be true of some of the most important goods, including having a good character and knowing important truths, that, once one has them, they are complete in themselves. The more we can appreciate our lives as achievement, the less we depend on future life. Second, if one is not too concerned with personal affronts and understands that vulnerability does not reflect on intrinsic merit, the Insult Factor will be less important. Third, if we appreciate the goods of life more than we crave the assurance that either they or we will not be permanently over with, we will ignore the suggestion, inspired by the Extinction Factor, that we should put off having goods of life in order to put off their end and ours.

NOTES

1. In saying that it is better if death, coming at a given time to a given person, picks him off healthy and happy rather than miserable, I mean to imply that he will have time until death to be happy rather than miserable. I do not mean that, of any two people—one who would be healthy and happy and the other who would be miserable and sick—it is better that death come to the healthy rather than to the sick one.

2. One cannot avoid the problem of a decline in moral character by failing to fulfill moral requirements that we are capable of fulfilling at one time in order to fulfill others at a later time. We must do what we should when we should. Preferring a state of affairs in which we improve rather than decline morally is permissible so long as our preferences do not affect our behaving as we are required. Choosing actually to lower our moral character at a given time in order to improve it later would affect others in morally indefensible ways and thus raise a moral problem.

3. I do not wish to settle the question whether just having had many pleasurable experiences is an achievement of which to be proud.

4. Another analogy is to aiding one's own child—a significant interaction with it—versus allowing others to aid it even better than one can. (Parfit discusses this issue in *Reasons and Persons*.)

5. This is not to deny another significant phenomenon, which also seems to speak against the view that having more and more goods is better and better. Speaking figuratively, some people seem capable of living on air. They ask for little and are happy with the little they get. While others may think these people are simply not aware of the real goods they are missing, I am loath to agree that extreme modesty in desires and achieved goods is a misfortune. Of course, the proper analysis of this condition may be that such a person has the particular goods of an appreciative state of mind and changeless equanimity to a great degree. The change that is introduced by too many different *types of goods* (rather than simply more goods) is a negative interference for him. A less-pleasing explanation is that such a person is an extreme negative utilitarian; he is primarily pleased to have escaped the great evils that are ever-imminent possibilities, and that is what his minimal goods represent to him.

Appendix: Inclines and Declines

The preference for an incline over a decline seems to play some role in explaining the asymmetry problem. It seems to me worth examining as it operates both within life and at the edges of life. Perhaps this preference is a brute fact—if it is a fact—but I wish to consider whether it can be explained. Furthermore, I wish to find an explanation that abstracts from the way that *awareness* of the pattern of one's life may operate. (For example, I wish to abstract from the fact that it is better for people to have something to look forward to since this adds some good thoughts to the present.)

I shall first canvas possible explanations, without endorsing any. I will group them (insofar as this is possible) into two categories: *active* (A), by which I mean that there is some significant causal chain, set up either naturally or by an agent, from past to future; and *passive* (P), by which I mean that there is some significance to mere change over time, assuming time's direction from past to future, independent of any causal connection between past and future.

Preference for an Incline Tempered

Two preliminary points should be made. First, the preference for an incline rather than an *equal* distribution of goods over time presupposes that we conceive of a person as a single, unified entity, with the same person who lost out in the past benefiting in the future. If we did not have such a conception of the person, we might prefer equal distribution over time. (However, preferring equality between life stages does not necessarily mean that we lack a conception of a single unified person. It may only indicate that we are averse to any low periods in our life.)

Second, it may not, in fact, be possible in our actual lives to incline in all respects simultaneously so what we aim at will be different from a complete incline. For example, it seems that physical decline is inevitable after a point. Suppose we, therefore, organize other goods of life (if this is possible) so that they occur on a big incline, thereby producing an incline over all, *over*compensating for physical decline. Then there will never be a period when all goods are simultaneously at their peak. There may be, however, a preference for such a coincidence of all goods at their high points—a peak in all respects, and this preference may dominate the preference for an incline that lacks this quality. So we would prefer to take a peak in all respects (if this were possible) in our youth and then decline. Another alternative is to seek an incline in some respects that is *just enough* to compensate for decline in other respects, thus exhibiting a preference for overall equality between life stages. (For example, as physical strength or biological fertility diminishes, psychological powers might increase.)

Having qualified somewhat the view that there is a preference for *any* overall incline, consider what might lead us to prefer inclines when we do prefer them.

The Active Factors

(A1) One possible explanation of the preference for incline over decline in life is that life is viewed as a productive process, with the "you" that exists at its end *the product* either of the agent's efforts or of a natural process. If *you* really amount to a product that lies at the end of the productive process, then there will be a preference that the end be the best.

(A2) Furthermore, if we decline, our efforts may seem counterproductive. That is, we hope that the more we learn and the more we experience, the better we will make things in the future. Despite more learning and experience, things would get worse if we decline.

(A3) We have an ideal of rational change, according to which good should breed good rather than bad (even what is bad only relative to good). The idea of "desert" is also part of our idea of rational change. If what we have done in the past does not make us deserve punishment, we may object to decline. (Death is often considered unreasonable because it is thought to be undeserved; if one does not deserve capital punishment, it might be said, one does not deserve to die.)

(A4) A passionate response to decline may be prompted by a competitive attitude: it seems bad to be bested by one's past in a way in which it is not bad to be bested by one's future. Analogously, a competitive individual can live with the fact that in the future someone will do better work than he, but he has failed if he does not surpass his predecessors.

The Passive Factors

(P1) Our ordinary model of rational decision making applied to action tells us not to move from our current position unless we can move to a position as good or better, at least eventually if not at each individual step. If we are moved (passively) into the future (given that we don't want to die), the future should be as good as or better than the past if our passive movement is to accord with this model of rational decision making. That is, if we want to keep going somewhere, we should go somewhere better or at least as good as where we are or have been. The last part of one's life is the part that is over last, and since we want to move only to as good or better places, to prefer that earlier stages be better seems like preferring that one's life be over earlier rather than later.

(P2) Even if one has an equal amount of contact with the good in declining and inclining life patterns, in a decline one is headed in the wrong direction, away from the greatest good, whereas one should be headed toward it.[1] This point emphasizes an inappropriate relation to what is valuable, rather than the mere irrationality of the moves in a decline. Both of these views emphasize *the fact of process:* in addition to the good or bad states one winds up in, the move from a lower to a higher state is better than the reverse move.

Notice that it is permanent decline that is the worst. A life of ups and downs imperfectly exhibits rational change and the appropriate relation to value, but it does not mean that heading toward greater value is over.

(P3) If events decline within a life, but life still provides enough good to be worth continuing, we have a conflict between two goods. As we get more of the good of simple existence of ourself, we must get less of the other goods of life *per unit of additional life;* in moving on we increase our total of the goods of life, but the per-unit amount decreases. A more perfect scenario involves simultaneous increases in simple existence and per-unit figures.

(P4) A decline, furthermore, makes the future anticlimactic. One will not necessarily experience only what one has already experienced, but the new will represent things worth having to a lesser degree than the old. Still, this factor of being anticlimactic seems to depend on awareness of decline, from which I intended to abstract.

(P5) Decline not only offends against the idea of the rational in development; it may affect our view of the value of the higher state that precedes decline. That is, decline may emphasize the vulnerability of a higher state and its inability to sustain itself.

(P6) The person in the decline loses what was already his, in contrast with waiting to get what is not his already but will be his. There may, of course, also be habituation to and identification with what we have had and what we were, which makes living without these things more difficult than being without what we have never had. However, decline, I believe, is seen as bad even without memory of the past or habituation to the better.

Inclines and Experienced versus Unexperienced Goods

The factors I have so far described apply equally to experienced and unexperienced goods. Indeed the preference for future unexperienced goods over past ones just seems to *be* the preference for an incline over a decline. By contrast, if we prefer an incline in experienced goods from a point in life, this is in part because it gives us future experiences, rather than simply because it gives us an incline.

Thus an incline, given other reasons already cited for why it might be preferable to a decline, might even overcome a preference for having goods in the present. That is, if having something later would provide much of what we want in wanting to have it now, why not have the additional benefits (cited above) of the incline per se? (One reason to have the goods now, however, is that this represents the fact that the good should be irresistible.)[2]

(P7) These proposed active and passive explanations of our general preference for an incline assume that the total goods in the declining and inclining life are held constant. However, the fact that this may be an unrealistic assumption is the basis for another explanation of the preference for an incline, namely that, having experienced an early high point in one's life, one cannot enjoy lesser goods as much as one would have enjoyed them had they occurred first. Thus the total good in a declining life will be less than in an ascending one. (This may depend on memory and comparison of past with present and future. As such it depends on awareness of decline or incline, a factor I said I would not rely on to explain the different values of incline and decline.)

It is true that the lower period before a rise is also comparatively bad. But knowing *abstractly* that one is not experiencing as much as one might is different from having *experienced* more and comparing the present *experience* with the already experienced past. (Not getting as much good in a declining life *because* one is depressed by the knowledge of the decline itself cannot be a total explanation of why decline is bad. This is because we should feel depressed only if we had some reason to think that the decline was bad independent of the depression it engenders. However, any depression arising from knowledge of the decline could be an additional bad fact about the declines of which we have knowledge. Similarly having something to look forward to is a benefit of inclines of which we have knowledge.)

Evaluating the Factors

Several of the factors described above seem clearly incorrect as justifications or explanations of the preference for an incline over a decline. Contrary to (A1), we need not see what we are at the end as who we really are. What I am essentially may be revealed by earlier stages of my life or by my life as a whole. For example, we recognize that someone was a genius, even though he was senile when he died. (The last events in such a person's life show only that the genius he had was not invulnerable.) And someone who had spent his life as an idiot might not be considered a genius because of sudden phenomenal insights during his last days.

Still, some things support the view that we are taken to be what we are at our last stage, at least where character is concerned. For example, there is the Christian view that accepting God in our last moment overcomes all prior unbelief. (It isn't clear, however, that final *un*belief can wipe out the effect on final judgment of a life of belief.) Analogously, a final decision, unlike our prior indecisive reflections, binds us and may be irrevocable. It may be that because the last moment of life makes impossible any further change, it is thought that, like a final decision, it is what we are committed to.[3]

To the extent that the real "me" can be identified with some earlier stage, living on to a worse, later stage still raises the problems that (P1)—the offense-to-rationality objection—is intended to highlight.

Explanation (P5) is suspect because one of the reasons we dislike decline is that it *does not* rob the high points of their great value: it robs us of more of what is still recognized as valuable. Notice again that factors that depend on someone's knowing that he is in a decline or even remembering the past, such as competitiveness (A4), anticlimax (P4) or total reduction in good (P7), are not as pure explanations of the badness of decline as are factors that do not rely on such knowledge.

It seems, therefore, that A2, A3, P1, P2, P3, and P6 survive as explanations and/or justifications.

NOTES

1. This is like the point Nagel makes about acts that aim at evil. See *The View from Nowhere* (New York: Oxford University Press, 1986). Though Derek Parfit has pointed out that Nagel's point depends on causation (our aiming at evil) whereas my point is about a passive drift, which is more analogous to the decay of our bodies.

2. Parfit notes that "irresistible" suggests that we should prefer even a *smaller* present good to a *larger* later good. I do not wish to imply this.

3. It may be especially important that the last period in one's life be good because it will be impossible to compensate for any badness in it. (This is different from saying that it is needed to compensate for the future disaster of death. Why can't past goods be seen as compensatory? Here again the preference for future goods reappears.) Still, a decline need not imply that the last stage is intrinsically so bad that it requires compensation. If compensation were required for the mere fact of decline, the inability to compensate for the final period that is the outcome of the decline would not explain what is wrong with decline.

II

SAVING LIVES: GENERAL ISSUES

5

Is It Worse if More Die: Agent Relative or Non-Relative Views?

> If A and B were drowning, and you could only save one of them, would you . . . have lunch or go to a movie?
>
> Tom Weller

If we are to save people from death, how should we do it? What does how we should do it tell us about the structure of morality? Some of the answers to these questions concern situations in which we save some people by leaving others to die, not intending their deaths but foreseeing them. Others concern situations in which we save some people by harming other people. We shall deal with the first sort of situation in Part II.[1]

In his article, "Should the Numbers Count?,"[2] John Taurek deals with conflict situations in which we can help some, but not all, of the people who need help, and we must choose whom to help. An example of such a case involves six people who need a drug to save their lives. I have the drug, but I cannot give it to all six because, say, they are located in two different places. Among my options are to give it to a group of five people on one island and to give it to one person on another island. (Henceforth, this is the Drug Case). The following are among the claims Taurek makes:

1a. If the five die, no one will suffer more of a loss than a single person would suffer if he died. There is no person who suffers five times the loss of the single person. If all six are strangers to us and their loss does not affect us personally, we care about the loss each person suffers because of the loss *to* him, not because of the loss *of* him. If we care about the loss to each, we should not care about a summation of individual losses that no single individual suffers. Therefore, numbers do not count in deciding whom to save. There is no reason to save the greater number just because they are the greater number. (Individual Loss Claim.)

b. There is no coherent impersonal sense of better and worse in which it would be a worse situation if the five people die than if the one dies. The fact that a certain situation is worse for more people does not mean that it is, in any coherent sense, impersonally worse. It is worse for each of the five if he dies, but worse for the single person if he dies, and so we cannot say that it is simply *worse* if the five die (or simply worse if the one dies). (No Worse Claim.)

2. If we want to show equal concern for all six people—though perhaps we needn't—we should toss a coin, thereby giving each of the six people an equal (50 percent) chance of getting the drug. (Equal Concern Claim.)

In this chapter I wish first to consider briefly how Taurek's views might apply to conflict-free situations. I then wish to consider the No Worse Claim, that is, whether it is true of the Drug Case that the state of affairs in which the five die is no worse than that in which the one dies. I will present an argument for the claim that it is worse if more die or suffer—dealing interchangeably with these two cases[3]—than if fewer do. However, I will then present an objection to saving the greater number merely because it is worse if more die, on the grounds that it may be wrong to produce the best state of affairs. Taurek's argument for not counting numbers is based on his evaluation of outcomes as not being worse if more die; his argument is based on his theory of the good. An alternative is to base an argument for not counting numbers on a nonconsequentialist theory of the right. And it may sometimes be right to do something even though it does not produce the best state of affairs.

It is useful to note that although conflict situations such as we will be dealing with often arise because a resource is scarce, and so there is not enough to go around, this is not always the case. Sometimes what is scarce is not the obvious resource we must distribute, for example, a drug; rather it is the time or personnel to deliver the item to more than one person or place. In that case we must still select to whom to give the drug as though there were a scarcity of *drug*. (The same problem arises if the item we have is plentiful but indivisible.)

More Specific Arguments

We have stated Taurek's conclusions and some of his supporting reasons briefly. Before proceeding it will be useful to consider in more detail some of the specific arguments he gives for his claim that it is no worse if more people die. We shall also consider some objections that have been raised to these arguments. This will allow us to locate Taurek in the landscape of different ethical theories, consequentialist or nonconsequentialist. By *consequentialism,* I mean the view which determines the rightness or wrongness of acts on the basis of their consequences. This view (usually) yields the conclusion that we always have a duty to produce the best state of affairs. By *nonconsequentialism,* I mean determining the rightness or wrongness of acts on grounds that include factors *in addition* to consequences. (Consequences are not necessarily ignored.) This view yields the conclusion that we do not always have a duty to produce the best state of affairs.[4]

My Friend

Taurek argues that if it were worse for five to die than for one to die, everyone would have a duty to save the five. Do we have such a duty? If the one was our friend, most would agree it would be morally permissible to save him rather than the five, if we were distributing our own medicine. But, Taurek claims, it would not be permissible for friendship to override a real duty. For example, if we had a *contractual* duty to save the five, the fact that our friend was the single person would not make it permissible for us to save him. Therefore, in the absence of the contract there is no duty to save the five and hence it isn't worse if the five die, for if it were worse we would have a duty to save the five.

Derek Parfit has objected to this argument[5] on the ground that it assumes that consequentialism is true. That is, in formulating this argument, Taurek seems to accept the consequentialist view that we have a duty to promote the best state of affairs and prevent the worse state of affairs. Therefore, for Taurek, if in a certain circumstance it is permissible to save our friend and there is no duty to save the five, this must mean it is not worse if the five die. But, Parfit claims, the nonconsequentialist will argue that a state of affairs may be worse, and yet we had no duty to prevent it. In particular, we have no duty to do a thing if the cost to us of doing it is too great. To lose our friend is a great cost. This does not mean there is no duty to save the five rather than the one when there is no great cost to us in doing so. This analysis is consistent with the idea of a personal prerogative to promote ends we especially care about at the expense of the greatest good.[6] Furthermore, the fact that friendship does not override a *contractual* obligation only shows that some duties are more stringent than others, at least on the measure of how much personal sacrifice we must make rather than abandon them. The stringency of the duties is not a function only of how bad the consequences are.

Someone's Own Refusal to Sacrifice

A second argument Taurek offers is based on the fact that we would not think it morally wrong for the single person himself to refuse to give his own drug to save the five. But, Taurek thinks, if it were worse for the five to die, it would be wrong of the single person to prefer the state of affairs in which he survives (the less good state of affairs) to the state of affairs in which the five survive. Therefore, it cannot be worse for the five to die.

Parfit objects to this argument that it is not necessarily morally wrong to prefer that the worse state of affairs come about when the cost to oneself of the better state of affairs' coming about would be great. The cost would be great for the single person who would die. This is another example of the personal-prerogative objection to pure consequentialism.

Identification with Another's Point of View

Taurek further argues that if the single person may prefer himself, *anyone* may permissibly identify with his point of view and prefer the single person, helping him rather than the five. Parfit argues that although the one person may prefer himself to the five because the cost to him of saving the five is great, this does not mean that anyone who will not suffer a great loss if the one dies may prefer the life of the one to that of the five.

It is important to note that Taurek's position implies that a third party may permissibly identify even with someone who would suffer a loss *less* than that which anyone else among the greater number would suffer. That is, so long as the loss is such that the single person would not be obligated to suffer it himself for the sake of protecting another person from a greater loss, a third party may prevent the lesser loss. For example, if the single person is not obliged to give up his arm to save five lives, a third party may save the one person's arm rather than the five lives, on Taurek's view. (To see the implication of this for social policy, consider that if someone is not morally obliged to give up his college education to save lives, it is permissible for *us* to put public funds into college education rather than into saving lives.)[7]

Taurek's Type of Moral Theory

These three arguments of Taurek's reveal his brand of consequentialism. It involves an *evaluation of outcomes relative to an individual's interests* combined with an *agent-neutral theory of permission to act*. That is, from the single person's point of view the outcome is worse if he dies than if the five die. From the points of view of each of the five, it is worse if he dies than if the single person does. (Such an evaluation of outcomes as "good for someone" versus "good, period," differs from the claim that the judgement of what is "good, period" can be relativized to individuals.) However, if an individual may perform an act on the basis of the evaluation of consequences for him, any agent may act as he would act. This means the permission to act is *not* relative to one agent rather than another; it is an agent-neutral permission.

In sum, Taurek combines an individual-relative conception of the value of states of affairs (i.e., what is valuable is what is valuable to a person) with an agent-neutral conception of action. Even if we each have a duty to produce the best outcome, we will fulfill this duty no matter whom we save, since outcomes are judged on a person relative basis. (The evaluation of outcomes for a person does not necessarily mean that *subjective preferences* determine the value of an outcome. There may be an objective standard of what is in the interest of each individual, and this standard can be used for the individual-relative evaluation of outcomes. There is accordingly an ambiguity when we speak of an "individual's point of view." Sometimes this means an individual's scale of values or preferences. This is the subjective notion. But other times it can mean what is truly, objectively best for that person, e.g., he prefers candy but spinach is good for him. I suspect that the world can be objectively worse for someone if a preference of his is not satisfied, i.e., there is something good in having one's preference satisfied. Nevertheless, it is possible for a greater good to come to someone if others act for his sake and against his preferences. I shall, henceforth, assume that seeing things from someone's perspective or point of view involves ascertaining whether states of affairs are truly best for him.)

It would be a stronger claim to say that Taurek recommended that an agent has a *duty* to produce a consequence judged best relative to some individual. Taurek does not seem to require this. For example, he does not insist that it would be wrong for someone to sacrifice his own individual-relative best consequence for someone else's. (This can be combined with the view that we would have a duty to sacrifice to save the five if their dying were the worst outcome.) Also he does not commit himself to there being no constraints on an agent's promoting the most valuable individual-relative consequences. That is, he does not say the one may kill the five to save himself. This puts him in the nonconsequentialist camp, strictly speaking. (Furthermore, he does not try to derive such constraints from their protecting an individual's own interest in not being someone who harms others. That is, he does not claim the constraints on one's acts exist because it would be a worse state of affairs for me if I kill someone than if I do not.[8]

Taurek does think that when the loss to someone is very small (e.g., the loss of his umbrella), he ought to suffer that loss to save another's life. (Presumably, on Taurek's view, saving more lives should *not* give a greater reason to do this than saving one.) This view seems to be in some conflict with the agent-relative evaluation of outcomes. For it may still be worse *for A* that he lose his umbrella than it is *for A* that B die. Is Taurek here succumbing to the idea that although it is worse *for A* to lose his umbrella it is simply worse (period) if B dies?

Direct Reasons for Nonaggregation

These arguments of Taurek's are supposed to provide *evidence* for the fact that five persons' dying is not worse than one person's dying. But he also argues more directly for this view by claiming that because there is no one among the five who suffers any greater loss than the single person suffers, there is no point of view from which the five's dying is worse than the one's dying. The only points of view for the evaluation of outcomes are individual points of view. There is no aggregate person who is the aggregate of many persons and in whom their losses are summed.

Taurek thinks that those who believe it is worse if five die than if one dies must believe (mistakenly) that there exists a point of view from which five times the loss that the one suffers is endured. Of course, even if there were a point of view from which the outcome of the five's dying would be worse than his own dying is for the single person, the five's dying would not necessarily be a worse outcome *for the* single person. That is, his suffering his own large but lesser loss will be worse for him than someone else's suffering an even greater loss. Taurek's argument against an aggregated point of view is, I believe, subordinate to his belief in the relativity of *any* point of view in the evaluation of states of affairs. There is no better or worse period, only better or worse for someone with *a point of view*. (So Taurek may accept interpersonal comparisons of utility and agree that someone who loses his life suffers a worse loss than someone who loses his arm. Yet it is not worse for the person who loses his arm that the other person loses his life.)

Persons and Objects

According to Taurek, people differ from objects, in that objects have no points of view from which states of affairs are evaluated. Objects can be aggregated from the point of view of persons. We might add that persons can also be aggregated from the point of view of another person. That is, it may be worse for me if I lose more rather than fewer objects and if I lose more rather than fewer persons about whom I care. But in the case of a person, concern for her rather than for ourselves involves seeing things from the point of view of her interests, not our own. It is that which supposedly rules out aggregation of persons.

Clear Case of Nonaggregation

Furthermore, Taurek notes, there are clear cases in which most people do not aggregate. Suppose one person will suffer a great pain lasting several years if we do not give him some medicine, but a million other people will each suffer one minute's small pain if we do not give each of them that medicine. We are not tempted to think that a million small pains add up to as great a loss as the long-lasting pain of the individual. Why then should we aggregate when it is a case of many people each of whom will suffer as great a loss as someone else will suffer? Of course, it is precisely here that most people do part company with Taurek on aggregation.

I

Conflict-free Situations

Assume for purposes of argument that The No Worse Claim (i.e., Claim 1b) is true; that is, it is not worse for more people to die than for fewer to die in conflict situations. On at least one interpretation of Taurek, it would also be true that it was not worse for more people to die when we could save all six people, that is, in conflict-free situations.

The interpretation of Taurek that would have this implication takes him to be arguing that, in general, what happens to people may be important for them, but it is not impersonally good or bad.[9] It might be suggested, therefore, that Taurek's argument against automatically saving the five in conflict situations also implies that it makes no moral difference whether we save all six or just one in conflict-*free* situations. If his argument had this result it would seem even more problematic.

I believe his argument does not have this result. We can justify saving the greater number in conflict-free situations in a manner consistent with not saving the greater number in conflict situations. First, in conflict-free situations, the failure to provide everyone with an equal chance to survive cannot be raised as an objection to saving the larger number. There is no such failure.

Second, Taurek's Individual Loss and No Worse Claims and a desire to show equal concern (Claim 2) are consistent with a positive reason for saving the six rather than, for example, tossing a coin to determine whether to save six or one: The concern for persons, which is part of equal concern, will lead one to want for each person that he live. A concern for equal treatment alone would be satisfied by tossing a coin to decide whether to save six or one, and then, if need be, throwing a six-sided die to decide which one. But concern for the loss to each person would lead to saving all six, even if it were not impersonally worse for all six to die than for one to die.

Another way to put this is that Taurek favors an empathetic point of view as grounds for saving a life. (This is concern for the loss *to* a person if he dies, rather than concern for the loss *of* the person.)[10] This empathetic point of view would lead him to save all six rather than just one. (As I understand this empathetic point of view, the loss of someone's life is a loss of the goods of life to that person and can be empathized with, even if it is not a loss *felt* by that person since he is not present when death is.) Yet Taurek would still be free to claim that it was only better for each person who was saved that he be saved, not impersonally better.

In conflict cases, this ground for saving more rather than fewer lives could be overridden by the desire to show equal concern for the single person, which, on Taurek's view, requires us to give each person an equal chance to be saved.[11]

II

Worse States of the World

Let us consider an argument against the No Worse Claim. Suppose that we begin with a world in which there are people but no one is in pain. (Call this *State of the World* I, abbreviated SWI). Then this world changes so that one person in it is in pain. (Call this SWII). Assuming it would be better *for him* not to be in pain, the SWII is worse *for him* than SWI was, even if it is not worse for anyone else. Is SWII also *simply worse* than SWI, not merely worse for him? It might seem to be Taurek's view that the change from SWI to SWII does not make a worse SW, only an SW *worse for* someone. On the other hand, Taurek may wish to say that if the change makes the world worse for someone and no better for anyone else, it is simply a worse SW.[12] That is, when there is no *conflict* of interest between individuals, when it is not true that an SW that is worse for one is better for another, we may say that the world is simply worse if it is worse for someone.

Now imagine that, instead of SWII, SWIII had come about. The same person who would have been in pain in SWII (call him Joe) is in pain in SWIII, but another person (Jim) who would have been all right in SWI *and* in SWII is *also* in pain. The two people suffer equally great pains. SWIII is worse for Jim than SWII is, but it is not worse for Joe or for anyone else. Is SWIII worse than SWII? Some might argue that it is not worse, even though SWII is worse than SWI, and it would become worse only if Jim suffered a *greater* pain than Joe. This is because the world is as bad as the worst suffering endured by any individual in it at a time.[13] But if we (including Taurek) could accept the view that a world was simply worse if it were worse for someone and not better for anyone else, then SWIII would be worse than SWII, as SWII was worse than SWI.

Perspective of Evaluation: Bias?

It does in fact seem reasonable to say that SWII is worse than SWI and SWIII is worse than SWII. But from what point of view do we say this?[14] As noted above, it is not from the point of view of the people in SWII who are *not* in pain since the world is not worse for them. (Let us assume that they do not suffer for those in pain.) Suppose they say to us, "Why did you say that SWII is worse than SWI, when it isn't worse for us? It is worse for someone else, granted, but to say that the world has gotten worse period is to adopt *his* point of view and elevate it to the level of an impartial judgment. That is biased. If it is worse for him but not worse for us, you can't say that it's *simply* worse. However, we may allow that, if it were worse for *everyone*, you could say it was simply worse."

Objective Value?

First, we should note that some people might reject even this last claim. They might reject it because they thought it committed them to the view that human suffering and death had objective importance, that is, that these things were not only important to people, but really important from a nonhuman perspective. They reject this view. If we do *not* reject this view, however, it also seems to make sense to accept the view that SWII is worse than SWI since something of objective importance, namely someone's being in pain, is added to the world, even though it hasn't become a worse world for everyone.

Human Value

However, suppose we did reject the objective significance of human suffering and death. We might still accept the claim that a world that is worse for *everyone* is simply worse, if only on a human, not objective, scale of value. But we could also say that something bad from a human point of view is introduced in SWII that is not present in SWI, making SWII simply a humanly worse world. This is because it is worse for someone and not better for anyone else.

The Point of View Outside Each Point of View

The important point in rebutting the charge that bias makes us say that SWII is worse than SWI is that we would not be saying this *because* we identify solely with the person for whom it is worse. So we could not be accused of bias. Rather we would be, in part, looking at matters from *outside the point of view of each person.* That is, we would check to see whether it is a worse SW from the perspective of each person in the world, but make our decision without identifying with any one perspective. Finding that it is worse for someone and no better for others, we say it is worse, but not because of identification with one rather than another.

This point can be reinforced by comparing SWII with SWIII. SWIII has twice as many people in pain as does SWII. Suppose we had decided that it was worse because we were simply identifying (biasedly) with the point of view of the second person who goes into pain. The SWIII would seem only one step worse than *SWI*. That is, it would seem no worse than SWII had seemed relative to SWI. But in fact SWIII seems even further removed from SWI on the scale of badness than SWII.

The conclusions of this section, then, are (1) as more and more people suffer losses such as death or pain without anyone's condition being improved, the world is getting worse and worse; (2) we judge that it is *worse and worse* from a perspective outside those of any of the individuals for whom it is getting *worse,* although from this perspective we take account of each individual's perspective; and (3) at each point at which we say the world has gotten yet worse, there are individuals for whom it has not gotten worse. There is, therefore, some sort of *aggregation* taking place from a point of view outside any of the individuals' points of view. Call this perspective the *impartial point of view*.

What would we do as more and more people suffer losses in these conflict-free situations, situations in which we can help them all? Presumably, we would aid as many of them as we could.

III

Equally Bad Conflicting Situations

Now let us consider our attitude to a set of SWs that alternate with each other. In SWIV, A is in pain, but B is not. SWIV alternates with SWV, in which B is in pain but A is not. That is, first A is in pain, then he stops being in pain and B is in pain, and then B stops being in pain and A is back in pain. This alternation continues. SWIV in its various instantiations is worse for A and better for B, SWV is better for A and worse for B.

I believe that if, as impartial observers, we examine these two SWs, we will say that they are equally bad. This is true even though the alternating SWs involve a conflict situation. That is, A's fate gets worse as B's improves, and vice versa. (Notice that the idea of alternating SWs is conceptually related to the fact that we save at least as many if we save the greater number as if we save the fewer. That is, within the side with the larger number is a subcomponent that is numerically equal to the side with the smaller number. Either they are saved or the smaller number are saved. Here the alternation is hidden.)

However, A might say to us, "How can you say SWIV is as good (or as bad) as SWV when SWIV is worse for me, and SWV is better for me?" B can say something comparable. The people in our earlier cases, who were not in pain in any given SW, could only say, "How can you say SWII is *worse* than SWI when it is *no* worse for me?" They could not complain that we said SWII was worse when it was better *for* them. In that sense, the interests of the people not in pain and those of the people in pain did not conflict. However, A cannot say we are partial to B if we say SWIV and SWV are equally bad. This is because being partial to B would involve saying that SWV was worse than SWIV. For a similar reason B cannot say we are partial to A.

The Perspective of Evaluation

Though A and B could say that SWIV and SWV are not equally bad for them, we would not, I believe, alter our view that the SWIV and SWV are equally bad, even if each, taken individually, is not as bad for A or for B. Since our judgment conflicts with the judgments A or B would make when they are looking at things from a personal perspective, it is made from a point of view outside of either perspective, although taking theirs into account. Is this point of view the same as that which led us to say that SWII was worse than SWI and SWIII was worse than SWII? Some might argue that it isn't because they can accept what was said about these three SWs but not agree that SWIV is as good (or bad) as SWV. That is, since it is worse for someone when one SW switches to the other, some might claim that they cannot say that one SW is just as bad as the other.

Interpersonal Comparisons of Utility

It might seem that this position must deny the interpersonal comparison of utility. That is, it must deny that we can say that A's loss is as bad as B's. But this is not true. For suppose that in SWVI, A loses an arm, and in SWVII, B loses both his arms. Someone (for example, Taurek) could agree that B will suffer a worse loss than A will. This would be the interpersonal comparison of utility. Yet he could still be unwilling to say that it is a worse SW in which B suffers his worse loss; it is only worse for B. That one person will suffer a worse loss than another person need not, on Taurek's view, imply that it is a worse world in which he suffers his loss than the world in which the other person suffers his lesser loss. Thus the view that SWVI cannot be said to be better than SWVII need not rest on the failure of interpersonal comparison of utility.

Still, even someone who takes the radical position of refusing to say that SWVII is *worse* than SWVI (consistent with interpersonally comparing utilities) can claim that the two states are *equally* good or bad—or at least each one's coming about is equally good or bad—even though they are not equally good or bad for each person. This would reflect his not preferring the interests of either person. This claim would put him close to someone who claims that SWIV and SWV are equally good or bad.

Although Taurek denies that something is a worse state of affairs when it is better for others, he could, I believe, agree that whichever state transpires things are just as good. When we are concerned for both A and B, I believe that from the impartial perspective we will think things have got no worse and no better when SWIV switches to SWV, and vice versa. (Though I also think that, for those who reject Taurek's views this will be a function of equal losses being suffered by both.) Furthermore, I believe, this impartial point of view is the same perspective from which we judge that SWII is worse than SWI and SWIII is worse than SWII.

Betrayal?

Nevertheless, it is interesting and very significant that we can say all this even though A, for example, may feel betrayed by the impartial point of view in a way he would not feel betrayed by it in the earlier comparisons of SWI, SWII, and SWIII. If A does feel thus betrayed by our response when SWV is replaced by SWIV, however, I believe he shows a failure to understand our equal concern for B. If B feels betrayed by our response when SWIV turns to SWV, I believe he fails to understand our equal concern for A. That is, though things have gotten worse for him, they haven't simply gotten worse because they have gotten better by as much for A.

Tossing a Coin: Fairness or the Value of a Chance?

What do we do if we must choose whether to aid A or to aid B when each stands to lose as much as the other? We might toss a coin. There are several ways in which we might justify doing this. First, it might be said that fairness demands that we give each an equal chance to avoid suffering a loss. Second, it might be said that it *is* as bad a world whichever person suffers his loss *only if* we have chosen fairly who will suffer. That is, from the impartial perspective, the world will be a *worse* place if one person suffers rather than another either through having been unfairly selected or in the absence of a deliberate attempt at fair selection. According to this analysis, not to treat people fairly is wrong, and the world is a worse place if wrong things occur in it.

The concern for fairness in both these approaches must begin with the insight that it is not as bad *for* A if B dies as if he, A, dies, nor as bad *for* B if A dies, as if he, B, dies. This is true even if it is equally bad whoever dies from the impartial perspective. That is, concern for fairness begins with a recognition of a conflict of interest.

A third approach to justifying use of a random decision procedure is also based on a recognition of conflict of interest, but it deemphasizes the role of fairness. Instead, it takes seriously the concern of each individual that he receive a 50 percent chance to win because it matters very much to him that he be the one who is helped.

Why is the third approach to the question of giving A and B an equal chance so different from the first two? They can be distinguished by considering a case in which there are a million people who need help but we can help only one. If we give each an equal chance to be helped, each has a one in a million chance of aid. This is far less than the 50 percent A and B would have if given equal chances. Will each individual care as much about this small ($1/1,000,000$) chance as about a large (50 percent) chance? Given that the small chance is the person's *only* chance, his concern to keep a small chance probably is not as diminished as is its objective status. That is, its subjective value to him does not decline as rapidly as its objective value. Nevertheless, it probably is less significant in his eyes on many measures (for example, how much he would sacrifice of his family's welfare to keep it) than is the larger chance.

Suppose we nevertheless care as much about seeing to it that everyone has an equal small chance as that everyone has an equal large chance. Then concern for fairness rather than simply concern for how much each individual cares about having his chance probably plays a significant role in the justification of giving people equal chances. (Although Derek Parfit points out that if a small chance at a good is a good, and numbers can aggregate, then what is at stake is a small chance for many people—possibly a great good. If having a chance at a benefit is no benefit, however, and only one person could truly be benefited, concern for fairness would alone explain concern for giving many a very small chance.)

IV

The Aggregation Argument

On the basis of what has been said so far, the following might be argued: If (1) it is worse if B and C die than if B alone dies (as concluded in section II); and (2) it is equally bad if A alone dies or if B alone dies (as argued in section III); then (3) by substitution, it should also be worse if B and C die than if A alone dies.[15] That is, where "$<$" = "worse than," if $B + C < B$ and if $A = B$, then $B + C < A$. Since this is an argument for aggregating losses, I call it the *Aggregation Argument*.

In response to this, suppose A says: "How can it be better if B and C live? It's better *for them,* but it isn't better *for me;* so it isn't simply better. In saying 'It's simply better if B and C live,' you have betrayed me altogether and biasedly sided with the points of view of B and C." An answer we might give to this complaint seems consistent with what was said in sections II and III. That is, it was understandable for us to say that the world was worse if more and more people died when no one's condition was thereby improved, even though from someone's point of view it *wasn't* getting worse. We also thought it was as bad when B suffered (as much as A) instead of A, even though it wasn't *as bad* for either B (for whom it was worse) or A (for whom it was better). Indeed this seems to be the crucial step in deriving the view that in conflict situations it is worse if more die than if fewer die. This is because, if this step is correct, it allows us to say that the world can be as bad even if it is worse for someone. Then we need not hesitate to say that it is worse if more die simply because it is better for the one who will survive. Nor need we hesitate to say it is better if more survive simply because it is worse for the one who will die.

In sum, if more are saved, we say "it is better" than if fewer are saved, rather than "it is just as good," because (1) B's being substituted for A (or vice versa) leaves things just as bad (or good) as they were, and (2) C's suffering in addition to either A or B makes things worse. This argument depends, crucially, on the substitution of equivalents, A suffering a loss and B suffering a loss.

As noted above, one is tempted to say that Taurek himself is committed to the view that states are simply better, even if they are worse for some, by his view that someone *should* sacrifice his own umbrella (that is, something of minor significance to him) to save lives. For it may be worse *for the person* who loses his umbrella that he lose it than that five people die. If he should nevertheless give up his umbrella, mustn't it be because the five's dying is *simply* worse than someone's losing his umbrella? Or can we stop the line of reasoning at the point where we say it is very bad for someone to lose his life and not very bad at all for someone else to lose his umbrella, and therefore the latter should help the former? (This reasoning omits the premise that it is worse if the *five* die than if the one loses his umbrella.) Perhaps one could derive Taurek's view on the umbrella without commitment to an impartial evaluation of states of affairs by noting that sometimes people sacrifice a great deal in order to save others from losing far less. That is, they produce what most consider a worse state of affairs from an impartial view to prevent a less bad state of affairs. If one thinks such a person is not necessarily wrong to act as he does, then Taurek's own injunction to suffer the loss of the umbrella in order to save a life might also be explained independently of any claim that one was acting to produce the better state of affairs. It is right to sacrifice though one is not bringing about the better state of affairs. Such an analysis is also reminiscent of one which Philippa Foot suggests[16] when she argues against the impartial evaluation of states of affairs, but in favor of helping the greater number. She says our fundamental moral ideas do not focus on best states of affairs, but on virtuous character. It is right to save a greater number because the generous person will do so. That is all we can say or need to know. But this is insufficient, I think, because someone who saves one person may be exhibiting as much of the virtue of generosity (e.g., sacrificing himself for the sake of another) as someone who saves a thousand. The worth of the act as a mark of generosity is as great. This may be one of the points of the saying that to save one life is as if one had saved a million. One is saving life, and exhibiting generosity in either case. We need some reason besides generosity that accounts for someone's choosing to save the greater number. Similarly, if Taurek thinks it is right to give up the umbrella, or a person of good character would do it, we need to know why attending to another person's loss which is much greater than one's own small loss is the thing to do.

V

Criticism of the Aggregation Argument

Is this Aggregation Argument satisfactory? I believe it is attractive, but I nevertheless wish to present a possible criticism. The basic point of this possible criticism can be phrased (somewhat cryptically) as follows: Saying that one state of affairs is worse than another, or as good as another, in the first and second premises of the argument *and* acting on this judgment is consistent with our retaining our links to each individual person. However, saying that one state of affairs is worse than another in the conclusion is not consistent with our retaining our links to each individual person. The conclusion would involve a shift in the degree of commitment to each individual, and even a shift in what we take to be the ultimate unit of attachment in morality. This does not mean that the conclusion is false—i.e., that it is not, in general, worse that more die. It only means that this conclusion is inconsistent with an attitude we were able to maintain in accepting the first and second premises. Therefore, we may face a conflict between acting on the conclusion and maintaining this attitude, a conflict that did not arise when we were acting on the first two premises.

More specifically, in step 1 we retain our tie to B and then add C, based on our tie to him; in step 2 we retain our ties to each of A and B when we give each of them as much of a chance as is consistent with retaining our tie to the other. However, in step 3, we add C to B when there is still a conflict between A and B, a conflict we have not first settled by tossing a coin between them. If we then save the greater number, this means severing our tie to A before giving him an equal chance.[17] This criticism claims that the commitment to maintaining a link to A, where this involves assigning equal chances to A and B, should take precedence over thinking of B's death as depriving the world of all that A's death would deprive it of (i.e., substituting equivalents) and then siding with B because C's life stands to be added to his. Step 2 does involve the claim that from an outsider's point of view it does not matter whether A or B dies. But because it leads us to give each an equal chance, step 2 also represents the fact that from A's point of view or B's it is more important that he and not the other survive. Step 2 does not engage in the substitution of equivalents. Tossing a coin allows the outsider to remain attached to each as an individual. (Acting on the toss, however, like saving the greater number, divorces us from some.) The criticism is that we should not act on the addition of C's death to anyone else's unless the *test of nonabandonment* of anyone is first met. Pairwise comparisons of individuals, as in step 2, allow us to retain links to all the individual units. The conclusion does not.[18]

Nonaggregation of Friends?

Let us now extend (and expand on) this criticism. We can perhaps get a better feel for the nonaggregative effect of a continuing tie to each individual if we imagine a conflict case that involves six of our *close* friends (Friends Case). This differs from the cases that Taurek discusses, which involve either six strangers or one close friend and five strangers.

In the Friends Case, I am imagined to care about each person intensely. What would I do if I had to choose between saving one and saving five? The suggestion is that my thought process would be best described as involving six unbreakable links stretching from me to each of the six people. Saving the five rather than giving each an equal chance would be impossible for me, *if* I were motivated to act just on the basis of equal concern for each.[19] I certainly would *not* think as follows: the loss of five friends would produce a bigger gap in my life than the loss of one, therefore I will save the five. This thought process would show concern for *myself*, rather than for the friends. If I persist in thinking about the friends as individuals to whom I am tied, each irreplaceable by another, each someone with whose loss of life I empathize then, it is suggested, no number of such individuals will add up to some higher, encompassing unit of worth known as "the sum of many individuals" or "the state of many individuals surviving." It is as if each individual cannot be made to stick together horizontally with another individual if I am truly linked on an individual basis to each. (Indeed, attachment to the individual who stands alone tends to "unstick" the others, to make me see them as individuals.)

As described in the Individual Loss Claim, Taurek believes that if the individuals whose lives are at stake are *not* friends of mine, I am concerned about the loss *to* them rather than of them. But, it seems to me, when the people threatened are my friends, my behavior is also determined by my concern about the loss *to* them. It is not that I do not also care about the loss of them, but this does not have any aggregative impact if I am not focusing on my own welfare—or at least that is the claim we are currently examining. In addition, I conceive of each of them as unique and irreplaceable, and am tied to each.

I can still say that it will be equally bad whether one friend dies or another does; it won't be better or worse if one or the other dies. Yet I cannot think of one substituting as an equivalent for another. If two things are equally unique and irreplaceable, or unique to themselves, the loss is as great if either is lost, but they still cannot replace each other.

Is it a mistake to apply (supposed) conclusions derived from a case involving a choice between friends to cases involving a choice between strangers, with which we are primarily concerned? It may, in fact, be true that we are (or even should be) more likely to forget about the status as individuals of strangers than of friends. However, it is also possible that friendship, in addition to the way it distinguishes friends from strangers, makes us aware of the true nonsubstitutable status of *all* individuals; it may teach us how to treat nonfriends appropriately, without thereby turning them into friends. At least, that is the claim that needs to be made if we are to draw implications from the Friends Case.

Nonaggregation of Nonpersons

An interesting characteristic of this phenomenon of nonaggregation, as represented in the criticism we are examining, is that the class of entities to which it applies is not limited to people. Taurek, by contrast, tries to derive his nonaggregative conclusions by emphasizing what the loss of life means *to* the person who loses it. For that person, his death will not be offset by the gain of many other lives. Further, there will be no greater unit (composed of many individuals) that suffers a greater loss *to* it than the one person suffers. Indeed, Taurek distinguishes between nonaggregation in the case of people and aggregation in the case of valuable commodities. But, I believe, it is possible to construct the same argument for nonaggregation with commodities or with moments of valuable experience in life. Yet these entities cannot be said to suffer a loss *to themselves*. Concern for the fact that each person cares more for his own survival than for the survival of another is not the only source of a desire to give equal chances.

For if we take seriously the irreplaceability of each entity or experience, then none of them can be replaced by another or by any group of others. We remain tied to each as an individual. For example, the claim is that it is only if we detach ourselves from our appreciation for each particular experience in its own right, and consider our life overall as a higher-order unit of value, that we would choose several good experiences over a single good experience with which they conflict. (I shall deal with the issue of higher-order units of value further below).

The claim then is that Taurek applies his nonaggregation thesis too narrowly. It can be made to apply to nonpersons as well as to persons and so does not essentially depend on the seriousness of the loss *to* the entity. It is important, however, to identify the different grounds for nonaggregation in nonperson entities and persons. First, theoretically, entities or experiences that were exactly alike could be substitutable one for the other. (Though the historical phenomenon of our having interacted with an entity otherwise indistinguishable from another would again distinguish them.) However, persons, even if indistinguishable to the same degree as nonunique entities, would still not be substitutable in the same way. This is because they are different *to* themselves. His replacement by an exact replica is small comfort to the person who dies. We might even be tempted to say that if he is not saved but another is, it is to him almost as if no one had been saved; as if no good had been done at all. To say it matters less to him that others are saved than that he is, because they cannot truly replace him, is here being extended into saying that if he does not exist, it is as if there is no value. But this is misleading. A person need not deny that valuable things and even things he values can occur in his absence, to yet contend that these valuable things do nothing at all to approximate the type of value that his own existence has for him. It is either me that is saved or not; one or all of the five is not even close to being me (even if there were such a thing as my "closest successor self.") Second, nonperson entities do not have a *claim* on us that we maintain our ties to each as an individual. However, if the argument for nonaggregation being given were correct, persons (even strangers) have a claim on us that we treat them in accord with the model of unbreakable ties, rather than seek to prevent the worst state of affairs.[20]

Suppose that we could be wedded to each good experience as an irreplaceable entity. This suggests that we can*not* extrapolate from the treatment of pain or other *bad* experiences to the treatment of good experiences (the sort of extrapolation Derek Parfit[21] makes). That is, with respect to bad experience within one life, we are unlikely to place value on the individual, irreplaceable experiences since we dislike each of them. So it is no wonder that we immediately choose to avoid the greater number of painful experiences and are not concerned about the loss of four individual experiences in exchange for having a different (bad) one.

Nonaggregation of Claims

Another item, it may be suggested, with which we can induce the nonaggregative response is a claim or a promise that gives rise to it. Suppose we have made promises to six people, but a conflict arises. We can keep five of the six promises if we go downtown and only one if we go uptown. Suppose we take our promises seriously and wish to show how seriously we take the claims to which they give rise. Then, the suggestion is, we should give each promise its chance to be fulfilled. That is, if we show the highest respect we can for the *idea* of an individual's claim on us, we will not immediately keep the most promises. *We thereby show both that each individual promise binds strongly and that it is each individual promise that binds.* That is, a bond does not stem from a new unit, namely a sum of promises. The proposal is, it is a mistake to think that we show greater respect for the idea of a promise if we automatically try to fulfill as many of them as possible in conflict situations. (Though this does not mean there is no other reason why we should fulfill as many as possible.)

Highest Respect for Persons and Toss of a Coin

Likewise, to return to people's lives, it might be said that we show the greatest respect we can for the individual person when we do not aggregate. This is because we remain tied to each as an irreplaceable individual—irreplaceable to himself, to us; or simply in fact—until, for example, a coin toss tells us what to do. It is a mistake to think that we show greater respect for the idea of such an irreplaceable individual if we automatically save the greater number of them in conflict cases; the rationale for doing that would require us to think of individuals as substitutable equivalents (perhaps, because each is equally irreplaceable to himself).

To act on a coin toss requires us to break attachments, but, as in (the few) cases in which a toss is used to choose between two absolute equals, it does not indicate that the pull on us of one side is greater than the pull of the other. It also allows us to prevent everyone from being lost. By contrast, a choice without use of such a random decision procedure *would* indicate that the pull of one side is greater than another's, perhaps because of aggregation. Would not our tie to each be even stronger if we let everyone die, a passive letting something happen, rather than actively breaking ties after the toss? Doing this would indeed seem to show even more the unbreakability of the tie to each. However, it is against the interests of *everyone*, whereas acting on a coin toss is not: We may break a tie when *each* person in the given situation would not benefit from its not being broken. By contrast, if we broke the tie in conflict situations because it is worse if more die, there is someone who would benefit if it weren't broken.

Higher-order Units of Value

A further claim that might be made is that to choose to save the greater number because they are the greater number is to *switch* from seeing the individual as the fundamental unit of attachment. We supplant the individual with the state of affairs (the number of persons being saved). This is not the way to show maximal respect for each individual—even if it is clear that our concern for the state of affairs is itself a function of our concern for the individuals in it. Being the ultimate unit to which we are unbreakably attached (until a coin toss) is not the same as being the unit from whose aggregation the ultimate unit to which we are attached is constructed. Supplanting the individual as the ultimate unit of attachment is already a diminution in respect. It is a move from depth of commitment to the individual unit to a greater superficiality of commitment. The individual unit is replaced by the different, higher-order unit. Or so it may be claimed.

Highest Respect for the Losers

Suppose that the fact that each individual is someone to whom we must retain our ties means that we should toss a coin between the one and the many. If the many lose the toss, and we save the one, the many will die. However, they die retaining their identities as individuals each of whom is such that we should not break our ties to him. Suppose we had a weaker notion of what we owed each person, so that it was easy to break a tie to one for the sake of saving many. Then each of the five, though he would live, would be thought of as a different type of individual, one whose status did not demand as much. In allowing ourselves to save the greater number of lives at the expense of one, without tossing a coin, we form a diminished conception of the persons whose lives we are saving—each is no longer the sort of person to whom we must retain our links. (Likewise in the case of promises, to break one in order to automatically go and perform the greater number is to fulfill a greater number of less important, less unbreakable, claims. If we must wait for a coin toss to see what we are to do, we do more to leave intact the binding status of each individual unit.[22] Or, at least that is the contention of this criticism.

"To Save One Life Is as if We Had Saved a Million"

It has been said that if we save one life, it is as if we had saved a million. There are various ways of understanding this saying. One way of reading it coincides with the view being presented here. The saying does not mean that we do as well to save one person as to save five when all could be saved.[23] It does not mean that a single life has infinite worth, if this implies that all the worth that could possibly be achieved is achieved if we save one life when we could save five more (because 6 × infinity is still infinity).

A point of this saying is, I believe, that we must retain the idea of the individual as the primary unit of respect, concern, and value. We do this when we treat the individual as an irreplaceable entity to which we retain our ties. Doing this is consistent with saving one person and (then) a second person and (then) a third. Saving more than one in conflict-free situations is, phenomenologically, like saving people in sequence. We thus respond to each. But retaining the individual as a unit, it is claimed by the view we are expounding, is inconsistent with automatically saving the greater number in conflict situations. Saving one is as if one had saved a million when doing so is the only course consistent with showing highest respect for humanity in each person. This shows itself in not abandoning any except as a result of a random decision procedure that prevents all from being lost.

Theory of the Right or a Revised Idea of the Good?

The idea of nonaggregatable links coming from each person is intended to represent a possible consideration stemming from the theory of the right that might stand in the way of producing the best state of affairs. However, if we accept the view that being the bearer or generator of such a link signifies one's greater *worth*, then we might raise an objection to aggregation from the point of view of the theory of the good. That is, if morality tells us to abandon the one to save the five, it will be representing a state of affairs worse than the state of affairs in which the one survives as a result of a coin toss. The state of affairs in which we should automatically save the greater number is worse because the worth of each individual who is saved would be less.

I shall continue, nonetheless, to assume that there is some straightforward sense in which it is a worse world in which five die than in which one dies, even if in some other sense it becomes a worse world if people are such that acting on aggregation is acceptable. This makes it possible to continue to consider a possible conflict between the right and the good, and it is this form of the argument I shall continue to focus on.

The Aggregation Argument Again

Let us return again to the Aggregation Argument. It is consistent with maintaining the link to each individual as an individual to say that saving B and C produces a better world than saving B alone, and then to actually save both B and C. It is consistent with maintaining the link to each individual to say that the world in which A alone suffers or dies is no better or worse than the world in which B alone suffers or dies and then to give each an equal chance, so long as this is said and done with a certain attitude. That is, suppose we maintain our links to each individual as an individual. Then our response to the changes in the state of the world, as A suffers and then stops suffering and B suffers and then stops suffering, should *not* be the same as our response would be to an unchanging world in which one person continues to suffer and one does not. We should instead register something like a change to a positive attitude for A's relief from suffering, while we register a change to a negative response to B's suffering. That is, we respond to the changes in each person's position rather than to the outcome described without regard to which individual occupies which position. We show our equal ties to each person by responding to the changes in the world that affect each one. This second step in the Aggregation Argument may depend on thinking of A's loss as just as bad as B's, but tossing a coin does not require us to substitute one equivalent for the other; it recognizes the conflicting points of view of each and does not substitute.

Problems arise when we get to the last step in the Aggregation Argument and combine it with the conclusion that we should save the greater number. In this last step we must substitute, for example, "A" for the second "B" in "B and C is better than B alone." Or, imagine that "B" is a substitute for "A" in "A $<$ B + C," where "$<$" signifies that someone's death is less bad than another's. If we act on the conclusion, we straightaway save B and C. Substituting and acting in this way involves breaking our tie to A for the sake of commitment to the greater worth of a *group* of individuals. No doubt we will have a negative response if A dies as well as a positive response if B and C survive, but we will still choose the side with the greater number. Doing this means weakening our commitment to the individual unit in a way in which it is not weakened in steps 1 and 2. This is because the last step, but not the first two steps, treats individuals as substitutable equivalents and requires us to cut our tie to one person for the sake of others, though the alternative to doing this is *not* allowing everyone to die.

Put yet another way, when we prefer B and C over B alone, we can prefer the agglomeration of the two without breaking commitment to B. Although we are indifferent between the outcomes in which A or B survive, giving each a chance reflects the equal pull of both without substitution of equivalents. But when we prefer B and C over A, our indifference between A and B does not lead to an equal pull of them both on us. The pull to A is broken by the addition of C to B together with the view that A and B are substitutable equivalents. The effect of adding B to C here—unlike the addition of B to C in the first premise—does not respect our tie to each individual as a nonsubstitutable unit. Step 3 represents aggregation of a totally different sort. To repeat, this third step, but not the other steps, depends on substitution of equivalents, and this involves abandoning someone when the alternative is not that everyone dies. The claim of the counterargument under consideration is that, given the type of thing that the individual and the tie to each individual is, more ties coming from one direction should not pull us away from the tie in another direction.

SUMMARY

In sum, this criticism claims that to reach the conclusion that it is a worse world if more die rather than fewer, and to act on it by straightforwardly saving the greater number, conflict with the strongest possible attachment to the individual as the unit of importance. It is possible for an individual to be the primary unit of attachment, even if it is an individual entity for whom it does not matter if it itself perishes or if others do. This does not mean that we would not be right to say that the world is worse if more rather than fewer die when it is not possible to save everyone. It is only that acting on that basis will conflict with retaining, in this strongest way, the individual as the unit of nonsubstitutable attachment, and this respect for the individual may be a component of right action. Acting on its being a worse world if more die rather than fewer when it *is* possible to save everyone does *not* depend on abandoning that unit of attachment. The requirement that we act in conflict situations so as to save the greater number is, therefore, *not* derivable from a requirement that we act similarly in conflict-free situations. Different issues are involved when there is conflict, notably our commitments to the individual as the unit of importance. This difference remains even if it is granted that it is no worse if one person rather than another dies. Or, at least, that is the claim of the criticism we have examined.

The Personal Point of View and Deontology

We have described Taurek's views on how an outcome is evaluated from the point of view of a particular person: each individual evaluates an outcome as better or worse for him. We have also considered the claim that if we remain attached to each individual's point of view, our conception of each person, including those left to die, is that of someone who cannot be abandoned. Let us consider briefly how these two positions relate to a certain sort of revisionist consequentialism that, supposedly, has results that are extensionally equivalent to the results given by a deontological theory. Here the topic is killing, rather than aiding.

Amartya Sen[24] has argued that each person as an agent should evaluate outcomes from the point of view he has given his position in relation to an act. But the evaluation is not about whether the consequences of his act are better for him. Rather the evaluation is said to be about whether the consequences are better or worse tout court, as evaluated from the position he occupies. (We noted above, that the judgment of whether an outcome is good for someone is different from the claim that the judgment of what is "good, period" can (and should) be relativized to individuals' positions.)

For example, Sen claims that an agent should decide on consequentialist grounds not to kill one person as a means to save five others from being killed, only because from his position in relation to the act (i.e., as the agent who would perform it), it is a worse outcome—not necessarily for him—in which he acts than in which five other victims are killed by someone else. What the agent sees from his position is not only his victim, but his act of killing the victim (as well as the five other victims and the acts of the agents who would kill them.) According to this form of consequentialism, the agent should not kill the one because if he does kill he will produce the worse state of affairs, as seen from his position. That he should not kill is the result that a deontologist endorses as well.

At least two questions can be raised about this revisionist consequentialism. First, is its account of consequences correct, that is, can we, or should we, evaluate consequences from a position we occupy relative to them, or should we always take an impartial perspective—a view from nowhere—in deciding what the consequences of our act will be? (I assume we may include in the consequences the agent's act itself.) My sense is that it is the impartial view that gives us a true account of the consequences, which everyone should evaluate in the same way for moral purposes. This is compatible with our caring more about the consequences in which we perform the act; that is, we may be more worried about the less bad consequences in which we kill one than in which five are killed by others. If the badness of the consequences are not determined in a position-relative manner, then a consequentialist theory will conclude that we may kill one to save five.

The second question about revisionist consequentialism is whether it can consistently give an answer that is extensional with the one deontology would give, even if we accepted that outcomes should be determined in a position relative manner. For suppose I set a bomb five minutes ago that will kill five people unless I now kill one other person by pushing him on the bomb as it goes off. Would a position-relative evaluation not say that it is a worse consequence if I become the killer of the five (in virtue of having done something a short while ago) than if I now kill one person? Again, would not a position-relative evaluation say that it is a worse consequence if I will kill five tomorrow than if I kill a different one today, when killing today would prevent my being available to kill five tomorrow. A deontologist will argue that we should not kill the one person even to prevent ourself becoming the killer of, or killing, the five in these cases.

There may be ways out of such problems for revisionist consequentialism. The ways out typically focus on giving greater weight to what we do now than to what we do at other times. But the primary point is whether these more complex variations will really be true to what should motivate us in not killing one to save others (when it is wrong to do so). My claim is that the correct account is given by deontological, not position-relative consequentialist considerations, but that, nevertheless, the deontological account is itself positional.

One way to contrast position-relative consequentialism and deontology is to consider what the deontologist thinks the agent sees from his position as potential killer of the one person: the agent sees his victim and the rights which any potential victim has against any agent; he need not see his own act (as his own versus another's) in that picture in order to be constrained from killing. It is the right of his potential victim that stops him.

This is a rights-based deontology. There could be a duty based deontology that prohibits a certain sort of act even if a victim has waived his right not to have that act performed against him. This duty-based deontology could also come into play if my potential victim would lose his life in any case, because if I do not kill him someone else will. (However, in at least some cases of this sort, killing may be permissible.) In these sorts of cases what comes into view for the agent from his position, and accounts for his not acting, is his perception of the sort of act he would have to perform, e.g., a type of killing. But even here, on the duty-based deontological model, while it is my act that I see, it is not that it will be *my* doing it as opposed to another's doing it, that stops me from acting; it is my understanding of the sort of act it is that stops me from acting. Even if others would perform more of the same sorts of act if I do not perform this one, I must not act, because the negative features of the act themselves make it impermissible for me to do it. (This is analogous to the rights of my victim constraining me, on the rights based deontological view, even if this results in other victims having their rights violated by other people.)

In cases where the characteristics of the acts do not make it impermissible to act, I may still regret that it is I who will (permissibly) do the act rather than that another do it. Here, finally, what I focus on from my position is that it is *me* doing the act. But the special concern for my behavior in this situation is not the sort of concern that drives deontological restrictions in general.

Finally, it is only because the right of my victim (or the characteristics of my act) stops me from acting, even though the rights of others will be violated, that every person—including those many actual victims—is the bearer of a right that is so stringent. This means that each person has the status of a person who may not be violated even to help others avoid violation, even if what happens to some of them is the violation of that right. This argument about the status of persons mimics the argument given by the anti-aggregationist, insofar as he derived the status of each person as someone who cannot be abandoned, even if this results in many persons in fact being abandoned.[25]

NOTES

1. The second sort of situation is dealt with in *Morality, Mortality,* Vol. II (New York: Oxford University Press, forthcoming).

2. *Philosophy and Public Affairs* 6, no. 4 (Summer 1977): 293–316.

3. Though I do not here distinguish loss of life from suffering other losses or simply suffering, whether a case involves one or the other may be important. That is, loss of life may function in a qualitatively different way from other losses.

4. The character of these theories is considered in more detail in *Morality, Mortality,* Vol. II.

5. In "Innumerate Ethics," *Philosophy and Public Affairs* 7, no. 4 (Summer 1978): 285–301.

6. We examine the prerogative in more detail in *Morality, Mortality,* Vol. II.

7. I owe this point and example to Peter Unger.

8. This is the way a pure individual-relative consequentialist might derive them. See *Morality, Mortality,* Vol. II.

9. There is another interpretation of Taurek, presented by Thomas Nagel in his paper, "Equality," reprinted in his *Mortal Questions,* p. 116 (Cambridge: Cambridge University Press, 1979), according to which Taurek means only that so long as a state of affairs is contrary to the interests of at least one person, it is not an impersonally good state of affairs. However, states of affairs that are in everyone's interest are impersonally good states of affairs. (A decision to save the greatest number is contrary to the interests of the one in conflict situations, but not in conflict-free situations.) On this issue, see also note 13.

10. Taurek, "Should the Numbers Count?," *Philosophy and Public Affairs* 6, no. 4 (Summer 1977): 307.

11. Taurek's views are also consistent, I believe, with its being better to save the greater number in what I shall call *partially conflict-free situations.* These are situations in which at least one person must die, but we have a choice whether more than one shall die.

Consider the following Helicopter Case, in which we are confronted with two choices, not one: There is a drug we must distribute to a group of five on one island or to a single person on another island. While considering this choice, we are told that a large helicopter has become available. If we wish, it can airlift four of the five people on the first island to a hospital for treatment. One person who cannot tolerate helicopter flight and who would die if airlifted will be left behind, and we will toss a coin to decide whether he or the person on the other island gets the drug.

Empathetic grounds for saving life should make the helicopter choice easy: Save four of the five people on one island when there is no conflict with a need to express equal concern for all six. Four people will be saved without giving anyone worse prospects than he would otherwise have had.

Some things that Taurek says about the death of five rather than one in conflict cases can be said about the death of five rather than one in the helicopter decision: If five die, no one of the five will lose more than the single person would lose if he died, and no matter what happens at least one person must die. Still we should save more of the group of five because we are concerned for the loss to each individual, and each additional person of the five whom we save has his condition improved without making conditions worse for anyone else.

12. As pointed out in note 10, this is the interpretation Thomas Nagel gives of Taurek's view in "Equality." This is the analysis of "worse than" that follows from Pareto optimality. Indeed, in conversation with me (in the fall of 1984), Taurek said he would go so far as to say this.

13. C. S. Lewis seems to take such a position in *The Problem of Pain* (London: Collins, 1957), pp. 103–104. It is analogous to the view that there is no more intelligence in the world if two people have IQs of 130 than if one does; only if one of them reaches new heights of intelligence is there more intelligence in the world.

14. David Wasserman emphasized this point to me.

15. I attribute much of this argument (as well as clarification of the distinction between fairness and the value of a chance) to David Wasserman. He emphasized step 2 and pointed out to me the substitution that could be made using 1 and 2. I believe it is implicit in the idea that when we save the larger number, we save at least as many as when we save the smaller number.

16. "Utilitarianism and the Virtues," in *American Philosophical Association, Proceedings and Addresses* 57, no. 2 (November 1983): 273–283.

17. This is true unless we think of deciding by seeing "where the greater additional number of people are" as itself giving A an equal chance with B. It would give A and B an equal chance if we assume that A and B had an equal chance to be next to C. (This use of counting numbers of people only takes greater number as a random decision device.) In fact, I do not think we conceive of counting numbers as involving giving an equal chance. In many cases we know there was no equal chance to be with another person(s), unless perhaps at a very far removed ex ante stage. I shall return to this point later.

18. After writing these pages, I came across Kagan's discussion of aggregation in conflict cases (in "The Additive Fallacy," reprinted in J. M. Fischer and M. Ravizza (eds.) *Ethics: Problems & Principles*). Kagan considers the following argument: If we had a choice between saving no one and saving one person, we should save one. If it is better that one person live than that none do, it is better if one *more* person lives than if fewer do when we can save all. Therefore, it is better if more people live than if fewer do in conflict situations. Kagan criticizes this argument by noting that factors may not have constant moral value in different contexts. (I agree with this point and have discussed it as the Principle of Contextual Interaction in, for example, "Killing and Letting Die: Methodology and Substance," and "Harming, Not Aiding, and Positive Rights." Kagan calls the failure to recognize it the Additive Fallacy.) This implies, he says, that (1) we cannot merely assume that one life added to other lives is a good thing, making an outcome better, simply because one life added onto zero lives is a good thing, and that (2) we cannot merely assume that if one life added onto other lives is a good thing making an outcome better in a context where all can be saved, it is a good thing making an outcome better in a context where someone will have to be left to die. My sense is that while we should not mechanically assume that a factor adds the same value in all contexts, it is true that one added to others where all can be saved makes for a better outcome and that one added to others in conflict situations also makes for a better outcome.

But, I have argued, just because it is in fact a better state of affairs if more are saved, this does not mean that in situations in which conflicts exist there might not be other wrongmaking factors which interfere with our automatically producing the best state of affairs. (I here assume that the goodness of states of affairs is evaluated independently of right or wrongmaking factors.)

19. I was interested to learn from Taurek that his concern for whether the numbers count originally developed when he had to deal with a conflict among his children, to each of whom he said he was deeply attached. The suggestion that he toss a coin in a conflict between two of his children and a third was his wife's, he said.

20. I owe this point to Larry Sager.

21. In "Innumerate Ethics."

22. I use an argument with a similar form in *Morality, Mortality,* Vol. II, against the view that we show maximal respect for individual rights if we minimize rights violated by violating comparable rights.

23. This interpretation was mentioned in note 17.

24. In "Rights and Agency," *Philosophy & Public Affairs* 11, no. 1 (Winter 1982):3–39.

25. For more on this see my "Harming Some to Save Others," and "Non-Consequentialism, the Person as an End-in-Itself, and the Significance of Status."

6

Is It Right to Save the Greater Number?

In this chapter, I will consider further the "maintaining ties" objection to the Aggregation Argument presented in Chapter 5. The central question is whether, as suggested, there is a conflict between the right and the good in substituting equivalents and counting numbers of lives. Although I will argue that there is no conflict, I will first present other cases in which there *is* a conflict between the right and substitution of equivalents. Then I will argue that in cases involving different numbers of lives there is no conflict, either because the theory of the right does not demand equal chances in such cases or because it actually requires counting numbers. In connection with the first possibility, we consider a consistency argument: those who wish to count numbers when saving people in conflict cases would be willing to sacrifice comparable good to avoid violating considerations of the right in many other cases. If they are not willing to sacrifice utility in this case, it must be because no such (or no weighty) considerations of the right are present. Then we consider in more detail what an objection to counting numbers based on fairness would amount to, in order to see whether not giving equal chances is unfair. Finally we consider whether there is a positive argument *for* counting numbers because it is right, that is, because it is owed to each individual that he be counted, rather than simply because counting will maximize overall good consequences.

I

Duty To Toss a Coin

But first, consider some preliminary points. The criticism of the Aggregation Argument's implications for action that I have presented depends on accepting the metaphorical idea of ties coming from each individual to the person who must decide which individual(s) will be saved. Each person has something that lets him put a "hook" directly into the person who must act, and these hooks are supposed never to reinforce each other to form weightier units. The conclusion is supposed to be that each individual deserves a chance. Is this Taurek's conclusion reached by a different route? Not quite. Taurek thought that we could help whomever we wanted and show equal concern *if* we wanted to. By contrast, if the Aggregation Argument proved that the smaller number's dying is a better state of affairs, then, barring greater personal sacrifice in acting, there would be good reason to bring it about, unless there were a nonconsequentialist consideration stemming from the theory of the right that stood in the way of bringing about that best state of affairs. If there were such a consideration, we could be obliged to give equal chances. It would not be a mere option. This is true even though an individual's need to live does not necessarily give rise to a claim to be aided in the way that contracting for aid would. That is, no one could have a right to be aided and yet each might have a right to be given an equal chance if anyone was going to be aided.

Comparable Cases Involving Negative Rights

Does the model of being tied to each individual as an individual imply that a case in which we choose whom to aid is like a case in which we choose whether or not to chop up one person for his organs to save five others from some disease (Transplant Case)? In the latter situation the negative right of the one (he has a right not to be chopped up) stands in the way of maximizing the good; so we may not engage in substitution of equivalents.

Strictly speaking, I believe it is not Taurek's conflict cases which are to be compared with cases in which we may not violate a negative right. There are, however, other cases involving conflict about whether to aid a smaller group or a larger group that do bear comparison to negative-rights cases. For example, suppose one person comes to me at *t,* needing a lifesaving drug. I know (with certainty) that if I give it to him, I will not be able to save five others who (I know with a certainty) will need the drug in a month and who will die without it (Present Need Case). It may be that I should give the drug to the person who is now in need, rather than stand by doing nothing when I could help. Later, when the five appear, I will not be able to help them, but neither will I stand by doing nothing when I could help. (For more discussion of this type of case, see pp. 141–142).

Despite significant differences, we can discern a structural similarity between the Transplant and Present Need Cases in the manner in which the one person stands in the way of serving the greater number.

Taurek's original Drug Case itself is analogous, in the realm of negative rights, to what is known as the Trolley Case. Here we must decide whether to allow a trolley to go toward killing five or direct it onto a different track where we foresee it will kill one. (The principle which justifies redirecting in the Trolley Case is meant to apply to, at least, all redirection cases, e.g., a case in which a plane already headed toward killing five people in one city may be redirected to killing a lesser number in another city, no matter how far away.) Without denying that there may be a morally significant difference between killing one and letting one die, we can see a structural similarity between directing aid and directing (or redirecting) a threat. Still, suppose the analysis according to which we have ties to each individual, unbreakable except by a coin toss, were correct. An implication of this analysis would be that we should treat the Trolley Case as similar to the Transplant Case, in the sense that numbers should not count. We should toss a coin in the Trolley Case. (In the Transplant Case, the one is protected not by a required coin toss but by a negative right, which takes precedence over any claims of the five to be saved and makes tossing a coin wrong.)

Substitution of Equivalents as Part of a Theory of the Right

Now let us turn to our central task: Can we rebut the idea that the theory of the right demands a coin toss? Can it be correct to act on the basis of the numbers? Can we act on the basis of the numbers without thereby shifting our attachment to any higher-order unit and away from the individual claims or needs? We can do all these things, I believe, if it is morally permissible to balance off equal and opposing individual claims or needs.[1] This balancing need not be understood as the canceling of these claims or needs, but should rather be seen as the recognition (1) that neither of two equal and opposing claims or needs can finally decide an outcome, the "unbalanced" members of one side must do that; (2) that whichever side we help, we will satisfy a claim or need that counts as much as any claim equal and opposite to it with which it is balanced; and (3) that each equal and opposite need or claim does not directly "hook in" and get for itself an equal chance to be satisfied, but is required to confront an equal and opposite (opponent) claim or need.

This model *does* indeed involve our abandoning a tie to a single individual or claim that is opposed by more, as described in Chapter 5. The position is that this is justified and, furthermore, does not necessarily involve a shift to using a higher-order unit of value. We are still counting individuals as individuals and understanding the personal perspective of each, according to which it is in his interest that he be the one to live, but we allow confrontation and balancing of individuals to make use of the *substitution of equivalents*. That is, the proposed theory of the right accepts rather than rejects the move that underlies step 3 in the Aggregation Argument.

Support for Not Substituting Equivalents

As noted above, despite the fact that I ultimately wish to defend the view that counting numbers is either permitted or required by a nonconsequentialist theory of the right that appropriately incorporates some substitution of equivalents, I think it is interesting and important to consider the range of aiding cases in which it is wrong to engage in substitution of equivalents. Here the model of remaining tied to each person is correct, even according to a theory of the right that permits counting in Taurek cases. Suppose, for example, that we have a choice between saving A's life and saving B's, and alongside B is C who has a sore throat.[2] Our drug that can save B's life can also in addition cure C's sore throat (Sore Throat Case). If we substitute equivalents, we conclude that it is right to save B and cure C's sore throat. (This is because we substitute B for his equivalent A and then also get extra utility.) Yet I believe it would be wrong to deprive A of his 50 percent chance to be saved simply in order to get the extra utility of curing C's sore throat associated with saving B. Here we should remain tied to the personal perspectives of both A and B given what is at stake for each of them. In this case it is right to toss a coin; the sore-throat cure in this case is what I call an "irrelevant" utility.[3] Yet we decide this way not simply because it is unconscionable to be concerned about a sore throat when lives are at stake. In other circumstances a sore throat might matter. Suppose we had a choice about the coin to be tossed in selecting between A and B whose lives are at stake: we could use an ordinary coin or a magic coin, which is such that whichever side it falls on a sore throat gets cured. Then it would be quite permissible and right to choose the magic coin. It is permissible to choose between random decision procedures on the basis of this extra utility, but not to choose between people on the same grounds.

Why is this so? Is it because a sore throat is something we should be willing to suffer to preserve another person's chance for life? Consider another case: we must choose between saving C and saving D, and only if we save D can we also reach E in time to prevent his finger from falling off (Finger Case). There again, I think, we should not deprive C of his 50 percent chance to survive, although a finger is more than E is obliged to give up to provide C with his 50 percent chance to survive when only one person would be saved whether or not the sacrifice is made.

What if we could save E's arm from falling off only if we saved D rather than C? At this point, I think it is no longer right to ignore the extra utility. At this point, I believe, we should shift from identifying with the perspective of each of C and D and focusing on how much a 50 percent chance of survival means to C. Instead of tossing a coin, we should give a greater chance of D and E's arm being saved. When the extra utility moves further up, to an additional life, that is save F or G plus H, then it is even clearer that we should save G and H.

I do not claim to be proving here that we should stop tossing a coin at a certain point. My aim in presenting these cases is rather to show in how many instances even someone who supports counting numbers of lives will still think that we ought to toss a coin and retain ties to the personal perspectives of each person rather than substitute equivalents.

Matters can become even more complex, however. The cases we have considered so far suggest that whether an additional utility is relevant or irrelevant is a function of the magnitude of the loss to the person who will suffer it. (Here I continue to use an objective evaluation of the loss to a person; i.e., even if he doesn't care appropriately for loss of an arm, it can be a big loss.) But, what about cases in which the chance at stake for each is less than 50 percent? Suppose each of one hundred people is on his own island and only one of them is accompanied by Joe. We must choose which one of the hundred to save from death, and only if we go to save the person on the island which also contains Joe can we also prevent Joe's finger from falling off. Is the finger relevant here since each person stands to lose a smaller than 50 percent chance of being chosen to live if we go directly to where Joe is, *or* is the finger even less significant because there are many more people to whom it matters what the outcome will be because they stand to lose their lives?

Second, suppose we face a choice of saving either five people on one island or on another island five who are accompanied by Joe whose arm we alone can save from falling off. Five people stand to lose a 50 percent chance of survival if we go directly to the island with Joe on it. Even someone who took the view that getting to save an arm as well was enough to justify giving a greater chance to one person rather than another, might reconsider his view about whether an arm was a relevant utility in this context. When a big chance to so many is at stake, the arm may be irrelevant.

Large Numbers

Now suppose 1000 people are on one island and 1001 people are on another.[4] Here, I believe, it may even be correct to ignore the difference of one life. If so, then in this context the one life has become an irrelevant utility. This would be true even if, in a choice between two on one island and three on another, the additional life should be determinative of whom we save.

It is sometimes said that when the number of lives at stake is large, for example, a billion, it no longer matters whether a billion die or a billion and one die. Our discussion suggests when (and why) this might be true and when it is not true. If we must choose between saving a billion or saving the same billion and one additional person, then it does matter whether a billion die or a billion and one instead. But when we are in a conflict situation, and it is a choice between a billion on one island and a billion and one on another island, then perhaps the additional one does not determine whom we should save. This is because we understand that the equal 50 percent chance to survive is important to the billion, and that from their points of view it is not just as good if the other billion people survive. We think that preserving this equal chance of so many is more important than saving one extra person outright.

What these additional cases suggest is that it is not only the (objective) significance of the additional loss to the person who will suffer it that counts. (For someone to lose his life is a great loss whether there is a choice between 2000 and 3000 or 1000 and 1001). In addition, the size of the chance for life that is at stake for others and the number of others whose lives are at stake may make relevant or irrelevant an additional utility that is irrelevant or relevant in other contexts. (This is a different point from the fact that also saving a finger is clearly relevant when the choice is between saving one person's hand or another's hand.)

I conclude that there are many cases where the substitution of equivalents is incorrect. (We will analyze some of these cases in greater detail starting in Chapter 9. Here we just use them as a preface to arguing for the view that sometimes substitution of equivalents *is* correct.)

What is going on when we move from tossing a coin to substituting equivalents? In the view of those who support the ties-to-individuals critique of the Aggregation Argument, what is going on is that we have allowed the lure of achieving the better consequence to override considerations of the right. This would assimilate the move, in a choice between C and D, from ignoring the finger to counting the arm, and thence to counting lives, to the move from requiring equal treatment for all to permitting an army general certain privileges in time of war because this will produce greater utility.

Counting Numbers and the Theory of the Right

There are two alternative positions to be contrasted with this view. These two positions share the view that a nonconsequentialist theory of the right does not require unbroken ties to individuals (and so a toss of a coin) when the extra utility achieved in helping one side rather than the other is sufficiently great (relative to the context of the case).

The first position also holds that the nonconsequentialist component of the theory of the right is agnostic on whether numbers of lives *must* be counted. But if no element of the right requires the tossing of a coin, then there is no bar to simply producing the best possible consequences. If this is a sufficient reason for action, then we ought to produce the best consequences.

The second position, by contrast, holds that a nonconsequentialist theory of the right requires us to count lives and, in general, to count certain extra utilities and to do this not merely because it produces the best consequences. Most crucially, this defense of saving the greater number insists that counting numbers is a requirement of the theory of the right, rather than of the theory of the good.

Agnosticism

Let us begin with the component shared by the first and second alternative positions. What evidence is there that when we count numbers we are not merely overriding a claim to be given an equal chance for the sake of utility? The general strategy of the following remarks is to consider in how many cases nonconsequentialists do not allow utility to override the claims of individuals to be treated in certain ways, and then to ask why these same nonconsequentialists would permit overriding of a claim in the case of saving the greater number. (We have already considered some aiding cases in which extra utility does not override equal chances.)

1. The criticism we have examined of the Aggregation Argument would lead one to believe that we face a conflict between producing the best state of affairs and abiding by a requirement of the right relation to individuals. On that model, saving the greater number by abandoning one is like saving the greater number by killing one as a means, a course of action typically rejected by nonconsequentialists. But if choosing to save the greater number and abandoning the one did indeed present a conflict between the right and the good, it would be hard to explain why nonconsequentialists, who will not kill one to save a hundred, are typically prepared to abandon one to save even two (let alone one hundred). It seems more reasonable to account for this on grounds that maintaining ties to individuals and tossing a coin is not a requirement of right conduct. (If it were merely a weaker requirement than not killing, we might expect it to be overridden for a large number not for one extra life.)

2. Those who would save the greater number in the Drug Case will not necessarily use a scarce resource to save a doctor rather than a janitor just because the doctor will then save twenty others from a fatal disease for which the scarce resource itself is useless. They may think it unfair to favor the doctor. But if they were concerned with promoting the greater good, they would override the claim of the janitor based on fairness. And if they do not override fairness here to save twenty, why would they override a claim to be given an equal chance merely to save two rather than one?

3. Those nonconsequentialists who would save the greater rather than the lesser number should yet, I believe, be willing to reduce the chances of the greater number by the proportional weight of the lesser number for the sake of giving the minority a

chance to be saved along with the majority. They should do this even if this increases the chance that all will be lost and decreases overall expected utility because the minority gains less of a chance to be saved than the majority loses. Here again consideration of the right would be allowed to trump utility.

4. Suppose it were possible to give the one his proportional chance to survive and the balance of chances to the more numerous, but the one might survive while the more numerous perish. Those nonconsequentialists who would save the greater number could be morally opposed to this scheme, though they would approve of reducing the majorities' chances for the minorities' sake when the majority and minority could survive together. If they were opposed to this scheme of separate survival, they would be sacrificing utility for the sake of a rightness consideration. This is because they would prefer a scheme that runs the risk of everyone's dying for the sake of avoiding (what they see) as the wrongness of the one's surviving when the larger number don't.

These pieces of evidence–which we shall return to consider in more detail below—are intended to suggest that if we think we should save the greater number of lives this is not because there is a rightness consideration that is being overridden by a utility consideration. There is no conflict of the right and the good when we count numbers. It is important to be clear about the nature of the argument. We take the responses a typical nonconsequentialist has to cases as indications of what factors do and do not explain these responses. This is not as powerful an argument as actually pointing to the factors in the cases which explain the responses. That is, the argument provides a reason for believing there is no unfairness in some cases by considering the pattern of nonconsequentialists' responses. This is not the same as showing what factors in the cases explain these responses. The latter would be a more powerful and direct argument.

Is the Consistency Argument Adequate?

We have proposed an argument from consistency. That is, how could utility's overriding a consideration of the right explain our counting numbers of lives, if we do not allow comparable utility to override other considerations of the right? One answer to this question is that the claim to an equal chance may be much weaker than, for example, the claim not to be killed to save other people or even the claim (based on fairness) not to have someone else's capacities (as a doctor) to save other lives determine whether one receives a scarce resource. That these claims are not overridden by utility would not show, therefore, that a weaker claim wasn't being overridden by utility.

In response we can say that if one extra life can override a persisting claim to an equal chance, that claim amounts to very little. If there were a serious claim to an equal chance, we would expect at least more lives to be necessary for overriding. Though true, these remarks would not really capture the point. For it seems appropriate to say that the claim of two conflicting persons to equal chances based on fairness cannot be overridden by the fact that, if we saved one of them, we could also prevent a second person's sore throat. (That is, the language of "overriding" seems appropriate here.) But it no longer seems appropriate to say that the claim of each to an equal chance based on fairness is "overridden" by the fact that an extra life is at stake on one side. Certain factors might *override* a still present claim based on fairness, but other factors just make it go away. This is what seems true in conflict cases involving a greater and lesser number of people. Perhaps the consistency argument cannot prove this, i.e., that more than mere overriding of a very weak claim to equal chances is going on. But it certainly suggests it.

Is Counting Numbers Unfair?

We have considered aiding cases in which smaller extra utilities do not override fairness and cases in which large additional utilities do not override other claims. Now, let us examine in greater detail the idea of fairness. We will consider a ground for the charge of unfairness and try to show that counting numbers does not succumb to it. This will involve a reanalysis of some of the cases we have already discussed in considering when substitution of equivalents is permitted and when it isn't permitted. (We are here still discussing the first agnosticism proposal, that the theory of the right is not opposed to counting numbers. We shall not yet consider the second proposal, that counting numbers is required by a theory of the right.)

What we would like to show is that in a case in which we must decide whether to save the greater number of people or a different group containing fewer people, there is no conflict between saving the greater number (bringing about the best state of affairs) and treating everyone fairly. In such cases, fairness does not require that everyone get equal an chance and the specific charge of unfairness in counting numbers—overridden or not—cannot be made to stick.

Conflicts between Fairness and Maximizing the Good

The standard type of case in which there is a conflict between the greater good and fairness involves giving someone more than his fair chance to survive because, if he survives, he will contribute a *great* deal to overall utility. John Broome[5] notes that we might give a scarce drug to an army general rather than give him the same chance to get it as an equally sick civilian. This is because without him the nation may lose a war. In such a case we may decide that the greater good overrides the consideration of fairness. However, we recognize that the requirement of fairness has *not* been satisfied.

Is this like saving the greater number in the Drug Case? Let us repeat some points made above. A very general reason to think it is not is that nonconsequentialists, who are often unwilling to sacrifice fairness to utility, find saving the greater number acceptable. Ordinarily when the greater good overrides fairness in a system that is not strictly consequentialist, a very significant difference in greater good must be achievable by overriding fairness. (The same is true when justice is at stake, e.g., we should not kill one in the Transplant Case, even to save one hundred). Yet nonconsequentialists are willing to abandon one to save *only two*. If so, can that really be a case of utility overriding fairness? It would be odd to think that the principle governing the nonconsequentialists' intentions is so inconsistent that it allows the very same consideration, fairness, sometimes to be easily overridden and sometimes to be overridden only with great difficulty.

In addition, again to repeat what was said above, suppose A and B both need a scarce drug to live. The fact that B (but not A) will save C (who does not need our drug) would *not,* I believe, be enough for a nonconsequentialist to override the claim of A to an equal chance based on fairness. This is so even though those who think that numbers count believe that we *should* save B and C rather than A, when C will be saved by the use of the drug we must distribute. This is what happens in the Drug Case. Nonconsequentialists cannot believe numbers count in the Drug Case on the ground that the greater good overrides the claim of fairness since they believe the very same greater good should *not* override A's claim to an equal chance when B will save C. It must rather be that they see no conflict between fairness and saving the greater number in the Drug Case.

Personal Characteristics versus Saving with Our Resources Directly

How does the case in which B would save C who does not need our drug differ from a case in which we save B and C?

Here is one suggestion (very roughly put) about what distinguishes these cases. In one kind of case we choose between people on the *basis of a personal characteristic that one of them has* but the other lacks; this raises the issue of unfairness. The capacity to save another life may be such a characteristic. By contrast, when we save B because *we* can thereby also aid C, so that C is aided but not because of any personal characteristic of B's, the question of whether to override fairness in order to aid B and C rather than A does not arise. In such a case, I shall say that C *directly* needs our aid because he can be *directly* benefited by the scarce commodity we have to offer. In the other case, C only indirectly needs our resource because he needs us to aid B with it. B will then aid him in some way not involving our drug. (The way I shall use these terms allows that someone who directly needs the drug for himself may get the benefit from it indirectly. An example of indirect benefit arises if his burying the drug in the ground makes a plant grow and consuming that plant saves his life. So "direct need" for the drug will allow for *indirect use and benefit.* The crucial point is that there is a distinction between someone himself needing to get the drug—even so that it will grow the plant—and someone needing another *person* to get the drug so that the latter can do something unrelated to distributing the drug to help him.)[6]

Revisions

Notice that we must offer a characterization of "personal characteristic" for this analysis to be complete. What if B can save C, who does not need our drug, because he happens to be next to C? This is not really a personal characteristic distinguishing B from A. Is it unfair to pick B rather than A for the drug because of his relative position? Whether it is unfairness or not, there does seem to be something wrong in picking B.

Suppose, however, that *we* could not get our commodity to C, who directly needs it. However, B, who is a fast runner and needs the drug as much himself, could get it to C. Would it be unfair to save B because he, but not A, can then give C a share of our drug? Here B's personal characteristic would be playing a role in our deciding to save B rather than A, and our action would not directly save C. Nevertheless, the fact that both B and C have as great a direct need for what we have to distribute as A does is, I believe, crucial in making it not unfair to save B because of his skill.

These two cases suggest that someone's personal characteristic if it helps better distribute what *we* have may be taken into account in deciding whom to aid, although a personal or nonpersonal characteristic that produces more utility in some other way should not be taken into account. On the other hand, there is a more general background limit on our goal: we do not do with our resource whatever will result in as much good as possible. Rather we try to achieve the best outcome for which our resource is specifically designed. This is certainly a nonconsequentialist characteristic since we are not maximizing overall good. Another way of putting this point is that we limit the *sphere* in which an item can maximize good.[7]

The Surgeon Case

In this regard, let us consider in more detail the Surgeon Case,[8] in which we must also distribute a scarce drug. We can use it to save 5 people in one part of the country or one person in another part of the country, but we cannot save all 6. Suppose the single person is about to perform surgery that will save the lives of 100 different people suffering from another disease. He is irreplaceable in the surgery, and they will die without him. To whom should we give the drug?

Some might suggest that we handle such a case by giving extra weight to the single person. This is because he has a relationship to the 100 that the 5 don't have. Some may object that giving the surgeon extra weight would not be to treat him and the 5 as equals. This objection depends on the claim that fair treatment as equals is owed to each individual *regardless* of his relationships to others, regardless of his instrumental role. There is an alternative to saying that we should in this case give the surgeon greater weight. We could instead say that, while each of the 6 individuals counts equally, we must also count equally the 100 who will be lost if the surgeon is not saved. That is, we should treat the Surgeon Case as though it involved a choice between saving 5 people and saving 101. Is there a reason for not counting the 100 people as 100 separate individuals on the side of the surgeon, though we should count the 5 confronting him?

In the Surgeon Case, the 100 people do not *directly* need the drug we must distribute. At most, if they could try to buy the drug to give it to the surgeon, they could claim that *they need it* in order to give it to the surgeon whom they need. That is, they need the drug only indirectly rather than directly because someone they need needs it. Their survival is dependent on his survival and their need for the drug is dependent on his need. In cases where they could buy the drug for him, they could only be said to need his having the drug, rather than the drug itself.

Another way to make this point is to consider a version of the Surgeon Case in which the 5 need the drug to save their lives, and the surgeon needs the drug to *cure a splitting headache* that prevents him from performing surgery. He himself would not die if he didn't receive the drug, though the 100 people he could help would die. Should he be a candidate to receive the drug nevertheless?[9] In this case, he still needs our drug directly, but not as much as each of the 5. If it were not for the 100 who do not need our drug directly, we would not consider giving it to him at all.

If the surgeon should be given the drug, wouldn't this be a case in which we think fairness is infringed for a great good, not a case totally in accord with principles of the right (i.e., rights, justice, fairness)?

Summary

A distribution of our lifesaving drug would be *unfair* if we distinguished between candidates who directly need our resource on the basis of a personal characteristic unrelated to the distribution of our resource for saving lives. A distribution would have something morally wrong with it for reasons other than unfairness if it distinguished between candidates who equally directly need our drug on the basis of a *nonpersonal* characteristic that does not help distribute our resources to those who directly need it. Counting numbers has neither of these two negative features.

Unfairness and such other wrong-making features could be overridden by significant utility. For example, in the case of the surgeon who has only a splitting headache, I suggest that we should not ignore the 100 he could save. But we should also not give them their full weight as 100 individuals versus the 5 who need our resource to live. Another way to put this point is that it would take more than 6 on the side of the surgeon to outweigh the 5 who need our drug. One additional person would not be enough. More than one additional person is needed to outweigh the factor of unfairness.

Complications

There are further complications in the direct/indirect need and personal characteristic versus nonpersonal characteristic distinctions. Consider the following cases:

1. Suppose two people are in deathly need of a doctor's aid. The doctor himself needs an organ transplant, but only to help him function up to par. He alone can save the two. We are about to give the organ to him *in order to* save the two people. Then a patient who needs the transplant more than the doctor appears. The point of this case is to see whether reversing the temporal order of our concern diminishes the sense that the greater good is achieved by unfair means if the doctor gets the organ. That is, instead of beginning with an organ that we must distribute, we begin with two people whose lives we want to save who do not directly need the organ. The organ is, at first, just a means to saving them. Does this altered gestalt change the conclusion we seemed to reach in other cases? Or should we still conclude that we may not do what will save the two if it conflicts with the best direct use of the organ?

2. Suppose that B has a characteristic A lacks, that his breathing normally will release a lifesaving chemical to save C. Here it is a personal characteristic of B's that would save C, though *not* his voluntary action. B needs our drug to survive; C does not. Does the fact that a natural occurrence rather than a human choice causes B to save C eliminate the unfairness of our helping him rather than giving an equal chance to A, who also directly needs our drug?

3. Certainly human choice is sometimes a consideration when we decide

whether to save the greater number. For example, suppose C will die if B does because he will commit suicide, not wanting to live in a world without B. I suggest that because C chooses to die, we should not count his as a second life at stake on B's side; A should not be made to pay for C's choice.

4. Suppose that if we do not help B, he will unavoidably give off a chemical *killing* C? Is it unfair that he get help because he poses a threat to others whereas A does not?

A Further Implication: Lesser Additional Utility

So far we have considered cases in which one person has a capacity to cause other lives to be saved. The saving of lives is a significant good. But our general point about the distinction between people having direct or indirect need for our good also applies in cases in which one person rather than another can produce only a small additional good.

Suppose it is right to ignore the extra utility-producing characteristic of one of two people in deciding whom to save. It might be thought that it is then strictly illogical ever to let the extra utility that can be produced if we save one person rather than another enter into our decision about whom to save. But this argument ignores the distinction between the extra utility produced by the person we save (e.g., a doctor who will cure someone's sore throat) and the extra utility that can directly be produced by what we have to distribute. The principle of fairness and of the direct use of our resource may rule out counting the extra utility in the first case, but not in the second. If it is impermissible to count the extra utility in the second case, it is for reasons other than that unfairness is at issue. For example, we might consider giving a drug to B to save his life rather than A's because B is located next to C, and only he can use our drug which alone can cure C's sore throat. I believe that we should not favor B in this case when he can also cure C's sore throat. (This contrasts with the correctness of our saving B rather than A if he could thereby also save C's life with our drug.) Yet this is *not* because a personal property of B's would be the basis for an unfair selection or because our resource is not directly needed. It is rather because the extra utility should be irrelevant. (We have already made this point and shall examine this issue in greater detail in Chapter 8.)

Recall also that *we* should at least give a greater chance to be saved to B than to A in cases where we can then make a significant contribution to C, even if not save his life. For example, suppose I had a choice of using my drug to save either A's life or the group consisting of B's life and C's leg. I believe it would be permissible to give a greater chance of help to B and C rather than A. This is so even if it is not permissible to choose B over A because he will operate on C's leg and save it, and not permissible to select saving C's leg alone over saving A's life alone. (That is, C's leg should not be a contestant against A's life on its own. For more on this, see Chapters 8 and 9.)

The Kantian Injunction

The distinction we have drawn between direct and indirect use of our resource and its relation to fairness is to be contrasted with the so-called Kantian injunction. That is, it has been argued[10] that we ought not to provide a scarce resource to one person rather than another simply because of his social usefulness because this treats people solely as means and not also as ends in themselves. Let us consider the "Kantian Objection." Imagine a case in which we must choose whether to save A or B, where B but not A will serve the useful function of saving C if he survives. It would not be treating *B* solely *as a means* if we aided him since in his own right he needs the scarce resource as much as A. Suppose B had a disease that was far less serious for him personally than A's was for him, but severe enough to interfere with B's saving C's life. Would we treat B solely as a means if we gave him the drug rather than A? It seems odd to object to treating someone *well* (rather than badly) because one sees him only as a means and is not really concerned with his welfare. Indeed, this case is construable as one where we compensate someone for treating him as a means, by giving him the drug for his lesser illness. (This fits the traditional model of not treating someone solely as a means if we pay him for his labor.)

Still, it may be said that we are treating A only as a means since we decide who gets aid by seeing what function each person can perform. A is treated worse simply because he cannot perform a certain function. In the standard case of *using* as a means merely, we use someone's services without considering his interests. Here we *treat* someone as a means because we consider whether he could be of use to us and reject him because he is not. It is true that here we do not ignore A's needs entirely: whether he or B is chosen depends on his usefulness, but we begin by considering the welfare of both A and B. If we gave A the drug, it would be *in part* because it would be good for him, not simply because he is useful.[11] Yet denying him the drug because he is not useful, when it is not in his interest to be denied the drug, is, I believe, adequate grounds for saying we are treating him solely as a means. So it does seem that the version of the Kantian injunction is violated.

However, suppose we give a drug to B rather than A because only B can give the rest of *our* drug to five others who need it also. Here, too, we seem to choose between A and B by taking a means perspective. Yet, I have argued, it is permitted by the Direct Need Principle.[12]

It seems, therefore, that violating the Kantian injunction does not always signify that our distribution has a morally wrong feature to it.

Justice

It is worth noting that even if it were not unfair to count numbers of people, it might be *unjust* to do so if counting conflicts with property rights. For example, suppose A and B both paid for supplies of a drug, but one of the only two bottles produced was accidentally broken. Furthermore, suppose it is morally appropriate that only those who pay would ever get the drug. Now, we must choose whether to give the drug to A or to B, when next to B is C, who needs the drug as much as A or B and whom we can help only by going to B. In this case there is a good reason to toss a coin. This is because there is good reason to think the matter should be decided on the basis of the needs of those who have property rights in the drug, without regard to C's need, which is unaccompanied by his own property right.

Conclusion

Let me now draw some general conclusions. I have argued that Taurek makes a mistake at least in arguing that being saved because one is in the larger group is like

being saved because one has a high IQ. If we save someone with the latter characteristic, it is because we think he has a personal characteristic that is either intrinsically more valuable than those of other people or will cause more benefit to
society in some way *other than* distributing our resources to those who directly need
it. This raises problems not raised by saving someone because he is with the greater
number or because he helps us distribute the resource we have to those who directly
need it. In the latter cases, we do not select on the basis of a personal characteristic
unrelated to distribution of our resource nor on the basis of a nonpersonal characteristic that has a causal role in distributing something other than our resource.
When we say that we saved someone because he was with the greater number, it is
misleading to infer that "being with the greater number" is a characteristic that
made us select *him* over a person in the smaller group. We do not save *him* because
he has this characteristic, we save him and every person he is with. But is it not true
that we save him *and* every person he is with because *each* one has
the characteristic of "being with the greater number"? Why select people with this
characteristic? Again this is a misleading way of putting matters. We focus on this
characteristic of each person in the larger group because if we save each of them, we
thereby save the greater number. We do not focus on the characteristic itself, as if
we were interested in selecting individuals on the basis of some feature irrelevant to
the direct need of people for the drug.

If there were no other ways in which to be unfair or otherwise go wrong in
selecting between people besides those we have been focusing on, we would not be
overriding fairness or committing some other wrong if we helped the greater
number because they are the greater number.

Other Grounds for Unfairness

Suppose the case in which we use our drug to save the five rather than the one does
not share the property that produces unfairness in such cases as the one in which we
save a doctor whose patients need him, or the one in which we save someone with a
high IQ. On what other grounds could it be unfair or more generally wrong?

If each of the six has an equal claim to be saved by us, we must give each of
them an equal chance. They might have this equal claim either because they each as
individuals had a claim to be aided or because they had a claim to be aided if anyone
else was going to be aided. If they each had claims to be aided, for either (or both)
of these reasons, then, it might be argued, when we cannot satisfy all claims, we
should give each claim an equal chance to be satisfied. We should do this even if this
means the greater number will not have their claims satisfied. (This is a fairness
argument which is similar to the original objection raised in the last chapter to the
Aggregation Argument.) In addition, it might be suggested that justice requires that
we take care of the worst-off person first. It may seem that this factor would not
distinguish among the six, each of whom faces the prospect of death. However, if
we automatically save the greater number, then each of them has an 100 percent
chance of survival and the single person has a 0 percent chance of survival. This
makes the single person the worst off in terms of probability of surviving. We could
make him better off, without making the others worse off than he is, by giving each
an equal chance.

Both these proposals for why counting numbers is unfair or unjust may assume that a person has not already had an equal chance to be in the more numerous group. For example, they are based on denial of the assumption that the single person was given an equal chance by nature to be in the position of someone who is with other people. For if each had had an equal chance to be in the more numerous group, then each would already have had an equal chance to be saved by us even if we do immediately save the greater number. (A similar rejection of the assumption of original equal chances would lead one to reject the argument that we should save a doctor who can aid five people rather than a nondoctor who cannot aid others, on the ground that the nondoctor had an equal chance to be the doctor.)

Suppose we limit ourselves to doing what we have already done, i.e., trying to show that counting numbers is not unfair because it does not select improperly on the basis of personal characteristics and then show that other reasons derived from considerations of the right—but not necessarily reasons of fairness—require that we *not* toss a coin. (These considerations may not be related to fairness, for if being fair involves only not selecting on the basis of improper personal or group charac-teristics, tossing a coin as well as counting numbers will be consistent with fairness, and *neither* will be dictated by it.) We will still have shown that numbers *should* be counted, independent of concern for the greater good. If numbers should be counted for reasons stemming from the theory of the right, then each person will not have a claim to an equal chance in conflict cases, nor should we take care of the worst 76 as described above. Therefore, unfairness will not arise by our depriving anyone of a claim to an equal chance. This way of arguing goes beyond agnosticism and was described above as the second proposal for rebutting the claim that counting num-bers involves a conflict between the good and the right. This second proposal goes beyond showing that we *may* act so as to produce the better outcome because there is no unfairness or other wrong in counting numbers. The first proposal said that neither fairness nor any other principle of right is contravened by counting numbers, but that the positive motivation for counting numbers is concern for the greater good. This made the argument for counting numbers depend on a denial of Taurek's No Worse Claim, that more deaths are *not* worse. Of course, the denial of the No Worse Claim could be part of a nonconsequentialist moral theory since such a theory need not deny that consequences are straightforwardly determinative when there is no conflict with rightness factors. But the second proposal does not depend on a denial of the No Worse Claim.

That is, the second proposal offers an argument for counting numbers in conflict cases as a matter of the theory of the right, independent of the theory of the good. That argument employs the idea described earlier, that balancing based on the legitimate substitution of equivalents is right at least in some contexts. The aim is to provide an argument that offers a justification for saving the greater number in conflict situations, which any reasonable person could accept as consistent with treating him empathetically and as an equal.[13]

Giving Equal Chances

As already noted, Taurek suggests that if we want to show equal concern in a conflict case like the Drug Case involving at least two possible outcomes (that five are saved or that one is saved), we should toss a coin. This view is supposedly based on treating all persons as equals. It has a further consequence: it requires us to give equal chances of coming about to all the different, realistically possible outcomes that are preferred by the people involved, at least when the people have equal stakes in the outcomes. In the conflict case in which either one person survives or five people survive, there are among the six people preferences for two outcomes—one in which five live, and another in which one lives. (The possibility that we save fewer than the five on one island is ruled out by empathy. So, though each of five may desire only his own survival, his survival will be brought about by the state in which five survive.) The first outcome is desired by five people, but since the object of their preference is the same, it is counted only once. When the object of this preference gets an equal chance, each of the people involved gets an equal chance. (And vice versa.) Suppose 5000 people prefer policy B and one person prefers policy C, and their interests are equally affected by the outcome. Then, if we do not emphasize the distinction between a preference and a claim, in Taurek's view, showing equal concern and respect for all 5001 people would involve a procedure like tossing a coin. This gives each one of them and each of the different policies affecting their interests an equal chance.

Counting Preferences

Consider an interpretation of treating all concerned as equals that does not require equal chances, yet does not depend on the view that it is worse if more people suffer in conflict cases. This interpretation requires that we count equally each individual's preference for a policy affecting his interests, where his preference is understood not as the *object* of his preference but as the *fact that he prefers* it. It is not enough just to count the object of his preference. We will not have succeeded in counting his preference for a certain state of affairs if the fact that he prefers it makes no difference in the process of deciding which state to bring about. His preference will make no difference in this process of deciding if we would proceed in the same way whether or not he had this preference. This will be so if we follow the policy Taurek recommends and toss a coin. For this policy would lead us to do the same thing whether it is a case of one in opposition to five; or one in opposition to a single other person's preference. If our policy results in counting only objects of preferences in this way, then a person's preference will be superfluous whenever one other person shares it. When we toss the coin, we "count each person's preference" only in the minimal sense that we examine his preference to see what it is—whether it is different from that of others. If his preference differs from anyone else's, then the state of affairs that is its object will be among those given an equal chance.

The reason for counting each person's preference need not be that this will result in more being saved—the better result in a conflict case. Nor because it is a better outcome in which more preferences are satisfied. The reason may simply be that treating people as equals involves counting each one's preference; this is something we simply owe each individual as part of treating him as an equal. (Of course, we need to explain why this is so.) Indeed, it might be that the greater number of individuals actually prefer that the single person be saved instead of themselves.

(Then they would have a preference that conflicts with an objective evaluation of what is good from their point of view, i.e., good for them.) In such a case, the view I am describing could recommend that the single person be saved even if it were impersonally better that the greater number be saved. Since what we would be doing would be based on counting each person's preference even when this conflicts with saving the greater number, letting each person's preference count cannot be based on the value of the greater number being saved. (For the sake of argument, I will continue to assume that in our Drug Case each of the five prefers that he himself be saved rather than that the single person be saved.)

The Trouble with Counting Preferences

There are limits, however, to the role of preference in this account. In particular, not just anyone's preference as to who among the six should survive is to be counted. It is only if one's own life is at stake that one's preference is to be counted. Therefore, it is a mistake to think of counting preferences of those whose lives are at stake as a form of general majority rule if the idea of majority rule suggests that just anyone can have his preference as to who lives counted. Furthermore, the idea of majority rule, even among the six, opens up the possibility that someone could vote his *external* preference.[14] That is, suppose we must choose between saving A and saving B, C, D, E, and F, but D, E, and F want A to live. If they vote for A and A votes for herself, there are then four votes for A and only one for B and one for C. If the vote is determinative, we must save A rather than the five.[15] But while we can agree that D, E, and F may decide for themselves that A should be saved instead of them, I believe we should *disagree* that their preferences may determine the fates of B and C. (Notice also that someone could vote his external preference for someone else on his own side. For example, B may not care whether he lives or dies but want C to live. C should not therefore be counted twice against A.)

The system of counting preferences that has a chance of being correct must count only (internal) preferences a person has for his own fate. Individuals may remove themselves from being counted because they do not care to live. However, if they do not care, they have no further right to have their preferences counted. If they do not remove themselves, this means they prefer to live. Then the counting of preferences proceeds, just as if we balanced off equals with opposite interests. Therefore, any of the five who prefers A's survival to his own may *indirectly* try to help A by leaving the contest up to A and whoever of the five does not prefer A's life to his own. Henceforth, these restrictions on majority rule should be assumed to be part of our description of balancing the interests of people with preferences for life.

From Preferences to Interests and Claims

This proposal has been phrased in terms of opposing preferences. Is it not more correct to think that we are considering people's interests (i.e., an objective evaluation of what is good for them), rather than their preferences, when we decide to save them? Further, are we not interested in their objective interests because we think these may give them claims on us? And should not claims (or rights) function differently from mere preferences; perhaps we can balance preferences but not claims (positive or negative)?

I believe we may allow the libertarian view that it is only if one *prefers* to stay alive that the objective interest one has in staying alive should be considered (given that one satisfies criteria for competence and so has a right to have one's preference counted). Of course, if we do not have information about people's preferences, we should assume a preference for life if this is in their interest, and then count equal and opposing interests in outcomes. I shall assume a preference to stay alive on the part of each person in the Drug Case and, so, speak of counting numbers because it is in each person's *interest* equally that he stay alive.

A common view is that someone's negative right not to be killed cannot be violated in order to help save others from being killed, although balancing would suggest it could be. Recall, however, that in redirection-of-threat cases (the cases involving negative rights most closely analogous to Taurek conflict cases), it *is* permissible to kill one to save five, and the justification for this at least looks like a matter of balancing. This shows that the structure of the case, e.g., whether we redirect a threat rather than start a new threat, not the presence of rights per se (negative or positive) will tell us whether balancing is permitted (as it is with preferences), or whether instead "rights are trumps" over maximizing utility or over minimizing violations of rights.

One suggestion, then, is that if we want to treat people as equals, we do this when we count their objective interest (which may give rise to a claim), rather than just the object of their interest. So we should not toss a coin in Taurek's conflict case. Other procedures for deciding in conflict situations, however, do seem to count each individual's interest when deciding what to do. One such procedure is majority rule. The following analysis of majority rule should make clear how it counts interests. It should also help us understand in more detail why we owe it to persons, as equals, to count their interests.

Majority Rule, Balancing, and Canceling

One way of arriving at a principle of majority rule is the following: In a conflict situation there will be at least one person with an interest in one outcome, call it x, and at least one person with an opposing interest in not-x. Consider a pair of such opposing individuals. Since their interests are opposed and of equal weight, it might be suggested *that they cancel each other out*. If we cancel them out, we will have counted each of these interests and given it all the weight it should be given consistent with equal treatment. The weight of these interests will have been "used up." Suppose we continue in this way, taking pairs of individual interests to balance each other out until no unused pairs of opposing interests remain. All the remaining interests (if any) will be for the same alternative, say x. The weight of these interests will decide the matter in favor of that outcome. (If there are no "unused" interests, we have a moral tie.)

The problem with this model is that it incorrectly gives the impression that equal and opposite interests are canceled, that they have used up their weight and so have no more weight in a final decision. It is as if together the equal and opposite interests amount to a zero, leaving only the unbalanced interests with any weight. But, as noted above, the balancing of equal and opposites need not be understood as cancelation.[16] It can be understood, rather, as the recognition that neither of two equal and opposing claims can finally decide an outcome (the "unbalanced" members of one side must do that), and, whichever side we help, we will satisfy an interest—it does not disappear as canceled out—that counts as much as any interest equal and opposite to it with which it is balanced. This is the substitution-of-equivalents component. (It should be emphasized that we are here applying this balancing model to a situation in which each individual stands to lose his life. As already noted, if some were to suffer lesser losses, balancing as described may not always be an applicable procedure. We shall discuss this further in Chapter 8.)

If equal treatment involves counting each individual's interest in an option, then majority rule seems to be one way to do this. However, when the margin of victory is greater than 1, the same result could have been achieved even if some of the members of the winning side had not existed. So even in majority rule an individual may be superfluous. Nevertheless, each "excess" member of the majority knows that if his side had not yet won, he would have been used to balance an opponent. It is only when he does not care whether or not he is thus used (that is, when the object of his interest has won) that he is not thus used. This is not so if a coin is tossed.[17]

More Than Two Incompatible Objects of Interest

In cases involving only two opposing objects of interest, the balancing-and-substitution-of-equivalents model for majority rule leads to the greater number prevailing. However, in cases involving more than two incompatible objects of interest, it is not so clear that this model of majority rule, independent of the denial of Taurek's No Worse Claim (1b) must lead to the greater number prevailing.

For example, suppose there are four mutually incompatible objects of interest, M, N, O, and P, supported by different numbers of people for equally strong reasons, as illustrated in the table below:

M	N	O	P
x	*xxxxx*	*xxx*	*xxx*

If we use the balancing model described above for majority rule, then, depending on the order in which we balance the groups against each other, different options will win. If we balance supporters for N first against those for M (leaving four for N), then against O's supporters (leaving one for N), and finally against P's supporters, this will leave two of those with an interest in P unopposed. So P will win, even though the group supporting P is smaller than the group supporting N, and only three people will be satisfied if P wins, instead of five if N wins.[18] We could arrange the balancing so that supporters of M, O, and P confront each other first. This will leave N with a five-to-one dominance over P. (That is, balancing supporters for M against those for O results in two for O, and these two confront the supporters for P, leaving P with a one-person margin of victory. If the five in N confront this one supporter for P, there is a five-to-one margin of victory. Then all five supporters of N get the object of their interests.)

However, we cannot argue that it is better to balance in the latter order because more people will attain the option that is in their interests and this is a better state of affairs *if* we don't want to depend on a denial of the No Worse Claim. After all, it was the function of the equals-balancing-equals analysis to provide a rationale for saving the greater number independent of any premise denying that claim.

I shall leave unsolved the problem of how the balancing-and-substitution-of-equivalents model deals with more than two objects of interest. I will only suggest that if we are to satisfy this rationale stemming from the theory of the right, we may have to look for a reason intrinsic to the theory of the right itself that requires us to balance equal-sized groups (such as those for O and P) against each other first, or alternatively (and perhaps more plausibly), that requires us to balance a smaller group first against the next largest group.

Why We Owe It to Individuals to Balance and Substitute Equivalents

We have already suggested that the possibility, and requirement, of balancing depends on permission to substitute individuals as equivalent to each other. If there were such a requirement, it would depend, I believe, on the further requirement that as outsiders to a conflict of interest, we always move back to an impartial perspective *outside* that of any of the contestants. That is, we first should adopt the empathetic point of view, seeing the world from the point of view of the objective interests of a contestant. We can do this for each contestant in turn. But if we see the world *only* from such points of view, one after the other, we will generate the "tied to each" position (described in Chapter 5) that favors tossing a coin. Furthermore, if we remain locked into the perspective of each, we may toss a coin even between those who stand to lose less and those who stand to lose more. After all, from the perspective of a person, preventing the greater loss of another does not substitute for preventing his lesser loss. In this approach, each individual is a token, non-substitutable for any other. By contrast, if our purpose in taking the empathetic point of view toward each individual is only to understand what each person stands to lose or gain, the result will be different. When we move back outside the perspective of any or all the individuals to the so-called "impartial perspective," we will take what we have learned from the empathetic point of view, but also see other things. First, as was emphasized in The Aggregation Argument, we see each individual as a token of a *type*. Each will be a token of a type, insofar as another individual has the same type of stake in an alternative outcome. This does not mean saving one is truly the same as saving another, since the need of that other person is satisfied only by his being saved; we still do abandon someone, yet from the point of view outside that of each of the personal points of view, we see that as much is gained in helping one as in helping another and in this sense they are equivalents. In the Aggregation Argument this was combined with the possibility of saving others. But we are now concerned with an argument from the right, not from the good. When we step out of the perspectives of each person, we also see the relationship of one person to another, rather than just focusing on each as an individual. This leads us to do pairwise comparisons, for example, looking for the worse off candidate and helping him before others, even if this is not for the greatest good, and even if focusing on the perspective of each individual, who is not compensated for his lesser loss by preventing someone else's larger loss, would lead us to toss a coin. The relation between candidates for help is established in matching or balancing, which involves some sort of substitution of equivalents (who are not identical).

Who Is Wronged?

Elizabeth Anscombe[19] has argued that in conflict cases such as we have described, no *one* of the larger group can complain that he is wronged if we aid the single person with an opposing interest instead. That is, no *one* individual can claim that he is owed rescue rather than the single person. How then, she asks, can the group of these single people claim that they together are owed rescue rather than the single person, and that they are wronged if not aided when the one is?

Our analysis suggests a higher-order complaint that each of the larger group can make: though each cannot complain if the single person is aided, he can complain if he is not given his appropriate role in the balancing process we have described. He is wronged if equals are not balanced against opposite equals. For this reason, given the outcome of such balancing, each person in the larger group is wronged if he, as a member of that group, is not aided.

Balancing, Substitution of Equivalents, and Consequentialism

Is this rationale for counting numbers, based on a supposed claim of each to be balanced against an opposite and equal individual, different from the consequentialist justification that we thereby achieve the best consequences? We ask this question because the idea of balancing opposite equals and substitution of equivalents just is the basis of consequentialist calculations to determine the best outcome. I believe that it is no embarrassment for a nonconsequentialist theory to have *as part of* its theory of justice the appropriateness, in certain contexts, of balancing and substitution of equivalents. These, the entire components of a consequentialist theory of basic justice—that each be counted for one and no more and be balanced against an opposite equal—are parts of a theory of justice (however wrong they may be as a complete theory). Endorsing them is different from endorsing the pursuit of the best consequences per se, even if we use them in deciding what the best consequences are. Indeed, given that a consequentialist would be willing to override justice for the greater good, balancing and substitutions of equivalents may be best justified in a consequentialist system as the only accurate way to determine overall good. Therefore, concern with counting numbers because of balancing is to be distinguished from concern with producing the best consequences.[20]

Ex Ante Self-interest

There may be another rationale for counting numbers different from what we have described. Some may consider it the most obvious rationale for making the numbers count; Taurek himself refers to it (p. 312). This rationale is that each individual, if he were ignorant about whether he would be with the smaller or with the larger group, would maximize his chance of being saved by agreeing to a policy of saving the larger number. He would do so because, a priori and barring special procedures that give individuals unequal chances for being with one group or another, he has a higher probability of being in the larger group. All that is required for this to be true is that he be given as good a chance as anyone else to occupy each of the six possible positions. Therefore, the claim is, even when he knows his actual location, he should agree that saving the larger number is justified.[21] This is (supposedly) because the policy he would have decided on when he was ignorant of his actual position and, hence, unable to bias a policy to favor himself, is the morally correct policy; the policy he is bound to abide by even when he knows his actual position.

Taurek rejects this rationale (perhaps mistakenly) for situations in which someone does know that he is in the minority position; he accepts it for conditions of actual ignorance. He must, therefore, reject the grounds given for commitment here and now to a policy that would, hypothetically, have been chosen if everyone had been in ignorance. Whether Taurek's rejection is justified or not, there are other questions raised by reasoning in ignorance.

First, when under conditions of ignorance (real or hypothetical) a policy of counting numbers is chosen (if it is chosen) because it is in the interest of each person, it is *not* chosen because it produces the best consequences over all. But neither is it chosen because, being in a position of ignorance where one cannot choose the policy that best serves one's interests, one chooses the policy that is right for some *principled* reason. That is, one does *not* say, "I choose numbers because, being forced by not knowing what my personal position will be to adopt an unbiased frame of mind, I can choose simply on the merits of the policy."

Second, on at least some people's understanding, part of reasoning under conditions of ignorance is the assumption that each individual has an equal chance of being in any position; then the truth of this assumption alone would be enough to satisfy those who believe that each is owed an equal chance. That is, if each had had an equal chance to be in his actual position or in that of anyone else, there would be no need to toss a coin; a coin (of sorts) would already have been tossed. We would then be free to pick the best consequences (save the greater number) without a conflict with the claims of each to be given an equal chance. We could do this without relying on an argument about reasoning from self-interest when in ignorance.

Third, it is not clear that deciding in ignorance should lead to choosing a numbers-counting policy, for there is debate about how to reason behind a veil of ignorance.[22] The procedure described above suggests that an individual consider what *his* probabilities (i.e., the probabilities of one individual) are of falling into any given position and into the more numerous group. But others have suggested that an individual reasoning behind the veil must consider what it would be like to be each of the actual people who will actually occupy the various real-life positions. This is a different procedure; the first may result in favoring maximal average utility as a policy, the second may result in maximin or, perhaps, equal chances for each in our Taurek conflict cases.[23]

In any case, my view is that there must be a more direct route to the conclusion that numbers should count than via ex ante reasoning which is in the self interest of each. Further, it seems that numbers should count even when ex ante reasoning does not yield this conclusion. For example, if it were clear that someone never had a chance to be with the larger group, and it was known who this person was, many types of ex ante reasoning would not conclude that we should count numbers. Yet, my sense is that counting numbers can be morally correct even in this case.

NOTES

1. I first proposed such a model in "Equal Treatment and Equal Chances," *Philosophy and Public Affairs* (Spring 1985): 177–194, though with too much emphasis on balancing as involving *canceling* out of opposing equals. Larry Sager pointed out to me that the role which canceling plays in that article is different from the alternative analysis of balancing I offered in a later paper, "The Choice Between People, Commonsense Morality and Doctors," *Bioethics* (Summer 1987)255–271.

2. I first discussed these cases in "The Choice Between People, Commonsense Morality, and Doctors." I consider them in greater detail in Chapter 9.

3. I use the term "irrelevant utility" rather than "insufficient utility" to emphasize that no amount of that type of utility (i.e., even large numbers of cured sore throats) could outweigh the claim to an equal chance to live. In this respect it is like the eye color of those whose lives are at stake: irrelevant. That large numbers of sore throats don't matter, is however, a claim that needs to be proven. (Parfit pressed me on why the use of irrelevant versus insufficient.)

4. Peter Unger mentioned this case to me, though he comes to a different conclusion about it.

5. In "Selecting People Randomly" *Ethics* 95 (October 1984): 38–55.

6. Here is an argument *against* its being unfair to aid B, who then saves C without using our resource: A and B had an equal chance of being in the position B actually occupies, of having the capacity to aid someone else. Since this argument appears in another context below, I will put off dealing with it now and simply assume for the time being that it is wrong.

7. This would seem to be related to the theory Michael Walzer puts forth in *Spheres of Justice* (New York: Basic Books, 1983).

8. First discussed in "Equal Treatment and Equal Chances," which the present discussion repeats.

9. This way of making my point was suggested to me by Deborah Helmers. Connecting appropriate distribution with concern that we distribute something so that it satisfies the most (roughly equally strong) *direct* needs for it, as I have done, should not be confused with the view that it would be unfair not to make the best use of something we have to distribute. For we might choose to let some resource that could save five go totally to waste in order to distribute some *other* resource to twenty people.

10. By James Childress in "Who Shall Live When Not All Can Live?" in Ronald Munson, (ed.), *Intervention and Reflection*, 3rd ed. (Belmont, Calif.: Wadsworth Publishing Co., 1988).

11. Derek Parfit pointed this out to me.

12. In addition, I argue in *Morality, Mortality*, Vol. II, that it is permissible to refuse to turn a fatal threat from five toward one if the one is a doctor who will save twenty lives if he is not killed. This is true even though it is otherwise permissible to turn a fatal threat from five toward one, thereby killing the one. Yet this is to choose between the five and one on the

basis of a "means test." Though we do not use the five as means to some end, we view people from the perspective of whether they can be means to some end.

13. Much of the material that follows was first presented in "Equal Treatment and Equal Chances."

14. This concept is owed to Ronald Dworkin.

15. The dangers of external preferences were emphasized by David Wasserman.

16. Larry Sager cautioned me to not identify balancing so closely with canceling as I had done in "Equal Treatment and Equal Chances."

17. In one sense of "count," *minority rule* also counts each individual's interest, but since it, in effect, deducts points in favor of an object of interest whenever someone has an interest in it, individuals' interests harm rather than help their cause. The individual's interest should make a difference in accord with, not against, his object of interest. The requirement that interests make a difference in accord with the interest (a positive difference) is what is commonly referred to as the positive responsiveness characteristic of majority rule. (This is also true when "preference" is substituted for "interest.")

18. This order of balancing could be seen as an abstract model of a situation in which several small political parties "gang up" on a big one: The large party loses it strength fighting with many smaller parties, defeating some of them, but losing enough in the process so that another small party is victorious.

19. In "Who Is Wronged?" *The Oxford Review,* no. 5 (1967) pp. 16–17.

20. I emphasize this in response to questioning by Amy Gutman.

21. I described this alternative rationale in "Equal Treatment and Equal Chances." Judith Thomson makes use of a complicated version of ex ante reasoning in her analysis of the Trolley Problem in *The Realm of Rights* (Cambridge, Mass.: Harvard University Press, 1990).

22. The term John Rawls uses in *A Theory of Justice* (Cambridge, Mass.: Harvard University Press, 1971).

23. I am here briefly summarizing the debate on this issue as analyzed by Scanlon in "Contractualism and Utilitarianism," in A. Sen and B. Williams (eds.), *Utilitarianism and Beyond* (Cambridge: Cambridge University Press, 1982) and also, the view Nagel takes on reasoning behind a veil of ignorance in "Equality," in *Mortal Questions,* (Cambridge University Press, 1979).

7

Ideal Procedure, Nonideal Alternatives, and Proportional Chances

In this chapter, we shall consider two alternatives to majority rule as described in Chapter 6. The first is what I call an "Ideal Procedure" for non-Taurek situations, in which some compromise between conflicting groups is possible. The second is an alternative way to give numbers weight: distribution by proportional chances.

I

The Ideal Procedure

This procedure is part of the theory of the right for dealing with individuals who press their conflicting claims on us.[1] Though I call it the "*ideal,*" it is intended to be so only against a certain background: I assume that, in the cases with which I deal, we have no right to reorganize lots given by nature to the point of equality if recipients of those lots object. That is, I will assume that those who are undeservedly (so far as we can tell) better off than the rest of us sometimes still have some claim against us that we not make too radical changes in the status quo in these life and death micro-contexts. I will not defend this claim here.

The basic idea of the Ideal Procedure is still that we should arrange for those in the less numerous group to confront, as individuals, those in the more numerous group. Each individual in the less numerous group will be paired off against an equal and opposite individual. However, this will be done in a different way than in majority rule as described above. The Ideal Procedure of balancing is not possible in situations of irreducible conflict between groups, situations with which Taurek presents us where all cannot be saved. In these cases, the closest approximation to the ideal is counting numbers; the larger number should get something if any subgroup does. But in situations where it is possible to reduce conflict so that everyone might get something, the Ideal Procedure says the following should be done:

1. Reduce the 100 percent probability of being saved (which the more numerous side would have if we automatically saved them) by as much as (but no more than) the combination of the proportional weights assignable to each member of the smaller group *if* this increases the minority's chances of being saved to at least a significant chance;

  2. Do this only if reducing the majority's chances in this way does not make it possible that the minority is saved when the majority is not saved.

The proportional weight of each individual (in the minority and majority) is found by dividing 100 by the total number of people. So if five people confront one person, the single person can reduce the probability of the five's being saved by one-sixth. This is the Ideal Procedure.

Why Balance in This Way? Solidarity versus a Claim to a Chance

This procedure lets individuals in the minority have an effect as individuals on what happens. Each one's proportional weight is pressed against the combined weights of individuals in the majority. This is a form of balancing that allows an equivalent and opposite individual to gain by taking away from others in proportion to his weight. Why let balancing take this form rather than the substitution of equivalents in majority rule? Because there is an important goal that can be satisfied by this sort of balancing, which is beyond our reach in cases of ineliminable conflict. This more important goal might be described as everyone receiving something in proportion to the power his weight gives him. This is a form of concern for solidarity; this helps explain Clause 1 of the Procedure as explained above.

   Why do we insist on Clause 2? After all, there would be no further reduction in the chances of the majority to survive if the minority had a chance to survive when the majority does not. (Clause 2, I believe, also rules out purchasing a *higher* chance for the minority to survive than the majority, even if we can achieve this by the same proportional reduction in the majority's chances.) The basic, intuitive answer is that we can be under an obligation to share (what would be ours by right if it were not possible to share), but it should not be the case that we wind up in a *worse* state than those who benefit from our fulfilling our obligation to share. (Thomas Nagel[2] argues that it is morally more appropriate, as well as psychologically easier, to sacrifice for those worse off than one is rather than for those better off. But our point here is that this may not be true if through one's sacrifice the worse off—unavoidably—become better off than those whose help they have received.)

   This intuition is more easily defended on the view that the desire for all to get something (solidarity) purchased at a fair cost drives us to reduce the majority's chances to survive for the minority's sake. The intuition is harder to defend if we think that the minority simply has a right to have a chance at the cost of a proportional reduction in the chances of the majority. For then how could we deny them this chance to which they have a right simply because it leads to their surviving when the majority doesn't? This point, furthermore, bears on the interpretation of Clause 1. For if the minority simply had a right to reduce the chances of the majority by the minority's proportional weight, mightn't it do this to get chances that were even far below its proportional chance and hence not objectively significant? (For example, one person might reduce the five's chance by one-sixth but thereby earn for himself only a 10 percent chance of survival.) Should it be part of the Ideal Procedure to allow this?

   Suppose there is no question of a right, analogous to a veto power, but rather a morally appropriate concern for solidarity. Then we might weigh the desire to achieve this goal against the return we get for what we sacrifice. Sacrificing a 16.7 percent (⅙) chance of saving five people may seem too much to pay to get only a 10 percent chance of saving the single person along with the five. (Could it be that the minority's getting even its proportional chance to be saved with the greater number is too small a return?) Of course, it may be worth a smaller reduction in the majority's chances in order to achieve the 10 percent chance. (We shall return to these issues below.)[3]

Reducing the Majority's Chances

The Ideal Procedure asserts that it is not always morally unreasonable to reduce the chances of a majority in order to improve those of a minority. So, it need not be because we think a majority's fate always takes precedence that we reject Taurek's recommendation to toss a coin in the conflict cases he describes. The fact that we are sometimes willing to reduce the chances of the majority for the reasons I have described, but are not willing to toss a coin in conflict cases, suggests that the latter is not dictated by a concern for treatment as equals. Indeed, if we were in a situation where we could certainly save one person but not another, we may (according to the Ideal Procedure) reduce our chances of saving one down to a 50 percent chance, if this will give us a 50 percent chance of saving both.[4] Possibly, on this view, the second person's proportional 50 percent weight may reduce the first person's chances of survival by 50 percent, even to purchase a 40 percent chance of survival for the second person *along* with the first even though this involves a reduction in overall expected utility. (Notice that this case differs from one in which each of two people has a 50 percent chance of being saved because they compete for our certainly saving one of them. Here there is no question of reducing anyone's chances for another, even if we alter our strategy so as to have a 50 percent chance of saving both together.)

It is important to emphasize again that the Ideal Procedure, unlike tossing a coin, risks losing all the lives. It also will not be employed if the one were to survive rather than the many.

Possible Outcomes of the Ideal Procedure—Smaller Outcome

Outcomes of Clause 1 of the Ideal Procedure could be either that the minority has a smaller chance of being saved than the majority (perhaps even smaller than the amount by which they reduce the chances of the majority to be saved), or that the minority shares the majority's higher (though reduced) probability of being saved. (I shall refer to these as Smaller Chance and Equal Chance respectively.) Let us illustrate the application of the procedure by considering a basic scenario and its variations.

Consider the Boat Case in which five shipwrecked people are in a boat. They will certainly be saved. There is one person in the water beside them. If he is not taken into the boat, he will certainly die. He will get a smaller chance of being saved than the five if a one-sixth reduction in the chances of the five purchases for him only a 16.7 percent chance of survival. (This is an example of Smaller Chance) This would occur if a rope were attached to the boat, dragging it down somewhat, but giving the single person a 16.7 percent chance of being saved if the boat continues afloat. Attached by the rope, he might drown even if the boat remains afloat. However, if he survived it would be because those in the boat did also. This is still a conflict situation because the option that increases the probability of one person's survival reduces the chances of five others. Still the conflict is not total; some compromise is possible.

Equal Outcome—Equal Chance to Share the Same Fate

There are at least two ways in which Equal Chance, sharing the majority's chance of survival, could occur. Everyone could have the same chance for a fate *shared by all* or everyone could have the same chance for a fate *not shared by all*. Consider the first possibility. Suppose taking the side swimmer in the water into the boat will reduce the 100 percent probability that the five people already in the boat will be saved by one-sixth. All six will then have five-sixths chance of being saved. I think there should be a strong preference for taking the single person into the boat.

In a case where we are at first asked to choose between saving either two people or one person, the Ideal Procedure says that we may reduce the chances of the two to 66 percent if this chance will be shared by all three to be saved together. This is a very significant reduction in the chance to survive of the original set. (In another case, if we could certainly save one person but not another, we may reduce the chances of the one to 50 percent if this will also give the other person a 50 percent chance of surviving with the first.)

Here again, as in the Boat Case, if we choose the Ideal Procedure we also indicate a preference for risking the loss of all six people rather than assuring the survival of at least one by tossing a coin between five and one. We may of course save all, but we will not use the Ideal Procedure if it meant one might survive when the larger number are lost. Still, in a case where the same fate will be shared by all, it is in the interest of the one to be taken in with the five rather than to have a coin tossed since his chances are greater of surviving with the five.

Equal Chance for the Same Unshared Fate

The equal chance to share the same fate marks the difference between taking the side swimmer into the boat and the following alternative solution to his problem. This would be to have each of the six people take turns in the water,[5] although it is known that the one who is in the water at the time of rescue will definitely die. (This is the second version of Equal Chance.) This alternative would also reduce each of the original five's chances to be saved by one-sixth and increase the chance of the original side swimmer to five-sixths. That is, each of the six would have a five-sixths chance of being saved, the same as if all six were in the boat in our previous example. This solution to the Boat Case differs from others in that we are certain that at least five people will live, though we are not sure who the five will be. On all solutions offered by the Ideal Procedure, it is never the case that a single person survives when five don't. However, in this version, a different person than was originally in the minority may die because someone who was originally in the majority may die.

Equality of Result

Preference for Equal Chance over Smaller Chance and for the first way of achieving Equal Chance over the second way, as well as preference for the Ideal Procedure over a coin toss in Taurek's case, would indicate a strong preference for *equality of result*. That is, there is a preference for all to sink or swim together (metaphorically, and in the Boat Case, literally). These preferences would indicate that (1) the same chance for a fate shared by all is preferred over even (2) the same chance for a fate not shared by all. The preference for equality of result could be so strong that it would overcome an alternative prospect of definitely saving five lives while providing each person with an equal chance to survive (the second way to Equal Chance). This preference would indicate that unequal results that may come of equal chances (as in Taurek's coin toss) are a negative factor.

There is another reason besides preference for equality of result why the greater number in the boat originally could reject the second way to Equal Chance. They could accept reduction of their chances for the sake of a shared fate or even giving the minority a lesser chance to be saved when the majority is also saved. Yet they could reject reducing their own chances when this would risk putting one of their number in the role of the side swimmer. This objection is analogous to that which underlies Clause 2 of the Ideal Procedure. That clause requires rejection of a procedure that would move us from majority rule so that the minority survives when the majority dies. In making it possible for someone who was in the *original* majority to become the side swimmer, we do not reduce his chances of survival any more than if we take the original side swimmer into the boat along with the original five. *However, we do make it possible for someone who originally would have lived to die when someone who originally would have died will live.* So while it is not the case that *a* side swimmer could survive when the five don't, it is possible that *the* person who was a side swimmer originally will survive when one of the original five won't. The fact that in this case a greater number will still survive does not assuage the complaint.

This bears on our understanding of Clause 2: The original majority can be obliged to reduce its chances in order to move toward equality of result. However, it is not just *any* greater number who must survive if the minority survives. It is the original majority. The ideal that the greater number should survive if anyone does is combined with a proprietary feature: that those individuals who were in the larger group need not cede *their* place in a good outcome to others. (It is at this point that our initial remarks on p. 123 about the claims against too radical a change in the status quo are relevant.)

Interestingly enough, however, if the side swimmer who could be saved, if we allowed the minority to be saved when the majority wasn't, would be one of the original majority, this would weaken the grounds for insisting on Clause 2. This is because the benefit of survival would go to a member of the original majority. But of course we cannot be sure that it would, and if Clause 2 were dropped the rest of the original majority could still be lost.

Of the three ways in which the conditions of the Ideal Procedure could be met, it seems that a shared fate with the minority getting the same chance as the majority's chance when it is reduced by the minority's proportional weight is preferable. This is because it gives the minority its greatest chance without violating the two conditions of the Ideal Procedure.

Result Proportional to Numbers

The Ideal Procedure reduces the chance of the majority to survive from what it was under majority rule by the proportional weight of the minority. It does not necessarily give the minority only a proportional (one-sixth) chance to win. Still the outcome that results if the six survive, which is a possibility, is perfect from everyone's point of view. Another procedure would alter the actual best result (rather than the chance for it). This would yield a result proportional to numbers that was not as satisfactory from the majority's point of view. (That is, the possible *best* result gets worse.) For example, in coalition government a compromise policy may reflect the position of members in proportion to their numbers. In this case, altering the policy so that the larger group does not get all that it wants will also not result in *both* the minority and majority getting something equally in accord with its preference. That is, the policy may give the majority only five-sixths of what it wants (a less-than-best result), but the minority will not also thereby get five-sixths of what it wants. It will get only one-sixth of what it wants. By contrast, if he is taken in, the side swimmer will get the same five-sixths chance to survive as the five, and the end result may be perfect (survival) for minority and majority. But of course, the end result may be disaster (death) for all.

Result proportional to numbers procedures can be used in situations in which it is possible to satisfy everyone to some degree. According to these procedures, we would not give each group with a conflicting interest an equal chance to win, or even a chance in proportion to the numbers composing it. Rather, we would create an end result that represents each group's interests or preferences according to the pooled weights of its individual members.

Proportional Chances and Pareto Optimality

As already noted, the Ideal Procedure allows for the possibility that everyone will die. This contrasts with Proportional Chances, which offers chances for opposed groups to be saved in proportion to numbers of individuals composing them. This proposal violates Clause 2 of the Ideal Procedure since the group with the smaller chance (and hence the fewer people) might be saved while the larger number die. However, Proportional Chances assures us that at least someone will live. It also diminishes the chances of the greater number in proportion to the combined weights of those in the smaller group. So if we reduce the chances of the majority to five-sixths by attaching a rope to the boat, and this gives the minority a one-sixth chance, all might perish. If we reduce the chances of the majority to five-sixths by taking a safety raft away from them, and then give it to the single person, we could give him an independent one-sixth chance to survive. Still, with this all might perish and all might survive. Suppose we toss a six-sided die, five of whose sides belong to the majority and one to the side swimmer's, to decide where to send a rescue ship. Then someone will definitely survive, and the majority and minority cannot possibly both survive. The last two scenarios represent Proportional Chances. Only the latter involves irreducible conflict (i.e., if one group survives, the other can't).

Suppose reducing the chances of the majority by the proportional weight of the minority brings the minority *a chance to survive along with the majority that is less than the minority's proportional weight.* That is, it gets less than one-sixth chance. Suppose also that this is consistent with both clauses of the Ideal Procedure. Then Proportional Chances, which represents either irreducible conflict or merely an independent chance, would be a Pareto-optimal alternative to the Ideal Procedure. This is because the majority is no worse off (i.e., its chance is still reduced to five-sixths), while the minority will be made better off, receiving a higher chance to survive, albeit not when the majority necessarily also survives. Suppose we prefer the Ideal Procedure to Proportional Chances, even when the latter is Pareto optimal. This could indicate that it is possible to believe that numbers should count for reasons other than that this maximizes expected utility since we are here foregoing a higher expected utility if we keep to the Ideal Procedure. (An alternative is that numbers count for the sake of higher expected utility but considerations of the right constrain our maximizing expected utility.)

Another Justification for Proportional Chances

There is a way of understanding Proportional Chances that provides a justification for its use in conflict cases like the Drug Case. This is a justification independent of its sometimes being Pareto optimal relative to the Ideal Procedure. In discussing the Ideal Procedure, we were concerned to justify the majority's losing any of its chance to be saved. We arrived at the majority's having its proportional chance to be saved by reducing its chance of being saved from certainty. Their claim to certainty was derived from a justification for majority rule. In the following discussion of Proportional Chances, we are concerned to justify the majority's having any more chance to survive than the minority—by contrast with tossing a coin—but we wish to justify it in a manner different from how we justified majority rule.

Proportional Chances claims to treat people as equals by counting each individual's interest in an outcome. It also involves one-by-one matching of opposite equals. It does not do the matching in the way that majority rule or the Ideal Procedure does. Majority rule involves straightforward substitution of equivalents. The Ideal Procedure allows the majority's chances to be reduced by the minority's proportional weight, a form of matching or balancing some individuals against the weight of others whereby an equivalent and opposite individual gains by taking away from those others in proportion to his weight. But it does this only when the minority cannot survive when the majority perishes.

The following is used to explain how unrestricted Proportional Chances might be understood: Consider a case in which we are presented with a *series of choices* between the claims of different individuals.[6] In the Fire Case, a house is on fire and we go in to rescue people. We can save only one person in the house since we must accompany him out. In the first room we enter, we find a person, A, who must use the front door to exit. (He is too big for the window.) To get him to the front door, however, we must take him through five other rooms. When we take A from his room into the next room we find another person, B. B could escape through the window, if we lift him through and exit with him. We cannot save both A and B. Whom shall we save?

If we want to treat A and B as equals, we might toss a coin or use some other random decision procedure (assuming that the flames will wait for our decision).[7] Suppose A wins. In the next four rooms through which we must go to save A, there are, respectively, persons C, D, E, and F. Like B, they can exit if we go through a window with them. This means that we may have to toss a coin between A and each of the others for so long as A wins his tosses. This involves up to five tosses of a coin between A and the other five people. He must confront, on a one-to-one basis, each individual with an opposing interest. This means that there is less of a chance of his winning than of one of the five winning. But still there is some chance.[8]

Serial versus Nonserial Confrontation

This case captures the element of one-to-one confrontation between equals with conflicting interests. But since confrontation occurs in serial order, the case is not one in which each of the five people A must confront has an equal chance to win. That is, each of the four, C through F, has less of a chance to win than the people confronting A before him have. That is, for someone like E, there is a chance not only that he will lose to A, but that B, C, or D before him will win first and exit with us.

To remedy this defect of the Fire Case, we can imagine the Lottery Case, involving people A through F, in which only one of six can win a prize. The equal need of each for the prize leads us to give each an equal chance to get it. If we throw a six-sided die, this gives each person a one-sixth chance to win and also involves each person confronting each of the five others. (We could also imagine that we decide which person to save in the Fire Case by throwing a six-sided die.)

Pooling of Chances

Now, suppose we alter these cases somewhat. For example, suppose B through F in the Fire' Case agree that if one of them wins his toss with A and exits, he will come back to rescue the other four by a method that we could not use and that they could not use to save A. In effect, B through F pool the *baseline* chances to be saved that they had in the original Fire Case. That is, each individual's chance to confront A in the Fire Case, which he had in virtue of having an interest equal and opposite to A's, also becomes a chance for the others to be saved in the Fire' Case.

Is it unfair to A if B through F pool their individual baseline chances to win? Shouldn't A still confront each individual who has an interest opposite to his, on an individual basis? Isn't the pooling that individuals do independently of their confrontation with A permissible without its altering the individual confrontations? Wouldn't this be true even if each of B through F now had five times the chance to win that he had previously and five times the chance to win that A has? Does it not seem incorrect to toss a coin and give each individual an equal 50 percent chance of winning simply because each of B through F has agreed to help the other four? Is this not true even though giving each a 50 percent chance would also increase the chances of B through F surviving over what they were to begin with in the Fire Case?

Likewise in the Lottery' Case, suppose only five of the six people are able to pool their equal baseline one-sixth chances to win the prize. (We can imagine that this prize, when shared, will satisfy each individual's needs just as much as his having it alone because, e.g., if jointly owned, it can be invested and produce a 500 percent profit, that, however, it is impossible to share with A.) Suppose we were to prohibit this because it gave each of the five a five times greater chance than A has to get a sum of money. Suppose we allow sharing of chances only if we can toss a coin between B through F and A. Mightn't each of the five complain that he was denied his equal one-sixth *baseline* chance to win and the right to use it as he saw fit? So long as A was not deprived of *his* baseline one-sixth chance and there was no attempt to exclude him from the pool, is there unfairness to him in their pooling their one-sixths and each getting even five times the chance to win? If not, it will be right to toss a six-sided die, even though there are five numbers such that whichever one comes up, each of the group of five will win.

Causal Relations between Winners and Pooling

In The Fire' and Lottery' Cases there is a causal connection between the person who wins and others winning who also need what we have to distribute. In Chapter 6 in our examination of fairness we discussed cases in which we can help B or A, and B but not A could help C get our resource that all three need, when we cannot reach C. This was contrasted with a case in which B but not A will save C from some threat for which our resource is not directly relevant. Fire' and Lottery' Cases present a different scenario. They involve someone who can help others who *directly need* what we have to offer when we haven't enough to supply more than one. I believe there is unfairness in our helping one person rather than another with, for example, the one kidney we have, simply because he will then get more kidneys for others who could also have used our organ. However, a choice like that is not at issue for us in the Fire' and Lottery' Cases. In those cases we are not thinking of outright *choosing* one of the five over A because of his relation to the other four. Rather we are asked to allow for the pooling of the chances each has, which increases the likelihood in a contest with A that the five will satisfy a need for which our help would be directly relevant *if* we could provide it to all.

It pays to see how the pooling of chances relates to our discussion of the Surgeon Case in Chapter 6. To treat as equals all individuals who *directly* and equally need something when only *one* of them can acquire it requires us to give each an equal chance in virtue of his direct need. Proportional Chances suggests that individuals may pool their equal baseline chances. Suppose this were true. The pooling may be prompted by causal dependence by some on another. For example, in the Fire′ Case, the pooling of chances that each already had in virtue of his direct need was prompted by the fact that each of five could come back to save the rest. (Partial pooling would occur if some people could come back to aid but not others.) In the Fire′ and Lottery′ Cases, pooling occurs after baseline chances already exist. These chances depend on need for what we have to distribute independent of any causal dependence on other people. In the Surgeon Case (in which the surgeon who directly needs the drug can save 100 people from a disease for which our drug is not directly relevant), the 100's *indirect* need for the drug *arises only* because there is a causal dependence relation that makes it possible for them to be saved when the surgeon is. They would have no independent claim on our drug.

In the Fire′ Case, according to the proposal being considered, A must confront each individual with an opposing interest. Treating each as an equal requires granting a right to confront A to each who has an equal direct need for our help. When the 5 choose to pool their individual chances to win, this may seem acceptable even if each then has five times the chance to win. But the 100 in the Surgeon Case do not have a *direct* need for the drug. *If* this means that each on his own were to have no claim to confront those who do have a direct need for the drug, how could the pooling of chances occur? One cannot pool chances that do not exist. If the pooling cannot occur because there are no chances to pool, then there is no ground such as exists in the Fire′ Case for giving each of the 101 people a 101/106 chance to win over 5 who directly need the drug. And it won't be correct to count the 100 on the side of the surgeon as we count the five who directly need the drug.

It is only if an *indirect* need can give each of the 100, on his own, a right to compete with the 5 that we can construct an argument for allowing all the numbers to count in the Surgeon Case. (Notice that if we constructed an argument for straightforward counting this would be different from giving each a proportional chance.) For example, suppose the drug is on sale at an auction and those with no life need at all (direct or indirect) are prohibited from bidding for it. Should someone who depends on the surgeon be allowed to bid as an equal for the drug along with the five who directly need it?

The Fair Way to Treat Someone Who Can Satisfy an Unsatisfied Need for What We Have

There are at least four different types of cases under consideration: (1) where we could save the greater number who directly need our resource; (2) where we could save someone who directly needs the resource and who then saves others who don't directly need it; (3) where we could save someone who directly needs our resource and he can produce more of the resource to save people who directly need the resource which we do not have enough of; and (4) where we could save someone who directly needs our resource and he can distribute our resource to others who directly need it when we cannot. (How do we interpret the Lottery′ Case? Since the money we can give can be invested to yield more, is it like our drug that someone uses to grow a plant? This was considered direct need with indirect use. Because there is indirect use, does this mean that *our* good can service everyone, and the one person who gets it is like the runner who delivers our resource? Here he does not deliver our resource, only its product once invested. Does this make a difference?) Suppose it were *wrong* to give a drug to a surgeon who will save people who don't need the drug rather than to someone who cannot save others but equally needs the drug. Suppose it were *wrong* to give a single available portion of a drug outright to a doctor rather than to a pianist though the doctor can manufacture more of the drug (not by employing it however) for 5 others who also directly need it. Recall that it is not wrong to give to one who can distribute our drug.

Our discussion so far suggests that it would be right to use a six-sided die to choose between the doctor and the pianist. That is, those who directly need what we do not have enough of should be permitted to get chances proportional to their number. This is because each of those who could pool their chances would have gotten a chance to confront A for the single supply of the drug, based on each having a direct need for it. And they could pool these chances by agreeing to give the drug to the doctor who would then save them all by other means than the resources we have.

Noncausal Pooling: Applying Proportional Chances to the Drug Case

Now in a conflict case like our original Drug Case, to return to it, there is no agreement among the five to help each other, and all five have a direct need for a supply of our drug, which is enough to service them all. (This contrasts with the Fire and Fire' cases in which what we have to offer cannot by itself service everyone or even five of six.) Further, in the Drug Case, unlike the Fire' Case, the possibility of pooling would involve no causal dependence to provide what goes beyond our resources: one of the five does not have to win first and then help the other four. Still, it might be said, nature makes possible the pooling of chances of the larger group. That is, all five win when one of their number does because they are all in one of the locations to which the drug can be sent. We might imagine that they started off on five separate icebergs, each then having his chance at the drug. The icebergs then floated into an island.[9] They do not deliberately exclude the single person from an agreement nor refuse to help him as well as each other.

The Fire' and Lottery' Cases were meant to suggest that there might be a way of giving equal treatment in those cases that had the effect of giving each group a chance of winning proportional to the number of people in the group. The chance each would have to win if he could win only on his own was multiplied by the number in the group who shared their chances. If giving groups chances proportional to their numbers is compatible with equal treatment in Fire' and Lottery', and with the No Worse Claim (1b) (i.e., that it is no worse if more die), perhaps it is also compatible with equal treatment in the Drug Case and other conflict cases. We determine the baseline chance of each individual by deciding which chance each would get if the six were isolated from each other and only one could get the drug. Then we allow for pooling of these chances. So we might toss a six-sided die in Taurek-type cases, too, even if this meant that five of the six people had a five times greater chance to win than the one did.

Like directly counting numbers, this procedure of giving Proportional Chances is consistent with Taurek's No Worse Claim, in that the rationale for it does not depend on holding that five dying is worse than one dying. It only involves considering the losses that may occur *to* individuals as significant to them and arranging for the appropriate confrontations between individuals with opposing interests as a requirement of treatment as equals. The single person must confront each one on the other side, which gives each member of the side with the greater number a greater chance of winning, given that when one of their number wins, all of them win. All win when one wins not because the winner helps the others, but because what the one wins is the distribution of the drug to all (given they are on the same island.)[10]

II

Choosing among Proportional Chances, Majority Rule, and the Ideal Procedure: Outsiders versus Insiders and the Appropriateness of Proportional Chances

It should be obvious that there is a conflict between Proportional Chances and directly saving the greater number. There is also a conflict with the Ideal Procedure. Majority rule and the Ideal Procedure *do not* allow the single individual any chance to win when the rest lose, but Proportional Chances implies that it would be unfair to deprive the single person of his chance to win when the others lose. I believe there are reasons for choosing between the procedures, and a difference between cases may make the reasons clear.

In the Lottery Case, the justification for giving each person an equal chance to win was that each had an equal need for the prize, only one person could win, and we wanted to treat all equally. In those circumstances, there was no other fair way of deciding who would win. But we might imagine another revised version of the Lottery Case, Lottery" Case, in which each of the individuals gets his chance for the prize by purchasing it (or undergoing another real loss for its sake). Perhaps in the Lottery" Case we may truly not deprive the single individual of his small chance to win, even if the five others pool their purchased baseline chances so that five would win if any of their number did. That is, in this case Proportional Chances *would* be correct, not Majority rule. It would also be preferable to the Ideal Procedure, allowing the one to win when the others lost.

Insiders versus Outsiders

Likewise, it might be that the six had some special duties toward each other, such that the single person had to be given a chance to win by each of the others. Then Proportional Chances should operate *between them.* Even *we,* as outsiders, would have to respect the prior duties they owe to each other. That is, suppose the impartial point of view tells us to match equivalents against each other by substituting equivalents, and save the greater number in the Drug Case. However, taking seriously the subjective views of each so that we became "tied" to each as individuals tells us not to count numbers at all. Both these perspectives tell us how to view the situation of individuals who have no obligations toward each other; both tell us to focus on the individuals simply as individuals, albeit to compare them as individuals to each other in the case of counting numbers as a matter of right. But it may be that we are not at liberty to focus on the individuals simply as individuals because as equals in conflict they are obliged to confront each other in some way. Then our treatment of them must respect such interpersonal requirements between them.

This gives rise to another way of conceiving of conflict situations, which, I believe, makes Proportional Chances seem most appealing, especially as opposed to majority rule and, perhaps, even to the Ideal Procedure. The cases discussed above involved our responding to people's need (assumed here to give rise directly to claims by individuals for our aid or to give rise to claims by individuals to our aid via a claim to equal treatment if another individual is helped.) We, therefore, had to decide how *we* would respond. But suppose the needed scarce resource is found by the six people who need it, and they must decide among themselves who will get it. Suppose, for example, that the drug is floating down a stream between two bodies of land, one of which has the five people on it and the other one person, and it cannot go in both directions.

If these people were to decide matters among themselves, it is reasonable to think that there would be *no one of them who could legitimately claim to be taking the impartial point of view.* Each is concerned with his own survival. Therefore, for the five to tell the one that the numbers should count, either for reasons of right independent of best consequences or for the sake of producing the best consequences, may, as Taurek notes, sound disingenuous.[11] This is so, even if the five would not thereby be saying anything false, and even if it were true that *we* should count numbers in this situation and it would be wrong for us not to produce the greater good. What we may have here are *position-relative factors* that may make it inappropriate for the six to recommend action or to act in the way we should. (This is a suggestion; I must admit I am not totally convinced of its truth.)

We could still disagree with Taurek when he says that we wouldn't expect the single person to accept *our* saying that it was a better state of affairs in which the five live than in which he does. In particular, if we as outside agents had to choose to whom to give the resource, we might well expect the single person to accept this as a correct reason for *our* acting. We might also expect him to understand our saying that, as a matter of right, we must deal with the claims addressed to us by counting numbers. It seems then that when the single person deals with someone who is taking the impartial view he might have to react differently from the way he would react in dealing with people each of whom is truly acting from his own partial point of view.

How may the single person and those whom he opposes for use of the drug decide to distribute it? The idea of one-on-one combat might, I believe, be of use here. The single person could claim that he has a right to engage in a one-on-one toss with each person with whom he stands in a conflict until he loses. If he confronts each person *one at a time* (serially), the odds of his winning (one-thirty-second), however, will not be the same as they would be if he confronted each other person by tossing not a coin, but a six-sided die. Only the latter arrangement really represents Proportional Chances.

Therefore, when the individuals present their conflicting interests to each other, perhaps it is permissible for them to confront each other as individuals according to

Proportional Chances. When they present their conflicting interests to us to judge, perhaps it is permissible for us to arrange the confrontation between individuals differently. I say "perhaps" since we have yet to decide between Majority Rule and Proportional Chances for that context. Let us turn to that question now.

Choosing Majority Rule over Proportional Chances

Proportional Chances does not seem indicated in the Lottery' Case (where there is pooling) if the way in which each individual came to have his baseline chance did not involve purchasing it or being owed it by opponents and if outsiders are deciding distribution. Suppose that in the Lottery' Case each individual began with his baseline chance only because there was no other *fair* way to decide among equals who would get the prize when only one could win. Then it seems that a baseline chance could permissibly be taken away if this were required by the right procedure an outsider should use in deciding who will get the money when more than one can win.

For the same reason, a baseline chance could be taken away *if* right treatment required it in the Drug Case. After all, a baseline chance would have been given to the single person in a situation where all six were on separate islands, because only one person could receive the drug, and an equal chance was fair to each person. There was no payment for this chance, it has not become a piece of property with some resultant entitlement to it.

So the question to ask is, Could right treatment in deciding who will win when more than one can win require depriving someone of a baseline chance altogether, as in majority rule? Or could it require excluding use of Proportional Chances, even though this would be Pareto optimal when the minority's proportional weight could buy it less than a proportional chance for survival by the Ideal Procedure?

I have already implicitly answered yes to both these questions, in defending balancing (with substitution of equals) as the best approximation to the ideal outcome when there is irreducible conflict, and in defending Clause 2 of the Ideal Procedure.

Here is a way to defend the straightforward substitution of equivalents over Proportional Chances (independent of considerations supporting the Ideal Procedure over Proportional Chances): There is a contrast between the model of strict balancing in which there is substitution of equivalents and that of nonserial combat, the model I have used to describe Proportional Chances. Strict (serial) combat involves two opposing equals confronting each other, with one of the two coming out victorious and, perhaps, going on to confront another opponent. The substitution of equivalents seems to better express the equality of opposing individuals and, hence, to be fairer. This is because combat calls upon some morally irrelevant differences between the individuals (in battle) or on some unequal factor outside of them (as in a coin toss) that can distinguish the winner from the loser. Nonserial combat also does this, since it depends on which way the six-sided die falls. (Serial combat presents an additional concern: if A wins each of his contests with the five others, it is as if he has been counted five times through the effects of luck. This problem does not arise when we toss a six-sided die, one reason why the die is more attractive from an egalitarian perspective). I believe it is understandable that proportional chances is attractive as an expression of the right over the good. Individual rights protect one person in the face of a greater good. The right to retain a chance no matter how many stand in opposition, even if they have a greater chance as a group, is an example of concern for the single individual. In real life, we are acquainted with cases in which a person can make of his small chances a great victory against the odds, coming out ahead of the favored many, and this seems perfectly consistent with moral rightness. But in these cases one also tends to think the one is shown to be superior to, not equal to, the others. This, of course, does not mean he has been treated unequally in being given his chance. But suppose we had been able to give a needed item to each person (all six), or even partially, to satisfy the need of each. This would have been the conduct deemed right, presumably. The outcome in which we balance equivalents by counting numbers comes closest to that outcome dictated by considerations of the right; an outcome in which one person wins, when five might otherwise have been saved, does not.

Ultimately, I believe, proportional chances often seems attractive as a policy because it combines certain features: (1) an unbroken tie to the personal point of view of each individual and vivid representation of the truth that the interests of one person are not satisfied if many others live and he perishes; (2) weight being given to individuals as individuals, so that (unlike what happens when we toss a coin), the equal chance to which each opponent is entitled is summed; (3) a clear sense that we are willing to sacrifice the good for our commitment to do right (if proportional chances is what is required by the right), a sense we lack when what we should do as a matter of the right coincides with what we should do as a matter of the good. However, that we would be willing to sacrifice the good for other values does not necessarily mean that justice and fairness would not be satisfied with counting numbers. Choosing proportional chances over counting numbers may represent an attempt to give weight to values that go beyond the right (understood as justice and fairness), just as the Ideal Procedure sacrifices simply counting numbers for the sake of solidarity.

Notice, however, that the attractiveness of proportional chances may be limited to cases in which the chance for the one to win is small, even though the expected utility of a small chance of a large loss is the same as the expected utility of a large chance of a smaller loss. For example, giving proportional chances to one against two, offers a one-third chance of losing an extra life, and this may not find favor for reasons of justice as well as the good, even if giving the one a smaller chance against the two does find favor. This leads me to suspect that giving an individual some chance, though not necessarily a proportional chance, has *symbolic value*, attesting to the personal point of view, and the ultimate nonsubstitutability of each person to himself. We may deprive people even of some of what justice says we owe them to recognize this value, but we may not deprive them of too much.

Notice also that we do not find proportional chances between one and many attractive whenever the one would suffer a lesser loss than the others, even if from his personal point of view the loss to him is not compensated by gains to others.

Suppose that equality is best expressed by balancing and substitution of equivalents and that we give equal chances in a situation where only one can win only because we want to treat all equally. Then in many situations where more than one can win, majority rule (as I have described it) would be preferable to the retention of a baseline for the minority as in Proportional Chances.

Notice the order of justification: majority rule is first justified over Proportional Chances. Then we can justify the Ideal Procedure over Proportional Chances, on the ground that we should not let the minority group win, for it should lose if any group has to, as shown by majority rule. That is the order of justification, even if the order in which we *rank* preferred outcomes places the Ideal Procedure first, ahead of majority rule. If proportional chances was not inferior to majority rule from the point of view of the right, and we did not supplement rightness considerations alone by saying that only majority rule is consistent with *both* rightness *and* goodness considerations, then we should not endorse clause (2) of the Ideal Procedure. Certainly this would be true if proportional chances was preferable to majority rule from the point of view of the right.

This does not affect what we have said above about specific contexts where Proportional Chances might still be appropriate. For example, it may apply where there is a causal relation of increased production of a resource between one in a group and the rest; all of them need our good, but *we* cannot provide it to all. Indeed, the contrast between those cases (which include Fire') and the Drug Case, where what we have to distribute can service everyone in the larger group, is what is ignored in attempting on p. 133, the unification of icebergs) to represent the Drug Case as a pooling of chances. Some of the special reasons that make Proportional Chances sometimes appropriate are not present when our resources are able to service everyone in the larger group, I believe.

All this does not mean that we could deprive the five of *their* baseline chances for the sake of giving all an equal chance, as Taurek suggests. The heart of both the Proportional Chances and majority rule analyses is that in conflict situations a procedure reflecting equal treatment is one in which individuals confront other individuals as individuals. (This is why A in the Fire' Case must confront *each* of B through F, even when they pool their chances.) When only one can win in a conflict situation, an equal chance for each is *derived* from the confrontation of each with all. Equal chance for each, then, is not a goal that must be maintained in all situations. Rather, it is a goal subsidiary to the goal of having individuals with opposing interests confront one another as individuals. When more than one can win, it is still required that those grouped on one side of the interest line be confronted *as individuals* by someone on the other side. If confrontation by strict balancing, which involves substitution of equivalents, is a better reflection of the equality of the individuals than (serial or nonserial) combat, then strict balancing is to be preferred, in these micro-life and death contexts.[12]

On any view that involves balancing, to give the one and the opposing five equal chances would be to ignore the individual identity of each of the five, to submerge each into the group, and to treat the group as a single unit. How can a balancing view claim to represent concern for individuals as individuals and yet associate each having an equal chance (which is the consequence of one and a group of five having equal chances) with ignoring individuals? Especially since the initial criticism of the aggregation argument claimed to take *individuals* most seriously, on the ground that we remain tied to each when we give each an equal chance? If individuals are not substitutable as equivalents, or if they do not have to confront each other as equivalents but rather just confront us without our seeing them as such in relation to each other, then individuals are taken most seriously when we toss a coin. But if identifying with individuals does lead us to see them in relation to each other, and from this point of view it is acceptable to take individuals to be substitutable equivalents seeing that we achieve as much if we save one person on one side as if we save one person on another—then one-on-one balancing will be taking individuals seriously. It is my sense that, at least phenomenologically, this is what happens: when only two people are in conflict, they confront us as individuals and we arrange for equal chances. When a third, who stands to lose as much as the other two, is added to one side, this forces us to assume a point of view in which the individuals do not just confront us but are seen in relation to each other. We perceive the first two individuals differently: we see them as substitutable equivalents. We are forced to this view when we give that third person's fate as much attention as we gave to the first two when they were alone. (For more detailed discussion of this phenomenology, see chapter 9.) All this is not to deny that the equivalents are not identical persons, and so someone's gain is not adequate to make up for another's loss from the other's point of view.

Choosing the Ideal Procedure over Proportional Chances

Let us review again the argument for preferring the Ideal Procedure to Proportional Chances. That is, suppose we can now argue the moves from Equal Chances to Proportional Chances to majority rule, and from majority rule to the Ideal Procedure. Could we then find ourselves moving back to Proportional Chances in almost a circular fashion? It has been argued that we should move, if circumstances allow, *from* simply saving the greater number *to* reducing the chances of the majority by the proportional weight of the minority if this gives the minority a significant chance to survive when the majority does (the Ideal Procedure). This need not have an egalitarian result since the minority may not share the same chance of survival as the majority. Yet the motive for the move does seem to be the desire to move in an egalitarian direction; I called this the desire for solidarity.

One motivation for the further move to Proportional Chances over the Ideal Procedure would be consideration of the greater good. We have already noted that such a move would be Pareto optimal relative to abiding by the Ideal Procedure when it reduced the chances of the majority by the proportional weight of the minority and brought the minority a chance to survive with the majority that is less than even *its* proportional weight. If we arrange matters according to Proportional Chances, the minority may wind up surviving although the majority does not. A second defense of the move from Ideal Procedure to Proportional Chances might be that the minority *has a right* to reduce the chances of the majority by its proportional weight if it thereby gains something, and it cannot be denied its right to do this simply because this means that it will survive when the majority does not.

Neither of these two arguments seems satisfactory, however. Take the latter first. We may deny that the minority has a right to diminish the chances of the majority by its proportional weight whenever this will increase its chances of survival. It may only be when the possibility of all surviving together is served that the minority has the right to reduce the majority's chances. This is the ideal of solidarity.

Now consider the Pareto-optimality argument. If we moved to the Ideal Procedure for the sake of common survival and common survival cannot be achieved, we are not driven to move to Proportional Chances even if it is Pareto optimal. If we cannot achieve the good of all surviving together, there is an even better way to improve the outcome, namely saving the greater number outright. This will not be Pareto optimal once we reach the stage of the Ideal Procedure, since it will make the minority worse off if we directly save the greater number. But that is not an overriding worry, if the balancing argument for majority rule is correct.

Conclusion

Majority rule, Proportional Chances, and the Ideal Procedure all claim to treat individuals as equals, yet they do not involve giving groups chances or shares independent of their numbers. On the other hand they do not seem to be *based* on the view that it is worse if more suffer that if fewer do. (While these three procedures do not *depend* on a denial of The No Worse Claim, they may lead to one sort of denial of it, different from the sort of denial we have examined heretofore. That is, if not treating people as equals is worse than treating them as equals, and these three procedures treat people as equals, it will be worse if, contrary to what these principles require, fewer are saved when more could be saved.)

III

Repeated versus One-time Distributions

In this discussion we have been concerned with procedures for deciding cases in which on *one* occasion we must decide between the many and the few. There may, however, be cases of repeated conflict, in which we must decide between the many and the few on several occasions. For example, suppose five people are on one island and one on another.[13] We can deliver ice cream to them once a month for several months, but we cannot go to both islands in any given month. It may be true that in multiple-conflict cases we should not apply *either* majority rule or Proportional Chances on each of the several occasions of choice. Rather we should deliver ice cream an equal number of times to each island. Does this show that there is something wrong with the use of majority rule or Proportional Chances in one-time conflict cases?

If we could deliver the ice cream only once, should we replicate as chances of each winning the proportions we maintained over the series, that is, equality? This could be achieved by tossing a coin. I do not believe that the fact that we would if we could provide equal deliveries over time to each island indicates by itself that majority rule or Proportional Chances for one-time conflict cases is wrong. For notice that if we could deliver ice cream an equal number of times to everyone, we would also *not* toss a coin on each occasion to decide where to send the ice cream. *So giving everyone an equal chance is also not the preferred solution in multiple-choice situations.* Therefore the fact that majority rule and Proportional Chances don't apply generally to many-time choices does not mean that they are less correct than coin tossing for one-time choices.

Furthermore, it is not true that commitment to equal shares when this is possible implies commitment to equal chances. One way to understand the desire for equal treatment in repeated cases, which is consistent with the equal-individuals-confronting-equal-individuals justification for Proportional Chances and majority rule, is as follows: If the five people get the ice cream the first time, the single person is in a worse state than they are in; he is the worst-off person, not having had ice cream even once. To improve the condition of the worst off, we give him the ice cream second. On this second round, there is no confrontation between him and the five people on the other island. This is because if they do not get ice cream again on the second delivery, they will not be as badly off as the single person would be if he did not get ice cream on the second delivery. But in one-time (or odd numbered) conflict cases we confront equal individuals as individuals because each will be equally deprived if he does not get what we distribute.

Present versus Future Losses

We have already examined some types of situations in which it is possible that numbers of lives should *not* count, for example, situations where fairness dictates that we ignore, at least to some extent, the capacity of someone himself to save others' lives if we save his. It is worth considering another situation in which they seem not to count straightforwardly. It has been argued that we should not count equally (1) lives, even of those who all presently exist, that will be lost *now* as opposed to lives that will be lost in the future, or (2) lives that will be lost by those who presently exist as opposed to lives that will be lost by those who *will* exist in the future. (Let us assume this is not because we discount the probability of those future losses occurring.)

How might we morally justify using our scarce resources to save one person trapped in a mine disaster now rather than use the same resources to prevent future mine disasters, affecting present *or* future lives, thereby saving more lives? One possible justification is that we wish to avoid having to stand by while someone dies. We want to avoid this even at the expense of preventing more disasters in which people will be beyond our help.

Sometimes, however, the choice is not between "curing" now and preventing irreparable future disasters, but between curing one now and curing many who could be cured later. In this case, we cannot argue merely that we wish to avoid being in a situation where we have to stand by doing nothing while someone dies. This is because if we do not refrain from aiding *now*, we will (by hypothesis) face *more* occasions in the future when we will have to stand by helplessly, doing nothing.

The reason why we may still choose to aid now, however, is that we seek to avoid standing by doing nothing *at a time when we have resources that could be used.* If we do aid now, we will not have resources in the future. In the future it will *not* be true that we stand by not helping *when we have resources* with which to help.

Suppose, however, that, convinced by this argument, we have started to aid someone. Then five other people come in whom we could aid as well with the resources we are in the midst of spending on the one. Why should we not stop aiding the one while we can still withdraw the resources and give them to the five? In this case, we *are presently standing by* while more die when we have resources to save them.

Some might argue that if we stop aid to the one, we would then be killing him to save the five, and this would be impermissible. But terminating assistance we ourselves have begun may not be killing and may be permissible, I believe.[14] Therefore, let us put aside this objection. One possible reason for not stopping aid would be that we are *committed* to the one, having begun to aid him. But it is not clear we are really committed in the sense of having a commitment (versus feeling committed).

If these are, in fact, some reasons why we do not use our resources to maximize lives saved, then we must seriously consider whether they provide reason enough.

Conclusion

If we save five rather than one, when we cannot save both the group of five and the one, we do let one die. This need not mean that we fail in our duty to the one: it is possible to let die by deciding to not aid in the absence of a duty to aid. (For example, if I must make supererogatory efforts in order to save someone and decide not to, I will have let the person die in the absence of a duty to aid.) Furthermore sometimes, it will be permissible to actively violate our duty to one person in order to aid a greater number. For example, suppose I have a strict contractual duty to aid someone (as a bodyguard), but I see that only I can save 1000 strangers. Then it may be permissible for me to break my contract, though I may owe compensation if such were possible. But this is not what happens when I save the group of five rather than the one with whom I have no contract. We have argued that the greater good comes about if the greater number are saved, and that the theory of the right either does not stand in the way of this or it requires that we count numbers. In aiding cases where there is no contractual duty our duty is to do our best, as a matter of the theory of the good, and to balance equivalents, as a matter of the theory of the right, given our resources and the limits of morally permissible demands on our energies. If we have done this, we have not failed in our duty to any individual we let die and we owe no compensation to the one left behind.

NOTES

1. I first described this procedure in a rough way in "Equal Treatment and Equal Chances."

2. In *Equality and Partiality* (pp. 79–80).

3. I am indebted to Ronald Dworkin for pressing me on whether there is a right held by the minority.

4. Notice that even though expected utility is not altered in terms of lives, were it not for considerations of solidarity, some might have a preference for the certainty of one life over the chance of two. The concern over certainty—both of ill and good effects—seems to play an important role in moral judgments where probabilities are concerned, and conflicts with using expected utility calculations.

5. This alternative was suggested to me by Bernard Baumrin.

6. The following discussion is taken from "Equal Treatment and Equal Chances."

7. This also assumes that having begun to aid A does not generate a commitment to him.

8. That there is less chance is itself puzzling since on each toss he has the same 50 percent chance of winning as the other person.

9. The joining of the icebergs as a way to make my point was suggested to me by William Wilcox.

10. Below we will point to a factor that distinguishes the Drug Cases from ones where proportional chances are appropriate.

11. "Should the Numbers Count?"

12. We do not use the substitution of equivalents model in a one-winner game since we would either (1) have no winner when the number of players was even, or (2) have to give each an equal chance to be the person left unbalanced when the number of players was odd, which would again involve throwing a six-sided die.

13. A case suggested to me by Kenneth Alpern.

14. See *Morality, Mortality,* Vol. II, and *Creation and Abortion* for more on this.

8

Are There Irrelevant Utilities?

Mixed Goods

In Chapters 5, 6, and 7 we examined in detail cases in which we had to choose whether to save a greater or a lesser number of lives. (We also applied our results to preventing a greater or lesser number of losses of a less significant sort when each person stood to lose in the same degree.) But we also looked briefly at cases in which the difference we produce if we distribute a scarce resource one way or another is a matter not of preventing additional losses of the *same* sort but rather of saving life and having some effect other than lifesaving. For example, a medicine might be used either to save one person's life or to save another person's life and cure a third person's sore throat as well. Or the choice might be between saving a life and doing something else. For example, a medicine might either save one person's life or cure twenty people's sore throats. In this and the next chapters, we are concerned to analyze in greater detail how our "commonsense" nonconsequentialist morality decides about the distribution of scarce resources in such "mixed" situations.

Furthermore, the decision how to distribute the scarce resource might be made by individuals occupying different roles: doctors, other professionals, ordinary moral agents, or agents of social institutions. We are concerned, first, with how ordinary moral agents should act, and second, if there is a divergence, with how these other agents should act.

The Distribution of Harms

Interestingly enough, many of the principles concerning the distribution of scarce benefits—as well as those that are not intrinsically scarce but that we cannot distribute to all—apply equally to the distribution of harms. These principles would be relevant, for example, in the following case: A public health official, who is redirecting infected material away from a large group of people, must decide whether to send it toward one person, thereby killing him, or toward another person, when this will not only kill him, but also harm some other community resource. I shall, therefore, discuss together the problems of distributing harms and benefits and draw attention where necessary to any divergences in applicable principles. We can also assume that in cases in which we redirect harms, numbers of lives count if they count in aiding.[1]

144

The Impartial Point of View

Our analysis will lead us to review the argument for saving the greater number of lives in Taurek-type cases. This argument will again emphasize that abandoning the fewer is best understood as involving a move toward an impartial point of view, from which saving one life (A's) is as good as saving another life (B's), without regard to the fact that, from A's *personal* point of view, it is *not* as good that B survive as that A survive (and vice versa). (In discussing the personal point of view, I continue to use an objective evaluation of harms or benefits to the person, rather than relying on some idiosyncratic personal preferences.) It is, of course, true that we adopt an impartial stance even if we toss a coin between many individuals, if doing so does not favor one person over another. Taurek obviously believes that giving equal chances to the larger and the smaller group is being impartial. The additional step in adopting the impartial view that leads to counting numbers is to reject the idea of a tie to each individual. This allows us to see each individual in relation to others who need our resource, not just in relation to us; and it leads to substitution of equivalents, I believe.

The crucial point we shall examine in detail in this chapter, having already made it briefly in Chapter 5, is that we should not *always* make the move to substituting equivalents; that move is not necessarily appropriate in those cases where, in helping one side, we can do all the good that we would do (impartially speaking) if we helped the other side, *plus* additional good as well. For example, in cases in which, whatever we do, we save the same number of lives, but one option also differentially produces a minor nonlifesaving result, we should not necessarily adopt the point of view that favors producing the most good. We have referred to the point of view from which we evaluate A's life as substitutable for B's as the *impartial* point of view. So it is possible that even from the impartial point of view we should ignore some extra good in deciding whom to save.

Direct and Indirect Threats

It has been argued[2] that if a threat is headed toward killing five people, we (that is, any bystander) may redirect it away from the five, foreseeing that the threat will then kill one innocent person as it travels in another direction. What I wish to consider here is the choice between possible direct victims of a redirected threat and the analogous choice between possible direct beneficiaries of a scarce resource.

To repeat distinctions we have already discussed, *direct* victims and beneficiaries are those who will suffer the harm or receive the benefit distinctively produced by the threat or scarce resource (as explained in Chapter 6). *Indirect* victims and beneficiaries are those who are harmed or benefited because a direct victim or beneficiary stands in a certain causal relation to them. For example, someone who would be mowed down by a trolley headed toward him would be a direct victim of the trolley; an indirect victim might be someone who depended upon the person who would be mowed down.[3] A direct beneficiary of a scarce resource is someone for whom that resource is useful. For example, if someone needs a medicine to cure his illness, that medicine is useful to him, and he would be a direct beneficiary. An indirect beneficiary of a scarce resource is someone who does not need that resource for himself, but would be benefited indirectly if someone else got it who was then able to help him. (I have allowed that a direct beneficiary of a resource may get *use* from the resource indirectly, e.g., if he plants the medicine and uses what grows from it.)

Irrelevant Utilities

Suppose we are able to redirect a threat away from five people in the direction of either Joe *or* Jim (Threat Case). I believe that, other things equal and given the time, treating Joe and Jim as equals requires us to use a random decision procedure to select between them. (A weaker claim would be that it doesn't matter how we choose, so long as we do not choose for certain bad reasons, e.g., color of skin.) But suppose that, alongside Jim, but not beside Joe, there grows a patch of beautiful flowers, which gives pleasure to a great many people, and these flowers would be destroyed by a threat redirected toward Jim. Sending the threat toward Joe, would, therefore, maximize utility (Flower Case). I believe that it would be wrong to decide against Joe and for Jim solely for the sake of this extra utility. I call the principle that articulates this result the *Principle of Irrelevant Utilities*.

Analogously, suppose a scarce medicine could be given to save the life of either Jim or Joe, but only if it is given to Jim will there be enough left over to cure a sore throat that Nancy would otherwise have for a week (Sore Throat Case). I believe that it would be wrong to decide against Joe and for Jim solely for the sake of the sore-throat cure. Notice that on the weaker claim, that it doesn't matter if we use a random decision procedure, so long as we do not choose for certain bad reasons, it is not held that we ought to give Joe and Jim equal chances. It doesn't matter whom we choose, as long as we don't choose for a bad reason. And now the claim must be that, if we choose to save Jim because we can then also save some other person from a sore throat, this *is* a bad reason. It may be harder to defend the weaker view that we should not select for a bad reason, than to defend the stronger view that we should give equal chances, since it doesn't seem a bad reason to act in one of two ways that, by doing so, we can save someone else from a sore throat.[4]

Indirect Beneficiaries of Victims and Causal Relations

At this point, we can again review why the distinction between direct and indirect beneficiaries and victims is important. It is sometimes held to be wrong to take into account such extra utilities as the saved flowers and the cured sore throat in deciding whom to harm or help *because of* the way in which such extra utilities come about. They may come about as a result of causal connections between what happens to a direct victim or beneficiary and what happens to the indirect victim or beneficiary; that is, one of the people whose life is at stake may, if he is saved, produce the extra utility or, if he is not saved this way, cause the disutility. For example, if one person rather than another is saved from a certain disease, many people who depend on that person for a cure of their sore throats might be cured; or if a married man rather than a single man is saved, the wife might be spared misery that would be caused by her husband's death. I have argued that to favor the person who can produce such smaller extra utility or prevent such smaller extra disutility is to treat people "merely as means" since it decides against the person who cannot produce the extra utility on the grounds that he is *not* a means. It does not give people equal status as "ends in themselves" and, therefore, treats them unfairly.

Direct or Indirect Extra Utility and the Charge of Unfairness

One could raise many objections to this argument, starting from what it means and proceeding to whether it is applicable to these cases. (I have discussed this in Chapter 6.) Here I will only remind the reader that the whole "means" objection to selecting victims or recipients on the basis of extra utility is sidestepped if we alter the example so that the extra utility is produced directly by our scarce resource, or the extra disutility is produced by our threat. This has been done in the cases (Flower and Sore Throat) we are presently considering. So consideration of whether the extra utility should count in deciding whom to save is separated from consideration of whether some property of one of the people (that gives him his causal connections to extra utility) should be allowed to count.[5]

Suppose that Jim, but not we or Joe, could get the medicine to Nancy, or could push the trolley from a patch of flowers that will be hit by it. Since Nancy's sore throat is directly helped by our medicine, and since the flowers are directly threatened by our trolley, the fact that Jim was saved for the sake of the causal connection between him and Nancy, or him and the flowers, would not fall afoul of a requirement of fairness. (Again, this was discussed in Chapter 6). Unfairness would be present only if Jim were saved because his personal property helped individuals who were not directly benefited or threatened by the benefit or harm we have for distribution, I believe.

Therefore, if we should disregard the extra utility in these variants of the Flower and Sore Throat Cases, it must be on grounds other than that to do so would be to give unfair preference to someone on the basis of his causal relations.

Choosing a Decision Procedure on Grounds of Extra Utility

Furthermore, it has also been noted that choosing against Joe and for Jim solely for the sake of the additional utility is different from choosing *between random decision procedures* on the basis of the utility *they* produce. I believe that it is consistent with the rejection of the first to approve the second. That is, we may permissibly decide against tossing an ordinary coin to select between Jim and Joe and in favor of tossing a *magic extra-utility* coin that causes extra utility when it is tossed—it might, for example, cause flowers to grow wherever it lands. Here we do not need to deny Joe or Jim his equal chance in order to get the extra utility we want.

It is important to emphasize this point since one might be tempted to say that the reason that minor extra utility should not be considered when deciding between Joe and Jim is that it would be "obscene" to think about flowers when lives are at stake. But if this were the reason, it would also be obscene to choose between random decision procedures on the basis of the extra utility. But it is not. Choosing against

Joe and for Jim for the sake of getting one life plus the extra utility is also different from using "where the extra utility is" as a random decision procedure itself. I shall return to these two points below.

Justifying the Principle of Irrelevant Utilities

I shall consider three possible justifications for the Principle of Irrelevant Utilities, but only one in this chapter. All these justifications involve detailed consideration of the way in which impartial and personal, objective and subjective points of view may be combined in our commonsense nonconsequentialist moral point of view. They are relevant to dealing with the general problem of aggregating losses and benefits across people.

I will discuss the first of these justifications in this section; it involves two steps:

1. Only equal or approximately equal individual interests or rights should be matched against each other in deciding who or what may be a *contestant* for a good.
2. The *contest* should be decided only by reference to the interests or rights of those who may compete for the good.

I ignore here the possible conflict between interests and rights, e.g., equal interests in the benefit but unequal rights to it, or vice versa. I include rights that arise from claims that individuals have directly in virtue of their interests or claims that individuals have if and only if others will be treated in certain ways, i.e., claims based on a right to equal treatment. The claim in step 1, that interests or rights only *approximately* equal (rather than exactly equal) may be matched against each other, needs defense. There are two defenses I wish eventually to consider but since one of them makes use of the results of the first section of this chapter, I will postpone discussion of that consideration.

Types of Irrelevance

The fact that equal or near-equal interests are required for being a contestant should not be misunderstood to mean that the individuals must be equal or near-equal in *all* respects if they are to be contestants and merit equal chances. It may be that it should be an irrelevant characteristic of a person that he can produce more good for society or that he is nicer, if his need for a drug to survive is approximately as great as someone else's. Our present discussion of the role of utilities that lie outside of the causal capacities of contestants *assumes* that we might be required to give equal chances to contestants who are overall very unequal. Possible justifications for this which we have already considered are avoiding unfairness and the Kantian injunction (when related to indirect versus direct need for our resource), and "separate spheres" for resources so that we not try to promote all types of goods with, for example, health resources. We shall, however, inquire further into the justification for making these other characteristics irrelevant as well.

It is, therefore, important to distinguish between *two types of irrelevance* with which we may be concerned. One type which is important to deciding who are equal contestants seems to be heavily tied to the ideas of separate spheres (i.e., not seeking to produce a good when it lies in another sphere), fairness and not choosing between people because they are means to the production of goods that are unrelated to direct need for our resource. If we refuse to select someone to live because she can produce music (versus life) for others, we are concerned with both the fairness/means issue and the separate spheres issue. The separate spheres issue could arise even if the extra good is produced in the person who directly needs our resource, e.g., if they will have a life with greater artistic achievement in it. (We have already noted that unfairness may sometimes be overridden. Strictly speaking, then, at some point utility produced in an unfair way will not be irrelevant.)

The second type of irrelevance (on which we focus when we discuss the Principle of Irrelevant Utilities) is concerned with losses or gains of a certain size. These losses and gains are in the appropriate sphere (e.g., life and health), stem from direct need for our resource, and producing them does not involve unfairness or selection as mere means. Here saying "a certain type of loss" is irrelevant really means that a loss of a certain size is irrelevant.

I will discuss this first justification of the Principle of Irrelevant Utilities using the Flower Case, although the Sore Throat Case could do as well. Step 1 means that Joe must confront Jim for a chance to live. Each has a right not be killed just considered as an individual and as much right as the other not to be killed to begin with. Let us also assume it is equally in each person's interest to stay alive. Joe would not, however, have to confront the flowers in a contest for life. That is, if there were a choice between sending the threat toward him or to a track where *only* the flowers lie, we would without question send the threat toward the flowers. (It might perhaps be said that Joe and the flowers are both indeed "contestants," but that Joe always wins. Let my use of the word "contestants," then, imply that there is a serious contest, a question as to who should win. We can use the word "candidate" to designate possible recipients of harms or benefits who are possibly very unequal in whatever respects are relevant to choice.) The flowers are not anywhere near as important as Joe's life. Furthermore, the loss to, or the right of, those who would have enjoyed the flowers is nowhere near as important as the loss to Joe of his life or his right not to be killed. The flowers or the flower lovers, who would not be contestants on their own, do not *become* contestants against Joe—that is, have anywhere near equal status *as individuals* to him—when the flowers lie beside Jim (by way of some peculiar interaction effect).

Using Extra Utility Consistent with the First Justification

Even within the framework of this first approach to the Principle of Irrelevant Utilities, it would be a mistake, I believe, to conclude straightforwardly on the basis of (1)—a principle that selects *contestants*—that (2) is true. That is, we cannot directly conclude from (1) that it is wrong to decide between contestants of equal weight on the basis of a factor that would not itself be fit to occupy the role of contestant.[6] Such a factor might well be of legitimate concern, in particular, when we are deciding between contestants who have an equal interest in getting a good, but have no right to the good per se, either via a right they hold as individuals or a right they have to be treated as other individuals will be.

Consider an analogy. We might decide to award business contracts only to black-owned firms (i.e., only black-owned firms shall be contestants) because we want to improve black business. We may even think that blacks *as a group* have a right to such help. We do not, however, base our decision on the belief that every black-owned firm has a right to the benefit of a contract. Rather, we believe that the group has a right to arrangements such that 50 percent of its firms will receive contracts. The claim is that, consistent with the decision to award contracts to 50 percent of black businesses, we could choose between two equally worthy black-owned firms as follows: we could give the contract to one rather than the other on the ground that, if we do so, we will have done all we need to do to satisfy the good of promoting black business and, besides, we will benefit other firms that are white owned without harming blacks. It is quite possible that, in pursuing our social goal, it would be *un*fair not to give an equal chance of getting a contract to each of two black-owned firms *whose effect on other parts of the economy would be the same*. That is, each of these may have a right to an equal chance of obtaining a contract *without* each having an individual right to a contract. But this right to an equal chance, based on fairness, need not apply when we can achieve our goal of awarding contracts to 50 percent of black businesses and achieve extra utility elsewhere as well by giving the contract to one firm rather than the other.

In this case it does not seem unfair to select one firm rather than another because this choice carries with it better effects, even though the other effects could not be a contestant on its own. It does not even seem that fairness is a consideration that must be overridden. I believe this is true whether the extra utility is produced directly by how we award the contract or even causally results from some property that one particular black business has, unrelated to the resources we have to distribute.

Notice how different this case is from the case in which we must choose whether to give a lifesaving drug to a doctor who will save other lives or to a different person who cannot. In that case, even if we do not think either has a right to the drug as an individual, we may think that fairness dictates that if either one is up for it, the other should get an equal chance, independent of extra utility. What lies behind this difference, I believe, is the view that *both* the doctor and the other person should be treated *if* one is treated—there is a right to equal treatment—whereas we do not think both black businesses should have contracts if one does.

According to the first approach to justifying the Principle of Irrelevant Utility, matters would be different if *each* individual black-owned firm had a right (and an equally strong right) to aid because of its individual characteristics alone, and for some reason aid could not be made available to all. Matters would also be different if neither had such a right to aid, but one had a right to be aided if the other one was.

Interests and Subjectivity

Let us first consider the attitude toward individual interests that *would* yield step 2 and the Principle of Irrelevant Utilities, leaving further discussion of rights for later. What might justify deciding the contest only by reference to the interests of contestants is the way in which personal and impartial, subjective, and objective views are combined in our nonconsequentialist moral point of view. I shall label *Subjectivity* that type of thinking which interweaves the personal/subjective and impartial/objective views. In what follows, we shall try to unravel the strands in this system and provide an anatomy of this way of thinking. Strictly speaking, the *objective view* can be described as that view from which events in the world are given the weight they truly have, all things considered. (We shall distinguish the objective view from the impartial view.) The *subjective view* gives something the weight it has from the perspective of an individual where this may be out of proportion to its weight from the objective view. The reasons for this may include idiosyncratic personal preferences. As described so far, the objective view is an all-or-nothing phenomenon. But there is a sense in which there are degrees of objectivity. We might say that there is the objective view, strictly speaking, and then there are views that are objective relative to subjective views. These relatively objective views contain in them elements of the subjective view.

The Interweaving of Subjective and Objective Elements

The strict objective view would acknowledge as contestants persons who, without the good, stood to suffer equal (not near equal) losses. However, because this view aggregates all sorts of losses, it need not search for *individuals* who would suffer such equal losses. That is, it will not matter where the losses occur or how many small losses to many people it takes to add up to an equivalent loss in one person. The view is *nongeographic*. The search for *individual* contestants who will suffer equal losses is, therefore, already a move away from the strictest possible objective view. At least this may distinguish, within the objective view, between an impersonal and an impartial perspective. One distinction between impersonality and impartiality is that impartiality is necessarily between individuals and so, unlike impersonal counting (which I consider the simplest form of objectivity), does not compare the loss to a single person with an aggregation of smaller losses over individuals. The reason that a less strict objective view looks for equal losses in *individual* contestants is that it shows concern for the loss *to* each person. This seems to incorporate a component of the subjective view, giving greater weight to aggregation *within* an individual life than to aggregation over lives, where the total aggregate is the same.

Recall that it is quite compatible with concern for the significance of his own death to each person to hold that death is bad for the person, even though it is not *experienced* as bad. Furthermore, it is compatible with concern for the significance of death *to* the person, that the person himself does not care about what is bad for him. This is an objective component introduced into understanding the subjective view. That is, we evaluate objectively (without regard to the idiosyncratic personal preferences of the individual) how significant the loss is *to* an individual. The "personal point of view" (as I use it) differs from the subjective point of view in thus evaluating the loss to the person's objective interests.

Assigning an objective weight to a loss, rather than weighing it according to the preferences of the individual, may conflict with giving individual decision making a strong role in the distribution of scarce resources.[7] It need not, however. In Chapter 6, when discussing Taurek's views, we said that if an individual did not want his life saved, we should not count the saving of his life as a factor in a conflict situation.

We did not then enter into the question of *why* he did not want his life saved. There may, however, be limits to the reasonableness of following his request. Suppose that he is known to be mentally incompetent; or that he falls short of incompetence but is still imprudent, not giving his own interests much less weight than those of others; or that he makes his request for psychologically inappropriate reasons, guilt perhaps, or extreme feelings of inferiority. Once we take these possibilities—and there are more—into account, we may no longer be sure how much weight to give to an expressed preference as against what we think someone ought objectively to prefer when considering what would be best for him. In addition, we must consider what we would do if there were no expressed preference (and no substituted judgment by others who know the person's preference). In such situations, objective weighing of interests from the personal point of view may play a greater role without conflicting with preferences.

It is possible that another element of the subjective view is introduced into an objective view if it acknowledges as contestants those who will suffer *near* equal losses. Whether this is a further incorporation of the subjective view depends on how it is justified. If it is because, from the subjective view, small differences are not noticeable, then the subjective view is involved. We shall return to this issue. A further addition that may come from the subjective view is restriction on the type of losses on which one must be only nearly equal in order to be contestants. Objectivity suggests that all types of negative and positive effects that will come of someone's being harmed or aided are relevant. But, for example, if only someone's need to avoid death were relevant, independent of the other goods or bads that life would bring with it, then not all effects are relevant. Which factors are picked as relevant may be a matter of the subjective view, if we include only certain effects because of how important they are *to* the person, e.g., whether he will live or die, in comparison with how unimportant other goods are to the person. Further, we can modify this subjective weighing by imposing objective standards on the comparison, thus making it part of the personal point of view to ignore certain effects.

To summarize the way in which I use these terms: Impartiality is a concept stemming from objectivity when the latter is restricted to some degree by concern for the subjective point of view. The personal point of view is a concept stemming from subjectivity when the latter has been restricted to some degree by the objective point of view. However, we have not yet completely described the way in which impartiality differs from impersonality.

Substituting Objective Equivalents

The type of relatively objective view I am contemplating at this stage has all these (possible) elements of the subjective view incorporated into it. This view is indifferent to which one of two equal contestants wins, other things being equal. It permits the substitution of equivalents. It would not matter from the point of view described up to this stage whether Joe or Jim wins *if* other things are equal. It is because, from this objective view, it does not matter who wins, that the increase in utility wrought by saving Jim in the Flower Case *can* decide matters from this view. For the same reason there might be no concern from this view that the selection procedure be fair: whether it is fair or unfair, only one person will win. (I shall deal below with the view that fairness is a good from the objective view.)

Likewise, if our only goal in having only blacks be contestants is to increase black business or satisfy a group right, this goal is achieved equally well whichever black business wins, and we are then free to seek to achieve other ends (such as increasing business in general).

Subjective Equivalents

By contrast, from a person's subjective view, things that an objective view would consider to be significantly unequal can be matched as equals against each other. For example, from Jim's subjective view, he might match as equals the loss of Jim's own arm and the loss of Joe's life. This aspect of Jim's subjective view may be incorporated into nonconsequentialist morality by giving Jim permission not to cut off his own arm to save Joe's life and in a prohibition against my taking Jim's arm to save Joe's life. Some philosophers (e.g., Taurek) would also have bystanders decide whom to aid and perhaps whom to harm by using such subjective equivalence scales relative to each person at risk. These philosophers would say that since Jim would not be duty bound to give up his arm to save the life of another person, a bystander should toss a coin to choose between sending a threat toward Jim when it would take off his arm or toward Joe when it would kill him.[8] Both the objective and the subjective views allow the substitution of equivalents. But the objective view matches what are objective equivalents, and the subjective view matches what are subjective equivalents.

Objective Constraints on Subjective Equivalents

There is a significant complication in understanding the role of the subjective view in general in accounting for moral permissions, related to its distinctness from what I have referred to as the personal point of view: The content of a morally permitted nonobjective scale of equivalents is itself objectively determined.

So the fact that someone values his cut-off toenail as much as someone else's life is not thought, on anyone's view, to make it morally acceptable for him not to give up the cut-off toenail to save a life. A morally acceptable subjective view sometimes allows *some* more weight to one's own concerns relative to those of others, but not just *any* weight, in particular, not just any weight that one subjectively desires. This is the objectivizing factor introduced into the role of the subjective view. Here there is an objective constraint on how the individual weights himself versus others. Previously we considered an objective constraint on how the individual weights his own losses, that is, even if he doesn't care about something it may be counted. From this combination of objective and subjective weighting that generates the personal point of view, we can say that, even though someone would not mind the loss of his legs, it would be objectively not unreasonable for him to count their loss as more important to him than the loss of someone else's life is to him. This does not mean that he would necessarily be unreasonable to prefer the loss of his legs if this saved someone else's life.[9]

Most crucially for our purposes, from the subjective view of each person, in contrast to the objective view, it matters a great deal whether Joe or Jim dies. That is, it matters to each of them whether he lives or the other person lives instead. To Jim, Joe's death is not a subjective equivalent to his own death. It also matters from an objectively permitted subjective view, that is, the personal point of view. I believe that the impartial point of view identifies with this concern of each person, and therefore, unlike the simple objective view, is concerned that there be a fair choice between the two people.

Sobjectivity

That part of the first approach to defending the Principle of Irrelevant Utility which is *concerned with how we view the interests of those involved* depends on a particular combination of the objective and subjective points of view. I shall refer to this combination as *Sobjectivism*[1] (abbreviated *Sob*[1]). An *objective* component in the Sobjective[1] View is that contestants for a good must have interests at stake that do not differ too radically on the objective view (an arm and life do differ too radically, for example). *Subjective* components in Sob[1] are that individual contestants are to be matched against each other by assessing size of expected loss to each rather than by aggregating just any set of losses, and (perhaps) that matching requires only certain losses to be only approximately equal. (To regard these as subjective components is to assume that a certain sort of justification should be given for the parts of this move.) In sum, what A would lose must be approximately as important to A as whatever B would lose would be to B. (It is not enough that what A would lose could reasonably mean as much to A as whatever B would lose could mean to A.) The third subjective component in Sob[1] is that we take seriously the recognition that, from their respective subjective points of view, both Joe and Jim are not indifferent to who wins the contest. *Indeed, for each, from his subjective view, his not surviving because the other survives will be almost as if no one survived.* Certainly to each the survival of the other will not be as important as his own survival.[10] Furthermore, from the *objective* view this is not an unreasonable subjective view to have. Finally, an additional *objective* component of Sob[1] is that *we* see that Jim takes the same subjective attitude to Joe as Joe takes to Jim, and we see them as equals. Therefore, Sob[1] taking into account *each* person's subjective view, assigns Joe and Jim equal chances. It does this instead of siding with the subjective or personal point of view of one or the other and instead of adhering to a stricter objective view that would give no weight to the desire of each to be the one who survives. This sobjective[1] view incorporates the personal point of view and impartiality.

Reaching a Conclusion

What do we get when we put the subjective and objective components together in this way? We conclude that we should not deprive Joe of an equal chance to live by directing a threat or a benefit in order to achieve something that we would not choose over Joe, or even treat as a contestant against Joe, if his life *alone* were at stake. That is, in our cases we should not determine where the threat or benefit goes on the basis of how we can save flowers or cure Nancy's sore throat.

For if we *do* save Jim on utilitarian grounds, then, from Joe's subjective view, it will be as if Joe were matched against the flowers alone. This is because Jim's being saved will have dropped out almost entirely from Joe's perspective. Matching Joe against flowers violates the *objective* component of choosing contestants who are near-equals. Put slightly differently, Joe and Jim would start off with equal chances if they alone were at stake because we see that, from each one's objectively permitted subjective view, it is almost as if no one survives if he does not survive. Suppose we allow a sore throat or some flowers to *alter this arrangement* of a 50 percent chance for Joe and to *determine* that Jim shall be saved. If giving Joe his chance were based on appreciating that he places a near-zero where Jim's survival occurs, then allowing minor utility to deprive him of his chance is, from his point of view, to allow the flowers or a sore throat to stand as a *contestant alone* against him. (Of course, if Joe sees Jim's survival as zero, he will see the flowers' survival as a zero, too. So, strictly speaking, it will be as if he loses out to no contestant at all. But because flowers *determine* the outcome, they become salient as a contestant from his point of view.) But this would violate the (essentially) *objective* component that contestants must be individuals who stand to lose something of nearly equal significance.[11]

The Black Businessmen

A similar analysis might be used in the Black Businessmen Case: It matters to each that he wins, he is not equally satisfied if another black wins. Further, let us suppose that a white businessman will suffer so much less if he loses out on business than either black businessman will that we would choose either black, if he were the only black, over the white. Therefore, we should give each black—who cares about *his* winning and to whom winning means so much more than winning means to the white—an equal chance. According to this analysis, we should not give the contract to a black on the basis of what also improves white business.

Still, though we *can bring ourselves* to see this case as we see the case of Joe and Jim plus the flowers, we must explain why our initial responses to these two cases do differ. That is, initially we said (p. 150) that there was no problem in letting the extra utility decide in the Black Businessmen Case (even if we owed a fair toss of a coin to each when no extra-utility was at stake.) There were also no other great objections to letting a gain to white business count. By contrast, there was, all along, discomfort with letting utility decide matters between Joe and Jim.

I believe this contrast is present because we think we ought to not harm both Joe and Jim if we could, but that we need not help all the black businessmen if we could (given the assumptions of the case). Just because we take black businessman A's interest more seriously than the white businessman's does not mean that we have to help A if we have already helped B. Unlike the businessmen, either Joe or Jim will lose out on something he ought to have—his life. (At the very least, in cases where we must aid rather than not harm, life is something each ought to be helped to have *if* the other is helped to have it.) If we alter our perspective so that we take very seriously the desire of each black to be the one who wins, we do not let extra utility be the determining factor. (This means taking the desire of each to win more seriously than when we merely gave equal chances when no extra utility was at stake.)

The Principle of Irrelevant Utilities and Nonaggregation of Significant Utilities

The analysis of conflicting interests presented above supports the view that, in deciding to whom a good or harm should go, only the interests of those whose interest in the outcome makes them contestants are relevant. If what is at stake for them does not make them contestants, they cannot be tie breakers, even if our resource would directly help them. It also means that we should alter our behavior toward Joe and Jim because of an addition to Jim's side only to the extent that we would alter our behavior in virtue of the addition by itself. This is a principle of nonaggregation. For example, we might have to create equal chances between Joe and each individual who would lose nearly as much as he, even if several individuals stand together against Joe. This may mean tossing a coin between one and five. (However, it might also mean giving proportional chances to represent a toss between Joe and each *individual* other candidate. On these issues see Chapters 4, 5, and 6.)

We should do this because, from his personal point of view, Joe sees a (near) equal opponent as a zero. We know that the other opponent(s) see Joe in that way, too. Therefore, *our* taking up the impartial view makes us give an equal chance to each. We may not deprive Joe of that equal chance (which we derived from our objective understanding of his having a subjective view), even if another person who will suffer an equal loss is added onto Jim's side. This is because the additional person (like the one he joins) *alone* should get no more than an equal chance, given Joe's subjective view and the way the objective view treats it. In sum, when we see that Joe takes the survival of each of any number of individuals as a zero, the impartial view arranges for equal chances between him and each of any number of individuals: Sobjectivity[1] leads to a Taurek-like view on conflict cases involving many lives. (It might, however, also lead to proportional chances, as noted above.)

Fairness

I believe that concern for fair decision procedures begins with taking seriously the subjective views of individuals and combining them with the objective view in the way described by Sob[1]. The concern that each have an equal chance stems, at least in part, from a desire to reflect the greater interest each has in his own survival. It might be suggested that this is not the entire basis of concern for fairness, however. This is because (as noted in Chapter 5, p. 85) as we reduce the absolute value of the chance, each person may no longer care very much for it. (Although it is true that its subjective value and its objectively reasonable subjective value may decrease much less rapidly than its objective value, given that it is all the chance the person has.) Suppose we still wanted each person to get this very small chance (e.g., one in a billion), rather than choose one person for the sake of the extra utility this would produce. This might show that the concern for fairness was independent of each person's concern for the value of a chance. (Though not if numbers count *and* the chance at life is itself a benefit, since aggregatively we would be producing a greater benefit in giving so many people a smaller chance.)

It might be claimed that fairness is a good and so should, straightforwardly and obviously be sanctioned by the objective view, strictly speaking. There are various problems with this position. If fairness is a good, it should be permissible to maximize it by inflicting unfair treatment somewhere to produce more fairness elsewhere. This, however, conflicts with the idea of fairness as a side constraint; we may not violate fairness even to minimize instances of unfairness.[12] Furthermore, if fairness is a good, from the objective view, it may be required of us that we forgo lesser goods in order to promote it. By contrast, an account of fairness as a side constraint would not necessarily say that we had to pay to promote it, though we would have to suffer losses *as a consequence* of the fair thing's being done. Finally, suppose that fairness were incorporated in some way into an objective view as a good. So long as the explanation of its goodness were in terms of its connection with individuals' subjective views, the point we were concerned to make would still have been made.

Summary

We could think of Sob[1] as an enriched objective view, incorporating some aspects of the subjective view, yielding a personal point of view and impartiality. Sob[1] results from the following moves: (1) a subjective component (having contestants rather than aggregating any losses); *to* (2) two objective components (contestants' having no significant differences in losses, where the losses to each are objectively weighted); (3) modified by (possibly three) subjective components (*near*-equal losses of only *certain* types and *nonindifference* to who lives this assigns opposing contestants a zero from each contestant's view, and, therefore, prevents flowers from facing Joe alone; to (4) one objective component (taking *all* the personal views into account).[13]

Equal Rights

Having considered the part of the first defense of the Principle of Irrelevant Utilities that focuses on interests and works through Sob[1] let us consider the part of the first defense concerned with rights. If the hypothesis about rights were true, that they are meant as protections of what the individual cares about from his personal point of view when this conflicts with what has value from the objective view, then we might connect Sob[1] with the defense of rights.[14] However, we need not accept that theory of the source of rights to agree that if a number of individuals each have a right to be treated in a certain way, then if only one could have that right met each has an equal right to a chance of being the one whose right is met. This right to an equal chance is a *proxy right*.[15] That is, the right to an equal chance may stand as proxy for an equal right.

Let us assume that Joe and Jim in our examples each has a right not to be killed and a right to be saved. The rights of both cannot be met. Assume that neither wishes to waive his proxy right to an equal chance to live merely in order to save some flowers. We should then not allow the aim of saving flowers to deprive Joe of his equal chance, any more than we would transgress his right not to be killed or to be saved in order to save flowers alone.[16] This right to an equal chance is derived from a strict individual entitlement. It stands up to the minor extra utility in a way that each black businessman's claim to an equal chance when no extra utility was at stake, based on fairness *between* group members, did not. When they were equal in total utility produced they had a right to an equal chance; when an equal utility was at stake they did not have that right. (That is, each black businessman did not have the right to be aided; each had only a right to a fair chance, in the absence of the possibility of extra utility. We had to alter our perspective and take extra-seriously the interest of each to be the winner to justify our ignoring extra utility.)

As noted previously (p. 150), a rights analysis may apply even if Joe and Jim do not have individual rights to be aided or not to be harmed, because each may have the *conditional* right to be aided or not harmed *if* the other is aided or not harmed. (Similarly, we may not think that anyone has an unconditional right to expensive medical care from state funds. Nevertheless, we may think that if some get the care, all have a right to get it.) The black businessmen do not have such a conditional right.

Rights or Interests?

Is our Flower Case best thought of in terms of the "interest" or the "rights" approach? If redirection of a trolley from five persons to one person is permissible, how can it be said that Joe and Jim each has a *right* not to be killed? We could say instead that each had a right not to be killed *unjustly,* say, if an *unjust* killing were at stake, or if we were denying one of the two his rights even in the absence of a competing claim from the other. If we conclude that they do not each have a right not to be killed in this case—one may be killed and one has a right not to be killed—then these two are comparable to the black businessmen who lack individual rights to aid. Each may only have a right based on fairness to an equal chance not to be killed when neither is associated with extra utility. We would then revert to using the analysis of interests given by Sob[1]: If we take seriously the interest of each in the outcome favorable to him, our concern to give each an equal chance could lead us to disregard extra utility.

I believe, however, that this analysis would be mistaken. Assume that in the Flower Case it is permitted to kill someone by redirecting the threat away from the *five*. It is a significant background fact that either Jim or Joe is still an innocent bystander who will be victimized by the redirection. Neither is someone who deserves to be killed. It follows that once we select the direction in which to send the threat, we would be under an obligation to help save the potential victim from the threat if this could be done. Judith Thomson[17] puts this by saying that the fact that it is permissible to infringe a right does not mean that the right does not exist. By contrast, once we had helped 50 percent of the black businessmen, we would, by hypothesis, not be under an obligation to help the rest. Therefore, I believe the individual-right model, as well as the individual-interest model, applies to the Flower Case.

Suppose Joe and Jim in the Sore Throat Case each had a strict entitlement to an underproduced and hence scarce medicine. Their rights to an equal chance to obtain it would be grounds for ignoring Nancy's sore throat, to the same degree that suffering a sore throat for two weeks would not *by itself* be weighed against saving a life. For example, suppose Joe and Jim had both paid for quantities of medicine that was underproduced. When such strict property rights to such an important item are at stake, the pressure to decide the issue between Joe and Jim alone seems to be even greater than it is if we consider just their interests on the model of Sob[1]. The plight of Nancy, someone with no claim to ownership, provides no reason why Joe should not benefit from what should have been his own property. (This need not mean, however, that we are, in general, more concerned with someone's property rights than with someone's interest in staying alive. For example, we might try equally to save someone who was dying because he could not get to a life raft that didn't belong to him, as to save someone who was dying because he could not get to a life raft that did belong to him.)

Again, even if neither Joe nor Jim had a strict individual right to be aided, they might each have a right to be aided *if* the other were aided. Here, too, Nancy's plight should be ignored.

What if we were obliged to provide medicine for only 50 percent of the population (because, for example, we were rightly concerned with the disease only when it resulted in an inadequate work force)? If we adopt a Sobjective[1] attitude to the interests of all concerned, extra utility (below contestant level) should still be ignored. However, we could not justify ignoring extra utility by using the argument based on the priority of giving rights holders equal chances to a commodity.

Prohibiting the Minor Utility

There is another type of case worth considering. This is one in which equal chances should be given, not because too many individuals have property rights to a certain good or because we treat each person's interest in winning sobjectively[1], but rather, because it seems appropriate to *prohibit* the consideration of any good other than that promoted by the characteristics that make individuals contestants. Suppose a university has one teaching position open and two equally qualified candidates. One candidate is far more personable than the other. May we decide to obtain the (supposed) added benefit of a very personable colleague without sacrificing intellectual standing? I believe we may not *if* collecting personable people (above a certain level of civilized conduct), not only should be morally irrelevant in selecting *contestants* for jobs at serious intellectual establishments, but also should not be a goal of a university *at all*.

Summary

We can see that the general claim that "other things equal (i.e., whichever way we go we only save one life), we may maximize utility" is not Sobjectively[1] true. It more likely derives from an objective view that is no longer concerned with the interests or rights of the contestants themselves once the feasible limit of saving one has been met.

Utility as a Consequence Rather Than as a Means

As we state this conclusion, it is still worth emphasizing that the losses we are willing to tolerate (e.g., the sore throat, the loss of flowers) are tolerated *as consequences* of giving Joe and Jim equal chances. This does not necessarily mean that we are thereby committed to suffering the same losses *as means* to giving equal chances. Indeed, this point can be generalized: The claim that rights trump utilities,[18] which does not, in fact, seem true in cases where we must redirect threats, is in a rough way acceptable only when the loss of the utilities is a consequence of respecting the rights. Compatibly with this, it may be permissible not to sacrifice the same utilities if doing so were necessary to enforce rights. For example, respecting someone's rights by not violating them may result, as a side effect, in a loss of public funds. However, this does not by itself imply an obligation to spend the same amount of public funds on services to protect that person's rights from being violated by private citizens.

Sob[1] and Extra-utility from Personal Characteristics

We have distinguished between extra utility that stems from the causal properties of personal characteristics of individuals and extra utility that stems directly from our resource. We have considered some justifications for ignoring extra utility stemming from the causal properties, even when we could not save more than one person whatever we did. We noted the unfairness of taking as relevant to distribution characteristics of the person not tied to his ability to benefit (or cause others to benefit) from our resource, the Kantian objection that persons would then be treated as mere means, and the view that there should be "separate spheres" for resources so that we do not have to be concerned with all sorts of goods at once. We also considered the possibility that an element of the subjective view was involved in deciding to ignore utilities, e.g., ignoring some differences because of how important someone's life was to him.

Sob[1] might be used to provide an additional justification for ignoring extra utility produced for others or in the lives of each candidate by the candidates' personal characteristics, though heretofore we have used it to discuss cases where *our* resource produces extra utility. Each of the candidates cares about whether he survives and is not indifferent between himself and another who offers somewhat more utility. If we are concerned with the great interest in, or right to, survival each person has, we will ignore extra utility that is small relative to survival in deciding what to do. Indeed, if Sob[1] tells us to give equal chances even when many lives face one, it might also be used to justify giving equal chances to two candidates even when only one offers a very large additional utility. For each person still cares for the large gain his own survival brings to him, even if the other's survival brings bigger gains overall. This might mean ignoring the fact that one person will live much longer than the others in deciding who are near equal contestants. This is because even though living much longer is not a good from a separate sphere and is the result of direct use of our resource, as well as personal characteristics, it is still true that the fewer years one candidate will have mean so much to him, that the extra years to another are irrelevant according to the reasoning in Sob[1].

Sob[1] and a Utility-maximizing Decision Procedure

Sob[1] need not rule out choosing a decision procedure that will select between Joe and Jim randomly on the grounds that it also maximizes utility. For example, Sob[1] does not rule out using the coin that miraculously causes flowers to grow wherever it falls instead of an ordinary coin. Sob[1] says we must not decide between Joe and Jim because we can save the flowers, but we may choose between decision procedures (that give Joe and Jim equal chances) because of the flowers.

Might we take this a step further and use the extra utility itself—where the flowers are or where the cured throat would be—as a random decision procedure? That is, if there will be, or ever was, an equal chance of the flowers or the sore throat winding up either with Joe or with Jim, might we send the benefit to where the maximum utility lies? Another case: Suppose that at random we assign one of two deathly ill people who enter a hospital to a floor where someone else already has a sore throat, having already decided to send to that floor the scarce medicine that can cure everyone (the Hospital Case). Requiring that we be ignorant of who is (or will be) next to the beneficiary of the extra utility at the time when we choose to maximize utility—what we can call the *ignorance requirement*—as well as the fact that there is a random choice of the person seems to make even this acceptable.[19] It contrasts with our already knowing who is next to the flowers or the sore throat and helping Jim because he is next to them. Choosing one person over another because he is next to the utility is different from wanting the extra utility and therefore making use of it in the process of giving each an equal chance.

A Utilitarian Interpretation of Equal Chances

Nevertheless, the temptation remains to interpret the straightforward utilitarian calculation as providing as much of an equal chance as anyone could want. We could reason in the following way: When Joe complains that he wants his equal chance, the answer to give is that *he has already* had his chance. Nature has already run a random toss, placing Jim rather than Joe beside extra utility. This is a toss whose results we know. Why toss a coin again?

If we do not routinely do what maximizes utility when we already know where the extra utility lies, or even when we do *not* already know where it is when it already lies somewhere, it may be because we are not sure that there was or will be an equal probability of the extra-utility factor being on either side. Our ignorance of what the probabilities actually are or were is not considered sufficient to make for a fair procedure. It is simply that we do not believe that it can truly be said that Nature gave someone an equal chance to be next to someone else who has a sore throat.

Though this may be true, our ignorance, at the time of selecting between people, of who is associated with the extra utility still seems to matter in itself, even if we know equal chances were given. (This condition is satisfied in the Hospital Case.) For only then do we *here and now* select between procedures, and not between people, on the basis of extra utility.

This same explanation seems appropriate when we consider why those behind a veil of ignorance would not decide to select between people on the basis of utility. That is, suppose that such judges were assured that each contestant would have an equal chance of being next to the flowers. They might still refuse to select according to utility on the grounds that at the time of selection it would be desire for the minor utility that determined the choice between Joe and Jim.

Notice, however, that even the recommendation to routinely choose where we know the extra utility lies has still emphasized equal chances at some point. That is, the motive for choosing the extra utility is not achieving the greatest utility *despite* unequal chances, but rather allowing extra utility to decide the issue *because* it signifies equal chances.

Sob¹ and Nonaggregation Again

We have already suggested, in discussing nonaggregation (p. 156), that the reasons given by the first defense of the Principle of Irrelevant Utility exclude our straight-forwardly sending a fatal threat away from five and in a direction where Joe sits, rather than in a direction where Jim *and Nancy* would both be killed. This is so even though the latter is a locus where *two* equally strong interests or claims to life confront Joe's. (Call this the Three Lives Case [1]). This first defense also excludes sending a scarce medicine to an island where Jim and Nancy will be saved, rather than to another island where only Joe will be saved. (Call this Three Lives Case [2]).

I will discuss this issue further using Three Lives Case (1), but details of Three Lives Case (2) could be substituted. A mark of Sob¹ is that each person's concern for the particular outcome in which he wins is given respect to the *very end* in choosing between people. So, when Nancy is added to Jim, Joe may according to Sob¹, legitimately say:

> Why should I give up my equal chance to save her? At most, she should get an equal chance also, given her equal right not to be killed and (approximately) equal interest in life. If I had had to face Nancy alone, a coin should have been tossed, just as when I faced Jim alone. The threat would not have been sent directly to me. In general, you may alter your behavior to me with *additions* to Jim's side only to the extent that you would alter it in virtue of any one of the additions by itself (Principle of Nonaggregation). So all three of us should have equal chances.

But all this also undercuts the initial assumption with which we began this chapter, namely that we may turn the threat away from five toward one. We need not even bother to toss a coin between Joe and the Jim/Nancy combination, for we will have to choose from among *three* policies: whether to let the threat continue toward the *five,* or turn it to Joe, or turn it to Jim and Nancy. If two lives do not outweigh one according to Sob¹, five will not either.²⁰

In Chapter 6,²¹ we considered arguments for the claim that we could take the personal view of each contestant seriously in conflict cases and still save the greater number. If *this* position is compatible with giving the personal view of each all the respect it deserves, it must be because our respecting the personal view of each person does not require us to think of each individual perceiving his opponent(s) as zero(s), and then arranging to give each an equal chance. (Nor does it require giving proportional chances, as would result by summing the separate equal chances each opponent has against the one.) Rather respecting the personal point of view requires us to arrange for individuals to confront those with approximately equal and opposing rights or interests on an individual basis, one by one, in a way which allows for substitution of equivalents. Seeing that this is done involves our permitting the substitution of equivalents at least sometimes and altering our behavior to Joe with additions to Jim's side. This is so even if the way we would treat Joe in relation to any individual addition alone would be no different from the way we would treat Joe in relation to Jim alone.

Suppose counting numbers is correct, and this indicates Sob[1] is incorrect. (I have allowed that there is no conflict between Sob[1] and proportional chances. If proportional chances, not counting numbers were correct, Sob[1] would not be impugned.) Then we must still explain how some lesser utilities are irrelevant and why the substitution of equivalents does not apply quite generally. (For if it did, we should substitute Jim for Joe—getting everything with Jim that we could get with Joe—and add the flowers.)

In the next chapter, we will again consider different accounts of why numbers of lives count, which stem from different explanations we will have to provide of the Principle of Irrelevant Utility.

NOTES

1. For a more detailed discussion of the issue of redirecting harms see *Morality, Mortality,* Vol. II (forthcoming).

2. See, for example, Philippa Foot in "The Problem of Abortion and the Doctrine of Double Effect," reprinted in *Virtues and Vices* (Oxford: Basil Blackwell, 1978); and Judith Thomson in "The Trolley Problem," *Yale Law Journal* 94 (1985). I have argued likewise in "Harming Some to Help Others," and in *Morality, Mortality,* Vol. II.

3. If a person who would help another injures himself, he may make the person he would have helped worse off than he would have been, but he does not harm him in not providing him with aid. However, if I, who am not aiding someone, injure the person who would have aided him, I do harm the potential beneficiary. I harm when I interfere with aid I have no right to control.

4. I owe this last point to Derek Parfit.

5. It has been suggested that if we should ignore the ability of people to contribute to overall good when we are selecting whose life to save with a drug, recognizing that each person has a right to equal consideration, it would be outright inconsistent with this commitment to equality to consider an additional good that can be produced if we redirect a threat or distribute a resource in one way or another. But this seems to be a mistake, since it ignores the differences between the causal role of a contestant and our causal role in providing the resource.

6. Remarks of Ronald Dworkin led me to consider more seriously the distinction between the contestant and tie-breaker role.

7. As described, for example, in James Griffin's *Well Being, Its Meaning, Measurement and Moral Importance* (Oxford: Oxford University Press, 1986). Griffin, I believe, follows

Scanlon, in "Preference and Urgency," *Journal of Philosophy* 72, no. 19 (Nov. 1975): 655–669.

8. See Chapter 5.

9. Derek Parfit drew this distinction.

10. That is, it is an exaggeration to say he cares nothing at all for the survival of others, but it is a useful exaggeration for this argument, I believe. We noted above (in chapter 4) that death of a person need not mean all that he values is gone, but still another's life is not a continuation of his.

11. Notice that this argument has essentially nothing to do with how high a percent chance Joe actually has to win. Even if the people among whom we had to select both had a very small chance of surviving, the argument would be the same. But what if a person's chance of surviving is very small, even if we turn a threat away from him and to flowers growing all *alone*. Suppose we should then save the flowers. If so, then someone with such a small chance of surviving should lose his chance relative to another person with the same small chance to survive who sits next to the flowers. The reason why a very low probability of surviving would lead us to pick flowers over a person must be essentially that, from his own personal point of view, a very low probability of surviving does not have any real value. It is hard to believe we could ever come across such a case.

12. However, might we introduce the idea of a good of *nontransgressable fairness,* which can only be maximally present by treating fairness as a side-constraint? That is, we could *not* maximize this value by transgressing fairness for the sake of minimizing unfairness. For more on this type of move in the area of rights, see *Morality, Mortality,* Vol. II; "Harming Some to Save Others," and "Non Consequentialism, The Person As An End-In-Itself, and the Significance of Status," *Philosophy & Public Affairs* 21 (Fall 1992):354–389.

13. I owe the request for the step-by-step analysis, and some aid in constructing it, to Shelly Kagan.

14. For a criticism of such a theory of rights see *Morality, Mortality,* Vol. II.

15. Lewis Kornhauser and Larry Sager emphasize that the right to an equal chance can stand as proxy for the equal right to a certain treatment itself, in "Just Lotteries," in *Social Science Information* 27 (1988): 483.

16. But recall note 11 and apply it as well to extremely small probabilities of having one's right met.

17. In "Some Ruminations on Rights," *Arizona Law Review* 19 (1977):45–60.

18. As expressed by Ronald Dworkin in *Taking Rights Seriously* (Cambridge, Mass.: Harvard University Press, 1977).

19. The question of the significance of the ignorance requirement was emphasized in discussion of this question by Ronald Dworkin, Jeffrey Gordon, Lewis Kornhauser, and Larry Sager.

20. Again, a proportional chances option, representing a chance for Joe against each individual, may be permitted by Sob[1].

21. And earlier in "Equal Treatment and Equal Chances."

9

Sobjectivity: The Anatomy of the Subjective and Objective in Moral Judgment

Let us now consider the *second approach* to justifying the Principle of Irrelevant Utilities. This approach also involves combining what I have described as the objective and subjective views. I call it Sobjectivism^2, abbreviated Sob^2. Sob^2 differs from Sob^1 in that it pits the various subjective points of view against each other differently, taking into account each person's moral responsibility rather than only his interests or desires.

I

Sobjectivity^2 and Responsibility to Sacrifice

Again, only roughly equal (relevant) rights or interests are contestants. Likewise, flowers are not tie breakers because consideration is given to the claims and interests of each contestant and to the nonindifference of each contestant to who will win the contest. Here the similarity ends. The argument to justify not using minor utility as a tie breaker proceeds differently: Anyone ought to be willing to give up flowers or a cure for a two-week sore throat (or move from a 100 percent to a 50 percent chance of having these) in order to give another person a significant chance at life. Subjectively weighing the certainty of flowers or a cured sore throat higher than someone's significant chance at life is a morally unacceptable personal point of view. That is, it is not an acceptable subjective view from the objective view. Indeed, on Sob^2 to take seriously each of the two contestants' nonindifference to who will win means that we should give up as much to preserve Joe's equal chance to survive as we should give up to save a single person when there is no such conflict. (In fact, we will not be definitely sacrificing flowers or a cured throat. We will merely be risking loss of these to protect equal chances of life.)

A distinction might perhaps be drawn between our risking losses that are worsenings and losses that are failures to be benefited. The first would occur if giving Joe an equal chance led not only to Jim's death but also to the destruction of the flowers. In a Sore Throat Case, worsening might involve Nancy's *getting* a sore throat because of the wind produced in turning a threat toward Jim. A loss that is a failure to be benefited occurs in the Sore Throat Case if we give medicine to Joe and so fail to help Nancy's throat, which is already sore; or in the Flower Case, if money meant for flower saving will be lost if a threat hits Jim, when the money is on him. Both harmings and not benefiting seem permissible costs with which to purchase equal chances. However, refusing Joe an equal chance because we can thereby benefit someone else in a minor way or improve a state of affairs in a minor way (rather than avoid making it worse) seems especially bad.

So far, the *results of* Sob[1] and Sob[2] as defenses of the Principle of Irrelevant Utilities are the same, though the arguments differ.

Larger Additional Utilities

Now suppose we are faced with a choice between turning a threat toward Joe and turning it toward Jim and Jane when Jim's and Joe's lives are at stake but Jane would lose her arm (Arm Case [1]).[1] Jane's arm by itself would not be placed in a contest with Joe's life if we had to choose where to send a threat. This is an objective component in Sobjectivity in general.

According to Sob[1], if something would not be a contestant, it cannot be a tie breaker. The view of Sob[1] is that whenever a pairwise comparison shows that anyone alongside Jim stands to lose significantly less than Joe would, that lesser loss is an irrelevant utility.[2] The reasoning behind this view is, first, that, from Joe's subjective view, if Jim is saved it is almost as bad as if no one (zero) had been saved, which is not an unreasonable personal point of view to have; Joe wants to be the person saved. Second, we would not toss a coin between Joe and a person who stood to lose significantly less than Joe would; we would ignore the lesser loss and save Joe. So from Joe's perspective there is no reason to add Jane and Jim, and no weight should be given to Jane on her own. We see that Jim has a similar point of view on Joe. Therefore, from the impartial view, we should toss a coin between Joe and the pair of Jim and Jane.

Sob[2] makes a different claim. It says that if one has a duty to give up something to save someone's life, one's retaining or getting that thing cannot be a tie breaker between people who otherwise have equal chances for life. If one doesn't have a duty to give up something to save a life, then the loss may be a tie breaker. Suppose a particular equivalence scale of someone's subjective view is permitted by the objective view. Then one would not have a duty to save someone's life at the expense of every loss that the objective view says could not be a contestant with someone's life. For example, Jane would not be duty bound to give up her arm to save someone's life, so she should not have to give it up to give Joe an equal chance to live. This is so even though her arm would not be a contestant. But, Jane risks only a 50 percent chance of losing her arm. Suppose she need not move from a 100 percent to a 50 percent chance of keeping her arm in order to save Joe's life. If this is so, Sob[2] says *we* need not see to it that Joe retains his 50 percent chance vis-à-vis Jim at such expense to Jane. Likewise, we may give a scarce medicine to Jim rather than to Joe if only then will there be enough left over to remove from Jane the 50 percent risk of losing her arm. All this is true even though Jane's arm alone, or the 100 percent rather than 50 percent chance of keeping it, could not be a contestant to Joe's life.

Brief Anatomy of Sob²

Briefly, analysis of Sob² in terms of its progressive subjective and objective components proceeds as follows:[3] A subjective component leads to *individuals* (rather than aggregates) being contestants, an objective component calls for no significant differences in potential losses between contestants, and (possibly) subjective elements added to this allows for those who are *near* equals in only *certain* respects being contestants. This is all shared with Sob¹. Sob², does *not* involve the radically subjective view that because someone is not morally required to give up his arm to save another's life, an arm may stand as a contestant to a life. That is, it does *not* take a permissible subjective weighting of equivalents in someone's personal point of view, which has some role in the existence of a prerogative not to save a life at the expense of one's arm, and use it to guide an outsider's choice in all respects. Rather the claim is that, so long as one of the two people whose lives are at stake will be saved, we may take into account in our third-person decision making that element of someone's morally permissible subjective view, according to which a person's arm is worth more to him than someone else's life. The fact that one person whose life is at stake will be saved no matter what we do will be apparent from the objective point of view—this is the substitution of equivalents—even if someone's subjective view treats the life of another as if it were a zero.

Detailed Anatomy

Let us now go over in greater detail the contrast in the way Sob¹ and Sob² combine elements from the subjective and objective views. Sob¹ requires that contestants be of relatively equal standing and, hence, excludes the possibility that someone who is not in the category of (approximately) worst off might win over those worse off than he. Sob¹ takes seriously Joe's concern for the outcome in which Joe wins, by seeing the outcome in which Jim and Jane win not only from their perspective but also from Joe's. Joe's perspective sees that outcome as almost like one in which no life would be saved. Since an arm alone is no contestant against a life on the objective view, an arm alone should not determine whether Joe loses an equal chance he would have had against Jim.

Sob² also requires contestants of relatively equal standing for the same reason as Sob¹. But it takes a more objective view of the situation in which either Joe or Jim would win, recognizing that a person will be saved regardless of who it is. This means that Jane's arm need no longer be weighed *alone* against Joe's life. For on Sob¹ it was necessary to weigh Jane's arm alone on one side of an objective scale against Joe's life. After all, if Jim were a zero and if Joe's life did not outweigh Jane's arm, we might wind up saving an arm rather than a life by giving them each an equal chance. On Sob¹, Jane's arm would be found inequivalent to Joe's life and, hence, not allowed to count at all. According to Sob², from the objective view (as against Joe's subjective view), when Jim is saved, a life *is* saved. Therefore, there is no threat that if Jane's arm is not weighed alone, by itself, on one side of an objective scale—and outweighed by Joe's life—we might save the arm instead of any life.

But Joe's and Jim's subjective concern as to who lives is also still taken account of by Sob^2. It is joined with the value to Jane of her arm relative to someone else's life, as weighed on her permissible subjective scale. This joining, however, does *not* occur by giving Jane's arm an equal chance with Joe's life if this means that because Jane is on Jim's side the outcome would not alter from equal chances for Joe and Jim. (Nor does it mean that it is joined by giving it an equal chance against Joe's life, which equal chance is summed with Jim's to give them a two-thirds chance to win.) Rather, joining the subjective value to each of Joe and Jim of his winning with the subjective value to Jane of her arm relative to someone else's life occurs as follows: Take it as a given that a maximum of one life would be saved no matter what we do (an objective-view factor). Then *we* (as the agents who must turn the threat or give the benefit) should identify with the personal perspective Jane would take if *she* were acting as agent instead of us and were taking seriously the potential victims' views of any outcome. If she took seriously the nonindifference of each potential victim to the outcome, she would do—at least according to Sob^2—as much to give each of them an equal chance as she would do to save a single life. But she need not do more. Therefore, this is how much of a loss *we* as agents should impose on her and not more. We therefore do not impose the 50 percent chance of losing an arm to give Joe a chance at life.

A possible alternative,[4] is to give a greater proportional chance to Jane and Jim. It may be that when the additional utility at stake is only an arm this would be the correct solution. Then only a great additional loss, e.g., Jane's paralysis, would be large enough to cost Joe his equal chance. (Still, even there the paralysis need not be large enough to identify Jane as a contestant in herself against Joe.) Notice that there was an interpretation of Sob^1 that allowed proportional chances to several contestants. Sob^2 might allow such chances to a contestant accompanied by extra utility in another person. I shall return to this suggestion.

Sob^2 and the Principle of Irrelevant Utilities

Sob^2 gives far less scope to the Principle of Irrelevant Utilities than does Sob^1. That is, fewer extra utilities will be irrelevant. Note that Sob^2 is supposed to be a view that even Joe himself could endorse; for example, he understands the moral acceptability of turning the threat away from, or directing a benefit to, Jim and Jane because of Jane's arm. This is true even though he would object on moral grounds to turning the threat away from, or directing a benefit to, Jim and the flowers because of the flowers.

If Sob^2 has this result in the Arm Case, it will recommend turning a threat away from five people toward Joe rather than toward Jim and Jane. Of course, the reasoning that would justify turning the threat toward *anyone* to save a greater number is not encompassed by Sob^2, strictly speaking. The reasoning needed to justify harming some to save a greater number involves more than merely showing that numbers count. (I will not discuss it here.)[5] Nevertheless, that the numbers count plays some role, and Sob^2 describes this role as follows: Whichever way the threat goes, at least one life will be saved. Jane or the five original potential victims are not obliged to take a big chance of losing a great deal in order to save Joe's life and so are not obliged to take that chance to give him a *chance* of living. We should decide on this basis.

Limits on Sob²

One limit on Sob² is its role in cases involving rights, e.g., property entitlements or rights to equal treatment rather than merely interests. Suppose only Joe and Jim have purchased portions of a lifesaving drug that is then underproduced. The fact that Jane's arm could also be saved if we gave Jim the portion of the drug we do have, should not make us deprive Joe of his equal chance. (The reasoning here is the same as given in Chapter 8, p. 159.) A second limit concerns fairness. If Jane's arm will be saved because Jim is a doctor who will cure her of a disease, there would be unfairness in depriving Joe of his equal 50 percent chance, in favor of Jim. This is because we would then be selecting between him and Jim on the basis of Jim's personal capacity to save Jane from a threat not directly related to her need for the item *we* have to distribute.

Sob² and Extra Utility from Personal Characteristics

Sob² at least suggests that if one person can produce more utility for himself than another can directly through the use of the drug we have to distribute, these extra utilities might be relevant in deciding who receives the drug and who are the (near) equal contestants for it. For example, if one person will live longer than another and would not have a duty to risk losing such an additional life span just to provide another with an equal chance to survive, we should not give the other person an equal chance. The substitution of equivalents applies as well when we are given a choice between certainly saving one person or having a 20 percent chance of saving another person: we get a 20 percent chance of saving someone no matter what we do, plus we get 80 percent more if we certainly save someone. We must then check to see whether the loss of the certainty of the additional 80 percent chance is too much to lose for the sake of giving the 20-percent person his chance.

We should not necessarily accept this view, first, because Sob² may not be correct, and, second, because even if it is correct when the extra utility is at stake for noncontestant, it may not be correct when the extra utility is at stake for a contestants himself. That is, a *distributed* extra utility may be treated differently from a concentrated extra utility.

II

Problems with Sob²

What are the problems with Sob²? One problem is that Jane would probably think herself justified in not risking as much to give Joe a 50 percent chance of life as she would risk to save a life when no one at all would otherwise live. This is because in our cases one life will be saved no matter what she does. This is a problem since it denies the equivalence of giving Joe his chance and saving a life when no one would otherwise live, though Sob^2 treats them as equal. (Jane would probably also think it permissible to do even less as the absolute value of the chance of life went down.)

A related problem with Sob^2 is that contrary to what it predicts there are losses large enough so that Jane is not obligated to deliberately suffer them in order to give Joe an equal chance at life, yet *we,* as third parties, *should* allow her to suffer them as a consequence of *our* giving Jim and Joe an equal chance at life. Hence, what *we* should do cannot be read off directly from what Jane has an obligation to do. Indeed, there are two points embedded here. First, suppose that Jane need not give up her arm, or even risk a 50 percent chance of losing it, in order to save a life. As third parties, we should nevertheless save a single life (not in conflict with other lives) even if this means that Jane will lose an arm. Second, when Jane's *finger* is at stake along with Jim's life, and we have a choice between saving Joe and saving Jim, we should give Joe his chance, even if this means that Jane loses a finger. We should do this even if this is a finger she would not be obligated to give up, or incur a large risk of losing, in order to save a life, let alone in order to give someone an equal chance to be saved when someone will be saved no matter what she does.

A Third Alternative: Sobjectivity^3

This means that we must provide an alternative principled distinction between losses if we are to distinguish the relevant from the irrelevant utilities. We cannot distinguish between a sore throat (irrelevant) and an arm (relevant) on the ground that someone is morally obligated to choose to suffer one and not the other. For one is not obligated to choose to suffer the loss of a finger to give an equal chance at life, yet an outsider may tolerate that loss to give an equal chance. What other principles might be suggested? Is a loss relevant if it is large enough so that, by *itself,* we would give it some proportional chance in a conflict with a life?^{6} Not if we would not give an arm even a proportional chance on its own, yet it is determinative against Joe's having an equal 50 percent chance when Jim will survive.

An elaboration on this proposal, however, might be supported by a somewhat different intuition about cases, which I find plausible: certain utilities would be irrelevant in a choice situation if they would receive no proportional weight on their own, no matter how many individuals suffered their loss, against loss of a life. For example, no matter how many individuals had sore throats, the aggregate would never weigh against saving one life. Utilities would be relevant in a choice situation in the sense of making the side to which they are added deserve a greater proportional chance of winning, if, even though they had no weight on their own in *one* individual when counted against saving a life, their aggregation could have proportional weight against saving a life in some choice situations. An arm might be such a utility, but, on this proposal, an arm should not *determine* the choice between Jim and Joe, even if Jane is not obligated to give up the arm to provide Joe with an equal chance. Her arm can only give Jim a greater proportional chance of winning. Finally, an extra utility should be *determinative* of our choice, when it is conjoined with Jim's life, against another life, if that utility on its own merits a proportional chance against a life when the choice is about whom to aid. (None of this is intended to apply when we must choose whom to harm.) So, for example, preventing complete paralysis might be such a utility when matched against saving a life.[7]

Recall, further, a point we noted in Chapter 6 (p. 103). That is, as we increase the number of lives at stake on both sides (e.g., 1000 in conflict with 1000), and thereby increase the number of people for whom an equal chance at life itself is at stake, the size of the lost extra utility that is irrelevant, at least to complete determination of choice, seems to increase, even up to a life. This seems to be true even though one would not be obliged to choose to suffer a 50 percent chance of such a loss in order to give a 50 percent chance of survival to the 1000.

Therefore, in addition to Sob[1] and Sob[2], we have now described a third proposal, *Sobjectivity³* (Sob[3]). Consider it again for the Arm Case. Against a background in which (only) one of Joe and Jim will live no matter what we do, we show too little concern for Joe's having an equal chance at life, if we value his chance less than flowers or less than a third party's sore throat. Again, it should be emphasized that we would not be showing unfairness to Joe in electing to save Jim because Jane's sore throat is near him and can be cured by what we are distributing to Jim, but we would be showing insufficient concern for what Joe's chance to live means to him. However, we show too much concern for his equal chance if we favor it outright over the 50 percent chance of Jane's losing an arm. (This is true even though, by itself, a 50 percent chance of losing an arm is not as bad as a 50 percent chance of losing one's life.) Let us consider what, phenomenologically, seems to happen as we think about the Arm Case: We consider what Jane stands to lose and what Joe stands to lose (including the probabilities of loss). Jane's loss of an arm retains its significance for us against the background fact that (only) one of Joe and Jim will be saved no matter what we do. The fact that from Joe's subjective view it is not as good if that one person saved is Jim loses its *saliency* at least to some degree. We are, in a sense, siding with the greater value Jane's permitted subjective view gives to her arm than to Joe's chance at life, though not entirely if we only give Jim and Jane a higher chance of winning. By contrast, in the Flower Case, the fact that only one of Joe and Jim will be saved no matter what we do does *not* cause Joe's subjective concern that he survive to lose its saliency.

It is important to emphasize that the *saliency test* does not provide any principle for selection. That is, it reports a psychological phenomenon. I have tried to describe the set of criteria that elicit this response to different degrees (above), related to size of extra utility lost, weight of loss on its own or aggregated, number of people who would want an equal chance, and whether what results is proportional or determinative weight.

Showing Appropriate Concern

Suppose that what was at stake for Joe and Jim was not mere death, but burning in hell for all eternity. Then concern for Jane's possible loss of an arm would, I believe, lose its salience entirely. (This is true even if Jane would not be obliged to risk the loss to save someone from hell when otherwise no one would then go to hell, let alone to give someone a chance of avoiding hell when someone will go anyway.) We would be concerned to give Joe an equal chance with Jim to escape that hell. That is, the contestants' subjective view of the outcome in which one rather than the other wins becomes salient again. So we shift between, on the one hand, an impartial and, on the other hand, a preferred view of the survival of one of the two men, depending on the possible losses to Joe and Jim and the possible losses to Jane. Sometimes Jane's possible loss is salient against a background in which one of the men will survive no matter what is done. Sometimes, Joe or Jim's loss is salient. When we ignore the flowers or the sore throat relative to Joe's chance for life, we are saying that we would show insufficient concern for Joe if we did not. When we side with Jane's arm, we are saying that we would show insufficient concern for Jane's arm if we ignored the fact that one person will live anyway; we would not be showing insufficient concern for Joe's equal desire to live if it were overridden at least in part by the risk of the lost arm, given that one person will live anyway. In all this, we never merely do an objective calculation of Jim and Jane's loss.

Sob^3 discounts Joe's subjective concern for a chance and often considers the objective fact that only one life will be saved no matter what we do. The chance to live is not always treated as equivalent to saving a life when otherwise no one would live. Sob^3 takes seriously Jane's permitted *subjective* weighting of the loss of her arm versus Jim's chance at life, although unlike Sob^2 it does not automatically make salient any loss she need not choose to suffer for the sake of saving a life or giving a chance at life.

Harm versus Not Aiding

How great Jane's loss must be to be at all salient relative to Joe's chance for life may also depend on whether we are to direct a trolley to Jim and her, thereby causing her a loss, or whether we are deciding to give a medicine that will prevent her loss. It will take a smaller loss to achieve saliency in the harming than in the aiding case, I believe.

Aggregation of Lives

Let us return to a choice between saving one life and saving several other lives. We could argue on the basis of Sob^3 as follows: Given that we will save at least one person no matter what we do, we would show insufficient concern for the additional persons on one side if we toss a coin between them and Joe. To do so would balance the 50 percent chance that they will lose their lives against Joe's equal chance to survive, giving his concern too much weight. Taking seriously what the others can lose and the probability of loss deprives Joe's desire to survive of its saliency. We then allow ourselves to substitute equivalents, balancing the equal and opposite interests in life of those on each side, allowing the individuals remaining to determine the outcome. With each additional person added to the more numerous side, the problem with tossing a coin increases. That is, there is aggregation. To repeat, from the impartial view, Joe's subjective preference to be the one who survives loses saliency against the background that in any case at least one will be saved and other lives are at stake also. The loss of an additional life is determinative, in keeping with the fact that it would merit a full 50% chance if it were alone confronting Joe; it does not merely give its side a greater proportional chance,

Saving Both Lives

It is very important to emphasize that the conclusion that we should not require Jane to suffer a 50 percent chance of loss of an arm, though perhaps a 30% chance, so that Joe and Jim can have an equal chance to live applies to cases in which either Joe or Jim can survive but *not* both. Suppose we could provide a 50 percent chance of *both* surviving, instead of a 50 percent chance for each to survive when the other does not. Then it might be correct for us to tolerate a 50 percent chance that Jane will lose her arm. (Notice that this claim is stronger than the claim that we should tolerate Jane's loss for the 50 percent chance of saving both Joe and Jim when the other option is that *both* will die.) The expected utility is the same whether there is a 50 percent chance that both survive or that one of two survives alone; that is $2 \times .5 = 1$ and $1 \times .5 + 1 \times .5 = 1$. Yet the 50% chance of loss of Jane's arm should be tolerated in order to give both the chance to live, even if it should not be tolerated when only one of the two can be saved no matter what we do. This is true even though *both* Joe and Jim may well die in the first case and even if Jane's loss would certainly occur whether both survive or both die.

Sob³ and the Ideal Procedure

This bears on the question of how Sob³ compares with the Ideal Procedure described in Chapter 7. Suppose that reducing the chance of saving someone from 100 percent to 50 percent offered a significant chance of saving both lives. The Ideal Procedure dictates that we do this. It would also allow us to forgo saving Jane her loss of an arm. (For example, suppose we could swim in the middle between two islands and could reach out to both Joe and Jim, who are on opposite islands, but not reach far enough to Jane, who sits next to Jim.)

   This conclusion is arrived at by (1) considering that we are permitted to have each of Joe and Jim reduce the chance of the other's being saved by 50 percent in order that he himself have that chance to be saved, and (2) giving no weight at all to the saving of Jane's arm when it is possible (to the permitted degree) to save both lives. The life and the arm should at least have a higher chance to be saved rather than give Joe his chance if it is not possible to save both lives. But Jane's arm alongside Jim does not diminish the permissible influence Joe himself can have in reducing Jim's chances if both have a chance to be saved. Here we treat the arm as we would treat it if we could certainly save one life, though the side effect of this was that we were unable to help Jane keep an arm.

   Again, I emphasize that the expected utility of using a procedure that had a 50 percent chance of saving Joe and Jim ($2 \times .5 = 1$) is the same as the expected utility of tossing a coin ($1 \times .5 + 1 \times .5 = 1$). The latter procedure would assure a life *and* possibly an arm; the former would assure nothing. Still the Ideal Procedure condones using the former rather than the latter, given a choice. The motive for this that we identified in Chapter 7 seems to be best expressed as solidarity, or perhaps equality of results.[8] Therefore, the Ideal Procedure is in no conflict with Sob³ since reducing Jim's chances by 50 percent to get a 50 percent chance of both surviving does not show either too much concern for Joe or too little concern for Jim and also Jane's arm.

Purchasing Less Than a Proportional Chance

If Jane's arm were not at stake as well, could we also reduce Jim's certainty of being saved by up to 50 percent if it gave Joe a 50 percent chance of being the *one* who we will save when only one can be saved? The Ideal Procedure does not, strictly, speak to this case. Since it was introduced against a background in which we first (tried to) justify the majority being saved if there were irreducible conflict, we argued that those who received a chance by reducing the majority's chances should not survive when the majority doesn't. But in a case where only one person begins with the certainty of being saved, there is no reason for him—as there was thought to be for the majority—to survive over the other one. Therefore, we might reduce the chances of the one by 50 percent to get 50 percent for the other one, even if only one will survive. Here there is no change in expected utility and no change in actual outcome.

Another problem arises when the significant chance purchased by reducing Jim's chance by Joe's proportional weight is less than Joe's proportional chance. In one scenario, we may go from a 100 percent to a 50 percent chance of saving Jim, but have only a 30 percent chance of saving Joe and Jim together. Of course we also lose out on saving Jane's arm (or cause her to lose her arm as the case may be). In a second scenario, which crucially does not retain the idea that we may save both lives, we may go from a 100 percent to a 50 percent chance of saving Jim to give Joe only a 30 percent chance to be saved if we do not save Jim. Jane's arm is lost as well. (For example, if Joe wins a toss of a coin, we must use a procedure to save him that is less than assured of success.) In these cases, expected utility is lower than if we certainly saved one, let alone one with an arm. Must we truly allow Joe to reduce the chances of saving one person by a great deal in order to purchase smaller and smaller—but still significant—chances of his own survival?

If the reason we allow Joe to reduce Jim's chances and endanger Jane's arm were a *right* that he has to do so, then it seems that any significant purchase would be enough. For example, suppose six of us are deciding to which restaurant to go. Five of us want meat; I want vegetarian. My one-sixth weight may rightfully have the power to cause a switch of restaurants, which results in a drop in the satisfaction of each of the five unmatched by my happiness rising to its proportional value. That is, I get very bad vegetarian cuisine, and they get pretty bad meat when they could have gotten superb meat while I would have had nothing at all. Yet this could be the morally correct choice if we think that I truly have a right to veto power in virtue of my being worse off if we go to one restaurant than the five will be if we go to another. But if the reason we reduce Jim's chance is the value of solidarity (or equality), rather than any basic right on Joe's part, then perhaps we have more leeway in considering how much we are willing to pay in the lower expected utility of saving life to get it. This could be true even at the expense of greater equality of results, since equality may be increased if the worst off has something at a very large cost to others, and though they would still be better off than he with the cost, we should not cause it. (Some may even attach a lower value to the same expected utility when it deprives us of the certainty of saving someone. For them, solidarity or equality has an even higher price attached to it, even if expected utility remains the same or even goes up.)

Solidarity or equality is a value in the case where both lives may be saved. It does not arise in the case where we can only save one person. Here we must consider that, from the objective view, when Jim is given a 100 percent chance, we get everything we would get if Jim were given a 50 percent chance of being the one to survive and Joe is given a 30 percent chance. But, in addition, we get a 20 percent extra chance of saving a life. Is the price of sacrificing this 20 percent too great? Does expending it show more concern for Joe's having his 30 percent chance than is appropriate, given the background fact that we could actually save one life otherwise? I suggest it does. (If we add Jane's arm next to Jim's life, of course, even giving Joe a 50 percent chance is ruled out by Sob^3.)

Sob^3 and Extra Utility from Personal Characteristics

If applied to the extra utility that can come to one person herself rather than to another, through her personal characteristics and the direct use of our resource, Sob^3 suggests that even when what both persons stand to gain is very significant, extra utility might be salient. If so, we should give one individual a higher proportional chance or give the resource to her outright. Such extra utilities would then be relevant in deciding who were near-equal contestants, at least if Sob^3 may be extended for this use, when the extra-utility is concentrated in one person. (Keep in mind that it may not be correct to extend it in this way.) However, in keeping with the distinction between Sob^2 and Sob^3, not just any good which is such that one party need not sacrifice it so another may have an equal chance for life will be salient and relevant.

Sob^3 and the Aggregation of Smaller Losses on an Objective Aggregative Scale

There is another way of understanding the reasoning in Sob^3. This approach is of significance, I believe, in answering the general question of whether and when the aggregation of smaller harms to many can outweigh greater harm to a few.

I have said that, in the Arm Case, Sob^3 takes seriously the subjective value to Jane of her arm and its equivalence on the scale of value of her personal point of view to Joe's life (at least as employed in decisions about whom she should aid). This does not mean that, in general, Sob^3 takes Jane's objectively sanctioned subjective view as its own. For Jane may, perhaps, permissibly refuse to give up a finger (or perhaps even refuse to do something that has a 50 percent chance of costing her a finger) to save a person's life. She need not risk such a loss when someone would be saved whether she did it or not, merely to give an equal chance of living to someone. Yet, according to Sob^3, *we* may do what will give Joe and Jim an equal chance for life even when it risks Jane's finger. That is, we take Joe's permissible personal view more seriously than Jane's, even in combination with the objective fact that someone will live no matter what she suffers. (As noted above, we might be more likely to do this when we risk not saving Jane's finger than when we would risk harming it.)

As described above, because Sob^3 takes Jane's subjective view seriously, it does not weigh her arm *alone* on one side of an *objective scale of equivalents* against Joe's life. This objective scale weighs individual (nonaggregated) items that are equivalents against Joe's life. If her arm were put there, Joe's life would win. (Sob^1 makes use of this fact. That is, from Joe's subjective view, Jim's being saved counts almost as a zero and Jane's arm would not be large enough on its own to determine an outcome unfavorable to Joe.) Interestingly enough, *not* putting Jane's life *alone* on one side of the objective scale amounts to placing it on an *objective aggregative scale*. It means counting the arm not as a possible objective equivalent to Joe's life, but simply as the arm it is, placing it on an objective scale that allows for aggregation of losses across people. That is, it means counting it along with Jim's life against Joe's. On this objective aggregative scale, we see that Jim's life and Jane's arm should together have a greater chance to be saved. (Jim's life and Jane's total paralysis should win outright according to Sob^3.)

In sum, the analysis I have given of Sob^3 also suggests the following: Suppose an individual will lose something that is greater than he should be asked to give up to save someone's life. That is, on the person's own objectively permitted subjective view, it (or the chance of saving it) is equivalent to, or worth more than, saving another's life, or a 50 percent chance of saving another's life, especially when someone will be saved anyway. *Also* suppose the loss is salient *to us,* in comparison to the loss of a life and the 50 percent chance of avoiding it, when only one person will live no matter what. Then (and only then) we shift that lesser loss to an objective scale where it carries its objective weight. One implication of Sob^3 is that if an arm stands alone against a life, we send a threat toward the arm since the arm is less weighty than the life. We also assign a higher probability of sending a threat toward one life rather than one life and an arm, having aggregated the arm and the life (the reasons for such aggregation being the interplay between subjective and objective views we have been discussing). This aggregation *can* override saving a life or giving equal chances. However, according to Sob^3, we do not aggregate arms on the objective scale until there are as many people on one side of the scale who stand to suffer a greater loss as there are people on the other side of the scale who stand to suffer (approximately) the same greater loss, for example, life.

Sob^3, therefore, allows us to judge that "the situation has got worse when an arm and a life would be lost than it was when a life alone would be lost," in a sense that allows the worse state to outweigh to some degree the less bad state.

The Coincidence of a Permitted Subjective View and an Objective Aggregative View

Suppose Jane refuses to risk losing her finger to give Joe a chance at life equal to Jim's, because the certainty of keeping her finger has more objectively permissible subjective worth (to her) than does Joe's equal chance for life. Then her decision coincides with a *simple objective* evaluation of the outcome. That is, one person will live no matter what she does *and* her finger will be all right if Jim lives. This is objectively better than if just one person is saved. She acts as if she had placed her finger on an objective aggregative scale. By contrast, when *we* allow her to stand the loss of her finger to give Joe his equal chance, we give more weight to Joe's concern for an equal chance for life (which concern stems from his morally permissible subjective view) than to her concern for her finger. We do this because we think that a chance for life is more important than the risk of losing a finger; the risk of her loss is not salient to us. Notice that we take this to be an evaluation from the same impartial view, a view from outside any person's subjective perspective that, however, takes seriously the subjective views of individuals. This is so even though, in showing concern for Joe's personal perspective, we have decided against a *simple* objective evaluation of the outcome that involves putting all items on the objective aggregative scale. We are impartial but not simply objective. Therefore, *we* refuse simply to count Jane's finger alongside Jim's life on an objective scale of evaluation of outcomes in deciding what to do.

Nonaggregation

Suppose an individual would lose something if we saved someone else's life, or gave someone else an equal chance at life, but it is something any individual ought to give up to save a life or to give an equal chance at life. *Or* suppose an individual would lose something not large enough to be salient to *us* in comparison with the chance for life that is at stake for someone else. (All things selected by the second criterion should include all things selected by the first.) According to Sob³, *we* as third parties may overlook the loss and either save the life or give it a chance. Then may we do this no matter how many other individuals will, as a side effect, also lose such a thing if we save the life in question? One suggestion is that such a sacrifice by each individual is *not* lifted onto an objective aggregative scale for any sort of weighing against the saving or provision of equal chances. This is true so long as the sacrifice is not salient to third parties in comparison to the value of a chance for life.

In sum, there is no aggregation across individuals of a sacrifice that each of them as individuals should be wiling to suffer *or* that is not salient to third parties against the provision of a chance for life—that is, no aggregation that would cause us not to give equal chances to such as Joe and Jim. (There is another form of aggregation we shall discuss below.) Note that any lesser loss that is not lifted onto an objective aggregative scale to be weighed against a *particular* larger loss could be lifted onto the scale to be weighed against a *different* larger loss. So, small headaches to many people do not aggregate against Joe's chance for life, but they may aggregate against Joe's chance to avoid a sprained ankle.

An Alternative View on Aggregation

There is an alternative view, however. It is that aggregation, leading us to give up on equal chances for Joe and Jim, is possible even if the losses are any given individual's duty or are nonsalient to third parties. It is hard to explain how this could be so. So long as we consider the lesser loss to each individual loser, and especially of each in isolation, the fact that in aggregate a great cost is being incurred to give an equal chance at life seems irrelevant. On the other hand, it is possible to simultaneously view each individual as someone who, for example, has a duty as an individual to suffer a loss so that another may get an equal chance at life *and* as a member of a society concerned with how much of the efforts and resources of its members[3] in total are spent on any course of action. From the latter perspective, the aggregation even of individual dutiful efforts and nonsalient losses may be possible. Here the society is identified with, and treated as though it were, an individual in whom losses aggregate.

Furthermore, there is another possible reason to aggregate such lesser losses, independent of social costs. There may be a strong concern with the *radius* of any given person's impact on others, independent of how strong an impact this is on each. That is, the fact that *many* people have lives which are affected by how we treat one person may be a strong negative factor. (In some cases, it would be better if a smaller group were more strongly affected. This is not to deny that there is also something to be said for dispersing a burden.)

We shall return to the idea of costs and how and when they are judged to limit the giving of equal chances. Here we note only that the type of aggregation of dutiful *or* nonsalient lesser losses we are here considering is meant to occur only after everyone who is worse off on one side already has his (near equal) match on the other side. The possible permissibility of aggregating nonsalient losses would imply that we should turn a trolley toward Joe (or give him less than a 50 percent chance of this not happening) rather than toward Jim, when Jim is accompanied by several hundred people who will each lose a finger. It would also imply that we should give the medicine to save Jim and several hundred people who each stand to lose a finger. (Some losses may be too low to aggregate even when many people suffer them, for example, sore throats. This makes them the pure form of irrelevant utility.)

Nonoutweighing Aggregation

If we reject this alternative view which permits aggregation of dutiful or nonsalient losses, it still remains open to us to aggregate such losses in a nonoutweighing sense. That is, we can still say that the situation is getting worse and worse as more and more individuals suffer these relatively small losses while we give equal chances for life, even though this worse situation does not outweigh the correctness of giving equal chances to Joe and Jim. This is true even though there is no one person for whom the situation is getting any worse than it already is for someone else. That is, though this situation would be worse for each new victim than it would otherwise have been for *him,* his situation is not worse than that of each person who already stood to lose his life or of each person who already also faced the lesser loss.

Sob[3] also allows us to say that as the number of people who lose an arm or become paralyzed increases, in addition to the one who would lose his life, we also think that the situation gets worse and worse, at the very least in the *nonoutweighing* sense described above.

Outweighing Aggregation

There is a further move, not necessarily a part of the reasoning behind Sob³, but stimulated by it. As the number of people on Jim's side who will lose a single arm increases, the situation gets worse and worse in the *outweighing* sense. That is, there is more and more reason to send the threat to, or the benefit away from, Joe. (This means reducing the chance of Joe's surviving further.) In addition, if it is wrong that Jane be totally paralyzed as a consequence of our effort to give Joe an equal chance, it will be a second wrong for someone else on Jim's side to suffer the same loss for the same reason. Furthermore, this second wrong will occur, in a sense, not only in addition to the first wrong, but because of it. This is because there was enough reason in the first wrong to make us direct a harm toward, or benefit away from, Joe. If we failed to act appropriately, the other wrong comes about on account of our failure. We originally had sufficient reason; now we have more than sufficient reason.

This reasoning goes beyond aggregation of one minimum tie breaker and one life. It aggregates across individuals all the losses that each individual need not have chosen to suffer to give a chance at life *and* that are salient to us in comparison to the larger loss. We can call these the *significant lesser losses*.

NOTES

1. This case, a crucial corrective to theorizing only with the Flower Case, was suggested to me by Derek Parfit.
2. Assuming that the loss to many people of their individual arms does not amount to a qualitatively new type of loss, e.g., the collapse of society.
3. Again Shelly Kagan helped in sorting out my intuitive moves as originally described in "The Choice Between People, Commonsense Morality, and Doctors."
4. Emphasized to me by Seana Shiffrin.
5. See *Morality, Mortality*, Vol. II, and "Harming Some to Save Others."
6. Suggested by Samuel Scheffler.
7. An alternative is that (1) an arm is sufficiently large a loss to give a greater proportional chance in conjunction with a life, but would not by itself even in aggregate get a proportional chance against a life in deciding whom to aid, and (2) several cases of total paralysis in aggregate should get a proportional chance against a life in deciding whom to aid, and one case is determinative in conjunction with a life, against one life. For more on the significance of the harm/not aid in this context, see pp. 182–183. I believe the need to move from Sob² to Sob³ may also bear on the adequacy of certain contractualist moral theories. For more on this see Chapters 10 and 14.
8. Derek Parfit suggests that the value in these cases is equality—we think it is bad that some should be saved and not others—not solidarity, which cannot, in any case, be at stake where people are strangers. I believe, however, that solidarity can be felt in virtue of simple humanity, feeling solidarity with others just as persons. And my sense is that, if our concern were with equality, we would demand more of a sacrifice than we do. But it may be true that we are just not willing to pay too high a price for equality.

10

Sobjectivity: Aggregation and Scales of Equivalents and Cost

Sob^1, Sob^2, and Sob^3 all require that only relatively equal interests be contestants for a good. For reasons grounded in a mixture of objective and subjective views, Sob^3 tells us to aggregate one life plus one arm (or other such lesser significant loss) for a greater proportional chance (or outright selection). (This all assumes there is no conflict with fairness. That is, we would not necessarily side with Jim's life and Jane's paralysis if Jane's paralysis would be prevented because Jim was a doctor who would cure a disease of Jane's. It also assumes that the scarce resource needed by Jim and Jane does not belong to Joe himself and is not something to which he and Jim have a conflicting property right, or a strict right to be treated in some way if the other is so treated. With respect to the latter right, the assumption is made that it is still better to have equal chances for one party or the other to get the good even if both can not have it.) It also seems consistent with, though not directly derivable from, Sob^3 that we should aggregate any number of additional significant losses that would occur on Jim's side. So there may be increasing reason to send the threat to, or benefit away from, Joe; that is, there may be increasing reason to override Joe's right to an equal chance.

I

Sobjectivity^4: Always Aggregating Significant Lesser Losses

Sob^4 is a further move in the direction of aggregation. Considering this view will also lead us to put into perspective the claim (made above) that an objective component of sobjectivity requires that equals or near equals alone be contestants. Sob^4 takes its cue from the claim, made in connection with Sob^3, that many arms may be aggregated to yield increased outweighing force. If we weighed one arm alone against one life on an objective sale, Sob^4, like Sob^1, Sob^2, and Sob^3, would recommend sending a threat to, or a benefit away from, the arm rather than the life. Sob^4, however, is unlike Sob^1, Sob^2, and Sob^3 in that it *always* aggregates across individuals any significant lesser losses (as already defined) that someone would suffer in situations where one would be saved no matter what we do. Crucially, losses of this *type* are aggregated even if it is not true that the same number of lives would be saved no matter what we did. (Sob^4 does not aggregate all losses that are merely larger than those someone would be duty bound to choose in order to save

180

someone else's life. For example, fingers are not aggregated when a life is at stake.) This aggregative sum across individuals has *certain* capacities to outweigh a larger loss to an individual (or to fewer individuals).

Consider one way in which *always* aggregating *significant lesser losses* for outweighing purposes goes beyond what Sob^3 allows. In Sob^3, an arm is lifted onto the objective scale for aggregation only once we are sure that the benefit of life will also go to one of the worst-off persons. That is, only if the person who would lose the arm is accompanied by someone who would lose his life will the arm be aggregated against Joe's life. Sob^4, by contrast, aggregates for outweighing purposes (giving a greater proportional chance or possibly complete outweighing) regardless of whether the worst-off person will be benefited.

Objective Scale of Costs Versus Objective Scale of Equivalents

To what scale does Sob^4 lift these larger losses for aggregation? It is an objective scale, but in the absence of someone on the side where aggregation of lesser losses occurs who is (nearly) as badly off as the worst-off person on the other side, it cannot, I believe, be called an objective scale of *equivalents*. It is, rather, an *objective scale of costs*. These costs can outweigh weightier losses faced by fewer people on the other side. Let me explain.

Suppose, contrary to what I have just suggested, that Sob^4 aggregated on a new objective scale of equivalents that allowed for *composite contestants* (made of several components). Also, suppose that enough people suffered what I call a salient loss (that is, a significant lesser loss). Then a type of loss that in some circumstances would only be a tie breaker or increase chances could, in other circumstances, be composed into a composite contestant against someone's life. That is, suppose we had to choose between sending a threat to Joe's life and sending a threat to twenty people who would each lose only an arm. It would then be possible that we would send the threat to Joe. This would violate the requirement that a person facing the worst loss be looked after first, with lesser losses only (possibly) being tie breakers or increasing chance when accompanied by the greater loss. It would also yield a different understanding of the objective view, one that did not lead to impartiality as described in Chapter 8. This is because the requirement that only relatively equal *individual* interests be contestants would be met only when one contestant could win on either side. When more than one could win on at least one side, the objective view would allow an aggregation of significant individual losses to constitute a group contestant. To win, the aggregate would have to be relatively equal to the other contestant (individual or aggregative).

I do not believe that Sob^4 raises the significant lesser losses to the level of equivalents. This is because I do not believe that commonsense morality would, in fact, endorse sending a threat or giving a greater chance of sending a threat toward Joe who would be killed rather than toward any number of people who would each lose an arm, if we had to send a threat somewhere. (For example, suppose we are partly in control of some already existing threat, such as a runaway trolley, and must now decide whether to direct this threat so that it kills one person or causes any number to each lose an arm.)[1] Likewise, if a threat were already headed toward any number of people who would each lose an arm, it would be wrong to turn the threat toward the one person who would be killed. This contrasts with the permissibility of turning a threat away from five people who would be killed and toward one who will be killed.

It is interesting to note that increased *probability* of a significant lesser loss and increased *extent* (number of people suffering it) of a significant lesser loss seem to function differently. We would not turn the threat toward one who would be killed rather than toward any number who would each lose an arm. Yet, we might turn the threat toward one who stood a very low chance of being killed rather than toward many others each of whom stood a high chance of suffering a significant lesser loss.

Sob[1], Sob[2], and Sob[3] are, in this respect, correct, I believe. There must be someone (or several people) on the side to which we do not send the threat who stands to lose approximately as much as the person (or several people) on the side to which we do send the threat before aggregation of significant lesser losses increases our reason for sending the threat as we do. Only when that condition is met can the aggregated significant lesser losses make one side truly more than equivalent to the other. (Note that I have discussed the distribution of threats, not benefits, in making this point. We shall discuss benefits below.)

Objective Scale of Costs

Yet, I believe that aggregation can take place on some other objective scale when there is no real equivalence to begin with. One suggestion is that once someone's objectively permitted subjective scale of equivalents equates a lesser loss to her with a greater loss to someone else, her loss is *always* elevated onto an objective scale of *costs*. Here the significant lesser loss is given its value from the objective view and aggregated along with the objective value of anything else that is also there, for example, a thousand other individual fingers. We should reject this view, I think. As I have argued above, it seems permissible for outsiders to allow to occur, or even cause to occur by redirection—though this is harder—larger losses to a given person than those which that person's personal point of view would equate with someone else's life (e.g., perhaps a finger).

So it is rather that once a lesser loss is salient to third parties, it is lifted to an objective scale of costs. There it is given its objective value and aggregated along with other such losses. Are losses to individuals that they are duty bound to suffer to save someone's life, as well as other nonsalient losses, aggregated on the scale of costs *as the number of people who have to take them increases?* Let us postpone answering this question for now.

Equivalents and Costs: Harming and Not Aiding

The aggregation as cost is reflected in the following facts. We might permissibly decide, if a threat is headed toward killing one person, *not* to benefit that person by redirecting the threat so that it takes off one arm of each of twenty people. Likewise, we might permissibly decide to give a scarce medicine to (benefit) twenty people, each of whom stands to lose one of his arms, rather than to save one life. We are here thinking in terms of costs, rather than equivalences. If we say "1 life = 20 arms," we do not mean equivalence, strictly speaking, as we do if we say "1 life = 1 life." (And, of course, here we do not mean identity; there is abandonment.) This is not the substitution of equivalents. Yet in the case of aiding or not aiding, calculation according to costs functions as though we had equivalents.

Put *very roughly,* in the rare cases where killing is morally permissible (e.g., redirecting threats)—at least, killing (and, in general, harming) someone who is not dependent on significant lifesaving effort from the person who kills him—requires calculation of equivalents.[2] Not aiding (e.g., not redirecting a threat away from someone to others who will suffer lesser losses or not giving a medicine) may require only calculation of costs. Taking care of the worst off (maximin policy), which typically interferes with consideration of aggregated lesser losses, applies to not harming, but it does not apply to aiding.[3]

Subjective Scales of Costs or Equivalents?

Given the distinction I have tried to sketch between scales of equivalents and scales of costs, it may be more appropriate to think of what I referred to as the objectively permitted subjective scale of equivalents—helping to constitute someone's personal point of view—as a scale of costs as well. For these equivalences allow our agent to refuse assistance; they are not used in deciding whether he may harm. For example, the agent may not direct a threat from himself to save his finger if he foresees that this will kill a bystander.

That we are often, as individuals and as a society, unwilling to pay the cost for what we think is, in fact, more valuable than the cost we refuse to bear seems puzzling. It is at the heart of the consequentialist critique of nonconsequentialism.[4]

The Relation of Sob[3] and Sob[4]

When we tried to identify a principle underlying the distinction between different extra utilities in Sob[3], we suggested the following: (1) An extra utility that gives rise to proportional chances for harm or aid when accompanied by a life is that which, in aggregate and unaccompanied by a life, merits proportional chances against a life when we must choose whom to aid; and (2) an extra utility that helps a life to override another life outright is one which alone, unaggregated, and unaccompanied by a life, merits proportional chances against a life when we must choose whom to aid. Sob[4] explicitly claims that both of these types of utilities, aggregated and unaccompanied by a life, can override a life outright, when we must choose whom to aid.

The positions that Sob[4] takes on overriding costs are close enough to the positions taken by the principle underlying Sob[3] to suggest that something like the analysis of costs provided by Sob[4] plays a part in the principle underlying Sob[3]. Perhaps we can get clear about both positions and bring them closer together by further distinguishing contexts in which the difference between costs and true equivalents is significant:

(A)   We should not send a trolley that is *at a crosspoint* and must go somewhere, to one person who will lose his life, but should send it rather to
many persons who will each lose an arm.

(A)' We should not send a trolley that is at a crosspoint and must go somewhere, to one person who will lose his life rather than to many who will be
caused total paralysis.

(B)   We may choose not to redirect a trolley away from one person who will
lose his life and toward many persons who will each lose an arm.

(B)' We may choose not to redirect a trolley away from one person who will
lose his life and toward many persons, each of whom will be totally paralyzed.

These four cases represent two different types of scenarios. These two types (A
and A' on the one hand, B and B' on the other) both involve harming those who will
suffer the lesser loss. (A) and (A)' suggest that total physical disability and arm loss
are *not* equivalents of life, and (B) and (B)' suggest that causing these lesser losses
can be a cost we may permissibly refuse to pay to save a life.

(C)   We may choose to give proportional chances to saving several arms (or
preventing one total paralysis) in contest with saving a life when we must
here and now decide whom to aid of several people currently in need.

(C)' We may choose outright to provide funding to cure a prevalent disease that
robs each person who gets it of one arm (or to cure a somewhat less
prevalent disease that results in total paralysis) rather than find a cure for a
rare fatal disease. This means we will be able to aid the first two (more
numerous) groups of people when they are actually ill and that we will not
have resources to aid the (smaller) third group when they come to us
needing (life-saving) aid.

Distinguishing between harming (in A and A' and B and B') and different types
of aid (C versus C') helps introduce consistency, I believe, between Sob[4]'s account
of costs (which permits directly outweighing by lesser losses unaccompanied by a
life) and the principle supporting Sob[3] (which permits giving proportional chances
to aggregated and sometimes nonaggregated lesser losses unaccompanied by a life).
That is, in cases where a larger loss of life is at stake on only one side, direct
outweighing as sanctioned by Sob[4] can occur when there are funding decisions and
decisions not to cause harm (by redirection) in order to save a life. Sob[3] sanctions
giving proportional chances in these cases when we must decide whom to aid here
and now, but does not allow proportional chances to lesser losses when we must kill
one. A possible alternative, with far-reaching implications, is that when a loss is
such that on its own it merits proportional chances against saving a life, then
inaggregate, unaccompanied by a life, it merits proportional chances in deciding
whether to kill one by redirection. This would alter the claim that killing requires
equivalents. (I assume in some cases that total paralysis is not the equivalent of life
itself.)

The Aggregate of Nonsalient or Duty-Required Costs?

As costs, rather than as equivalents, and for the purpose of deciding whom to aid rather than whom to harm, may we aggregate nonsalient costs or even those costs required of individuals as a duty? The more people who will lose out on fingers, for example, the more our perspective may shift to the total social cost. This will be true even when there is no one on the side of this aggregation who will be as badly off as the person who stands alone. Again, it is puzzling to explain why this should be. The reasons given previously (Chapter 9, p. 177) for aggregating salient lesser losses in similar circumstances, and for aggregating nonsalient lesser losses when they accompany a life (or other greater loss) may play some role here as well.

Special Roles

Notice that occupying some special roles may make it inappropriate to act according to objective aggregated costs of even salient losses in the way Sob[4] recommends. A doctor, for example, should go to save the patient who will die without her rather than to the group of twenty people each of whom would lose an arm. (Even Sob[3] would permit an ordinary moral agent here and now to give proportional chances to many arms. I have not said how many.) A doctor should be concerned with equivalents and about who will suffer the most *as individuals*. I suggest that a doctor, qua doctor, should not be concerned with what saving a life costs in terms of individual lesser losses. (This is consistent with the doctor's choosing to save five lives rather than one, or the group of one life plus one arm rather than one life.)

   This contrast between the doctor and the ordinary moral agent suggests that even the ordinary nonconsequentialist moral agent we are thinking about is, in some ways, close to a social agent. That is, he is in some respects like someone who acts on behalf of society at large and so must be concerned that all of us not pay too high a cost for something. So we have said that it may be right for the moral agent to aid the many, each of whom stands to lose an arm, rather than the single person whose life is in danger, having given a greater proportional chance to saving the life. We may compare this to deciding which sorts of medical procedures society will provide, given different numbers of people in need of each procedure. We may choose to fund procedures that many will need for saving arms versus procedures for saving lives that few will need. This is not to deny that there is a difference between funding procedures and denying someone lifesaving aid at the very time he needs it. To employ a point made in Chapter 8, if we do not fund, we will not be in the position of having to deny someone something we have. This will not be true in the cases where here and now we must aid, and then we give proportional chances in various ways.[5]

Sobjectivity[5]

I believe that Sob[3] and Sob[4] in combination, rather than Sob[1] or Sob[2], most accurately represent our commonsense morality. They are also to be contrasted with what we will call Sob^5, in which everything of concern to individuals is always allowed to be aggregated on the scale of equivalents, no matter how small. This includes the losses that are nonsalient to outsiders but that matter from someone's subjective view, including even those someone would be obliged to make to save a life. Sob^5 is just straightforwardly utilitarian in aggregating everything. Because aggregation is on the scale of equivalents, it is used to make decisions about harming as well as not aiding.

The Anatomy of Commonsense Morality

It is worth noticing that the progression from Sob^1 to Sob^5, which gives increasing weight to the subjective concerns of individuals, also coincides with a more and more strict objective view. For example, when Sob^3 (but not Sob^1) allows an arm to count in deciding between lives, it takes account of the fact that on Jane's subjective view her arm is worth more than Joe's life and proceeds to give the arm its objective value. As we move to Sob^5, any items, even minor, that someone cares about are put on the objective aggregative scale. There is no prior consideration of whether it is *objectively* permitted for such an item to be rated as equivalent (or as cost-equivalent) to someone's life on a subjective scale of value. So, as we skip the objective evaluation of the subjective views and allow even pure, uncensored subjective views, we move, in fact, toward weighing in a totally *objective* manner.

Therefore, as we give the subjective view something, we take something away from it. What do we take away? Concern for the fact that from the subjective point of view of each person who stands to lose his life, it matters who wins, and because it matters more to someone if he is the one to suffer a big loss than if he suffers a small one, this should make certain utilities become irrelevant. There is a general progression toward objectivity as we take subjectivity more seriously in just one sense.[6]

To repeat, suppose we take seriously every loss that has subjective value to someone, without first weighing it objectively against what someone else stands to lose. Then we do not care whether it is anywhere near as objectively large as what someone else stands to lose, or even whether the objective view permits the subjective scale of equivalence (or costs) of a particular individual. We simply place the loss on an objective scale used to evaluate possible alternative outcomes. This is to return to a completely *objective* aggregative morality such as utilitarianism, which simply and straightforwardly gives objective weight to every subjectively discernible loss or gain. We would be doing this if, in distributing a scarce resource, we weighed saving a thousand people from each suffering a headache against saving one person's life. By contrast, not counting every such *subjective* loss on an *objective* scale used to evaluate outcomes may *reflect a different concern for the subjective point of view* since, according to this subjective view, it matters whether I or someone else suffers some loss and how large the losses to *individual* persons (rather than aggregated over any geographic locations) contributed are. Consideration of this leads us to treat some utilities as irrelevant (as in Sob^1).

This analysis supports the view that *commonsense morality* gives weight to the concern of each person to be the one to survive in a way that prevents the straightforward substitution of equivalents. It does so when the cost of doing this is not too great. (Sob^3 represents this especially.) It does not endorse a totally objective view, nor does it endorse giving as much weight to the nonsubstitution of equivalents as Taurek's position recommends.

Imperceptible Benefits

The argument for nonaggregation of small utilities to different individuals has an interesting application to a type of problem that Jonathan Glover,[7] Derek Parfit,[8] and Michael Otsuka[9] have discussed. Suppose each of us, individually, can only improve (or worsen) the condition of a group of 100 people by an imperceptible amount. But together, 100 of us, each doing the imperceptible amount, which is not zero, can do a significant (x) amount to help each of the 100. On the other hand, I as an individual can make a modest contribution ($x - n$) to someone else. What should I do? I agree with those (like Parfit and Otsuka) who argue that imperceptible improvements are really improvements and that when aggregated, they may amount to the greatest utility. I am concerned, however, to consider what one should do if, for example, 99 others have already each made their imperceptible contributions which will be distributed among the 100. Now it is my turn. With what I have, I can cause an imperceptible improvement to each of the 100 people in need, or else cause a significant and perceptible improvement to one person. This one person, without the improvement, is still better off than any of the 100 will be, even once the 99 aid them. He is not the worst off.

I believe that even if we agree that I do produce the greatest utility overall by helping the 100, because imperceptible improvements are something, and when aggregated amount to a great deal, it is still right for me to produce the lesser but significant (not imperceptible) gain to one person. This view depends on two claims: (1) It is significant gains (or losses) to individuals that are important. A significant gain to one person should not be outweighed by aggregated small gains to many people. (2) Once others have already acted as we *all* should act *if* we all had to act in the same way—that is, they have all together produced the best result to each of the 100 people by each producing their imperceptible difference to each of the 100—I may do what, in that context, is the better act. (This is not the act that maximizes utility, as claim 1 explains).

This second claim depends on a revised notion of universalization. I could will it that everyone else do as I do, if they also act in a context where 99 others have already done something else. Would the reason the hundredth aider has for acting be available to the ninety-ninth, and if to him, the ninety-eighth, ninety-seventh, and so on, so that all would have a reason not to aid the 100, thereby producing the worse result? The ninety-eighth and ninety-seventh may have a *similar* reason, that is, if 96 have already aided, the additional good each does (or even the three together do) is not as perceptible to each of the 100 as the good they can do for the single person. But suppose only 50 people have so far aided. No one of the 50 left can will that the other 49 act on the maxim "when 50 have aided the 100, aid the single person" since then there will be a very significant perceptible difference to the 100 not aided by the 50 and these 100 will be worse off than the one in whom we could produce the modest good. So, just because the hundredth person and a few others have reason to aid the one person to degree $(x - n)$ does not mean everyone else does.

II

Why Only Approximate Opposing Equals Are Sufficient

We are now in a better position to discuss at least one aspect of the claim, embodied in several forms of Sobjectivity, that there must be an equal or approximate equal as contestant on either side of an equivalence scale. I wish to consider the possibility that Sob[3] itself helps us explain *why* approximately equal rather than exactly equal is enough and *how* approximately equal such contestants must be. (I am assuming that the criteria for which this issue arises are the needs and benefits which are directly served or produced by our resource, in keeping with the fairness, Kantian injunction, and "separate spheres" points already made.) So far we have been dealing primarily with cases in which extra utility or disutility arises in some locus other than the locus of primary utility or disutility. For example, the extra utility is Jane's arm, which belongs to Jane, but the primary utility at stake is to Jim, his life. Cases involving single candidates whose stakes are unequal involve added disutility or utility in the *same* locus. That is, the extra good or bad would come to the same person as the primary utility or disutility. If contestants are defined as candidates who are approximately equal, we are interested in who such candidates are. (We have made short side-remarks on how each Sob applies to cases where candidates are unequal. Now we deal in greater detail with this issue.)

Broome's Answer: Proportional Chances

Before considering the answer that Sob[3] suggests to the question why contestants for a good need have only *approximately* equal stakes, I will consider an alternative answer suggested by John Broome.[10] Suppose that, of two people to whom we can give a benefit, one will be slightly worse off than the other if he does not receive it. Broome suggests that we should toss a coin between them only *if* we are unable to give each a chance in proportion to how badly off he will be. Consider the case in which one person, A, will suffer fifty-one points of harm if not aided and someone else, B, will suffer forty-nine points of harm. According to Broome, A ideally should have a 51 percent chance of help and B a 49 percent chance. Suppose we cannot meet such a standard. It would be *more unfair* to straightforwardly help A rather than toss a coin between A and B. Therefore we ought to toss a coin. The reasoning here is that if A receives 100 percent probability of getting help when he deserves 51 percent, then he gets 49 percent more than he deserves, whereas if B gets 50 percent probability of getting help when he deserves only 49 percent, he gets only 1 percent more than he deserves.

An implication of Broome's proposal, therefore, is that it is only once someone deserves a greater than 75 percent probability of being helped—that is, a probability more than halfway between 50 percent and 100 percent—that we should, without further ado, choose to aid him rather than toss a coin. For then the difference between what he is owed and what he gets if straightforwardly aided will be less than the difference between what the other party is owed and what he would get if a coin were tossed (that is, $100 - 76 < 50 - 24$). Then contestants for a toss of a coin would be individuals whom it would be more unfair to automatically choose between.

Broome believes that we ought always ideally to give chances in proportion to need, even when we are faced with very great need and very small need. (Need is here being understood as degree of expected harm if not helped.) On Broome's view, therefore, aiding the much worse off before the better off (maximin) is an incorrect ideal solution to distribution problems. This is because the correct way of distributing a good should make it possible for the better off to have a small chance of getting an item they need to a small degree.

Any commitment to proportional chances yielding the latter result seems to me to be incorrect. Does such a commitment stem from mistakenly treating need in the way we should treat a property claim? If two people owned unequal shares in an individual piece of property, it might be correct to give each a proportional chance to get it. (We discussed the case of a lottery prize for which tickets were purchased. There we concluded the minority's chance should not be taken away so that the majority can get the prize). Need, I believe, functions differently, with much greater need between candidates swamping any prima facie claim generated by a lesser need. This could be so even if the greater need is not greater by so large a degree that, on a scale of proportional chances, it would deserve more than a 75 percent chance. That is, a 70 point need versus a 30 point need would be enough. The question is whether only a slightly larger need also swamps a smaller one. Are proportional chances ideally correct here at least? Before answering, let us consider what Sob[3] recommends.

Sob[3] and the Irrelevance of Some Added Losses

Sob[3] can generate the following proposal for these cases: Consider how much worse off one party would be than the other if he were not aided. Suppose the difference is such that one person ought to suffer such a loss to save someone else's life *or* the loss is not salient to third parties as grounds for giving the resource to one party over another. Then the ideal (not approximate) solution is to toss a coin. Such degree of being worse off will be irrelevant. The candidates will be what we have called contestants. So as the ideal solution (not second best), we should toss a coin between a person who will lose both legs and one who will lose both legs and a finger. This is true even if the second person is not duty bound to give up a finger to save someone's legs.[11] Another way of understanding this is that what both people stand to lose swamps the slight additional loss one person would suffer (and additional utility we could produce.) The person who stands to lose less should not be deprived of his equal chance to avoid a major loss, the loss that is the primary concern. In other words, the small additional loss that is not the focus of concern should not privilege one person with respect to his chances to avoid the major loss.

Suppose that someone would stand to lose a hand *if* he made some other small sacrifice to save someone else's life. He would not then be required to make such a small sacrifice. This, however, does not mean that *we* may not treat an additional smaller loss as irrelevant, even though its being treated in this way is what may lead to a further, greater (salient) loss should this person lose a toss. The fact that smaller and larger losses are joined for a single person does not, I believe, mean that we may not treat the smaller loss as irrelevant and decide that it should not count against tossing a coin.

Of course, we may not be able to evaluate the significance of the additional smaller loss that faces one person without considering the bigger loss each person would be subject to. That is, if C stands to lose one hand, but D stands to lose a hand plus a finger, then we must consider what it means to be without a finger if one is *already* missing one hand, so as to be reasonable in determining how much worse off D would be than C.

A different problem arises when each party faces the same disaster, but one could wind up in a better state than the other. (That is, in the previous case one party will be worse off if not treated; he faces a worse disaster. Here the two can avoid the same disaster but one will come up better than the other.) For example, suppose two people face death and are (it at least seems correct to say) equally needy of life, but one will have a somewhat higher quality of life if he lives, though both will have adequate life quality. According to Sob^3, the enormous size of what each stands to lose—and gain—namely, life itself, swamps the difference in potential gain to one. The difference becomes irrelevant relative to this particular primary potential gain. (This analysis implicitly rejects the view that the person who loses out on the better prospect is threatened with a worse fate if he loses, i.e., death through loss of a fantastic rather than mediocre future is not considered a worse end state. Another analysis need not; it may accept that one is facing a worse disaster but only insist that the difference in degrees of badness is irrelevant.)[12]

In these cases where differences between candidates are not salient, we have contestants, and where Sob^3 recommends equal chances, Broome's approach ideally recommends proportional chances. It is important to reemphasize that the approach here recommended says not only that utility not directly produced for candidates by our resource is irrelevant (or at least must overcome weighty consideration to be counted). It also claims certain differences in direct effects of our resources are irrelevant.

Significant Additional Loss and Gain

On the other hand, helping the saliently worse off person will also conflict with proportional chances. Suppose the additional loss is a salient lesser loss. If we ignore it, would we then be showing insufficient concern for this lesser loss and too much concern for the equal chances of the two people? It might seem that the approach suggested by Sob^3 implies that we may routinely help the person who stands to suffer the saliently lesser loss, that is, that we treat as a noncontestant the person who stands to lose less than the person with the salient difference. This result would disagree not only with Broome's recommendation of proportional chances, but also with Broome's *nonideal* approach, which calls for equal chances until one party has more than 75 percent of a proportional desert, for salient difference may not mean that the person who stands to suffer more would suffer a loss, great enough to put him above 75 percent on a scale of proportional desert.

A similar analysis employing Sob³ can be given of cases in which each of two parties would be equally badly off without aid, but one party would be better off if aided than the other would be if aided. For example, suppose E would gain an additional twenty years of life and F would gain only an additional year of life. We consider the overlap in gain, that is, what is achieved no matter who lives. Then we consider the additional gain if we save one of the people. Suppose the additional gain is not only large enough so that someone would not be duty bound to give it up to save another person, or give him an equal chance, but also involves a difference salient to outsiders. Then the loss of the additional gain is something we should not allow someone to suffer. We should save the life that will give a greater number of years. Or so it might seem.

Dispersal Versus Concentration of Benefit

Two significant factors, however, temper this result. First, there may be a preference for situations in which additional significant benefits are distributed widely rather than concentrated in one person. That is, we may find it easier to decide straightforwardly to aid one side in cases like the one involving Jane's paralysis. In these, the additional utility at stake accrues to someone *other* than the person who is a contestant for the primary good. By contrast, when the person who stands to gain at least as much as someone else will also gain a great deal more, dislike of concentration of benefits may be a factor that pulls against routine aid for him.

Suppose that the concentration as opposed to dispersal of benefit reduces our tendency to choose the side with greater potential utility. This, I believe, argues *against* the view (mentioned above) that we should help the person who will live longer because he will be *worse* off than the other person if he is not aided. He will be worse off, it is claimed, because he comes to die *through* losing out on more, i.e., his absolute level is the same (dead) but this is much worse as it comes by way of a greater loss. On this view it is not only where one ends up, but also how far one has fallen that determines how badly off one is. But if the person in whom benefit would be concentrated would be worse off if he died than the other contestant, there should be more, not less, of a tendency to help him than there is to help the side that will have the greater benefit *dispersed*. After all no one of the individuals on the side with greater utility at stake in the cases involving dispersal would be worse off than their single opponent on the other side. Yet I believe we are somewhat more likely to look favorably at dispersal than at concentration of benefit.

Second, in the case in which we try to avoid a worse outcome, I believe the difference required for salience will be smaller than that required when we try to promote the best outcome. (Our discussion of concentration ignored this point.) That we do not find production of additional benefit above a shared baseline as urgent as avoiding a worse baseline and that we are somewhat opposed to concentration help to produce this result. Underlying both these views may be the idea that just because someone is lucky enough to have the possibility of a better prospect should not give him outright preference.

Still, a very significantly better outcome is a good event and its concentration in one person makes for a radically better life. And these facts count as well. Be we need not conceal the simple fact that it is better behind the inegalitarian, perhaps even elitist, view that the person who loses out on a great deal is therefore worse off than someone who loses less, though they fall to the same baseline.[13] All this means that a lower total in expected benefit aggregated over several people, than an expected benefit concentrated in one person, is necessary for salience, relative to the yet lower expected benefit of a competing person; bigger differences in expected benefits will be consistent with contestant status.

A Role for Proportional Chances

Suppose we accept this Sob^3-derived proposal rather than a proposal based on proportional chances across the board. It is still appropriate to give proportional chances in some cases. For example, using the model of the arm case, Sob^3 recommends use of proportional chances when a difference between two candidates is salient and such that by itself it would not be a contestant against a life, but, if present in and aggregated over several separate individuals, it could deserve a proportional chance. Then when added to a greater loss in one candidate (as when added alongside him) it could yield a higher proportional chance for that candidate. Here is another mark of cases where the policy of proportional chances is legitimate: Whoever wins, we do not sense that the wrong person has wound up with the benefit *so long as* there was a differential probability of each one winning. These are cases where a differential is salient but not large and a proportional chance gives us what we want. The difference merits some sort of additional chance. Here process is more important than outcome. (In the cases where equal chances are appropriate, process matters, but not as *compensation* for what would otherwise be the wrong outcome.)

In another sort of case, the difference in possible bad outcomes is sufficiently large and would, other things being equal, determine an outcome for one party. However, letting it determine an outcome in favor of one party would produce some other difference between contestants that would pull us not strongly in the direction of favoring either party. Then we might simply give a higher proportional chance of winning to the person who faces the worse prospect, allowing that he may nevertheless lose. An example of this is if one person will be worse off than another in a salient respect, but both stand to gain a great deal relative to what they each would get if not aided. Then helping the person who is worse off will deprive the other person, who is not much better off, of a great deal. Here the difference we will create between the people is much greater than the salient difference on account of which we would outright help one rather than the other. Here proportional chances may seem most appropriate.

Summary

We might summarize our position this way. If there is a very great difference between the two candidates (for example, the additional loss added to a greater one would deserve a proportional chance on its own), we shall feel that the wrong person has gotten the resource if the one who will not be as badly off or the one who will not do as well gets it. (More so in the former than the latter case.) This will be true even if the other candidate was given a greater proportional chance to get the resource. If the difference between the candidates is nonsalient, there will be no sense that the wrong person has gotten the resource, whichever candidate gets it. But there should also be a sense that it would be wrong for one candidate to have had an even slightly greater chance of getting the resource based on his slight difference in need or outcome. The difference should be irrelevant. If the difference between candidates is salient but not overpowering, there will be no sense that the wrong person has gotten the resource, whichever candidate gets it *only if* the worse off candidate or the one who stands to gain or lose much more did have a greater chance to get it.

In the next chapters, we shall consider in more detail the use of proportional chances and the notions of greater need, and of better and worse outcomes.

Sobjectivity and Scanlon's Contractualism

In conclusion let us consider the possible relation between sobjectivity and contractualism. Contractualist moral theory, as recently developed by Thomas Scanlon[14] and employed by Thomas Nagel,[15] asks us to seek policies to which it would be unreasonable of anyone to object (given the aim of getting unforced, informed agreement). A wrong act is one which would be disallowed by any policy to which it would be unreasonable for such people to object. This involves checking the objections that each person might have to various policies and deciding whose not unreasonable objection to a policy is strongest given the possibility of other policies. The need to move from Sob[2] to Sob[3] indicates that the reasonableness of someone's complaint against *making* a sacrifice is not necessarily definitive of what is morally correct policy for us to follow. Furthermore, it is not only the person who would have to give up a finger to give Joe an equal chance at life who could not unreasonably refuse. Joe could not unreasonably refuse to give up his equal chance for life to preserve Jim's life and someone else's finger. But this does not mean *we* are in a moral stalemate. For it may still be unreasonable for Jane to object, if we (not she) are responsible for preserving Joe's equal chance for life at the possible cost of her finger and Jim's life.[16]

The move from Sob[2] to Sob[3] emphasizes that in this process of testing which objections are not unreasonable we should distinguish between someone's objections to *his* making a sacrifice and someone's objections to tolerating our doing what may or will result in a loss to him. That is, on Scanlon's model it seems that each person must raise an objection from his own point of view. But, as our rejection of Sob[2] implied, we did not think that any loss an individual could not unreasonably object to *making* was one that would be salient to us as outsiders when choosing between that individual's loss and someone else's desire for an equal chance.[17] Must Scanlon's account make room for a point of view outside that of any of the parties'—our point of view—from which losses to them can be considered, a point of view whose conclusions we would expect them, from their own points of view, to find it reasonable for us to reach? Perhaps not, and in the case we are considering all that is needed is for Scanlon to distinguish between what, from some individual's point of view, it is not unreasonable to object to donating on one's own and what, from that same point of view, it is not unreasonable to object to third parties doing (or permitting to happen) to one as the consequence of a policy.

The questions at issue here may be the basis for an objection to the broad use to which Scanlon wishes to put his model of contractualism. That is, Scanlon believes that the desire to find policies that could be agreed to because they could not reasonably be rejected by anyone (who is seeking informed, uncoerced agreement) just *is* what taking the moral point of view amounts to. But, as he admits, there may be situations in which it is not unreasonable of one opposing party to reject the other side's proposal and also not unreasonable of that other side to reject the opposing party's proposal. He says in this case that there is then no policy endorsed by the moral point of view. For example, we may agree that it is not unreasonable for the rich to reject making very large sacrifices for the sake of the poor. But we may also agree that it is not unreasonable for the poor to rebel and cause the rich those great losses, if that is the only alternative to the status quo.

Yet in this particular case, I think, we should agree that there is no simple moral symmetry between the two proposals. There is a sense in which the poor have right on their side even if the rich are not morally unreasonable to resist; not all objections which it is not unreasonable to make are created equal. Evidence for the morally asymmetrical status of the complaints of the rich and the poor is the fact that if the rich were to be willing to suffer the large loss their conduct, would be considered supererogatory, morally fine and indeed beyond the call of duty. By contrast, if the poor were to cease objecting and drop their complaint, we might think they exhibit certain vices, such as excessive self-abnegation, lack of self respect, etc. But from what position do we think this? From what position within Scanlon's model of moral reasoning could we reach the conclusion that morally the poor are in a better position to object to a proposal, if our moral reasoning is supposed to end when we discover that each party can not unreasonably object to the other's policy proposal from its own point of view? Notice that here the rich can also not unreasonably reject a policy which allows outsiders to help the poor to revolt when this will cost the rich a great deal, even if they are not asked to actively undertake the sacrifice. That is why their evaluating our actions (versus their own) from their point of view does not seem to offer a sufficient way out.

Perhaps this case, as well as the move from Sob^2 to Sob^3, indicate that Scanlon's is not a complete model of reasoning from the moral point of view. It seems there is some point of view from which we do more than consider individual's not unreasonable complaints and *that* is the moral point of view. (Perhaps some iteration on the perspectives of individuals would suffice?)

Contractualism as Scanlon and Nagel describe it, is concerned with pairwise comparisons, i.e., seeing if any one person will personally have a greater complaint than another. As noted above, some might argue that this procedure results in unbreakable ties to each individual whose loss would be at all significant. Nagel and Scanlon, in fact, seem to allow for substitution of equivalent *types* of complaints. They also allow for taking care of the worst off first, even if the loss to the less badly off would be significant as well. That is, one worst off person can be matched against an equal and opposing worst off person. Sob^2 and Sob^3, however, are concerned with when such substitution is and is not permissible. Both these procedures begin by considering when it would be not unreasonable for someone who will suffer a smaller loss than others to object to his making a sacrifice, given that only one person will live no matter what he does. It can, therefore, sometimes be reasonable for the person who will suffer the smaller loss to object to a policy because of what will also be happening to others. He may have the strongest complaint even if he suffers a lesser loss, given that only one will live no matter what he does. Scanlon allows that the biggest loss does not always give one the biggest justified complaint. This makes possible some aggregation when there is already substitution of equivalent, larger types of losses, (The scale that seems to underlie Sob³, telling us which lesser losses help give proportional chances and which help a larger loss override its equivalent competitor, might be used to make more precise the contractualist model.)

Sob⁴ distinguishes costs from equivalents, and on these grounds permits some aggregation of significant lesser losses even unaccompanied by a larger loss. By contrast the pairwise comparison which is at the heart of contractualist reasoning, seems (for the most part) to prohibit favoring those who would each suffer lesser losses while those who face greater losses go unsatisfied. Scanlon, however, argues that if the position of the worst off will not be very bad, and what we could give to him is small, foregoing a great gain in the better off would be too high a cost to pay for helping him. Could this limited use of a "cost argument" be expanded to allow us to consider the cost to many, each of whom faces a smaller significant loss—as Sob⁴ does—even when the worst off is very badly off in absolute terms and could be helped a great deal? This would expand the scope for aggregation.

Finally, in discussing Sobjectivity we have distinguished between comparing how badly off people will be and comparing how much people will gain. When Sob⁴ aggregates the cost to those with significant lesser losses, it considers how badly off they will each be if not helped (e.g., without an arm, paralyzed). This is different from considering as a cost the absence of a great gain to someone who will not be badly off even if he is not helped. Yet it is the latter notion of cost which Scanlon uses in arguing against always helping the person who will be worst off. That is, the absolute level to which they fall is not determinative; how much better off they could be is considered in determining the loss required to help the worst off.

NOTES

1. Assuming, of course, that the loss to many people of their individual arms does not amount to a qualitatively new type of loss, e.g., the collapse of society.

2. For some suggestions as to the rules covering killing in these other cases, see *Morality, Mortality,* Vol. II, and *Creation and Abortion.*

3. This point calls upon and, I believe, helps support a distinction between killing and letting die, harming and not aiding. For more on this issue, see "Killing and Letting Die: Methodology and Substance," and "Harming, Not Aiding, and Positive Rights," and *Morality, Mortality,* Vol. II.

4. For example, see Shelly Kagan's *The Limits of Morality,* (Oxford University Press, 1989).

5. Sob⁴ is not relevant to the question of what extra utilities to candidates themselves, produced by their personal characteristics and from the direct use of our resource, are relevant

or irrelevant to determining who are equal contestants. This is because Sob[4] begins by assuming that none of components of the composite contestant are anywhere near equivalent to the candidate on the other side.

6. Although I noticed that taking seriously someone's subjective view of his arm involved adding it to an *objective* aggregative scale, it was Shelly Kagan who emphasized to me the general progression.

7. In "It Makes No Difference Whether or Not I Do It," *Proceedings of the Aristotelian Society*, Suppl. Vol. 49, 1975.

8. In *Reasons and Persons.*

9. In "The Paradox of Group Beneficence," *Philosophy and Public Affairs*, 20, no. 2, (Spring 1991): 132–149.

10. In "Selecting People Randomly."

11. This proposal goes beyond the claim that certain differences ought not to matter because from people's subjective views they are not noticeable, like a slightly greater pain that is not detected.

12. The "worse fate" view was suggested to me by Thomas Nagel. I first made this claim in "The Report of the U.S. Task Force on Organ Transplantation: Criticisms and Alternatives." I discuss the issues raised by such cases further below and in Chapter 13.

13. Derek Parfit criticizes the view that we should take size of loss into account in deciding who is worse off somewhat differently. He writes (in correspondence): "The claim seems to be that how badly off someone is partly depends on how much better off he might have been, and that this is so quite generally, or as such—and is not a mere consequence of the disappointment he may feel. This is the view that I *think* you should not take seriously. First, the moral point which is expressed in this view can be perfectly well expressed in other terms. We can say that the strength of someone's complaint depends *both* on his absolute level *and* on the size of his 'loss,' or on how much worse off he is than he might have been. (On the view that I call 'Minimax Loss,' it depends only on his loss.) If we distinguish absolute levels and losses, that leaves it entirely open what their relative importance is.

"Second, it's extremely confusing to take the size of someone's loss to help to determine his absolute level. If we're even to state this view, we need to employ the other notion of an absolute level, since the size of someone's loss depends on the difference between his absolute level in this primary sense and the absolute level at which he might have been. Since we must employ 'absolute level' in this primary sense, the most we can do is introduce a secondary sense of 'absolute level' which we confess to be different. We would then say that the person who is best off in terms of absolute level in the primary sense might be the person who is worst off in terms of our secondary sense, simply because he could have been so much better off. This secondary sense isn't what we ordinarily mean by how badly off someone is. Suppose I get one piece of cake when my only feasible alternative was two, and you get two pieces when you might have been given 100. In this secondary sense, you are absolutely worse off than me, simply because you could have had so much more. Why speak in this bizarre way, when we can easily express the substance of this view by giving weight, directly, to the size of people's losses? . . . Your objection is that this view is inegalitarian or even elitist. My objection is not to the substance of this view, but to the willfully obscure way in which it's expressed. The inegalitarians should simply say that, in their view, what matters most is not someone's absolute level but how much worse off he is than he might have been.

"In Chapter 8 of my unpublished draft *On Giving Priority to the Worse Off*, my main claim is that, if we follow Nagel and Scanlon in giving priority to making the *single* greatest weighted loss as small as possible, our view is not, as they suggest, egalitarian. It's anti-egalitarian. We shall prefer giving a smaller total benefit all to one person than to giving a larger total benefit shared between many people who, even after receiving it, would all be worse off."

14. In his "Contractualism and Utilitarianism."

15. In *Equality and Partiality* (New York: Oxford University Press, 1991).

16. An additional problem arises in seeking the strongest objection: If we merely compare welfare losses, no one will have to make larger sacrifices to avoid imposing a smaller loss on someone. This means that we could not generate strong negative duties not to harm.

17. It is clear we could allow to happen to someone a loss which is greater than he would have to bring about on himself. There are only very limited ways in which we can cause him such a loss, e.g., redirecting a threat, and it is puzzling that we may do it at all.

III

SCARCE RESOURCES: THEORETICAL ISSUES, SPECIFIC RECOMMENDATIONS, AND ORGAN TRANSPLANTS

11

Acquisition of Organs

"I know I have the body of a weak and feeble woman, but I have the heart and stomach of a king, and of a king of England too."

Queen Elizabeth I, speech to the troops at Tilbury
on the approach of the Armada, 1588

So far, we have considered some general theoretical problems in the distribution of resources that cannot be given to all who need them. In the rest of the book, we consider more specific problems in distributing and acquiring scarce resources. To focus the discussion, we examine the issue of organ transplants using organs from human donors. It is important to emphasize that the factors we examine, especially in the distribution section, apply to any scarce resource, including money, needed to pay for the use of nonscarce resources (e.g., organs from nonhuman animals). Because it raises interesting issues, and not necessarily because it represents current practice, we first examine certain proposals for acquisition and distribution made in the Report of the U.S. Task Force on Organ Transplantation (henceforth referred to as *the Report*).[1] In this chapter, we summarize some of the Task Force's major proposals on acquisition and distribution, examine scientific criteria for death and then discuss acquisition issues in more detail. In the next chapters, we consider proposals for distribution in detail.

I. THE TASK FORCE'S VIEWS ON ACQUISITION AND DISTRIBUTION

Acquisition: Original Owner and the Family

A proclaimed aim of the Report is to describe a fair distribution of scarce organs. This is to be done on the assumption that the organs are voluntary gifts by donors who are not paid. According to the Report, this makes the organs a national resource.

In fact, it is often not the person whose organs they are (who I shall refer to as the *original organ owner*) whose decision determines donation. The original organ owner's decision to give, which could be acted on legally, can in effect be overridden after his death by the family's decision not to give. Furthermore, if the original owner has made no decision, the family may make the decision to give. The Report[2] suggests that families, not original organ owners, are the crucial factor in acquiring organs, and the Report raises no moral objections to this state of affairs. In particular, although the Report comes out against presuming consent to donate on the part of original organ owners and states that "present efforts should focus on enhancing the current voluntary system rather than on reducing the role of actual consent," the actual consent it is concerned with is not that of the original owner but that of next of kin (p. 31).

The Report notes that physicians are reluctant to act on donor cards without the consent of next of kin (p. 29), and it specifically places no emphasis on increasing the number of original owners who fill out donor cards or on registries of original owners who are willing to donate. The Report concludes, "as the organ procurement system now operates the primary focus is on securing permission from the family member rather than from the actual donor.[3] There are good reasons to think that this will continue, and that the system can be made more effective without introducing a national registry" (p. 51). One reason that the Report gives for recommending that next of kin have control is that, according to it, the family is comforted in giving a dead relative's organ. Physicians who know this will also find it easier to offer the kin the opportunity to give.

A policy that allows the family to override an original owner's desire to donate may seem to exhibit a willingness, out of respect for family wishes, to tolerate loss of some organs. However, if it is known that families are more likely to donate than original organ owners, giving the family power is really, over all, a policy for increasing organs donated. (More on this to come.)

Whole-Brain Criterion for Death and Criticism of It

Let us now put aside discussing the Report, to say a word about death in connection with organ acquisition. Currently organs may be removed after a whole-brain-death, rather than a cardiovascular-death, criterion is met. (This means organs can be alive and in better condition for a transplant.) That is, even if breathing could be maintained by machine, the person is declared dead when *no* brain function is reported. However, organs may not be removed if there is only higher-brain death. In general, the use of the whole-brain rather than mere higher-brain-death criterion (i.e., death of cortical areas responsible for consciousness and personality) is somewhat puzzling. This is because the whole-brain criterion may, in fact, be a disguised "natural" (machine-independent) cardiovascular-function criterion. That is, breathing independent of a machine depends on lower-brain function. Suppose that all brain function except that which controls breathing had stopped. Would we declare dead someone who was still breathing? If we say no, I believe we are merely concealing a natural cardiovascular criterion behind a total-brain-death criterion. To make this point even clearer, imagine, hypothetically, that breathing were not controlled by the brain at all, but by the liver. Then *total* brain death would be possible, though breathing continued. If we would not declare death when brain function ceased in this case, this would show that a natural cardiovascular-function criterion for death is truly what is operative. We would then have a *whole-liver criterion of death*.

But then why stop with a *natural* cardiovascular criterion? That is, if we value a particular function, we would ordinarily value its presence whether this is caused naturally or artificially. For example, if we value consciousness, then if someone could retain consciousness only via an artificial brain and such a device existed, we would make use of it. We certainly would not declare dead someone who was conscious through the use of such a device and could not be conscious without it. This would be true even if we had a higher-brain criterion of death. On this model, therefore, if cardiovascular *function* is valued, artificial sustenance of it should be sufficient to declare someone alive. However, if we reject this functional criterion for continuing life because the function of breathing is not in itself important, then we should be willing to declare dead the individual whose liver supports breathing. And if we are willing to do this, we should be willing to declare dead the person who has only brain-supported and, hence, natural cardiovascular function.

One objection to this argument is that even if the function of breathing is not in itself of worth, regardless of how it is achieved, we do value some *natural* integrated organ functioning, a sign of which is breathing, but could be anything else. This would imply, however, that if breathing were maintained artificially, but there was natural functioning of the gall bladder and nothing else, we should not declare the person dead. Is this is a reasonable result? Alternatively, some may be interested only in any *natural brain* functioning, whether it leads to breathing or not. This may be because the brain is the most "honored organ." But if none of its valued functions (e.g., consciousness) are present, why continue to honor it?

I believe that conceptually we should be interested in loss of the functions of consciousness and personality, and that a whole-brain rather than a higher-brain criterion should be used only because we are not sufficiently certain which higher brain areas are necessary for these functions, and we prefer to err on the side of safety.[4]

If we reject natural cardiovascular functioning as a sign of life of the person (rather than of his body), this need not mean we would bury such breathing dead people. Just as we may pull out the plug of a machine that keeps breathing going, we may wish to deliberately stop the natural breathing of a dead person whose body is breathing.

Distribution: Need and Outcome

The Report considers degree of need and degree and likelihood of successful outcome to be the primary considerations in deciding who shall get an organ in conditions of scarcity. The Report's notion of need is roughly equivalent to urgency, that is, how soon someone would die, or how badly someone's life would go in the future, without the organ. "Successful outcome" is a function of the additional length of medically adequate life that someone will have as a result of the transplant, compared to what he would have had without it. Its probability is also relevant. (This is not just successful surgery, but further consequences.) The Report does not consider possible conflicts between additional length of life and differing degrees of quality of life. Medically adequate quality is treated as equivalent to superior quality for purposes of deciding on a distribution. It is clearly the good to the patient, not the good to society, of additional time alive that the Report uses to measure successful outcome. This means that social utility and number of dependents are ignored.

From a philosophical point of view the idea of identifying "outcome" with "additional medically adequate years of life" is problematic. One reason is that it implies that we consider only number of additional years and disregard their distribution; that is, we do not consider whether the distribution is fair or equal, or even whether it improves the condition of those most urgent. Philosophers sometimes recommend that we evaluate one outcome as better than another only if it provides that additional years be given to the person who would otherwise be worst off.[5] We should be mindful of these two different notions of outcome. For purposes of this discussion I shall use "outcome" to signify the narrower notion, of additional years of medically adequate life. I shall use the term "state of affairs produced" to signify the broader notion which includes how the additional years are distributed. "Expected outcome" includes reference to probability.

Successful outcome is said to be predicted by such factors as (1) how perfect tissue matches are, (2) the age of the recipient, since the old are less likely to live as many additional years as the young, and (3) other illnesses (which the old are also more likely to have). There is much emphasis on the view that perfectly tissue-matched recipients should be offered organs first, both in order to maximize outcome and to prevent sensitization of patients with imperfect (medically inadequate) matches. This de-emphasizes the use of immunosuppressive drugs in creating a good outcome and gives the Report a "perfect outcome comes first" orientation. (Under UNOS [United Network for Organ Sharing] rules that now regulate distribution, such perfect matches are in fact given precedence.) Success is also a function of patient compliance with the requirements of treatment and of a support network to care for the patient. However the committee suggests that it is desirable to use social services for support, thereby compensating for absence of a family, rather than exclude potential recipients on this ground.

The Report recognizes a conflict between taking care of the most urgent and producing the best outcome since it is an important fact that those who are most urgent from reasons of sickness tend to produce the worst outcomes. This is because the sickest patients are too far gone to benefit much from an organ, unlike those with less severe conditions. However, we should note that while absolute outcomes may be better in the less urgent, it is differential outcome (i.e., the difference between outcome with and outcome without an organ) that is relevant. If those who are less urgent could be treated in other ways besides being given transplants, they would do well even without transplants and might yield even lower *differential* outcomes with transplants than the more urgent.[6] Further, those who are likely to die before others because they are difficult to match may also be considered urgent, though they are not sicker than others, and so they do not necessarily offer poorer outcomes with an appropriate organ.

The Report does not offer a final answer on whether to treat first the urgent who offer at least some significant outcome or the less urgent who offer a better outcome. In practice, the urgent are most likely to be treated. This may be because there is a belief that scarcity is only temporary. One price that we may pay for this, even if there is only temporary scarcity, is that outcomes in general get worse, at least if there is then a long wait by others for another organ when no alternative therapy is useful. This is because the longer someone waits for an organ, the sicker he tends to become and so the worse his outcome tends to become. If scarcity is not just temporary but permanent, some will die, since such scarcity *means* not all who need and can benefit (at least to some degree) are treated. If the urgent are treated first, those who promised better absolute or differential outcomes will die.

Time Waiting and Line Jumping

The longer one waits the more likely one is to become urgent because one becomes sicker; the one who waits longest is more likely to be someone who is sensitized or who is difficult to match. But should time waiting, per se, independent of these associated factors, be relevant in distributing organs, even if one's urgency is lower or the outcome one offers is not as good as that of others? The Report only says that if candidates' urgency and expected outcomes (i.e., length of medically adequate life times probability) are equal, time waiting should be determinative.

Line jumping may permissibly occur for three reasons according to the Report:

1. Individuals who develop the greatest need, usually likelihood of death, move up—or move from outside—the line to its head. What if someone on the line (or off it) develops good prospects for the *best* outcome? Should that person jump the line? I do not think the Report gives a clear answer. It might be that expected outcome is used (in some way) in forming a line, but not for line jumping on an established list.
2. Already sensitized individuals with the same expected outcome as nonsensitized patients, as predicted by tissue matches, are offered an organ first. (This is because they are less likely to match any future organs.)
3. Blood type O material is either (a) offered first to O people otherwise similar in need and expected outcome to blood type A people or (b) offered only to O people. The Report recommends both policies. (This is an error since the two policies are inconsistent with each other and both are inconsistent with other recommendations, as we shall see below.)

These three reasons can be seen as amplifications of the "need-as-urgency" criterion since they represent, in descending order, increased likelihood of someone's dying before receiving an organ. This is because of the greater difficulty, in decreasing order, of the sensitized getting an organ, and of O versus A people getting a suitable organ if O organs are routinely given to A people as well. Blood type O people are more likely to face death because As can use either A or O organs, but Os can use only O organs.

Finally, the Report excludes ability to pay as a ground for distributing organs.

II.   QUESTIONS ABOUT VIEWS ON ACQUISITION
Consent, Dissent, and Conditional Consent

A good deal of the following discussion concerning the role of the original organ owner, his family, doctors, and the state in acquiring organs, is concerned with whose consent is required in order to acquire organs and whether consent can be bypassed entirely.[7] As a background to this discussion, it may be useful to present a brief discussion of the general role of consent in the medical context.

The modern right to give consent is really the right to give or *refuse* consent, after having been provided with information relevant to the risks and benefits of a procedure and its alternatives. The consent at issue is the actual consent of a real person, not the hypothetical consent of a perfect rational person [although, in the course of our discussion of transplants, we shall make reference to the actual consent of people *ex ante* (i.e., much earlier than the occasion when consent about a procedure would have to be made) to waive their right to consent to the procedure].

In fact, many patients do not either simply consent to a procedure or refuse it. Rather they give what I call "conditional consent", i.e., they agree to a procedure if and only if something else is done (e.g., if they are promised a follow-up visit or assured that a certain drug will not be used on them, etc.). While informed consent forms to be signed by patients are now routine, I know of no forms that doctors are required to sign showing that *they* have consented to abide by the conditions the patient has pressed. (It might be useful to introduce such forms.)

Rights, Waivers, and Duties. The right to give informed consent to a procedure gives the medical personnel a duty to ask for it before doing the procedure, but no duty to provide whatever procedure the patient consents to (e.g., there may be scarcity of services, or it may violate a doctor's code to provide the service consented to). That is, informed consent is not a sufficient condition for action by medical personnel (though it might be argued that it is a necessary condition). The exercise of many rights may be waived. One may waive one's right to give informed consent in at least two ways: (1) by not listening to information at all, where this amounts to an implicit "no" to a procedure; or (2) by waiving and transferring one's right to decide to the doctor. Is it possible that there is not only a right to give consent but a duty to do so (i.e., an unwaivable right)? If one emphasizes the responsibility of patients to participate in treatment decisions, one may conclude there is a duty to be informed and to consent or dissent oneself.

Foundations of a Right to Give Informed Consent. So far, our discussion has consisted largely of conceptual analysis. What is the rationale for the view that there is a right to give informed consent, so understood? Decisions in certain legal cases can be read as founding the right in (essentially) a right of self-ownership. If one owns one's body, one has a right that it not be interfered with without one's consent. If there is an unconsented-to intrusion, assault and battery has been perpetrated. If consent is necessary (with exceptions in certain circumstances, e.g., emergencies) and if persons are rational beings, i.e., capable of acting on reason, they will need information about alternatives, risks, and benefits in order to make reasonable choices. Such information should be given outright and independently of a patient's questions. (Presumably, since the information is what "any reasonable person" would need in order to make a reasonable choice, particular follow-up questions by particular patients can pick up on what any particular person wants to know.)

This two-pronged rationale (right of self-ownership and the needs generated by rational decision making) is different from the following (weaker) reasoning: (1) There is a right to give informed consent because it is necessary to avoid harm. Such a foundation might imply that if one is not harmed by a procedure to which one has not consented, one has no complaint. (2) There is a right to give informed consent because if one does not give such consent one's liberty (to choose differently) has been impeded. Such a foundation might imply that if one would have consented to the same procedure one actually undergoes without consent, then one has no complaint. (By implication, on these two views, if a procedure could not be harmful and would be chosen by any reasonable person, the opportunity to give informed consent would not be necessary.)

By contrast, the self-ownership/rational choice foundation makes clear that one can be *wronged* even if one is not harmed or has not had one's liberty to act on an alternative interfered with. One has a ground for complaint if one was not asked because one's right to control what belongs to one was not respected, through failure to obtain consent.[8]

Problems: Consent to Nonintrusive Behavior. One problem with the self-ownership justification is that it is so closely tied to the issue of bodily intrusion and to legal defenses against assault and battery (though this perspective *is* most pertinent to acquiring organs for transplantation). It would fail to predict that one is wronged in the following case: a doctor decides, without telling his patient, not to pursue chemotherapy, which could extend the patient's life by a bit, because he decides that it would be too painful and that overall the costs would outweigh the benefits. In this case, there is no bodily intrusion, rather a failure to intrude, so the justifications offered for informed consent above do not apply. Yet it seems clear that there should be informed consent to such a nontreatment. Though this does not mean that consent to treatment is sufficient to oblige a doctor to treat; and that absent consent to nontreatment, the doctor must treat. Informed consent here is required if this particular doctor-patient relation is to continue; the patient may seek a different doctor if he is informed and cannot consent to nontreatment.

Kantian Justification. One alternative, Kantian-type justification for seeking informed consent which would cover such a case focuses on a duty to promote those (morally permitted) ends of rational beings which form part of their own personal conception of the good. This is a way of promoting autonomy. (But note that autonomy may be more than a value we should promote; its exercise may be thought of as a right then we may not sacrifice its exercise in one person merely to maximize its presence overall in other people.) This view does not reject the idea of self-ownership and indeed must make use of it as well, for one's consent to procedures cannot ordinarily legitimate their use on what one has no right to control, e.g., a stranger's body. But it does provide a broader non-paternalistic view, that one should not act even nonintrusively and for someone's sake without consulting him and his own conception of his good. Note that even if one could bring about the fulfillment of a persons's own conception of the good better without consulting him, one should still get consent out of respect for his right to rational self-governance. (On this view, it may be more justifiable to fail to promote someone's conception of the good in order to protect one's own interests of—or those of others—than to do the same for *his* sake. As rational beings, persons not only form a conception of their own good, but can act on reasons and so should be reasoned with. Yet we are creatures of only limited rationality, especially when subject to illness. In recognition of this fact, we should try to help people exercise as much of their rational faculties as possible, not make decisions for them. On a Kantian view, the role of the right to informed consent, as of rights in general, is to preserve equality to as great a degree as possible and ward off servility and submission.

Possible Limits on Informed Consent Relevant to Transplantation. We have already mentioned the possibility that being informed and giving or refusing consent may be a duty rather than merely a right. If this were so, it might be required that someone be informed of the fates of those who will not receive organs because she will not donate or because she takes an organ for herself when there is scarcity. My own sense is that one has no duty to be informed in this way, and that one can set limits to the information one receives.[9]

If one had a duty to perform certain acts, e.g., arrange for donation of one's organs after one's death, then there might be less pressure on medical personnel to get informed consent to take the organs, since proceeding without consent only makes a patient do what he has a duty to do. In general, emphasis on patients' duties, e.g., to participate in experiments, should raise serious concerns insofar as it plays such a role in arguments for bypassing acquisition of consent. The legitimacy of bypassing consent for this and other reasons in the context of transplantation is a topic we shall discuss in greater detail below.

Acquisition by Gift

If the only (or primary) means of acquiring organs is through donation, one might think distribution of the gift should be solely up to the donors. This is what happens when donors who will continue to live give up their organs to others selected by them, as in live kidney or liver-section donation. This implies, contrary to the Report, that if the organs were seriously thought of as gifts, we would not treat those acquired after the donor's death as a national public resource. Rather, we would treat them as private gifts to be distributed in accord with private preferences, unless they were donated with no designated donee. In fact, the Uniform Anatomical Gift Act allows the donor to specify a donee.[10]

The government might be worried that private designation would not lead to distribution according to greatest need or best outcome and would allow gender and race discrimination.[11] However, designating a particular donee is not the same as designating on the basis of a suspect category like race.[12] In any case, my point here is that it should not be thought that distribution on the basis of "fair" criteria is implied simply by the fact that the organs are gifts.

Notice also that the fact that donors do not receive money for organs (this being what "gift" is usually thought to amount to)—in fact, donors are now prohibited from receiving money—may suggest that distributors of the organs should not reap a personal profit denied to the original organ owners. But the fact that organs are gifts does not imply that recipients should never pay for organs. That the organs are given as gifts is consistent with recipients being selected by "fair criteria" and having to pay if they could afford to. The money could go to a worthy cause, not to the donor. (I return below to the issue of distribution by ability to pay and its connection with means of acquisition.)

The Family's Role When the Original Owner Has Decided: Who Is Harmed or Helped?

Why should a family be allowed to override the original owner's (legal) decision to give? (The family does not have the right to override the original owner's express *refusal* to give.) It might be argued that the family members are alive and will suffer if we do not abide by their wishes (and more so if their wish is not to take, versus to take, organs), whereas the dead person can no longer be harmed if we do not do what she wanted. (Of course, in the case of a difficult match, the person who does not receive the organs may well be irreparably harmed. Let us put that to one side at this point.)

But it is a mistake to think that the dead are beyond being harmed or benefited. We can harm them by defaming their reputations after their deaths or by destroying the projects they completed in their lifetime. (We could do this even if such harms were permitted and so did not *wrong* them.) We may benefit the dead by completing their projects. The fact that they do not know they are harmed or benefited does not mean they have not been harmed or benefited. One reason they *would* be angry or happy *if* they did know what we had done, is that what we have done is either harmful or beneficial for them, independent of their knowing of it.[13]

If we do not satisfy the desires someone had that his organs be transplanted, do we harm or rather merely fail to benefit him? It might be suggested that we come closer to failing to benefit than to harming, but that is still something. The dead person did not necessarily have (only) the desire that he should know that his wish to donate was satisfied. Rather, he had the desire to donate. We can still satisfy his desire that his organs be transplanted, even if, because he is dead, he receives no felt satisfaction from this. In carrying out his wishes, I believe, we will have helped him, though he doesn't know we have. This is a reason for so doing with him in mind, as much as if we carry out the comparable wish of a living person (or a dead person's will). However, since the object of his desire is that others be benefited, it may not, strictly speaking, be correct to say that we benefit him, the person whose desire we satisfy. But we do help him to satisfy his desire.

Wronging the Dead

Suppose the original owner not only desired that his organs be transplanted, but had a moral right to control the fate of his body, even after death, with a concomitant right that others not control it against his wishes. (This right would be comparable to his rights over his property if he is permitted to write a will.) Then we wrong him, by violating his rights to control his body, if we recognize a right in someone else to override his wishes. I do not believe a family has a moral right to control the original owner's body superseding his own right simply because their feelings will be hurt if his organs are taken, any more than they may arrange for taking when he has explicitly refused. (Not allowing organs to be taken is to exercise control as much as directing that they be taken.)

However, suppose we refuse to carry out the original owner's wishes because the cost to us (society) is too great. (For example, suppose we would alienate the public from organ transplants if we acted against families' wishes. Then the cost in terms of lives lost might be great.) We would then not literally accord others a right to override his decision, and so we would not wrong him in this way. And he may have no right that we obey his wishes at large cost to ourselves. We might even refuse to carry out his wishes because we simply desire not to hurt the family's feelings, without thereby recognizing any right of the family to override his wishes.

But if the family does not have a moral right to override the dead person's choice, is it truly right that they should have de facto power to affect our behavior in this way, especially when other lives are at stake? And should we not rather stem public alienation by explaining that the family best shows respect for the dead by following his wishes?

Of course, if the original organ owner's *expressed desire that his family be satisfied* were stronger than his desire to donate, his family may override his desire to donate. But then, it is *his concern for them and our respect for that, not their concern for his organs per se,* that would give them the right to make a decision.

The Family's Role in the Absence of the Original Owner's Decision: Substituted Judgment?

How does the family acquire a moral and legal right to decide to give a dead relative's organs when the relative has made no decision on organ donation? The family's right may arise because their decision is an instance of "substituted judgment." That is, they may be deciding as they think the dead person would have decided. In most other situations of substituted judgment, the family acquires a right because its members are thought to know best what their relative wanted, though she or he did not make a public commitment. Or an organ owner may have feared that a public commitment to give his organs would lead doctors not to treat his illness aggressively. He may therefore have expressed his desire to his family in private. The family then becomes a conduit for the dead person's views. If a patient's instructions could be read from a sealed document opened only after his death, this last need for the family's role could be avoided.[14]

The "Best Interests" Argument

In many situations not involving organ transplants, the family is allowed to make decisions, even if they are not claiming to know the person's desires, on the ground that they will decide in her best interests. In the case of organs, however, the family seems to be deciding a question not about the best interest of the deceased family member, but about using her organs for someone else's best interests. There may be a very stretched sense in which they are acting for her best interests: Suppose that a life in which a person has helped others is a morally better one, and that one could make someone's life better by having that person play even a nonactive role he has not himself chosen in a project that contributes to greater good. (This is a controversial claim.) Then something comparable could be said about the dead and using their organs to help others. This is true even though we may not literally have made the deceased person's "life" better.

In deciding *not* to donate, the family could also be protecting the decedent's interests. Suppose the decedent's losing an organ would, for example, jeopardize his eternal survival in a life after death. Then the family could be acting to protect his interests if they decline to donate his organs. More generally, suppose there were self-interested reasons why someone ought not to donate his organs or self-interested reasons that justified someone's reluctance to donate. Then a family who acted on these reasons would be acting in the interest of the decedent. (Below we shall consider some nonreligious reasons that could justify reluctance to donate.)

Concern and Ownership

Finally, the family may be thought to have a moral and a legal right to decide because, next to the original owner, they care most about the organs in question, as *parts of the original owner*. Because they care, they may need the organs in order to come to terms with the death of a relative. (This, however, would imply that they have a veto over organs being taken, not power to donate.)[15] Alternatively, ownership of the body may simply pass to them. Of these two, only ownership could yield a moral and legal right, I believe. Neither caring most, nor the fact that they will be comforted by keeping or giving an organ, would seem to be a strong enough basis for a moral and legal right to decide. The thought may be that if those who care most about the body are willing to give parts of it away, it must be all right to do this. But my caring most about something does not, in general, give me a right to control its fate. And it is also possible that, although the family cares more for this particular body than anybody else does, they do not care enough.

Suppose something like property rights in the body would be sufficient to yield a right to donate. Presumably it is such property-like rights that the original owner has. Should a family, independent of the original owner's willing it, acquire all the original owner's powers of ownership of a body, as they do over unwilled furniture? Although one's own body may be appropriately thought of as one's property, conferring a great deal of control over disposition, it is harder to think of the body as *simply property,* which can pass (unwilled by its original owner) to relatives.[16]

A Proposal

The modern controversy has, in part, been over whether to recognize that a person, and not only the family, should have legal rights to arrange for the disposition of the person's remains after death. But there have been recent attempts to argue that neither a person nor the family should have property-like rights in the remains, which are, rather, community property to be used for the community's benefit.[17] The view I propose is that a person has property-like moral rights in his body and on this basis can have a legal right to decide about his remains. He can pass on or deny these rights to others by will, but the rights do not pass by intestate succession (without being willed and in the absence of active denial) to the family. Ideally, if a right to dispose of the organs is not willed, the use of the bodily organs would come to an end with the original owner's death. The familial right or duty to bury follows from a limited stewardship role. However, there is reason to believe that this ideal could be overridden, as we shall see below.

Why We Want the Family to Have a Right

Some, who assume the family does *not* care as much for their relation's organs as he did, may *wish* the family could automatically get an owner's right. This is because the family is likely to give if it cares less about the organs. Alternatively, they may be comforted by giving his organs, and this, too, will increase the pool of organs. That is, people may be reluctant to will their own organs (for reasons having nothing to do with fear that their illness will be treated less aggressively), but not be so reluctant with other people's. If the reluctance to will one's own organs is not truly rational, but is permitted to determine outcomes nevertheless, and if the family's response is more rational, society may wish the family to decide. At least, they may wish for this when it does not override what we or they know to have been the original owner's wishes. Notice, however, that if one deliberately waits to ask permission of the family when one *could* have asked the original owner, this suggests that one knows the owner's answer would have been negative. Giving the family control when we could have asked the owner, but did not, seems like an attempt to override the owner's negative wishes.

Alternatives: Selling Organs

What are some alternatives to the present means of acquiring organs? Organs might be sold by original owners if this would increase the number given or distribute those given more in accord with need and outcome. That is, donors might be paid, and so become sellers. This does not imply that recipients would pay; the government, or the hospital might. Subsidized purchases and fixed prices might be an alternative to a market.[18] An objection to any sort of money sale, especially an open market, is that more appropriate criteria for who gets the organ than who pays for it should be in place. These are issues of distribution. But, as noted, payment could be offered to a seller by the government or hospital, with distribution determined independently. The poor would be more likely to sell than the rich and less likely to be able to pay for organs if the government did not subsidize purchases. Paternalistic fears that the poor would be imprudent and endanger their health by selling organs for money might be dealt with by not permitting sales by the living who will go on living; allowing only the dying to sell organs taken after their death. (Sale by the living of replenishable body parts, e.g. blood, is less worrisome.) The price could be set high enough to encourage a sale but not high enough to encourage a poor person to induce an immediately life-threatening condition for the sake of a sale. Quality control could be introduced to deal with the (sometimes supposed) effect of a market or any sale mechanism, that poorer quality material is elicited than through altruism.

Is there still something further morally wrong with selling one's parts? On some views, the person is a nonphysical entity (a soul) in a very intimate relation to a body. On such a view, selling body parts could not be selling oneself, strictly speaking. On other views, the person *is* the live body, or perhaps a part of it (e.g., the brain). No one takes the view that a person *is* the dead body. But it is the organs kept alive after the person is dead that are donated. Still, donating a person's live parts (perhaps excluding the live brain) is not the same as donating the person.[19]

The idea that a person may not sell himself is given one defense in Kantian ethics: Things that have value because they are valued by rational beings have a price, but rational beings have worth in themselves, independent of whether anyone values them. Therefore they have no price, but rather dignity. This is an argument against the commodification of persons. Some would extend this to an argument against commodification even of labor. But why should these views affect the permissibility of arranging for the sale after one's death of a nondead body part, which by itself will not be oneself, nor (unlike labor) a part of oneself at the time another uses it. There will be no (apparent) risk to one's welfare, and compensation is given to the original owner herself. To see people as the source of commodities is not necessarily to see them *as* commodities.

It is sometimes thought that one should not commodify anything to which one is intimately related and should only give such a thing as a gift. But then should not the prohibition on selling a body part be related to how psychologically, rather than physically, intimate that something is, how involved one's personality is with that part? One's personality is less involved with one's kidney than with one's sexuality. The "stupid" question, "What is your favorite internal organ?" makes this point nicely.[20] Therefore, sale of a kidney (even during one's lifetime) might be permissible, even if prostitution is not. (It is usually thought permissible to take money for the use of parts of oneself with which one's personality is involved if this use is good *for oneself,* e.g., money to model one's face. Disputes about sale may arise when the use is not good for one. Likewise, one may accept payment for use of one's skills because this promotes one's development, but this is different from accepting payment to allow one's talents to rot.)

Coercive Offers

The concern that the poor, rather than the rich, will sell organs is a concern independent of commodification per se. Even if a rich person sees a part of himself as potentially a commodity for sale, he nevertheless does not feel tempted to sell it. This raises the issue of coercion, and coercive offers, which are concerns whether donations are during life or after death. Like the offer of money for some jobs, to which the poor are also more susceptible than the rich, the offer for organs may be coercive. This is in part because what the poor must give up is something they would much rather not give up, but their desperate straits prompt a sale. Some countries have allowed such sales by the poor; such sales may even be Pareto optimal for them. That is, the poor can then feed their children, who matter more to them than their organs do. Yet all this is not enough to endorse such sales. For we might strongly prefer that the poor feed their children in some other way, for example, by improved welfare payments. Then they will not be driven to selling organs. Passing laws against such sales might be justified if this served as an impetus to welfare payments.

One reason money sales may seem objectionable is that they could often involve "selling one's principles" as well as one's body parts. That is, suppose someone has personal or religious reasons for not wanting to give body parts (his own or others). Then he is offered money. If he accepts, it becomes clear to himself and to others that he has sold his principles. It may be best for society not to offer the opportunity for such weakness of will.

Finally, there may be objections to someone other than the original organ owner arranging for a sale, objections that do not arise if the original owner were to sell. If family do not have property rights over a body, they may not sell even though the original owner might have. If they should only do what the original owner would have wanted, they may not sell unless they know he wanted to sell.

Organ Trading: Insurance

A way of acquiring organs from *nondying* donors that could be prudent would involve organ trading. People might give organs not necessary for their good health, in exchange for the assurance that if they were to need an organ in the future, they would have a better chance of acquiring one. (This is a form of sale.) The dying might also use organ trading, giving their organs in order to improve the chances that a loved one would get a needed organ. Here people give in order to get. They may also first get, contingent on an agreement to give later, perhaps after death. Those who are unwilling to agree to later donation might be put behind those who are willing to donate or have donated when they themselves are on line for receipt of an organ. In these schemes, giving or willingness to give helps one to get, and getting commits one to giving. They are like insurance schemes, connecting distribution with acquisition, either as an incentive—if you give, you will get—or as a price—if you've gotten, you must give.

Retaining Altruism

One organ distribution system incorporating aspects of such insurance schemes, but retaining noninsurance altruism, would treat individuals who for medical reasons cannot spare organs on a par with individuals who can donate. Individuals who are medically able to donate, but won't, would be treated less favorably on a waiting list. The distinction between inability and unwillingness to donate is crucial in this scheme. (Similarly we can distinguish between rejecting people as friends because they have no money to spend on us [wrong] and rejecting people as friends because, though they have money, they will not spend any on us [sometimes permissible]). Those who trade may do so for insurance reasons, but altruism has a role in helping those who cannot reasonably buy insurance, and willful free riding is eliminated.

A system in which all donations were more clearly altruistic (not paid for, not part of an insurance scheme) might also involve a clause giving lower priority to those medically capable of donating but not acting altruistically. It could do this without becoming a nonaltruistic insurance system. Mutual altruism is expected in friendship, and we may break off friendships with people who are not reciprocally altruistic in the relation. Yet friendship is not an insurance system *if* we give when we know we will not need in return and do not exclude as friends people who lack resources with which to be altruists. The Report itself presupposes such an analysis in its discussion of the distribution of some U.S. organs to nonresident aliens (pp. 93–95). It suggests that we give a certain amount to aliens of other countries for altruistic reasons and encourage other countries to reciprocate. But it also considers not giving aid if other countries do not reciprocate. Encouraging reciprocation in others does not make the system cease to be altruistic and become a mere insurance scheme if countries who truly cannot donate are still not denied benefits and if we donate even though we do not need in return. (Individual nonresidents who receive scarce organs might be required to give in return, on the grounds that access to organ transplants is not a universal human right but a society-relative benefit. If one has overcome the religious or traditional objections to transplant's that impede their development in one's own country, one should be able to overcome objections to eventual donation in return for treatment, so as to replenish the organ pool in the guest country.)

Presumably, reciprocally altruistic donors would be even more willing than self-insurers to provide organs for those truly unable to donate. The likelihood, of course, is that any system that both contains an altruistic element and punishes attempted free riding will induce potential free riders to adopt an insurance motive for joining the scheme as a way of not losing out on benefits.

In thinking about these various schemes, it is interesting to see how an insurance scheme that is altruistic toward those incapable of donating *and* not altruistic toward those who will not donate is extensionally equivalent to reciprocal altruism that covers those incapable of donating and excludes those not willing to donate.

Taking in the Face of Opposition

Another alternative policy of acquiring organs is simply to take them after death. Taking is not literally a policy of presumed consent (although some may call it this) since it presumes nothing about the intentions of the original owner. Consider an analogy: Suppose five people are adrift in the sea after a shipwreck, and one of them dies of unavoidable natural causes. Are the other four justified, not merely excused on account of mental distress, if they save their own lives by taking the organs of the dead person when the deceased or family's wishes are not known? If they are too weak to take, may a third party who is in no need help them to do so? What if they or the third party know that the decedent or the family would be opposed to such taking? *If* all agents were justified in taking in all these circumstances, this would support the view that third parties may, in general, take organs no longer being used for the sake of those who would otherwise die. To those who would classify the postshipwreck case, but not the general need for organs, as an emergency, it is useful to remember that lives are lost when transplantable organs are not available. Furthermore, how many lives will be counted as lost may be in part a function of how many organs we have. For, if we know we have few, we may eliminate as even possible candidates the old and those with a prognosis for a low quality of life. These tend to be classified as "futile," or hopeless, but in fact they only offer a low probability of a minimally good outcome. This may lead us to ignore these deaths when counting how many die because of scarcity.

Reasons for a Duty to Give and a Right to Take?

What reasons can be given to support such taking? If the original owner or family had a duty to give, this would help us to argue for taking from recalcitrants. (It would not be conclusive support for taking because someone may have a duty that others must nevertheless not enforce.) Some of the reasons for thinking we have a duty to give organs that we are not using are also reasons for taking, even if we have no duty to give and also object to giving. One two-part reason involves the (supposed) insignificance of the harm done to us if our organ remains are used when they would otherwise rot and the significance of the good done with them.[21] We can accept such a reason without thereby justifying general utilitarian reasoning wherein *any* lesser harm is outweighed by *any* greater good.

Why is there only insignificant harm? Suppose I take organs for transplantation from someone who is dead and who wanted his organs buried. I do not injure (cause bodily damage to) *him* or violate *his* liberty to act in the future. He is dead. We damage his remains, but they would have rotted anyway. I do violate his liberty in the sense that I prevent his wishes from being carried out, i.e., refusing his organs for donation. And I do fail to respect his right to control his body. That is, even if he is not harmed and even if he would have donated if asked, I do not respect his right to make the decision. In these ways I can wrong the dead. However, it has been argued[22] that, even when we deal with the living, a right to control property and act on a preference may permissibly be infringed to save a life. For example, suppose someone's toothbrush is old and unused by him so there is no damage to him if we take it, and it can be used to save a life. Then, even if he refuses to donate it, it seems morally permissible to take it.

If we take the toothbrush, we may still agree that we have not respected its owner's property right nor liberty in the course of doing the overall right act. We may, therefore, think the owner has a right to compensation for these wrongs. However, suppose we cannot compensate him because, for example, it is physically impossible to do so. It does not follow that we may not act.

Suppose someone who is still alive has had his kidney removed and keeps it in a preservative jar in his back yard, unused and forgotten. In this case, the kidney would not rot anyway if we do not take it, and the owner is still alive. Nevertheless we would not need to interfere with him physically while he is alive or interfere with any liberty of his except deciding how the kidney will be used. Furthermore, he is not using the kidney for any other significant purpose, so his interests are not set back in this respect. These factors make it easier to justify taking his kidney to save a life.

Suppose it is permissible to infringe a property right of the *living* in this way when there is no bodily damage to the person and no physical liberty interfered with, even when we cannot compensate. Why may we not infringe the property rights of the dead, even if this infringement is some other wrong to them? After all, there is no bodily damage to the person (only to his remains), no interference with his liberty of action after death, and his organs would rot in the ground anyway. Further, his family may be offered compensation. This reasoning is similar to the justification of eminent domain by the government.

What is called for here is a judgment in the particular case. This does not commit us to saying that we are always free to take all things that people discard and that will rot anyway (e.g., their garbage) for any purpose we wish. They might, for example, strenuously object to our purpose, our purpose could be morally wrong, or we might profit from the use of their former property when they could have profited instead. These factors may often make taking morally impermissible. Furthermore, although a single taking to save *one* life is theoretically permitted on the argument I have described, if there is much (even unjustified) social opposition to taking, it may not pay to take unless *many* lives could be saved. Notice, also, that we may have to treat differently items that are deliberately discarded (like garbage) and items over which someone cannot help losing physical control (like their body remains). It seems that it should be easier to take the former than the latter.

The Family

If a policy of taking did not seriously infringe the dead person's rights, would it nevertheless harm or wrong the family seriously? Even if they have no right to give permission for an organ to be used, might they have a veto over a taking? If there were significant psychological damage to them in not having the complete body of a relative buried, should we conclude it was wrong to take it?

Suppose we agree that we could not demand a large sacrifice from someone to save another's life. Could we then argue as follows: The family need not sacrifice much to save another's life; suffering at a relative's dismemberment is a large sacrifice; therefore, we may not impose it on them?

Not straightforwardly. If the relative's body does not belong to his family, taking his organ is not, strictly, taking something from them. This, therefore, cannot be their *sacrifice*. If they suffer, it is as a side effect of our taking what is not theirs in order to help others. Further, this is not imposing a sacrifice on them for the sake of another; their suffering is not intended because it is causally efficacious in saving the life. Likewise, if we use a procedure to save a life that causes emotional upset in the community, the community is not having a sacrifice imposed on it intentionally for the sake of saving a life.

To repeat, the concern of relatives does not give them a right to control the bodily remains of their relative; so, in using his body, we do not make them sacrifice by taking what is theirs, and their suffering is not a sacrifice we impose for the sake of another. Nevertheless, I understand the impulse not to take if the original owner has not donated, in the face of the family's suffering. One explanation of this might be that the remains of my relative *are* mine to keep in the condition consistent with the family's burial practice, though not mine in a complete sense, for example, to give away. I have *some* of the rights of ownership.

Suppose I have a right to maintain a certain relation with my relative's remains, a right that these remains play such a part in my life (so long as the relative did not object to this). Then it is a sacrifice to make me give this up to save someone else's life, especially if giving it up causes me much suffering. It might be asked, How could this sacrifice outweigh the fact that someone will die if it is not made? We must consider what type of people we want to be, that is, shall we be people who also have the option of having this relation to their relative's remains, or people who place saving life above the possibility of such a relation?

Suppose the family has this right to maintain a personal relation with a relative's remains. Still it is true that when no family members are in opposition, the state might permissibly override the dead person's wishes not to donate or take from original owners who have not explicitly donated.

An Intransitivity

Suppose the family's feelings do provide a veto over the state's taking organs that were not donated by the deceased. That is, Family Desire > State Action. We have also argued that the decision of the deceased about his organs should dominate a family's feelings. That is, the Deceased's Desire > Family Desire. From these two premises should we not conclude, *by transitivity,* that the Deceased's Desire > State Action? We have, of course, argued that State Action > Deceased's Desire in a taking policy. Is this wrong, or is one of the two premises wrong? Can they all be true, despite the apparent intransitivity?

I believe we have an example of a permissible sort of intransitivity.[23] That is, where ">" means "dominates":

1. Deceased's Desire > Family Desire
2. Family Desire > State Action, but
3. − (Deceased's Desire > State Action), and indeed
4. State Action > Deceased's Desire.

The explanation of the reasonableness of this intransitivity depends on our understanding that each dominance relation depends on a different factor.

For example, we can explain the first claim if the deceased's desire takes precedence because family members should stand in an egalitarian relation to the original owner and therefore their felt suffering at his decision should not override his rights over his own body; this is so even though he will not experience suffering if his wishes are overridden. (The egalitarian impulse in not overriding someone's will is not present if the deceased is a child.) We can explain the second claim if there is a right of the family to have the remains play a role in their life and if their experienced suffering if the remains are taken is significant enough to override the claims of another person's life. Then the state, which represents that other person's interests, must back down. Finally, we can explain the third claim if the state, in its role as representative of the interests of the needy stranger, can override the deceased's rights over his body in part because neither the state nor the stranger stand in a relation of intimacy that requires egalitarianism. There is insult only if a family member acting on behalf of the stranger, not the state or a stranger himself, overrides our directives over what was our body.

Taking in the Absence of Opposition

A more moderate scheme than taking in the face of family opposition involves taking organs from the dead *if* there is no expressed opposition. Requiring the family or original owner expressly to refuse permission, rather than waiting for them to make a donation, still increases the burden on them in several ways. Obviously, it means they must do something if the transplant is to be prevented. But, more importantly, it also puts them in the position of interfering with the commencement of life-support procedures for the stranger, which would automatically occur if they did not act. People usually find it somewhat more difficult to interfere with on-going life support, or a process that will lead to such life support, than merely to stand by, not initiating aid. This problem for the donor's family increases the likelihood of getting an organ. But the true voluntariness of owners' or families' consent is correspondingly decreased. In sum, it is not as easy to stop a process of the organ going to the recipient that would have begun automatically, as it would have been to refuse to give when explicit donation was needed to start the process rolling.

Deriving the Family's Right from the State's Right

Suppose there was no family veto, i.e., society had a moral right to take even over the opposition of both the original owner and family when the harm to each is not great. Still, society might *wish* not to upset living relatives even to this lesser degree. Suppose, in addition, that we knew that relatives would be more likely than the original owner to agree to let organs be used and that the original owner has not explicitly refused. Society could then grant the family a legal right to decide to give. In this case, the family's legal right to decide is derived from (1) society's prior moral right to take when no great cost is involved, and (2) certain information about probable family behavior. As long as enough organs for transplantation can be got from families willing to give, society's moral right to take without family consent when there is no great harm done to them, and the lack of any fundamental right on the family's part to decide about donation (as argued for above), need never make any practical difference. (Note that this way of deriving a family's rights to donate applies even if the family does have a veto on a state's right to take.)

Three conditions should limit such a granting of rights to the family, however. First, although society may often permissibly override the original owner's express refusal to donate, it seems inappropriate for family members who should have stood in an egalitarian relation to the original owner to be granted that power. It is especially humiliating to think that one's relatives (rather than society as a whole) have powers to override one's decision, *including* one's decision that their preferences not be determinative. Saying that society has the strong right to take, and that the State can be its agent in taking the organs, is really a way of saying that it is for the best that the organs be taken. But to say it is for the best does not mean that just anyone can carry out the act of taking. Second, granting the family the right to override the original owner's decision to donate would also hinder the goal of acquiring organs. Third, a policy requiring that medical personnel request organs of families rather than wait for volunteers seems most efficient, and, unlike waiting for refusal, does not diminish voluntariness.

Returning the Family's Right to the State

Although society might permit the family to make the decision to donate, the family may wish society would relieve them of the burden. Contrary to the opinion of the Report that families find solace in giving a relative's organs, responsibility for authorizing removal of organs may produce great strain in a family member. Likewise, the individual who faces impending death may himself find deciding to give organs too great a strain. This strain could exist even if, when considering the matter before being called upon to make a decision, everyone in the society believed it would be best for all needed organs to be removed and transplanted. Further, this strain could exist even if, at the time a decision must be made, family members, or the original owner himself, wish the organs to be removed, *though not by their directive*. No one wants responsibility for the decision. All could want to be forced to do what they cannot bring themselves to do voluntarily.

To avoid the strain of actual decision making, individuals could make another decision ex ante (that is, prior to the actual decision-making time): Let the government take the organs when a death occurs. Here, instead of the society simply taking organs for reasons of necessity, the citizenry is granted the right to vote on the specific policy of "taking on occasions when it is necessary." This is a way in which society could be said to waive its moral right simply to take the organs to save life, instead allowing individuals to decide on government policy. Then citizens might decide ex ante to bind themselves by taking the later decision to remove organs out of their own hands and putting it back into the government's. (Somewhat analogously, they might now decide on a policy to have themselves taxed later, recognizing that they would not have the moral strength to donate money voluntarily to the public good on the later occasions when it would be necessary.)

Suppose one did *not* believe that society had a right to take organs, a right that it could transfer to the family and that the family could, in turn, transfer back. (A veritable "hot potato.") One could still derive society's right to take via individuals' ex ante decision to cede any fundamental decision-making authority they had to the government. They do this in order to avoid the strain of actually donating organs that, ex ante, they think they should donate. After such a social decision, and at the time of a particular taking, *consent* of the organ owner and family would be *presumed*. This is consistent with some right to object on the part of the minority who voted against taking. We should not, I think, presume general consent without such a vote, however.[24] I believe only this sort of reasoning justifies calling a policy one of Presumed Consent.

Why Object to Donating: Unended Use-history?

If there are good arguments for simply taking organs, perhaps they are held in check to some degree by trying to understand some people's discomfort with even voluntary donation by original owners of body parts. The problem in understanding this discomfort lies in locating a wrong that is not an injury to, or violation of the future liberty of, a person, and is more serious than a property-right infringement and infringement of a past choice, and would befall dead persons when we take their organs for use. This must be a wrong or harm that does not befall them if their organs rot in the grave instead. One suggestion is that the harm or wrong consists in *the use-history of something to which the person was intimately connected, or that actually was the person when he was alive, not ending with the end of the person's own history.*

Consider these analogies: Your pet for many years has died; you must decide whether to give away his water dish or bury it with him. Or your husband has died; you must decide whether to give his wedding ring to someone else for that person's use or to bury the ring with him. In each of these cases, I believe, we can understand the claim that the more you cared about your pet or about your husband, the more appropriate it is that you not allow others to use what had regularly and solely been used by them. (Perhaps you might keep the items, but that is not really an option with organs.) In the case of the ring, I believe, this is because we think your husband would have considered himself harmed by the further use; he would have opposed the use on the grounds that (somehow) it diminishes a relationship in which he was involved. You are, therefore, protecting his interests in not giving it. (What counts is not necessarily his having these beliefs, but whether it would be understandable if he had them.)[25]

One's relation to one's body is, at the very least, regular, intimate, and associated with the person one is. If we take its parts and give them to others (but *not* if we let them rot in the ground), we prevent their use-history's ending with the person. *Their identity as belonging to the person alone is not retained.* Furthermore, if we take organs of the dead for use by others, the bodies of those who are still alive could be thought of as on loan to them, something to be used for a while and then to be passed on to others. (We might even feel pressured to treat our organs better, in view of the fact that others could get them.) *Our treatment of the dead changes our attitude to our own bodies while we are alive.* Our sense of ourselves as *different* embodied people may diminish, for good or ill.[26] From the survivor's point of view, there may be some difficulty psychologically separating from the dead person since his organs remain alive in others.

Degrees of Intimacy and the Significance of Ending Use-history

A person may have a more intimate relation to some of his body parts than to others; he may identify more with one part than with another. For example, if *total face transplants* were physically possible, there might be many more refusals to donate than there are for kidneys. (Why, rather than pride that one's most distinctive characteristics go on, as when one's children resemble one? Perhaps, because a *stranger* will have one's most distinctive characteristics.) This suggests that the more we "see" the person himself in the body part, the more significant it is if its use-history does not end because we take it after death for someone else's use.

Therefore, unlike the property right we infringe when we take the toothbrush, a more significant harm or wrong can be done to a dead person when a body part is used by another: The use-history of an item intimately related to the dead person does not end when he dies, and this is worse to the extent that the item was more closely tied to the person's identity. Of course, people do give up intimate things that have been theirs alone. The claim is only that the act of detachment involved in this giving up can involve a significant sacrifice. This is true even when the person would no longer be able to use the item himself, and it would be destroyed. Nevertheless, the location of a more significant harm or wrong that can occur if organs are used by others does not imply that if the need is great enough, we may not simply take the organ. We just understand better the harm involved.

Dismemberment and the Invisibility of Decay

Are there other sources of discomfort with the use of organs from the dead even when consented to? Suppose we buried people's organs, so their use-history ended with the person, but we dismembered the various parts of the body before burying them. The fact that the person's body had been dismembered might be disturbing to many. Is the fact that the whole decays gradually crucial then? But suppose we did not bury bodies, but allowed them to decay gradually *in our presence*. The fact that we saw the person's body come to naught might be disturbing. Likewise, dismemberment of inner organs seem to be less disturbing than visible disfigurement. It seems important that the last contact of the living with the dead should be with what *seems* to be an intact body; anything else may take away a continuing illusion of life. People may prefer that the undeniable evidence of death and radical change that a dismembered surface or decayed body presents come to exist beyond sight. But this would not interfere with internal organs being removed or visible dismemberment that occurred out of sight of relatives, at least if the reaction of nonrelatives was not crucial. However, there may be an additional preference that known radical change actually happen at a point *in the future* when the death has faded from memory somewhat.[27]

The practice of cremation raises a question about whether people do in fact react this way. Nevertheless, let us suppose such reactions exist. Should they not be grounds for speaking of the harm, or perhaps only offense, that the taking of organs causes *to the living* and not to the dead? After all, the dead person is not robbed of the illusion that he is still alive. The possibility exists, however, that we may all prefer that others see us, finally, in an undecayed, undismembered state and also prefer that we be thought of as whole even on the inside at the time of the most intense response to our deaths.

An Alternative View of Personal Identity

What lies behind some people's opposition to donating and to receiving organs is the belief that a person's identity inheres in all parts of the body.[28] (Such a view has been expressed to me by some doctors.) To give away an organ is, then, to give away not merely a bodily part that supported one's existence before brain death; it is to give something that retains traces of one's personality. Likewise to receive an organ from someone else is to receive something in which that other person's personality inheres. On such a view, it would be permissible to take from the deceased person an *artificial* organ he had been using, but not an organ with his own genetic code. The first is not thought to have his personal characteristics.

This view of personal identity certainly seems to be radical. Since it insists that personality-bearing items live on after brain death, it may call into question the brain-death criterion of death. If it were true it would not be clear that one should even bury a brain-dead body whose organs were still alive or terminate life support to it. However, it may be possible to distinguish between the person still being alive and an information program for the person continuing on. This would make sense of the objection to transplants, if personality characteristics "came to life" again in the recipient. It is important to emphasize that there is no evidence for the truth of such a view of personal identity, without denying brain death as criterion for death.

SUMMARY

A strand of current social thought tends to de-emphasize the individual and the impersonal state, and emphasize middle-level social units such as the family. Nevertheless, I believe we are morally more justified in emphasizing individualism and donation from the original organ owner, and instituting policies that ensure his wishes are carried out. Such a policy might, for example, *allow potential recipients to sue if the decedent's expressed will to donate is not acted on.*[29] We are also justified in deriving society's and the State's right to take for reasons of social need, perhaps limited by the family's veto. But we seem not to be justified in locating in the next of kin a fundamental right to make donation decisions, other than those based on the principle of substituted judgment, especially decisions that override an original owner's dominant will to donate. Deriving a family's right to decide *directly* from society's need for organs is also problematic. For it seems a social need would most directly give society, not the family, a right, and it is only fear of a too powerful state that would lead us to deny this.

The view I have presented here is twofold. First, persons have a property-like relation to their own bodies, but the family should not automatically have similar property-like rights in a relative's remains. Second, social need may sometimes permissibly override the original owner's property rights. A subsidiary claim is that the family's suffering can veto the state's but not a relative's decisions. Society's right to take organs from corpses is closely connected to the fact that taking organs from the dead is non-liberty-violating after death and a noninjurious transgression. However, it can interfere with an alternative choice (a liberty infringement) and be a property infringement, showing a lack of respect for individual decision making. It can also be an attack on our intimate relations to our bodies. Furthermore, out of concern for the family's feelings and the desire to increase the supply of organs, as well as out of concern over a too powerful state, the original owner, or society, may grant the family a right to decide on the disposition of organs (not merely to veto state action). But society should not grant families the right to override the original owner's decision, negative or positive. And required request by medical personnel of the family should be the rule.

Family members and original owners may also decide, ex ante, to avoid the strain of an actual decision and so empower the state to take. This makes possible a policy of presumed consent, to which original owners or family members are sometimes permitted to object on the occasion of a taking.

In fact, families seem to have been given the right to decide because it is believed they are likely *to give* when original organ owners would *not*. Therefore, they cannot be seen as playing the role envisioned by substituted judgment, figuring out what the original owner would have wanted. (Can we truly imagine that the original owner would have cared more for his family's satisfaction in giving than for his own preference *not* to give? Should we leave it to the family to interpret his preference ordering in their favor?) If substituted judgment is not the source of their right and if the family have not been willed the right by the original owner, they can have the right to decide only because society's representative (usually the state) has a right in principle to take organs and delegates its power to them. Suppose we gave the family decision-making power, rather than make greater efforts to inquire into the wishes of the original organ owner. Then we are, in effect, seeing to it that the wishes of original organ owners are circumvented by never being made explicit. Therefore, even if we do not allow families to override explicit refusals by original owners, the state, in not emphasizing request of the original owner, would still be using families to circumvent the wishes of the dead. It would be letting families serve as agents of the state's right in principle to override the decedent's wishes. Those who oppose the state's right to override or to circumvent the original owner in principle should then oppose the family's right, except when substituted judgment is operational.[30] Those who oppose the state's actually having the right for fear of giving it too much power, need not oppose delegation to the family.

Organs from Fetuses

The Report does not discuss the possibility of acquiring organs from fetuses. I wish to make only a few remarks in this connection. Suppose a fetus would be aborted for the ordinary reasons of the woman not wanting a pregnancy or an offspring. Assuming the abortion causes death of the fetus, the use of organs from such a creature that would be aborted anyway seems, intrinsically, morally permissible (though questions arise about who has the right to make the decision to give organs). This would be true even if abortion were morally impermissible, since even if we may not intend an evil, it may be permissible to make good use of an unavoidable evil. Problems arise if a pregnancy is begun for the ordinary reasons or causes, that is, desire for a child or failed contraception, but the *reason* for termination is to acquire fetal tissue for transplantation. One might seek to acquire the tissue either for someone else or for the woman who is carrying the fetus. The problem here is that, whereas in ordinary abortion we kill the fetus to stop its imposing on the woman, an imposition from which it benefits by getting continuing life, here we do not kill the fetus to end any problem *it* causes or from which it benefits. Rather, it would be killed to end a problem arising quite independently of it, that is, someone else's illness which gives rise to a need for its organ. We use it to make the world a better place, when it not only did not contribute to its present bad state (i.e., it did not cause someone's needing a transplant), but its life is not a benefit to it of that bad state (i.e., it is not a beneficiary of someone else's needing a transplant). Even if abortion is not a moral evil because it is permissible to end the fetus' imposition on a woman *in order* to stop the imposition, it may not be permissible to end the imposition for just any reason at all.

Further problems arise if the pregnancy is started for the sake of ending it. That is, the fetus is created so as to have organs to give to someone who needs a transplant. Then the *entire life* of the fetus was a mere means to satisfying that other person's need.

If the fetus is a person, then even if abortion for the sake of stopping imposition were permissible,[31] neither killing it to acquire organs nor creating it in order to kill it to acquire organs is morally permitted. But suppose the fetus does not have the rights of a person because it is not a person. Why should these types of abortion not be permissible? For example, why can we not deliberately create a nonperson and kill it for the sake of people, before it develops into a person? One possible answer is that it may be permissible to end the life of such a being (despite its potential to become a person) for some reasons, but it is still inappropriate to bring into existence a being that has potential to be a person for any reason but to see that the potential is fulfilled. It may also be inappropriate to end its life for some reasons rather than others even if it were brought into existence appropriately. (A possible, though not perfect, analogy: It may be easier to break an engagement that has only the potential of leading to marriage than to end a marriage. Still, it may be morally inappropriate to bring an engagement into existence for the sake of ending it and inappropriate to end it for reasons other than that the relations between the two people involved are not satisfactory.)

Organs from Live Donors

Donation from living donors has commonly occurred where risk to the donor is not great and where protections are in place to prevent coercion to give. Recently, however, there have been liver-section donations from live donors that raise the issue of significant risk to the donor. An ethical problem, for doctors in particular, is whether they are permitted to impose significant risk of harm on a patient when there is no greater probability of benefit to that same person, but only benefit to another person. In dealing with this issue,[32] the attempt has been made to do separate cost-benefit analyses for the recipient and for the donor of the organ, so that we do not merely weigh costs of the donor against benefits to the recipient. This move avoids the utilitarian failure to take seriously the separateness of persons and seems consistent with a doctor's duty not to harm or risk harm when no greater benefit is at hand for the patient who is harmed or risks harm. On these analyses the benefit to the donor is said to be psychological. For example, in the case of relatives who are donors, it is thought that the loss of a loved one would be a greater cost than the loss of part of a liver. The reasoning here presumably is like that employed to justify a procedure that risks physical harm (e.g., plastic surgery) when a person will suffer psychological damage (e.g., disfigurement) if that procedure is not undertaken.

There seems to be a difference, however, between ordinary cases in which psychological benefits are weighed against physical harm and cases of live donation: the person who donates does not *aim* at his own psychological benefit or the avoidance of his own misery when he donates. He aims to save his loved one, though the side effect of doing this may be psychological satisfaction and avoidance of misery. Any argument that assumes the motive of such a donor is his own psychological satisfaction commits the fallacy of psychological egoism. This is the view that we can ultimately desire nothing but our own satisfaction, the proof of which is supposed to be that when we get what we desire, we experience satisfaction. But for our satisfaction to come as a side effect does not show we aim at it. Indeed, someone who was interested in saving someone else's life might well be willing to take a drug that induced depression and misery in him but saved the loved one; this alone would show that he aimed at the survival of the loved one and not at the avoidance of his own misery.

If psychological satisfaction is a side effect, not one's aim, does this rule out counting it in a cost-benefit analysis? Perhaps not, since the donor will be benefited in some way. But it does suggest that someone should be allowed to donate from simple concern for another person, regardless of whether it causes him satisfaction or helps him to avoid misery. This would be especially true if there were a duty to help the others, even while there is no duty to improve one's own mental state. If we can believe that concern is the true motive of a stranger—rather than masochism— even strangers should be allowed to be living donors at some risk to themselves.

How does this accord with the doctor's duty not to cause or risk harm? Doctors already cause or risk harm to people for their own physical or psychological benefit. They should still refuse to cause or risk harm when this will be to no one's benefit. But they may cause or risk harm to *a willing individual* who autonomously chooses to sacrifice for the benefit of another person. To insist the overriding benefit come to the person who risks harm is to practice a form of paternalistic reasoning.

However, all this does not mean that doctors have a duty to do whatever individuals consent to have done. Especially since parents may be willing to risk harm to themselves that is greater than any benefit it could buy for their child, doctors may refuse to participate in an activity that is wasteful of *their* energies, without being accused of paternalism. (And protections against coercive pressure on potential donors is especially important in live donation.)

A Modestly Radical Approach to Acquiring Organs: Killing to Save Life

In conclusion, I wish to consider proposals for acquiring organs that are at the farther reach of public acceptability. It is ordinarily wrong to kill one person to save many. For example, it is wrong to kill one healthy person against his will even to provide each of his organs to save several people. Perhaps, however, it is sometimes morally permissible to kill someone intentionally in order to acquire his organs to save another (or others).

The most modest proposal along these lines—given that these are already radical lines—is to kill one of two people who need an organ to survive in order to save the other. This is the alternative to letting both die.[33] That is, suppose that to live, Smith needs Jones's liver and Jones needs Smith's pancreas. If nature takes its course, each will die before his organ can be of use to the other. It maximizes the chance of each to live if they both agree to a toss of a coin that will determine whose vital organ will be removed for the sake of the other.

This proposal only endorses killing someone who would die shortly anyway, when it is in his interest to agree to the coin toss. Additionally, such an agreement may be acted on only with the actual consent of the participants. This proposal does not depend on a simple utilitarian justification. That is, it is not based on the principle that one may always kill someone to maximize lives saved, for this principle would permit us to kill a healthy person to save others. The proposal is based, first, on its being in the interest of each person ex ante to agree to being killed if he loses a toss; *and,* second, on a person losing only a small bit of life he would otherwise have had without the scheme.

An Objection and Response

If we think of killing someone who will die shortly anyway as depriving him of only a few days of life, this helps make the "modest" proposal seem modest. But killing a person is also destroying a certain type of entity. Standing in the killing-relation to a person may be inappropriate, even if it does not deprive anyone of much time. (See Chapter 1, p. 21.) If we focus on this, then we may not find the modest proposal modest after all. That is, even if it is in someone's interest to agree to such a proposal, the killing required to carry it out may remain forbidden.

Suppose this objection were valid. (It is not clear that it is.) A different proposal might still go forth if the removal of the organ needed by each person for life were not itself the cause of death. That is, if a single lung were needed for a person who had none functioning, or a single kidney, removal of this would not cause death of the donor if he had another lung or kidney. Then *both* lives might be saved if there were an exchange of organs. Therefore, the proposal might be made *even more modest:* The arrangement could be restricted to those who need for survival organs whose removal from another would not be a cause of death. Under this rubric there is one more (highly hypothetical) possibility: Suppose that the organ each needs from the other to survive is not needed for life by the original owner unless he receives the organ he needs. This means that one of the two would not die by our removing his organ to give it to the other, yet still only one can be saved, and one is left to die. This is because the one who receives an organ will no longer be able to give his to the other without dying, and the other will die of his unrelieved need, not the organ donation. Here we toss a coin to pick the survivor, but do not kill the loser, who dies of his already present disease.

A More Radical Proposal

Imagine a case involving only two people. Suppose Smith will die in four hours unless he receives an organ from Jones, who will die in two hours unless he receives an organ from Smith. When Jones dies naturally his organs could be used to save Smith.[34] My suggestion for this case[35] is that the distinctions between killing Smith to save Jones and merely letting Jones die, and then using his organ, is *not* necessarily morally determinative in this case. Likewise, the difference between intending Smith's death to save Jones and merely foreseeing Jones's death and then saving Smith is *not* morally determinative in this case.

Smith, without aid from Jones's organs, will live only two hours past Jones. This is an *intrinsically* insignificant amount of time (except perhaps as a buffer to death

[as described in Chapter 3, p. 52]). It is also insignificant *relative* to the total years
either Jones or Smith might live if he got the other's organs. The two hours are
valuable to Smith only *instrumentally,* as a way of outliving Jones so that he may
get Jones's organs. I suggest the following: Suppose the large advantage brought by
an intrinsically insignificant period of time involves benefiting from losses incurred
by another person, and that the other person could himself greatly benefit if there
were no such advantage to that intrinsically insignificant period of time. Then equal
concern for each could lead us to toss a coin to see whether Jones will die naturally
and then have organs removed, or whether Smith will be killed to acquire his
organs.

The same result might be achieved if we recognized Jones's right to determine
whether his organs shall be used by Smith after his (Jones's) death. Jones might
refuse to let them be used, in order to make it in Smith's interest to agree to a coin
toss. With the coin toss, Smith will have at least some chance of getting a significant
additional life span.

Inappropriate Bargains

Of course, Jones might want to make these moves even if Smith could live *a year*
without Jones's organs and Jones's organs could (hypothetically) be preserved and
given to Smith (who can use no organs besides Jones's) at the end of the year when
he needs them. Yet it would be morally impermissible for Jones to strike a bargain
for a coin toss that might result in Smith's death in these circumstances, I believe.
This is because a year is an intrinsically significant period of life. It is only when the
intrinsic worth of what Smith stands to lose if he is killed, that is, what he would
have had without the use of Jones's organs, is small that this policy of tossing a coin
might be morally permissible, I believe. Suppose Smith could live another five
years before needing the organs Jones will lose in two hours. (Let us assume we
could keep the organs for five years before use.) Then if Smith *lost* the coin toss
with Jones, we would again, in killing him, be depriving him of a significant period
of life that he would have had without any benefit from Jones's organs. This would
be wrong.

The Survival Lottery

This policy of strictly limited coin tosses strikes a balance between a prohibition on
killing Smith and a "survival lottery" (Harris's term) between two people. In the
survival lottery,[36] we may select from among healthy people someone to die in
order to save others, or someone who will share a fair risk of death with another.
Here, even people who would lose significant periods of life that they would have
had without the assistance of others' organs are involved in the choice of who lives
and who dies. Indeed, Harris would object to saving some by using only the sick
who without aid would die shortly anyway. Excluding the healthy from those who
might be killed to save others would favor the lucky (healthy) over the unlucky
(already sick), he claims.

The position I have described distinguishes between (1) the luck of those who can turn an intrinsically insignificant advantage of a few hours into the possibility of benefiting greatly from the loss to others who themselves might otherwise benefit, and (2) the luck of those who can have an intrinsically significant advantage, independent of others. On the view I propose, the latter should *not* be killed to get organs for the sick. Nevertheless, it may well be morally permissible for the former to be killed as the result of a fair coin toss. Furthermore, they might be killed even if this does not result in more lives saved, but only represents giving equal chances for survival to two different people, as in the case I have described.

Objections and Responses

Unlike the modest proposal described first, this more radical one is not in the best interests of both parties ex ante, at least if the ex ante judgement is made at the time when each knows that Jones will die before Smith. One of the parties would definitely survive via the other's organ if we did not intervene (assuming that Jones does not refuse permission to let his organs be used in order to force a bargain). The toss of the coin, however, gives him only a fifty percent chance of surviving. This may be raised as an objection to the proposal. It is not devastating, however, if we think a moral distinction can be drawn between depriving someone of (1) a long period of time he would have had without the organ, and (2) a long period of time he would have had only with another's organ plus the short time he would have had independently. Furthermore, the objection is not devastating if we are in favor of altering the course of nature to make things fairer, at least to the extent that someone does not benefit from an intrinsically insignificant difference.

Finally, the same objection and response raised to the modest proposal can be made here: We are killing a person, not merely depriving someone of some time. In addition, since someone would definitely live even if we did not interfere—this is unlike the scenario for the modest proposal where both would have died—we are killing *only* in order to make who lives a matter of humanly organized fairness. The trauma of responsibility for death may not be worth the gain achieved. Better to stay with "Nature's Lottery" wherein the intrinsically insignificant difference of a few extra hours plays the role of "where a coin lands." (We need not take it as a visible correlative of who deserves to live, though some may.) This assumes we can accept the view that nature's lottery gave equal chances to be in the positions of Jones and Smith.

This last objection would not hold if we applied the radical proposal to a situation in which *many* people, who will die naturally slightly earlier and thereby provide Smith with organs, could be saved by our killing Smith. For in such a case, more than the gain of humanly organized fairness is at stake; more total lives could be saved. Suppose we did endorse some scheme involving killing Smith, who will live only a short time without the organs, in this situation. I believe it should involve the same fair coin toss between both sides. That is, Smith should have an equal chance to win. He should not merely get his proportional chance, in accord with the numbers of people at stake, nor should he automatically lose on grounds of the majority counting. The latter two proposals may be reasonable for distributing a scarce resource that we have to give, but not when we must take something from another person for use by yet others, and when the alternative is that he could gain from their loss. In general, I believe, when we would take away his life from someone (considering that he stands to lose a substantial period of life) for the sake of many individuals, each of whom stands to lose no more than life if not aided, we should not aggregate the losses of the many or give greater chances to them in proportion to their numbers. Ordinarily, I think, there is a complete prohibition on sacrificing someone for the sake of many others if this is done in some way that does not involve redirecting a threat.[37] But the case we are dealing with may be an exception, because (1) the person would not lose much life that he had independently of the help of others anyway, and (2) he stands to gain from the loss of the many simply because he will outlive them briefly.

Furthermore, the objections to killing would not apply, even where the choice is only between two individuals, if we need not kill the person who loses the toss. That is, the objections will not apply if we remove only organs necessary for life in the recipient but not necessary for life in the donor.

These various schemes we have described have as their aim increasing the supply of organs. It has been suggested that scarcity in organs is a blessing-in-disguise: If we had enough organs the cost to transplant everyone who could get even minor benefits would be wasteful of money and medical time. This is a point worth taking seriously, but it only means that principles for scarce resource distribution, which we are about to discuss, should be applied more generally, to time and money.

NOTES

1. Committee of Public Welfare, "Organ Transplantation: Issues and Recommendations," Department of Health, Education, and Welfare (April 1986).

2. As well as a Hastings Center report: *Ethical, Legal and Policy Issues Pertaining to Solid Organ Procurement* (October 1985).

3. A linguistic oddity: the Report here uses the word "donor" for someone whose organs are taken, though he or she does not personally donate them.

4. This is a view argued for by Robert Veatch in "Whole Brain, Neocortical, and Higher Brain Related Concepts of Death," in John Arras and Nancy Rhoden (eds.), *Ethical Issues in Modern Medicine,* 3d ed. (Mountain View, Calif.: Mayfield Publishing Co., 1989).

5. Derek Parfit emphasized this point.

6. Dr. Thomas Starzl emphasized this point to me. They warned against a practice in which the less urgent who could use alternative therapies are transplanted, merely to produce very good outcome statistics.

7. These remarks are based on a talk on informed consent given at the Kennedy School, Harvard University in May 1992.

8. In this respect, the reasoning in *Canterbury v. Spence* seems more "liberal" than that in *Cobbs v. Grant,* since the second but not the first decision requires that some harm take place through failure to be asked to give informed consent and that evidence be given that a reasonable person might have chosen a different procedure than the one that caused harm, if they had been informed.

9. For further discussion of this issue in the context of abortion, see my *Creation and Abortion.*

10. The Uniform Anatomical Gift Act, 57 *Georgia Law Journal* 5 (1968–1969), sec. 3, no. 4.

11. It might also have a chilling effect on honesty and dissent in human relations. If we feel our lives are at the mercy of others' free choice, we may be afraid to speak and act as we believe we really should.

12. As was emphasized to me by Lewis Kornhauser. In fact, it is claimed that under current distribution policy, which is not dominated by donor choice, blacks and women are much less likely to get organs than white males. It is not clear that this indicates discrimination.

13. Thomas Nagel, "Death."

14. A sealed document may also be useful in helping avoid the reported intrusive presence of doctors, waiting for a death of a publicly declared donor in order to quickly retrieve organs. If they do not know he is a donor, they will continue to treat him simply as a patient to the end and not disturb the peace of a dying patient. Would this affect efficient acquisition of organs too much?

15. I owe this last point to Gregory Dees.

16. It has been argued that the right (and duty) of relatives to bury a relation indicates only a quasi-property right, not full-blooded ownership: M. Sadler and B. Sadler, "Transplantation and the Law: The Need for Organized Sensitivity," 57 *Georgia Law Journal* 5 (1968–1969). The notion of "stewardship" has been used.

17. J. Dukeminier, "Supplying Organs for Transplantation," 68 *Michigan Law Review* 811 (1970).

18. I owe the suggestion of fixed prices to Andrew Schauer.

19. Some may believe that any part of one's body somehow carries one's personality and so be reluctant to cede an organ for this reason. But if this were true, would the person not yet have died if any parts remain alive? Perhaps there is a difference on this view between the person and a program for his personality, which leaves it open that when the program from an already dead person is put in the body of a still living one, the former's personality characteristics "come to life."

20. T. Weller, *The Book of Stupid Questions.*

21. In fact, it is *beliefs* about the insignificance of the harm that are practically relevant. If someone believes that great harm would come to him, for example, the absence of a complete body at the time of the Resurrection, his body part should not be taken after his death. A public debate over the truth of the belief, or disallowing reliance on it, would be too socially divisive to be worth considering.

22. Judith Thomson, "Some Ruminations on Rights."

23. I first discussed this type of phenomenon in "Supererogation and Obligation," *Journal of Philosophy* (March 1985): 118–138.

24. Opinion polls are too unreliable.

25. In the case of the pet, we need not anthropomorphize by imagining the pet's having a belief that giving its water dish diminishes something about its life. Rather, the truth of the content of purely hypothetical beliefs is important. That is, would it have been right to have had these thoughts? It is possible, however, that in the case of the pet it requires anthropomorphization just to think that it would be appropriate for it to have such beliefs.

26. Roy Sorenson raises a countercase to this analysis: Suppose someone has had a wooden leg all his life. Would we have the same attitude toward taking it to give to someone else as we have toward taking someone's natural leg? The distinction between our natural and non-natural parts may be crucial. We do not see *ourselves* in the wood, though we may see ourselves in the flesh.

27. The sight of a nonintact body may be one of the causes of the discomfort experienced in seeing relatives hooked up to machinery in an intensive care unit; here the last experience before death does not maintain the impression of ordinary life. I owe this point to Dan Moros.

28. We have earlier made these points in note 20.

29. I owe this suggestion to Dr. Joel Zinberg.

30. In its decision in the Cruzan Case, the Supreme Court also distinguished between an individual making a decision prior to her terminal illness to have treatment discontinued and her family's deciding to have his treatment discontinued. The former is permitted though the latter is not.

31. I have discussed this question in *Creation and Abortion*.

32. See D. A. Singer, et al. "Ethics of Liver Transplantations with Living Donors," *New England Journal of Medicine* 321, no. 9: 620–621; and my "The Doctrine of Double Effect: Theoretical and Practical Issues," *The Journal of Medicine and Philosophy* 16 (October 1991): 571–585.

33. This proposal is mentioned by John Harris in "The Survival Lottery," *Philosophy* 50, no. 191 (January 1975): 81–87. Harris does not endorse this modest proposal but something more radical, as we shall see.

34. This case is owed to Daniel Dinello in "On Killing and Letting Die," *Analysis* 31 (1971), reprinted in Bonnie Steinbock (ed.), *Killing and Letting Die* (Englewood Cliffs, N.J.: Prentice-Hall, 1980), pp. 128–131.

35. Contrary to Dinello's recommendation.

36. As described by Harris in "The Survival Lottery."

37. For more on the distinction between redirecting threats to save a greater number and other cases of killing to save a greater number see "Harming Some to Save Others," *Philosophical Studies*, 57 (1989):227–260, and *Morality, Mortality*, Vol. II.

12

Distribution of Resources: Need and Outcome

In this chapter and the next two as well we will consider some fundamental conceptual and substantive issues in the distribution of scarce resources. The factors discussed and the situations described are relevant to any scarce resource, including money necessary to fund procedures employing nonscarce resources. To focus discussion, however, we consider organ transplants involving scarce human organs. (To generalize the discussion, merely substitute the word "resource" or "procedure" most everywhere "organ transplant" occurs or is implied.) Again we shall begin by using certain recommendations of the Task Force Report as a basis for discussion. Among the crucial general issues are (1) the concepts of need and urgency, (2) need versus urgency, (3) how to characterize outcome, (4) need versus outcome, (5) urgency versus outcome, (6) differential outcomes, (7) time waiting, and (8) the role of money in distribution. These issues are so complex, for example, how helping the worst off can produce inequality, that we can only hope our analysis points in some directions worth investigating further. (One possibly important consideration, responsibility for need, e.g., if one brought one's illness on oneself by a bad lifestyle should one be disfavored in distribution, will not be dealt with.)

In connection with the analyses of crucial concepts, we shall consider hypothetical distribution cases. Only in Chapter 15 will we consider in more detail actual procedures for distributing resources, why procedures are desirable in general, and whether we should move from a qualitative to a quantitative procedure.

Types of Scarcity

As a preface to the discussion of distribution, we should distinguish three possible contexts in which distribution decisions might be made: true scarcity, temporary scarcity, and uncertainty.[1] In *true scarcity,* if we give an organ to one person rather than another, the person who does not get it will never get another of the same type. No other organ will come along for him. The assumption is that someone who to some degree needs an organ, and who to some degree could benefit from it, will not get it. If he needs it very badly, he will die without it. In *temporary scarcity,* the person not given an organ now must wait for another organ. This wait need not be without cost to him, but he will not die. We know we have at least temporary scarcity of something if a line forms. In *uncertainty,* we are not sure whether we are in a condition of true or temporary scarcity with respect to a given individual waiting for a given type of organ. In reality, we are most often in a condition of uncertainty, I believe. We must keep in mind these distinctions in deciding on principles for distribution.

I. NEED AND URGENCY

The Concept of Neediest Rather Than That of Most Urgent

To say someone to some degree needs an organ is to say he will in some way be badly off without it. But there are different ways of being badly off: being badly off from now on, and being badly off because one's life overall will have gone badly if one doesn't get an organ.

Therefore, at least two subquestions are embedded in the question, Do these people need an organ equally? (1) Do they need an organ equally to survive? and (2) Do they need to survive equally? The answer to the first subquestion may be Yes, while the answer to the second subquestion is No. Two people may need the organ equally in order to get the additional years an organ can give, but they may not need more years equally.

The Report's notion of need is derived from subquestion 1, though it too can have two subparts. This is so since its notion of "most needy" is concerned with who needs an organ to avoid the earlier death, or who needs an organ to avoid the worst quality of life in the future. The judgment of need is here being made in a forward-looking way, in the way we commonly use "urgent," and I shall use the term "urgent" for it henceforth.

I shall refer to how *soon* someone will die without the transplant as urgency^T ("T", for time) and how *badly off* someone will be without it *soon* as urgency^Q, ("Q", for quality of life) respectively. In the case of kidneys, urgency^T is not usually in question because of the backup of dialysis. With livers and hearts, urgency^T is at stake. Urgency^T can be related to being sensitized, so that it is hard to find an organ one will not reject, and to having blood type O, as well as to being very sick.

But there is an alternative account of "most needy" that arises from considering subquestion 2. On this other account the person who will die having had the least by the time he dies is the neediest. I shall use the term "need" so that it correlates with how much a person will have had by the time he dies.

If the neediest will have had least, least of what? At least two different measures might be suggested: least of adequate conscious time alive, or least of the other goods of life. Under the "other goods" one may include both good experiences (e.g., hedonistic pleasures) and the structural or formal features of life, such as particular achievements, or even the overall achievement of having lived a full life, moving through all its distinctive stages. These two broadest categories, conscious time alive and the other goods of life, correspond closely (though not exactly) to the distinction between medically adequate time alive and more refined quality-of-life judgments.

If we included hedonistic and formal goods in measuring neediness, the neediest need simple time alive in part because it is the means to the achievement of these goods of life. This focus on these goods leaves open the question of whether adequate conscious life itself is an intrinsic good (and more life means more of this intrinsic good) or only an instrument to other hedonistic and formal goods.

A Modification

One modification which I believe we should accept of the view that neediness is having least by time of death is that the person who has had *both* the least opportunity for adequate time alive (and whatever other goods we count) *and* the least of these has the greatest need not to die. He has the strongest need for the organ and needs most to be saved. (An alternative "most needy," is the person who will have had least of these goods *despite opportunity for them* if he dies. We should choose our wording to avoid two problems: (1) if someone has had the least opportunity for goods of life but managed to get the goods anyway, it would be foolish to call him most needy; (2) if someone has had few of the goods of life but much opportunity for them and was at fault for not acquiring them, it seems wrong to treat him as most needy.)

Another Modification: Which Goods Count the Most

Should we consider hedonistic and formal goods in determining neediness or just adequate conscious time alive? Having the least and the least opportunity for which types of goods constitutes greatest need? (We should keep in mind that in answering this question we may also learn what sorts of goods we should use to judge outcomes that come from getting an organ.)

In discussing death,[2] I considered the view we take of our lives from the outside. I suggested that from that outside perspective, we value the formal or structural features of our life over the experiential ones. For example, I suggested, we do not give much weight in our assessment of a life from the outside to how much pleasure or pain there was in it. An alternative view was that we do think our life with pain in it is worse than the life without the pain, but we are often not courageous enough to pay the price for the better life; e.g., we are not willing to suffer moderate pain in the future rather than have it be true that we suffered more pain in the past. I have tried to cast doubt on this alternative by noting that even if we had a choice between its being true that we suffer a very small amount of pain in the future and a very large amount in the past, we would not pay the small price for the sake of having had the less painful life. Paying this small price does not require great courage, and yet we do not prefer it. It remains possible that though we have had a worse life if there is much pain in it, it makes no difference whether we have had a life worse in this respect once that life is over. We will prefer suffering in the future if this is an indication of greater past achievements, not of less pain. This is because a painful life can be a bad life and yet not reflect badly on us. It was also noted that we have a different attitude to other people's lives, preferring to suffer ourselves rather than have it be true that they have suffered greatly in the past. We might connect this asymmetry with the Kantian view that we have a duty to promote the happiness of others but have a duty to promote our own virtue.

Furthermore, I suggested that the person who has achieved the formal goods of life needs to go on living less than someone who has not achieved these (p. 61). This is true even though the first person may live a better life in living on just because he has achieved certain formal goods.

I also suggested that in actually living our life, we may choose the experienced values over the formal features. So, we may refuse to give up pleasure in order to complete an important project. We may even refuse to give up a period of simple adequate conscious life (i.e., die earlier than otherwise), even if it has no great hedonic experiences in it, although this refusal costs us the completion of an important project. Sometimes, of course, we do sacrifice good experiences or conscious life to complete a project.

When deciding who is neediest for purposes of distributing an organ, I believe we should take most seriously the concern that each person has simply for continuing on in adequate conscious life and the intrinsic worth of such life even if its worth does not reflect on ours. That is, we should take the modest view from within life that, I believe, most of us adopt if we face death, that values more adequate conscious life. We should not focus on the "courageous" view from without concerned with the structure of life or even the view from within that is concerned with positive experiences. This would mean, roughly, that the person who has had less adequate conscious life is neediest on the internal view, even if the person with fewest achievements is neediest on the external view. I shall postpone considering factors supporting the view that adequate conscious life counts more than other sorts of goods in determining neediness in a medical context until we discuss the analogous question of whether adequate conscious life or other values should be used to rank different outcomes. This standard for need will, in a sense, favor men over women, at least in our society. That is, men will have more achievements to their credit earlier than women (though not if we include reproduction and raising of children as achievements). If absence of formal goods is not a criterion for need, women may die more frequently than men without the nonreproductive formal goods to their credit.

Implications

If we accept adequate conscious life as the measure of need, the needier will, in general, be the younger rather than the older person. (Even if we included formal or experiential goods, however, these are likely to be fewer in younger than in older. If we assigned a random chance of their being greater in younger or in older people, there will still usually be a difference in adequate conscious life between younger and older people.) One person could be needier than another but less urgent. For example, if a twenty-year-old will die in a year if not given an organ, he is needier on the account I have given than the fifty-year-old who will die tomorrow. He will be twenty-one when he dies, whereas the other candidate will die at fifty. Furthermore, the younger candidate may on occasion offer a less good outcome than the older and/or more urgent one and yet still be needier.[3]

But notice also that one can come to have least adequate conscious life by having poor prospects, as well as by dying. (Also, by having had periods of nonadequate conscious past life, two people of the same age can be different in need.) For example, suppose a person will have much pain but not die if he does not get an organ. This opens up the possibility of comparing a needier person who doesn't face death with a less needy person who does. I shall put this possibility to one side for the time being, and assume we are concerned with individuals whose lives are at stake, unless otherwise stated. (These are four possibilities, of course: needier versus less needy both have life at stake or both have quality of life at stake; or needier has life at stake, less needy has quality at stake, and vice versa.)

Why Do the Needier Have a Greater Claim?

Suppose we have correctly identified the neediest as those who have had the least opportunity for and the least of adequate conscious life by the time they die. Then the question remains why this factor of greater need should count in favor of their receiving the organ. The ground might be that they necessarily offer a *better outcome* because there is a *Diminishing Marginal Utility of Life* (DMU). That is, the same absolute number of years of adequate conscious life may be more valuable to someone who has had less conscious time alive so far because they produce more good. This means that we should multiply the absolute years of "expected differential outcome" (i.e. the difference in outcome with and without an organ) of the younger person by a factor representing his comparative and absolute need (i.e., how much younger he is than the other candidate and how young he actually is) in order to get the true value of the years we can give him. (We can get such a factor for one candidate by assigning factors to each candidate on the basis of his absolute years alive at time of expected death. Where only two candidates are involved, we can get the factor for one by setting a zero base for the other.) For an example, see Table 12-1. In that table, need is represented as a combination of age at time one needs an organ and urgency^T, which is how long one will live without the organ. The combination of age and urgency^T tells us how old someone would be at time of death if he does not receive an organ. The multiplicative factor is "f" (whose value I choose arbitrarily simply to illustrate a point). Outcome is how many medically adequate years of conscious life would be had if transplantation occurs now. Differ-

Table 12.1

Need			
Age	Urgency^T	Outcome	Differential Outcome
20	1 month	2 years	$f(3) \times (2 \text{ years} - 1 \text{ month})$
50	1 month	4 years	4 years $-$ 1 month

ential outcome is the difference between outcome and urgency^T, that is, the difference in outcome that the organ makes. (It is this outcome that is most relevant in deciding what is the outcome of a transplant to a person.)

It is possible that an absolute outcome of two years to a 20-year-old would offer a more valuable "need-adjusted outcome" than four years to a 50-year-old.

It is worth noting that DMU may be present even though the amount someone would offer to pay for the remaining years of his life would not diminish as he gets older. That is, when one's remaining years are everything that one could have, their subjective value will not diminish as rapidly as their objective value.[4] Nevertheless, I believe that one can still understand the reasonableness of the claim that the remaining years are more valuable if one has not had as many past years.

A second reason why outcome to the younger person may be more valuable is due to formal or experiential features. For example, it may be that the period from twenty to forty is structurally a more significant period than that from fifty to seventy. Relying on formal or experiential features may not, however, yield a straightforward DMU of life since better formal features (e.g., achievements, powers) may be present later in life than earlier. But if we ignore such factors as formal and experiential goods of life in determining need, should we use them in reasoning about outcomes and why the neediest should be helped?

A third way of understanding the idea that each year of life brings more benefit to the person who has had less, is that a given unit of additional time makes a bigger difference to his life overall because it gives him a larger proportion of what he has already had. For example, one year to a ten year old increases his life span by one tenth over what he has had, one year to a 60-year-old only gives him $\frac{1}{60}$ of what he has had. We could double the life span of a 10-year-old by giving him ten years, but only increase by $\frac{1}{6}$ the life span of the 60-year-old by giving him ten years.

Still, it is not clear that this impact on someone's life as a whole matters, in addition to absolute numbers of years. It is different from a year which makes one life involve diversity of experience, but adds only repetition to another life. (This is not to say that the latter difference should matter in distribution decisions.)

Why the Needier Have a Greater Claim: Fairness

Suppose we could not produce a better outcome for the needier person, even when we consider need-adjusted outcome (see Table 12-2, in which we make the unrealistic supposition that an organ can provide a twenty-year outcome when in fact a good outcome currently is only between five and seven years).

Table 12.2

Age	Urgency^T	Outcome
	Need	
20	1 month	$2 \times f(3) = 6$ years
50	1 month	20 years

Still, the needier person may have a claim to the organ based on fairness or equality. That is, because he will have had less if he dies without the organ than if the older person dies, we should help the worst off person before helping someone who has already had more get even more. This is the maximin strategy. This might be true even if the twenty-year-old's need adjusted outcome is six, while the fifty-year-old's is twenty. If we reject simple maximin, we could still represent the value of fairness in helping the worst off by multiplying his outcome in-absolute years by *a second multiplicative factor* (f'), which also varies with his absolute and comparative need. This result might also be overridden by higher absolute outcome in the less needy.

In sum, we should not only multiply the neediest's differential outcome to indicate its greater value in virtue of DMU, but also multiply it again to indicate that this valuable thing is going to the neediest. That is, because a certain number of extra years goes to the neediest, it is a thing of greater value because of DMU, and that it goes to the neediest has separate additional value (due to fairness).[5] As noted, the factors by which we multiply the outcomes should reflect not only relative neediness, but absolute neediness; the suggestion is that the more absolutely needy someone is, the more the additional years matter.

Note that when we multiply *for the sake of fairness,* we are thereby giving need (at least somewhat) greater weight in our distribution scheme than outcome,[6] and indicating that it is morally more important that a given outcome go to the worst off than the better off. When we multiply outcome because of the DMU of life, we do *not* thereby indicate that need counts for more than outcome in our distribution scheme. We only indicate that some outcomes are better than others because of DMU. (That a better outcome arises through DMU is also different from preferring the younger because they tend to live longer as measured in absolute numbers of years.)

If we should give to the neediest for reasons of fairness rather than, or in addition to, DMU, it will matter how we determine who is neediest. That is, if there is DMU of life, this means each year brings less, the more one has had in absolute terms. Comparative DMU is simply a function of how much one person has had in comparison to another. One way to measure degree of neediness is also to compare how much one person has had in comparison to another. But it is also possible to determine relative neediness (by determining who is worst off) in another way: First we consider how much life a person should have (given the biological limits on length and quality of human life). Then we get the figures for how much each person has already had of this ideal. The degree of neediness is determined by comparing how far away from the ideal each person is, given how much they have had. This second procedure for giving sense to the idea of neediness is irrelevant for determining DMU, and will give different answers to how much needier one person is than another than an answer based only on how long each has lived. For example, suppose A has lived ten years and B twenty years, and a "reasonable" life is seventy years long. If we determine comparative neediness by seeing how many years A has had relative to B, we shall say that A is two times as needy as B. If we determine comparative neediness by seeing how relatively far A and B are from what they should have, the ratio will be 60 versus 50; so A will be 1⅕ as needy as B. On both ways of determining degrees of neediness, those who have had less will be needier and that will be sufficient for our discussion to proceed (until a much later point).

The results of these arguments in favor of making age a relevant factor in distribution, are quite different from the recommendations of others who also think that age is relevant. Most such writers wish to find a cutoff point, e.g., 70 years, beyond which costly life-saving aid would be denied government support. The years before 70 would be treated equally. The arguments that have been presented here suggest, in contrast, that almost all differences in age, e.g., the difference between 20 and 50, should affect distribution decisions. This is a radical result: it does not tell us to favor the young over the old; it tells us to favor the young*er* over the old*er*, at least to some degree.

Diachronic Model

A further argument to support some preference for the younger distinguishes age discrimination from race, sex, and other types of discrimination, on the grounds that everyone has a chance of being in the category "older" in a way that everyone does not have a chance of being a different race or sex.[7] Put more accurately everyone will have been younger, even if they do not get to be older. This means that the decision whether to aid the older or younger of two people can be translated into the decision whether to arrange for aid for oneself when young or for oneself when old. This is the diachronic model. Instead of comparing two different people, one young and one old synchronically (at the same time), we compare the same person at different stages. In order to get the benefit of being assured treatment when he is younger, so that he first gets to have at least some of what an older person has already had, each person can take the risk of not getting treated when he is older. He sacrifices treatment in one part of his life for the sake of treatment in another part, an insurance policy of sorts. Instead of sacrificing something in youth to save for old age, one sacrifices something in old age to improve one's chance when young of getting to be older.

If this model is correct, one does not sacrifice a totally different person in favor of oneself, as one would in practicing sex or race discrimination. Of course, at the time when the youth is preferred, he wins out over a different older person. But that older person will (theoretically) have had the insurance of being treated better in his youth, and the younger beneficiary himself accepts the risk of being treated less well if he is older.

It might be argued that insuring oneself against death early in life is a maximin policy we do not, in fact, select. That is, we engage in many activities in which we risk our lives for the sake of formal goods and even for the sake of extending the length of mere adequate conscious existence. But in these activities, we take a risk for the sake of the possibility of what we see as a greater good for ourself. We do not often choose certain death for the sake of other goods. (We logically could not choose certain death for the sake of lengthening mere conscious life.) And we would choose certain death, if we could help save the life of the younger and chose not to.

Might we argue as follows: Suppose we are behind a veil of ignorance, which deprives us of information as to our specific status in society.[8] We do not know whether we will be someone, A, who faces death at twenty years of life or someone, B, who faces death at 40. Suppose we have a policy ensuring twenty additional years to the 20-year-old rather than giving him an equal chance for those years to the 40-year-old. Then we try to ensure that everyone lives to 40. But wouldn't we prefer to have a 50 percent chance of living to 60, even if it meant a 50 percent chance of dying at 20? Considering that we do not know whether we will be A or B, we may take the risk of dying as A since we may thereby buy ourselves the chance of living to 60 as B.[9]

Consider two possibilities for such "veil of ignorance" reasoning. One (Harsanyi's) tells us to assume that we have an equal chance of being in any one person's position. On that assumption, if we decide that the twenty years should certainly go to the 20-year-old, we give ourselves a 1 in 2 chance of the greater benefit (on the assumption of DMU) since we have a 1 in 2 chance of being in that person's position. Suppose that we decide instead that the 20-year-old and the 40-year-old should each have a 1 in 2 chance of getting an extra twenty years. We then give ourselves, from behind the veil of ignorance, a 1 in 4 chance of the greater benefit which goes to the 20-year-old and also a 1 in 4 chance of the lesser benefit which goes to the 40-year-old. That is a worse prospect than a simple 1 in 2 chance of the greater benefit.

A second possibility (Rawls's) is that we have no idea, behind the veil of ignorance, what our chances are of being in any one person's position. Some argue that, here, too, we should maximize our expected benefit. That would again tell us to decide that the twenty years should certainly go to the 20-year-old. Rawls argues, instead, that we should make our worst outcome as good as possible. But then we would choose the same policy. On none of these lines of thought would it be rational to prefer that the younger and the older be given an equal chance.

Are these the ways to reason from behind a veil of ignorance? Should we imagine that we have a chance to be A or B, or rather is the veil a device which forces us to identify with whoever will occupy the positions of A and of B? Thomas Scanlon has argued that the latter is the correct way to understand the veil of ignorance. That is, we should identify with each separate person rather than decide as one person who has a chance to be in one position or another.[10] This, he thinks, will give the person with the strongest complaint against a proposal a veto over it.

Suppose we do identify with both A and B. Suppose further that receiving the organ would make it possible for A to live to 40 *and beyond*. Could we argue that then it is in A's own interest to tolerate a 50 percent chance of dying at 20 in accord with a policy that gives 40-year-olds a 50 percent chance to get an organ? For if *he* gets the organ, *he* himself could then benefit from such a policy as well if he lives on for twenty years (assuming we would give one person two organs). Although it is true that, if A himself lives to 40, he might then on another occasion get his 1 in 2 chance of another twenty years, his expected benefit from that must be less than his expected loss if he goes down from a certainty of getting an extra twenty years now to merely having a 50 percent chance of having these years later.

It is important to understand that if there are good moral arguments for an older person's not having as strong a claim on a resource as a younger one (i.e., if he has no claim to equal treatment), this is consistent with his being treated as an equal. Persons can be shown equal concern and respect (to use Dworkin's phrase) but be treated differently if they merit the different treatment. It is also important to emphasize that the fact that a younger person should be preferred to an older one in distributing a scarce resource is consistent with its being wrong to permit the resource to become scarce and wrong precisely because it means that older persons will not get it. This further implies that although a younger person's life might be preferred to an older person's, an older person's life might be preferred to lower taxes and to a higher standard of living for a younger person; raising the taxes of the younger person might make some resources less scarce.

Problems: Arguments Against the DMU of Life

Let us now consider some problems with these reasons for helping the person who will be worse off at the time he dies. (Henceforth, I shall assume the "no opportunity" clause is met.) To say that there is a diminishing marginal utility of life is to say that each additional year of life produces less happiness or less of any other true goods of life (for which we will loosely let "utility" stand). In fact, this does not seem to be true, in general. For example, there seems little reason to believe that one year at 40 will bring less happiness or satisfaction, or involve doing fewer good things than one year at 20. (Possibly there is, in general, DMU after a certain late point in life.) If we abstract from the structural features of a life, and just consider adequate conscious life, people's capacity to derive satisfaction from this also does not seem to diminish much with each additional unit they have had. Alternatively, it might be that the rate at which the value of adequate conscious life diminishes is so slow that it is insignificant for making one outcome better than another. This means that it is incorrect to use anything beyond minimal multiplicative factors to produce need-adjusted outcomes based on the DMU of life at least before a certain late point in life.

It could also be pointed out that, strictly speaking, we have not employed the notion of DMU at all. Usually DMU is applied to money; it is said of those who *currently* have in hand much money that an additional unit of it is worth less to them than a unit of it is worth to someone with less money *currently* in hand.

This claim does not necessarily imply that an additional unit of money today is worth less to someone who *had* a great deal of money yesterday than a unit today is worth to someone who did not have a great deal yesterday. But it is the second claim which most closely matches the claim we have made about years of life.

Rather than focus on how equally capable of providing good more life is despite different pasts, it may be suggested that we also focus on how equally important it is to all to avoid the evil of death. That is, it might be suggested, that the length of life a person has already had pales into insignificance in the face of the prospect of total extinction. Someone who has had more of life should not be more likely to face total extinction sooner than someone else who has had less. Analogously, imagine a very bad experience (e.g., torture). If we *had* to choose someone to have it, the fact that one candidate has had a *much* better set of experiences so far than another should not make us select him to be tortured. Whatever good has already occurred to the person can fail to be relevant in comparison to the evil at stake, even if the good added to the evil makes one life much better than another overall. (A similar analysis would also seem to lead to the view that future quality of life should not count in selecting who will avoid extinction. This is because life itself is the only way to avoid the great evil of extinction, so differences in quality pale by comparison.)

Another reason that might be suggested for denying both the DMU of life and the role of fairness is that it is rational to discount the past. Cases presented by Derek Parfit (and first discussed in Chapter 2) can be used to argue this point. For example, suppose one wakes up in a hospital under the effect of amnesia and is not sure whether it is, of two alternatives, the day after very painful surgery or the day before mildly painful surgery. Though there will be less pain in one's life if one will have the surgery tomorrow, it seems understandable to prefer to have had the much more painful surgery yesterday. We discount the bad that is in the past. Likewise, we discount the good that is in the past. (This point was made in discussing the asymmetrical attitude to prenatal nonexistence and death.) If it is indeed rational to discount the past, then it might be suggested that we should deal with the young and old, those with much life and those with little, simply on the basis of what the future holds from now onward.[11]

Responses: In Support of the DMV of Life and the Fairness of Counting Past Benefits

It is hard to accept the view that there is much DMU of life. Still, someone who has never had certain experiences does often get more from them than someone who has had many such experiences. Furthermore, experiences of adequate conscious life should not be treated only as an achievement some of which (in the young) suffices, but rather as something of which more can be better than less.[12] We argue both that the value of adequate conscious life may diminish some and also that its value is not exhausted by having had some.

Even if there is not much DMU of life, it can still be true that it is morally more worthwhile or valuable to give an outcome of a certain degree of utility to those who have had less than to those who had more. This means there is a sort of Diminishing Marginal Value (DMV) of life. This implies that even if there were no scarcity of organs, something more valuable would be done if a certain good outcome were given to those who had less than if it were given to those who had more. In situations where what we have to offer is scarce, so that not everyone can get something, fairness is the crucial moral value which is in question when we decide to give to those who have had less. We could, therefore, multiply the differential outcomes by a factor which represents the greater moral value of giving to those who are worse off, and in particular represents the moral value of fairness.

Does the evil of death make what life one has had pale into insignificance? A large part of what makes death bad is that one has no more time alive and hence no more goods of life. Death is not, like torture, a great experienced evil.[13] Therefore, given that the amount of additional time and goods of life at stake is always finite, i.e., there is no question of avoiding extinction altogether, the significance of the loss of future years and goods should, I believe, vary with how many years and goods one has already had. This is the DMV of life. This might not be true if an infinite future were at stake. For then finite past goods would pale in comparison with the vastness of the loss of infinite future goods that would be at stake.[14]

Further, we cannot just ignore a person's past, treating past goods as though they had not been enjoyed, even though they may be discounted by him. This will be especially true if we are concerned with fairness in distribution. Hence, if we assign multiplicative factors according to years of life, it should be primarily from concern for fairness, and for DMV rather than for DMU of life. The outcome multiplied by such a factor will also be a need-adjusted outcome. Note, however, that the factors by which we multiply the outcome vary with the absolute and comparative neediness of the candidates. This implies either that it is more unfair to favor, for example, a 60-year-old over a 20-year-old than it is to favor a 40-year-old over a 20-year-old, or else that fairness counts more in the first case than it does in the second.

Problems: Exceptional Ages

The thesis of the DMV of life implies that it is always worth more to give an additional year of life to the younger person than to the older. But this fails to account for a fairly common feeling that it is less important to save those who have just begun their lives than to save those who are older. So, at least to some, it seems more important to save a 20-year-old rather than a 1-year-old, even if we could provide them both with long lives.[15]

This point rests on its being at least not clear whether we want to say that a life that ends at one year is worse than one which ends at 20. But in another sort of case, it can be clear that a life ending at one point rather than another is worse, yet we might still object to the DMV of additional life. For example, it could be worse to have a life end at 10 than at 20, but the five years from 10 to 15 might still not be worth as much to the 10-year-old as the five years from 20 to 25 would be worth to the 20-year-old. However, to explain this we may have to reintroduce the distinction in formal features: the time from 10 to 15 is preparatory, whereas the time from 20 to 25 is likely to contain more accomplishments. DMV, as we are using the notion, says that more of the same thing is worth less. But if the later periods of life contain different goods in them, this will not be more of the *same* thing.

How shall we deal with these points? I tend to think that five years is worth more to the younger person than to the older person when we consider it simply as time experiencing adequate conscious life. However, it is not necessarily worth more when we consider its role in producing a life with an important certain structure to it. Which of these factors should dominate, or do they cancel each other out? As much as we care about the structural characteristics of a life, including its being a complete type of thing, I suspect the multiplicative factor should favor adequate conscious experiencing of life in the evaluation of outcomes from an organ. (Some seem to think of youth as *only* a time for preparation, mere investment that bears fruit in middle-age accomplishment. But this, I think, ignores the simple goods of adequate conscious experience, as well as the achievements which youth also contains, and emphasizes achievement over everything else. It emphasizes the view from outside one's life over the view from inside.)

If we emphasize adequate conscious life then, other things equal, the five years should go to the 10-year-old rather than the 20-year-old. This does not, however, defeat the idea that at very early periods of life, the person is not sufficiently established to make the loss of more life to him worse than the loss is for someone older.

Problems: Against Overall Fairness

One objection to the view that those who will be overall worse off have a greater claim because a strict maximin ideal of fairness is correct helps us locate yet a *third notion of need*. This is in addition to urgency and being worse off overall at time of death. If what we can provide to the person who is needier does little to alleviate his greater need, it may not be worth helping the worst off. That is, we must ask whether he has greater *need for that which we have to offer* because it satisfies his need. Giving two years to the 20-year-old, even if it is adjusted to get its true value as outcome, may do little to ameliorate the fate of the younger person. That is, dying at 22 does little to ameliorate the complaint of dying at 20. In addition, suppose we can provide much more to the older person, and he will also not have had much more if he dies without the organ than the worst-off person. Then it may be correct to satisfy someone other than the person who will be worst off if he dies without an organ.

The model for this analysis which decides against helping the worst off (see Table 12-3) may be provided by cases based on ones used by Derek Parfit.[16]

Suppose it is worse to be blind than to be deaf. Then Joe will be the worst-off person if we do not help him. (He will also be worst off if we do help him but not as badly off.) Yet it is probably right to help Jim instead. It might be suggested that this is because we can do little to ameliorate what makes Joe worst off but can still do a great deal to help Jim. Making a big difference to those who are not worse off is sometimes worth more than making a smaller difference to the worse off for this reason.

Objection

It is not clear that we should be concerned with how much of the worse off's need we can satisfy, as a factor independent of how large a gain (in absolute or need-adjusted terms) we can provide him with, or how big a loss we can help him to avoid. For how much someone's need is satisfied seems to be a structural feature of a life, and we said we would ignore these. Furthermore, if it were relevant, we

Table 12.3

	Already	Future Outcome If Not Helped
Joe	Blinded	Lose finger + Blinded
Jim	Lost finger	Become deaf + Lost finger

should compare it with how much what we can give to the better off satisfies *his* need. Theoretically, we might be able to satisfy the need of an older person more easily (given that his need is less) with even fewer years (in absolute or need-adjusted terms) than we can give to the needier. Yet should this weigh in favor of helping the older person? It seems not.

These points suggest, I believe, that we should not place too much emphasis on whether we have done a lot to satisfy the need of the worse off; it is more important to compare the need-adjusted years we could offer to the needier person, his absolute and comparative level of need, and the cost in need-adjusted years to the less needy. For, as noted above, making a big difference to the better off is sometimes worth more than making a smaller difference to the worse off. This is especially true as the absolute condition of the worse off is better or the comparative difference between better off and worse off is less. [17]

But how shall we deal with the Parfit-like examples in which we can prevent the loss of a finger to the blind or prevent someone who has already lost a finger from going deaf? Here we prevent a bigger loss to the less badly off person than to the worse off person, as well as do more to satisfy a need. It is the former fact we should emphasize. For if we could prevent a much bigger loss (do more good) to the one who is much needier, even if we did not satisfy much of his need, we should help him rather than the better off.

(Intuitively, we might object to maximin even if the worst off receive a significant benefit and are absolutely and comparatively needy, simply because the less needy stands to lose out on a sizeable chunk of life, for example thirty years. It is possible that our reasoning here may mimic the sort of reasoning we would engage in if the impermissible course of taking a sizeable chunk of the less needy person's life, i.e., killing him, to save the needier person were proposed. That is, even though we would not in fact be taking, but only refusing to provide someone with, additional years, we may think he is asked to pay too high a price in order to provide more life to the worst off and that he should retain a 50 percent chance (or close to it). That is, we do not distinguish between killing and letting die. But this seems to be a mistake in our reasoning.)

Security versus Respect for Humanity and Rights

There is more to be said against favoring the younger. It might be suggested that even the younger would exchange the security of having at least as many years as the older for the benefit of being treated as a certain sort of being throughout life. (This applies even to the younger person who already knows he cannot get to be old. Identifying with that younger person, we must think of *him* as someone who at some point will have decided how he wants to be treated as a person at all stages of his life.) That is, he tolerates the increase in the risk of dying young because this alone is consistent with his being the sort of creature, throughout his life, whom it is impermissible to abandon or treat differently on account of age. Being this sort of person actually contributes to the quality of his life even in youth, it is claimed. To do this is really to maintain the ideal of equal treatment for each person's life (perhaps allowing for differences in accord with expected outcome in absolute or

DMV terms). (It is also possible to think of such an exchange of security by someone who expects to grow old and is concerned with his status as an older person). Is such an exchange merely the reflection of a person's preference? Or is there something about giving the older less chance vis-à-vis the younger solely in virtue of age difference that is intrinsically wrong, and so a scheme excluding it ought morally to be preferred?

This difference between a mere preference and intrinsic wrongness can be thought of as the difference between not *wanting* to be treated in a certain way and a rational person's not being able to *will* such treatment.[18] That is, some might *say* that it would be wrong to treat the old differently because we, even when younger, would not agree to such treatment for ourselves. But it is not the simple refusal to agree that makes difference in treatment wrong. It is rather the intrinsic wrong-making property of different treatment that makes it wrong to agree. Or so it might be argued.

But what is this wrong-making property? Could it be that distributing resources so as to help the neediest treats humanity inappropriately in the older person, counting that humanity for nothing in him, and so radically alters our idea of what sort of being we as persons are, even when young? But why should taking care of greater need, where this involves an overall evaluation of years lived, mean that we ignore the worth of humanity? We do not, in general, think that giving something to someone who has not already had a great deal treats humanity in the less needy as nothing.

An alternative view might hold, for example, that all those who have not yet had a "full" life at the time of death (i.e., 70 years) are equally needy. Then the 20-year-old and 50-year-old will be equally needy. I find this an odd result. Even if we think the structural feature of leading a full life, in the sense of one that spans significant stages, should be considered, this view gives no differential credit for how far from or close to living such a full life one is. If there were a *right* to have such a "full" life, this might make formal sense of ignoring differences in degrees of satisfaction of the right. The analogy here would be to property rights: you have as much right to be protected in your property as someone else who has had his for a shorter time and who needs his in daily life much more than you do. But, I believe, while such protection of property independent of need is common where negative rights (i.e., rights to noninterference are at stake), it is not as crucial in the area of positive rights (i.e., rights to aid). In distributing the latter, need might play a role.

Attachment and Power

Empirical factors may diminish the role of age. Attachment can develop to individuals who have been with us for a long time, with greater attachment the longer the person has been with us. Many of the elderly are, therefore, our most treasured relations and most deeply embedded in the family network. We cannot imagine our world without them. A protective attitude also develops to the elderly, in particular; we tend to see them as more like children. However, the tendency to give them preference in contexts where we would give children preference is an error based on confusing them with real children. The protective attitude toward the elderly may be misplaced, in general: surviving for many years is probably an indication of hardiness, or the ability to use others (perhaps by unconsciously feigned weakness). Along these lines of the survival of the fittest, we may think those who have survived to a certain point have proved themselves to have a stronger hold on life. Life is here seen as a struggle in which one must kill or be killed, or something like a game of musical chairs—the seats available diminish for each age group, and one must struggle for a seat or be eliminated. God or Nature, not other people by way of explicit policies, will eliminate some from the competition. Associated with this may even be the idea that having struggled to survive, one gains privileges and is owed a preference in the receipt of medical care, especially in one's most powerful years of middle age. We are fearful of denying the powerful. In the middle years especially, Oedipal concerns are probably also at work; because one sees the young threatening one's place in areas of life where this is not appropriate, one resists in a medical context. All these are common and perhaps natural views, but not necessarily morally appropriate for all that.

Additional factors may apply in particular cases only. These include gratitude to the old for past and present services rendered. Also, the social inefficiency of losing those with well-developed skills. The draft applies to the young, for this reason. But if the distribution of scarce resources would not affect many people, inefficiency resulting from an age differentiating policy should not arise.

Perhaps these considerations should temper the criterion of need that would give the young almost automatic preference for an organ. However, I continue to believe that differences in age should be given some weight primarily because of fairness considerations, and especially when life and death is in the balance, and that this does not deny the older person respect due him in virtue of his humanity. Nor does it interfere with its being true that it is appropriate for us to have an elevated conception of ourselves at all stages of our life.

A Proposal

The final proposal of this section is that age be given some weight in decision making in virtue of its role in identifying the neediest candidates. This means not only having a dividing line between those above and those below a single point, like seventy, but holding it as a factor in someone's favor that he is younger than someone else at most points in life. If preference for the younger should have this

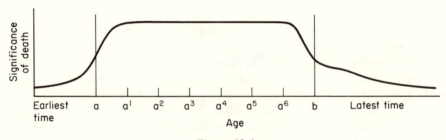

Figure 12.1.

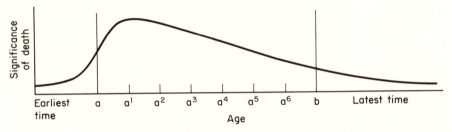

Figure 12.2.

place, any younger person may, of course, waive that preference in favor of older individuals. All this does not mean that an overall evaluation of how the life will have gone may not be outweighed by other factors, e.g., differential urgency.

We could also conclude that younger age should be given some preference (even if not a great deal), even if we thought that experiential and formal properties of past or future life should be counted in determining need or value of outcome. This is because, even if we assume that there is equal likelihood of these latter properties being present in the younger or older person's past or future—though presumably more experiences and achievements are typical in older rather than in younger people's pasts—there is still some weight to be given (e.g., via DMU and fairness) to a clear difference in amounts of adequate conscious life which correlates highly with age.

Many would draw the following curve with respect to the significance of death (see Figure 12-1). This view may reflect, at least partially, the opinion that formal and experiential goods count and are most prevalent after (a) and before (b). It may reflect the view that as a person one always has an equal claim to avoid death until all significant life stages are complete. The view for which I have argued is different. While agreeing about pre-(a), it de-emphasizes the formal and experiential goods for purposes of deciding who lives, and is willing to give some preference not only to the period from (a) to (b) over the period past (b), but to give differential positive weight to the intervals from (a^1) to (a^6) *in descending order*. This results in the curve seen in Figure 12-2.

II NEED VERSUS URGENCY

The Here and Now versus Overall Evaluation

A different problem with helping the neediest (as I have defined this term) may arise because we think differences in urgency[T] cannot be ignored.

For example, consider the case in Table 12-4 where X or Y must be given transplants now though they are not equally urgent[T]. (Suppose we will not be able to operate on X later, or that no other organ will appear for him within a year.) The outcome in years is equal and there is true scarcity, so that if one person gets an organ now the other person will die according to his degree of urgency[T]. The table represents the alternative characterization I have given of need, a combination of age and urgency[T]. Combining age and urgency[T] gives us age expected at death

Table 12.4

| | Need | | | Differential Outcome |
	Age	Urgency[T]	Outcome	
X	20 years old	1 year	3 years	2 years
Y	50 years old	1 month	3 years	2 years, 11 months

without an organ. The outcome is intended to represent number of years expected with an organ if there is transplantation now. To find the differential outcome (additional time due to organ alone), we must subtract the urgency[T] figure from the outcome figure. (There are unequal differential outcomes in this case. We could modify the case so that there is unequal outcome but equal differential outcome.)

The push toward helping the most urgent[T] who will die sooner, like the push to producing the best outcome, is future oriented. That is, rather than look to the past, what has been and cannot be changed, and its contribution to an overall life (20 + 3 years versus 50 + 3 years of life at the time of death), we just look forward from now (1 year versus 1 month before death).

However, the future orientation based on helping the most urgent[T], unlike the future orientation based on differential outcome, might be seen as a requirement of treating persons with respect. That is, the thought is that we treat persons dis- respectfully if we do not deal with their *present* pressing circumstances. It is wrong to detach ourselves sufficiently from the current complaints persons present to us to do an overall life calculation, or for that matter to do a future-oriented outcome calculation. This may be another aspect of the problem of moral distance. That is, we tend to think we should help the dying person on our doorstep if not the one in a foreign country. The here and now imposes itself.

If we are concerned that here and now someone is more urgent than someone else, we are concerned with helping who is worst off at this time. Need, as I have described it, may seem to be concerned with overall equality in the lives of people. But of course, it is possible that helping the neediest results in more inequality than it alleviates, for in helping the person who would be worst off if not helped, we may do him so much good that he winds up overall much better than the person who was originally better off. For example, if we help a 20-year-old rather than a 40-year-old, he may live to 70. Nevertheless it may be right to help the worst off person. Even if helping the neediest coincides with producing more overall equality in lives it can conflict with producing equality between people's *current* conditions. If I am your slave one day and you are my slave the next day, though there is overall equality between us, there is no time when we stand in a relationship of equality. Rather we stand in alternating subordinating relations. More equality would be present if we were never each other's slaves, for example, if I made my bed and you made yours each day rather than if I made yours one day and you made mine on another.[19]

One way of understanding the weight of urgency is that it represents the attempt to take care of those worst off here and now, and this may coincide with producing equality in people's current, rather than overall, conditions. For example, we take care of the person who is in greater pain now so that he is in no more pain than another, whose less significant pain we ignore, even if the more urgent person will have had less pain overall in his life than the other overall. Notice that equality henceforth may conflict with producing equality in only current coinciding conditions, because, for example, producing equality now will lead to greater inequality in the future.

A strong argument for coinciding equality exists when giving preference to someone who has had less in the past would put him in an intrinsically unjust relation to another. For example, if one party dominated in the past, and domination is intrinsically wrong, putting the other party in the dominant position will also involve a wrong relation. But even here, the call for punishment of the previously dominant party, and even the educative function of experiencing a subordinate relationship, might argue for *overall* equality. In cases where no intrinsically unjust relation is involved in compensation, the case for overall equality becomes even stronger. However, another argument against sacrificing coinciding equality in one respect exists when another sort of coinciding inequality, e.g., political inequality, will follow upon it. For example, if young and old live together and interact as citizens, current inequality in health or economic status will be bad. But if we face a life and death decision, where only one person can live, the younger or the older, there will be no further interaction between the loser and other people. Then overall equality may be an appropriate goal, even though it is more of a loss to the loser to die than to live on with an unequal status. This will, of course, mean that when the young and old do interact, they may be aware of the unequal claim they will have on truly scarce resources in life and death situations.

Finally, there may be "mixed decisions" in which we must decide between someone who will die in a short time if not given an organ now, and someone who will have poor quality of life but not die. If "need" is defined as how overall badly off in terms of adequate conscious life someone will be when he dies, then neediness is affected not only by when one dies but also by future poor quality of life (e.g., inadequate conscious life). The most morally problematic choice for the neediest over the urgent^T would occur if we chose someone who was neediest *because urgent*^{Q} over someone who was less needy but urgent^T. For example, if we chose a young person who would have a long life of pain if not transplanted now versus an older person who will die shortly, with the assumption that there is true scarcity and we must act now or never. In such "mixed" decisions one would need to know whether the outcome which is not adequate life is still partially adequate, and so better than death, or "a living death," for this would be very significant in deciding whom to help. At least one would need to know this if we are willing to forego always helping whomever will have had the worst life overall if not helped now. I shall continue to assume we are doing unmixed comparisons, i.e., the neediest and nonneediest are both facing death, unless otherwise stated.

Some may even think that we must leave it to God to act on overall evaluations of a life even when this is restricted to amount of adequate conscious life; people must not try to do this. Keeping in mind that the more urgent^T someone is, the worse his expected outcome tends to be, some may still be willing to count differences in expected future outcomes in conditions of true scarcity. But the grounds for doing this cannot be respect or concern for the here and now or coinciding equality (as it might be for urgency^T) or fairness (as it might be for need).

(Cases in which we refuse to aid the most urgent^T, when we have aid to offer, in order to keep on hand a resource to give to someone else *later,* raise different problems. [We have noted this in Chapter 7.] For if we help the most urgent^T, we will literally not be able to aid the other person later because we will have no aid to offer, but if we hold on to resources that could be used now, we do nothing when we could aid. As noted above we seem to prefer to avoid the second situation, and not only because we worry that we may be denying someone aid now that others will turn out *not* to need later. However, this specific problem would arise in Table 12-4 only if we would put off transplanting X for a year.)

A Proposal for Need and Urgency^T

One possible proposal is that, despite the psychological salience of urgency^T, it should not have great weight as an aspect of respect for persons. Rather, differences in need should take almost absolute precedence over different (as well as identical) urgency^T scores, in situations of true scarcity. That is, we should be much more concerned about how badly off someone will be when he dies than with how soon he will die. In situations of only temporary scarcity, or no scarcity, however, it would still be permissible to distribute according to urgency^T. (We shall discuss this in more detail below.)

We may also face situations in which two candidates will be equally badly off at the time of death, but one is more urgent^T than another. In Table 12-5, both candidates will be twenty when they die if not given transplants. Both would die at thirty-two if treated, but one will die in a year, the other in ten years. (These cases are unrealistic, but still useful for theoretical purposes.) Assume true scarcity and the necessity of giving a transplant to either person now to achieve the benefit. In this case, should urgency^T be taken as a relevant difference? It is hard to ignore it. Yet suppose the possible differential outcomes were twenty to each if transplanted. We might object to someone losing out on a chance for a much longer life just to deal with the more urgent^T claim of someone equally needy. (Discounting a death simply because it is further in the future seems irrational, given equal need.)

In real life, of course, uncertainty about the future—both absence of precise knowledge of outcomes and uncertainty about age may lead us to deal with the most urgent^T person. Further, if need (as a function of age) is not given too large a role (perhaps for reasons mentioned in Section I), then it would not totally dominate

Table 12.5

	Need		Outcome	Differential Outcome
	Age	Urgency^T		
X	19 years old	1 year	13 years	12 years
Y	10 years old	10 years	22 years	12 years

urgency^T. But if need had at least some weight, weight of urgency^T would be diminished. For example, we would take care of a 20-year-old rather than a more urgent 60-year-old, even if differential (and DMU-adjusted) outcomes were equal.

So, the final proposal is that the weight of urgency^T should be modified to some degree by need.

Urgency^Q as Worse Life

How do cases in which urgency is a matter not of how soon death comes but rather of how poor one's quality of life will be operate relative to my notion of need? Suppose someone is more urgent^Q because he will live his remaining five years in great pain while another candidate will live his remaining five years lacking energy. Then we make a bigger difference to someone's future if we help the more urgent^Q avoid pain than if we help the less urgent^Q retain energy. We also produce more equality between the two from now on. That is, the difference between adequate quality of life and low energy is less than the difference between adequate quality of life and pain. But suppose the more urgent^Q patient has had forty years of satisfactory life and the less urgent^Q only twenty years. The 20-year-old may be worse off overall if not treated than the 40-year-old will be; the 20-year-old will never have had the twenty years of vigor the 40-year-old has had.

Even if we accept a large role for need in general, it may here be correct to forget about the unalterable past which makes one person much needier than another. That is, we should sometimes just try to make the most difference to a candidate by helping the one who will be worst off in the future, even if he would not be the worst off overall if not treated. (It may also be relevant that the loss we prevent in the 20-year-old would in any case not do much to compensate him for his shorter life, though I have suggested we should not focus on this factor.) The model to use in discussing this case is again suggested by cases represented in Table 12-3.

On the other hand, it is a significant gain to have five energy-filled years, and the comparative and absolute difference between more and less needy persons is significant. (That is, one is twenty years younger than the other, and, in absolute terms, will die at a young age.) This is a case in which attending to pain is very costly.

A Proposal for Need versus Urgency^Q

I have suggested that when urgency is a matter of how soon someone will die without treatment (urgency^T), it should be balanced at least to some degree against overall need *when there is true scarcity*. So the needier but less urgent^T person may get the organ even if differential outcome is the same. When urgency is a matter of how badly off in life someone will be (urgency^Q), what weight should need have relative to it assuming quality of life is at stake for needier and less needy?

To say need has less weight relative to urgency^Q then it has to urgency^T implies that someone less needy who will die soon may be given less consideration (relative to a needier person who will die later) than someone less needy who will live poorly if not treated will be given relative to someone who is needier and faces a less bad quality of life. This may sound odd, and hence we should conclude that need will count for more against urgency^Q than it does against urgency^T. How we think about these cases truly depends on whether we think greater need counts very much against greater urgency^T. Those who think that in matters of life and death, urgency^T counts above need will not think it odd that greater need is taken into account more against urgency^Q. On the other hand, those who think greater need should above all count when life itself is at stake for both parties (i.e., urgency^T) will think this explains the less needy being given more consideration with urgency^Q than with urgency^T.

Although I am not sure, I shall here side with the view that greater equality in treatment of more needy and less needy should reign in matters of quality of life. This means need carries more weight relative to urgency^T than to urgency^Q, in part because it costs the more needy less to have the needs of the less needy met when it costs them in quality of life rather than in life itself. By contrast, if it mattered more who is currently worse off than who will be overall worse off, we might emphasize that it costs the currently worst off less to sacrifice quality of life than life itself, and so conclude that need carries more weight relative to U^Q than to U^T. If we recognize the weight of both (1) overall equality and of (2) coinciding equality, the question becomes whether (1) is dominant and must give way to some degree for (2), or whether (2) is dominant and so must give way to some degree for (1).

We might represent whatever added weight this need has by multiplying the face value of the quality of future life of the neediest by some factor, correlated with absolute and relative neediness. This factor would be smaller than the factor used when death is at stake for needier and less needy. Only after doing this should we compare the future life of the needier to the significance of the loss we prevent in the person who at face value is more urgent^Q.

Urgency^T Versus Urgency^Q

It is worth noting the following: the emphasis in medical circles on producing the best outcome is sometimes presented as a concern for the diminished quality of life of someone who is not treated because we treat someone more urgent^T. That is, we are presented with a conflict between urgency^Q and urgency^T. For example, we are told to consider the suffering of a child who could live normally if we did not help the more urgent^T person whose outcome cannot be as good, no matter what we do.

This argument, however, ignores the fact that the urgent^T person will die rather than have some sort of life, whereas the person who misses out on the best outcome will not die. Both will at least have some life if we treat the most urgent^T and forego the best outcome possible for another individual. The dead are highly invisible, of course, and we can produce a prettier end-state picture among those still living if we produce the best outcome (i.e., largest number of medically good quality years). But this is not necessarily the morally correct choice.

I am here assuming some significant outcome is possible for the most urgent^T person, recognizing that, in reality, the most urgent^T may have very bad prospects. I am here also implicitly assuming that need is held constant between the candidates with differential U^Q and U^T.

Use of Type O Products

A factor in distribution decisions that relates to urgency^T is blood type. As noted above, it seems most reasonable to give O products special attention as a function of concern for what we are calling urgency^T, that is, as part of a concern for who is more likely to die before receiving an organ. The Report provides two directives for the use of material from O blood type donors: (1) O material should be offered first to suitable O recipients (p. 82), and (2) O material should be offered only to O recipients (p. 74). Obviously these directives have inconsistent implications. The second policy would require that we never use O material on people with blood type A. The first policy would permit such use provided that no O recipient is either available or expected to be available in time to use the organ. The first policy is obviously better in respect of an efficient distribution of organs.

Both policies, however, conflict with an aim of giving preference to urgent^T and sensitized individuals, who are considered part of that class most likely to die before another organ appears. This is because, if urgent^T or sensitized persons were A type, O material would clearly not be offered to them by the second policy and would not be offered by the first policy if "suitable Os" does not include "as urgent as others." If we are concerned with O material for urgency^T-related reasons, the most reasonable policy seems to be: Offer O material first to an O recipient as urgent^T as other potential recipients, where 'as urgent^T' includes 'as sensitized,' given that sensitized are even more likely to die before another organ is found than O people. This policy means that A people may often get O materials. This revised policy, in effect, distributes consistently according to degree of urgency^T. It may be superseded by a policy that says that we must treat or give some preference to the neediest (as defined above) before the urgent^T. I assume that the neediest and most urgent are treated only if they offer an outcome that is of some significance to them. And it is worth repeating that the bad outcomes associated with those who are urgent^T because of sickness need not be associated with those who are urgent^T because of sensitivity or O blood type. Even if we should not treat those with poor outcomes in true scarcity this rule would not apply to these urgent people.

III.   NEED VERSUS OUTCOME

How Should We Evaluate Outcome?

Need represents concern for fairness as taking care of the worst off overall, and for DMV of life. Urgency represents concern for the pressure of the here and now and for coinciding equality, taking care of who is worse off now. Outcome is what I refer to as a maximizing factor; emphasis on outcome indicates a concern for the best possible future state of affairs where the standard for judging states of affairs is narrow, i.e., how many additional medically adequate life years can we produce.[20] The Report emphasizes length of medically adequate life in measuring outcome, rejecting more refined notions of "quality of life" that it thinks would involve deciding on the merit of different life-styles. It also considers only the good of the outcome for the person whose life is at stake, not for the community at large. For the most part, I believe these two moves are to its credit.

Take the first point first. Why shouldn't we make refined quality-of-life judgments where these involve only consideration of the worth of a life *to* the person
living it rather than its social usefulness? (The discussion of this question bears on
our earlier discussion of how needy someone is, in which we asked whether refined
quality-of-life judgments about someone's past should be included (if it were possible to make them) in our deciding how needy someone is.) Is it because it is not
possible? I do not think so. It *is* possible to say of some lifestyles that they are better
than others for the persons who lead them, I believe.

There are three commonly discussed "philosopher's" criteria for how good
one's life is. The first is how much happiness there is in one's life. The second is
how much satisfaction of desire there is in one's life. Assuming that people desire
things other than happiness, this second criterion is based on the idea that what is
intrinsically valuable is the satisfaction of desires. These are two different versions
of a utilitarian test. They both raise problems about the interpersonal comparison of
utility. That is, if we want to decide whose life is better we will, for example, have
to compare the degree of intensity of desires and their satisfaction.

A third criterion is referred to as the Objective List Test.[21] According to this
view, certain experiences and achievements are objectively valuable, for example,
happiness, meaningful work. One way of interpreting this is to say that they would
be the objects of perfectly rational desire. These are desires in accord with the true
value of their objects. Satisfaction of desires per se is not (or is only minimally)
intrinsically valuable; its value is in accord with the value of the objects one desires.

According to each of these views, some lives can be judged better than others.
Some lives are happier than others, some have a greater degree of satisfaction of
desires, some have a greater amount of objective goods.

So ways have been suggested to decide whose life is better for the one who lives
it. Why should we refrain from using them? Is it because to each person, her life-
style is as important to her as somebody else's (perhaps better) life-style is to him?
After all, it is all she has. This may not always be true, for it is probably not true that
someone cares just as much about his poor quality of life as another person cares
about his better quality life. On the other hand, someone may care as much for the
five years of life he could get from a transplant (given that is all he can get) as
another person cares for the twenty he could get. (This is not to deny that someone
would care more for having twenty than having five *if* he could have twenty instead
of five.) Yet we may want to allow that we could favor the person who will live
longer, even if not the person who will have a better life.

Should we refuse to consider these refined quality-of-life judgments in comparing life to be gained by one person with life to be gained by another, because the
difference is not significant in comparison to the difference between living at all and
dying?[22] That is, even the person who will gain a less good life if he lives will (we
are assuming) gain a medically adequate life. And is not the gain of life in comparison to death many times greater than the gain of finer quality life in comparison
to lesser quality life, or greatly appreciated life to less appreciated life? In other
words, is not finer quality an irrelevant utility?

Even this does not seem quite right as an account of why we should not attend to
refined notions of quality of life. For what if someone would sacrifice much additional adequate conscious life to have a better quality of life? Then, we could not say

such quality pales in comparison to simply adequate conscious existence. It does not seem that we are dealing with an *objective* judgment about the significance of adequate conscious life itself versus quality of life, or with how much one cares for one's life. Rather, if someone is relatively satisfied—by which we mean satisfied enough—with the life he will have, this seems sufficient to make us ignore other differences. His "subjective accommodation" to his type of life can dominate any other criterion of judgment when we make life-and-death decisions for the sake of the candidates themselves rather than for society.

Is this different from the criterion we used in deciding how badly off someone will be when he dies? There we used a more objective standard, roughly, how much adequate conscious life one has had. I mean the standard for future outcome to be less strict than the standard employed in judging past life. For example, if someone's future life will be full of pain—I take this to be less than (medically) adequate life—but he can accommodate to this, that is all we need to consider. That is, subjective satisfaction is sufficient; it need not be necessary, since objective medical adequacy can be reason for saving a life even if someone rejects it subjectively. However, it is usually improper to force treatment on someone who does not want it. Since many people will reject a life (especially bought at the trouble of a transplant) that is not an adequate conscious life, and will accept one that is, in most cases the two standards will overlap.

What Counts in Outcome: Further Considerations

We may be able to clarify why we should not seek other achievements, even when we are only concerned with enriching the person's life for himself through the use of our resource, by using a doctrine of separate spheres in which different criteria rule.

Suppose someone would rank adequate conscious life higher than all other things except a certain achievement. Further, suppose that another candidate could live to achieve the very thing for which the first would sacrifice much conscious time alive if he could be the one to have the achievement. This does not mean that the first candidate now cares less for his own adequate conscious life than he cares for the other person's achievement. But should he understand if *we* give the organ to the person who can achieve what he cannot achieve *because* he himself would sacrifice conscious life for his own achievement? That is, while he cares only for *his* achievement, the fact that he would sacrifice years of life to have this type of achievement in his life is based on his view that the achievement has greater worth than mere conscious life. Can we make use of his own value judgment to favor the other candidate who can achieve?

I suggest that the first candidate could reasonably object to this. For suppose (what is hardly likely) that we would all sacrifice five years at the end of our lives in exchange for completing a work of philosophy. Suppose also that we argue from this to the conclusion that an organ should be given to a production philosopher who will live five years rather than to someone else who will complete no comparable project in the equal number of conscious years we can give to her. Then should we not also give the organ to someone who will finish a philosophical work, though he does not live anywhere near five years?

Should we not also funnel funds that might go to organ transplants directly to the completion of philosophical works? That is, suppose it were true that *all* the people who needed transplants would live many years of conscious life, but would complete no projects for which we could understand exchanging five years of life. Then should the reasoning that distinguishes between outcomes on the basis of projects in them also lead us to support the National Endowment for the Humanities rather than organ transplants? Or, at least, should we not fund life extension only when it is connected with the completion of projects?

Does the following proposal seem outlandish? Suppose there is a shortage of funds for lifesaving procedures, but we also, quite separately, still wish to fund cultural pursuits. If some worthy philosopher is dying, may we fund a transplant for her that we would not otherwise fund at all, as a grant in the humanities? (Might we even invest in research for the illness she has as a way of keeping her productive?) Or must we rather open up the competition for the extra transplant to needy people in general? If it were permissible to reserve certain transplants as a means to meeting the interests of a sphere other than health care per se (e.g., philosopher's achievements or getting one's astronauts to the moon), this still would not mean that one may, in general, use this extra achievement as a factor in selecting recipients of organs.

It might be argued that preferring some projects over others is elitist, or at least that a liberal state should not be involved in favoring one project over another. But the questions I have asked apply even if we have a highly abstract description of projects, such that there is widespread agreement on its being reasonable to sacrifice the last years of one's life to complete them.

My sense, accordingly, is that, as important as structural and hedonistic experiential factors are, they should still take back seat in the choice between people's lives to the continuation of conscious life of whatever kind that is satisfactory to those who must lead it. The fact that someone would give up conscious life to achieve some goal does not mean he would want to lose the only thing he can have, adequate conscious life, so that someone else may achieve such a goal. Therefore, the extra-utility achievable in only one life could be considered by all to be even larger than the good we can produce whomever we save, and yet if the latter utility is significant enough, giving equal chances for it could take precedence over achieving it plus extra-utility.

But this does not seem to be true in general. That is, suppose the extra-utility is twenty additional years of life, so that with an organ one candidate would live twenty-five extra years and another would live just five years. In this case as well, the extra-good is so great that someone would risk or give up the base utility (five years) to get it (for a total of fifteen extra years). In this case, as well, we can ask ourselves whether one candidate should lose out on his chance for the great good of five years of life just because he was not lucky enough to be able to also achieve what even he recognizes as worth more than the minimal good he can have. Yet (as we shall discuss further below) I believe extra years are not irrelevant, even if such things as cultural achievement are.

What is needed to supplement such an argument for ignoring some large extra utilities, I believe, is a doctrine of separate spheres or specialized aims.[23] In the sphere of lifesaving enterprises, completing projects is not a relevant consideration.

In the sphere of lifesaving, if we take seriously the point of view of each individual, to whom it is important that he rather than someone else lives, we cannot say that we will have satisfied the requirement of the sphere, namely to save life, if we save one life and go on to produce a cultural achievement as well. The good of lifesaving rather than this extra utility must continue to be our paramount objective. Under a theory of separate spheres or specialized aims, health resources are to be used to produce adequate conscious life and/or what people are willing to live for if it is less than objectively adequate. They are not specifically directed at other achievements *unless* the persons whose lives are at stake choose to exchange life for achievement in their own cases or for the sake of others. In this sphere, we do not treat people as means to goods other than their own survival with adequate conscious life unless with their consent. Separate spheres, each with its own criterion for the distribution of a good, might be defended on grounds of equality, i.e., if we distribute not only arts funds on the basis of talent but also life or health, the same people, or class of people, will receive both kinds of benefits and this will result in inequality that would not exist if the different benefits were distributed on different criteria. But this does not seem to be the primary problem. For suppose artists who were heavily funded worked harder and hence got sicker more frequently than others. They would also get health care more frequently than others, but this would not be problematic. Separate spheres are better justified on the grounds that the goal of improving health or saving life is sufficient unto itself, and there is corruption in the achievement of this aim if achieving some other good is combined with it in the selection of persons, even if as much life or health is attended to. (Again this does not exclude selecting a random decision procedure on grounds that it, like the magic coin, produces a good from another sphere.)

This idea of separate spheres may also be related to a variation on the idea of direct use of resources. In distinguishing above between direct and indirect uses we distinguished between someone's needing a drug and someone's needing someone else to have the drug. But we might also make use of the distinction between a person's needing an organ for life and his achievement's requiring that he have life (since if he lives he can make possible the achievement). That is, the organ does not directly make the achievement possible. (We can refer to these as indirect' versus direct' uses.) But separate spheres goes beyond indirect' use, since the latter may involve an effect that is still the health of the person, as when an organ makes possible someone's survival for another operation for a different illness.

Ignoring most differences in quality of life need not be inconsistent with the maximin approach that gives greater need (at least) some greater weight when need is a function of how much adequate conscious life someone has had already. There is a moral difference between giving to someone because he has had less adequate conscious life than others have had and giving to someone because he will then produce a better quality life for himself than others will produce for themselves.

Cases

Consider some of the implications of this view of relevant outcome: In a choice between a 20-year-old and a 40-year-old, each of whom is expected to live an additional twenty years, the fact that only the 40-year-old could provide us with that significant structural feature in his outcome, namely, a full life if he dies at 60, is not grounds for our selecting between them. (It is worth repeating that an expected outcome of twenty years is unrealistic in the area of organ transplants, where a good outcome is currently between five and seven years. But our discussion should apply to other scarce resources.) In a choice between two 20-year-olds, each of whom is expected to live an additional five years, we give no extra weight in deciding who lives to the one who will complete a significant project in that time period. (There may be exceptions, for example, for those who can complete projects that have truly exceptional social importance. I consider these to be projects which contribute not merely to the life of the person involved in the project, nor are they socially important *merely* because they result in an aggregation of small gains to each individual in society. Fairness is being overridden when such a great good is made relevant.)

Final Proposal

The proposal we suggest for this topic is that outcome in the medical context *not* be judged as better or worse on the basis of formal or structural goods; that outcomes are to be considered qualitatively equal if conscious life, acceptable to the individual living it or objectively so, is present in each. However, the length of such conscious life may be considered in selecting between better and worse outcomes— we have yet to give a detailed defense of this view—and structural goods that are judged important for extraordinary social reasons might override fairness. All of this is not meant to be incompatible with the fact (if it is one) that those who yearn to complete projects may be more likely to survive than those who do not have such projects. This fact (if it is one) need not be reflected in our distribution decisions except insofar as we think such a yearning will increase expected number of adequate conscious years of life.

Family Dependents

What about counting as part of the outcome the usefulness of a life to society or to close dependents, in distribution decisions? Consider the latter question first. Why not save a father on whom five children depend rather than a single person?

The first suggested objection to doing so when an organ is needed for life is that no one of the children will suffer as large a loss if the father dies as the other organ candidate stands to lose if he dies. Further, since each child's potential loss is less than the single person's, we should not aggregate the losses to each child. Only the losses of those who could stand against the single person as a contestant in their own right should be counted against him.

This objection, however, conflicts with some of our conclusions in Chapter 9. There we considered the Arm Case, in which we must choose between Joe's life and Jim's life plus Nancy's arm. What Nancy stands to lose is less than what Joe stands to lose, and she would not be a contestant against him alone. Nevertheless, we concluded, her loss could be aggregated with Jim's to outweigh giving Joe an equal chance to live (though perhaps not to outweigh any chance). Why should not the children's loss be counted like the arm, and the loss to several children be aggregated, as many arms next to Jim's life would be?

Several distinctions between the cases suggest themselves. First, it may be that a permanent physical loss, such as a missing arm, should count more than the emotional or financial loss the children suffer.

As a test of this hypothesis, suppose there were no causal relation between the father and the children's suffering (which there, in fact, is), but we had the following choice: (1) to save the life of the single person, or (2) to save both the life of the father *and* also make a serum of part of our organ to alleviate emotional suffering the children experience as a result of going through some life crisis unrelated to their father. Suppose that without the serum the emotional suffering would not be permanent and adjustment would take place, though at a lower quality of life. I believe we should not automatically help both father and children, rather than give the single person his equal chance to survive. I believe we tend to think that emotional suffering to unfortunate events in life passes, or at least should be coped with in ways other than by the serum. Economic loss is of less significance and to some degree compensable. (We certainly must not think that living with some psychological pain or damage is worse than death, just because the dead are highly invisible and their suffering is over.) More important, economic security (and perhaps even normal psychological welfare) are goods in a separate sphere from the goods we seek in health care. (This would be true even if, by some fluke, our resources directly produced economic security.)

Another distinction between the case of father and children and the Arm Case (as well as the variation just described in which our serum cures emotional suffering) is that in the Arm Case there is no causal relation between Jim and Nancy, that is, we do not save Jim rather than Joe because *Jim* will then save Nancy's arm. It is we, with our scarce resource, who will save Nancy's arm. But if we save the father without giving the single man a chance, we do so because *he* will (by hypothesis) play a causal role in maintaining the emotional welfare of his children. This means that the single person fails to get the organ because he cannot fulfill the same role as a means. This in turn suggests that we are not evaluating him as an end in himself, but distinguishing him from another on the basis of whether he is a means. This may introduce unfairness. (Ordinarily, it is said, it is permissible to treat someone as a means if we also treat him as an end in himself. Is this test satisfied in our case? If we consider whether the treatment is in the single person's interest first and then eliminate him because he fails as a means, have we met the test? That is not the way the test is meant to be applied: It is permissible to treat someone as a means if we also actually *give* him an organ, not if we merely consider whether he needs it for his own sake and then eliminate him on means-grounds.)

Can we always raise this objection to focusing on someone's role as a means? I have suggested (in Chapter 6) that we cannot raise this objection if the person's causal role aids the distribution of the very scarce resource we are trying to distribute. So if the children also needed our resource to avoid some significant permanent physical damage, and we could not reach them but their father could, there would be no unfairness in favoring him. In this case, but not when we ordinarily would count dependents, direct use of our resource and the satisfaction of the "separate spheres" criterion are both present.

Where there is unfairness, this is *a* reason for not counting the children. But unfairness is not an absolute bar to counting such considerations as the children's misery. What the presence of unfairness suggests is, rather, that a greater amount of bad is needed to override unfairness than would be enough to allow us to favor Jim over Joe when no causal relation distinguishes these two. In the choice between Jim and Joe, greater extra utility than the minimal (sore throat) was necessary for it to be permissible to favor Jim. One child's significant loss may be insufficient to override the unfairness of paying heed to a father's role as a means, but several children's significant loss (by aggregation) might be sufficient to override unfairness, at least if the loss were in the relevant sphere. It remains true that there should be no aggregation over many children of small losses to each child, and that consideration of losses in different spheres is problematic.

Finally, if we select the father because of his dependents, it might be suggested that we violate the liberal view that state policy should be neutral between different conceptions of the good life, not favoring those who have chosen to be parents over those who remain single and childless. (Counting dependents is even worse if individuals remained childless even though they tried to have children, or are childless because of some unfairness in their social position, or are childless because it is morally better to be childless.)

This objection may miss its mark, however. For liberal institutions to be neutral, it may only be required that they not *aim* at favoring one lifestyle over another. They will still be neutral even if they have the *unintended* effect of putting one life-style at an advantage over another.[24] So, if there were strong reasons independent of favoring child rearing for counting the effect on dependents, for example, the harms to them simply as other persons, then counting them would not violate neutrality. That is, it would not consist in intentionally favoring having children.

Social Usefulness

In most cases of family dependents, we are dealing with emotional losses that are significant but less than the loss each organ candidate faces. By contrast, what if society is dependent on the services of one of the candidates? Here the benefits are most often in a different sphere, and the candidate is usually not truly irreplaceable; his role can be filled by someone else. If he or she is irreplaceable, and the loss each member of society will suffer in this person's absence is small as well as in a different (e.g., economic sphere), there should be no aggregation of the small losses added to his side. Suppose the loss each would suffer is significant, but less than that which each organ candidate faces and in a different sphere. Then selecting him on the basis of his causal role raises the issue of unfairness. Nevertheless, this objection might be overridden on the basis of a great enough social effect.

Suppose, however, that we must choose between giving the organ to a janitor or to a doctor who is irreplaceable in saving the lives of twenty people. (The doctor may already be providing them with care that would stop if we do not help him— this is like a mother's relation to her children—or if he is saved he will begin to save people who are about to die.) In this case, each of the people dependent on the doctor stands to lose as much as each of the candidates for the organ stands to lose, and the loss is in the same sphere. Should we consider this to be a straightforward case of one versus twenty-one? If the doctor is needed because only he can deliver our scarce resource to the other twenty who need it as well, then there is no unfairness in selecting him. Then the case should be treated as one versus twenty-one, despite the causal connection. Indeed we might select the doctor if *he* needed the organ only to cure a headache that prevents him from delivering the rest of the organ to his twenty patients.

However, suppose the other twenty do not directly need the scarce resource we are distributing. Then saving the doctor rather than the janitor raises the issue of unfairness, since he is selected because of his causal relation to the twenty when they do not directly need our resource. Unfairness can be overridden. However, to override it we will need more than the one extra life on the side of one candidate that would suffice if there were no causal relation. If there were many lives dependent on the doctor's, it might be permissible to prefer him in distributing the organ. This could be true, even if he did not personally need the organ as much as the janitor did.

Nonindividual Losses

I have insisted that we consider the losses to individual social or familial dependents and that if the losses to each are not large and in a different sphere then aggregation is not permitted. But, it may be objected, even if losses to each dependent individual are small, the type of benefit one organ candidate provides to society can still be large. For example, a great musician contributes a cultural product that is large even if it provides only a few minutes of pleasure or insight to a few people. Indeed, the large cultural product is not to be identified at all with the aggregation of the smaller gains. It is (barely) possible that the exceptional products of talented individuals may override the unfairness involved in preferring them over others.

Better Outcomes by Direct Use of a Resource

There might (theoretically) be cases in the area of organ transplantation that involve direct use of our resource for several people to produce a sphere-appropriate good. For example, suppose several people who could be saved by using parts of our organ confront one person who needs the whole organ to survive. (More realistically, one person may need multiple organs, when each organ alone could be used by each of several other people.) Here, the number of lives should count, if there is approximate equality among candidates in relevant criteria for distribution. We might also face another situation in which our organ (or a dialysis machine) can either save A's life or save B's life and protect C from many sicknesses. Then the ratios discussed in Sob³ (and Sob⁴) are relevant. If the additional utility is such that when many instances of it are aggregated they should be given proportional chances against a life, then when one instance of that utility accompanies a life the two together may be given a higher chance of getting the resource. Also, if the additional utility would be large enough to merit on its own a proportional chance for the resource against a life, it together with a life should directly outweigh another life. (This analysis attends to what we should do when confronted with the needs of individuals here and now. It does not speak to decisions about funding transplant procedures versus other procedures. Our discussions of Sob³ and Sob⁴ in Chapters 9 and 10, however, are also relevant to this funding issue.)

Final Proposals

In sum, in determining differential outcomes there should be no aggregation of small lesser losses in dependents, but significant lesser losses of the appropriate sphere (even when not alleviated by direct use of our resource) may aggregate along with the death of one candidate to the point where they override the unfairness of evaluating candidates as means. Significant lesser losses of the appropriate sphere alleviated by direct use of our resource by several people can affect distribution of the resource.

Conflicts of Need and Outcome

We have just considered whether the idea of outcome as medically adequate years is sufficient, whether other effects should count as outcomes that we compare among candidates. Now we can begin to consider conflicts of need and outcome.

Above, we considered the concept of need and suggested that one reason for helping the neediest is that we may thereby produce a better outcome because of the DMU of life. If there were DMU of life it would reduce conflicts between need and outcome. But it has already been suggested that the utility of life may diminish very slowly.

Even if we multiply the increment for the neediest by a large f, however, that outcome may not always outweigh a bigger absolute increment to the less needy. Yet the gain to the neediest may still be significant. Therefore, possible conflicts remain between satisfying the neediest on grounds of fairness and producing the best outcome. If fairness is the reason why we should help the neediest, it may nevertheless not be overriding.

Using Table 12-3, we considered the view that if we can do little to satisfy the complaint of the worst-off person, at the cost of a big loss to the person who will not be worst off, it may be permissible to help the person who will not be worse off. It might be said that this is true even if the gain to the worst off is significant, for a significant gain (e.g., a need-adjusted outcome of a year) may still not do much to alleviate the need of someone who will otherwise die at twenty. However, we raised objections to counting how much the need was satisfied independent of how large the gain was. The case for helping the nonneediest will, of course, be even stronger if the need-adjusted outcome is, arguably, not even significant, for example, three weeks. Another reason has been given for not attending to differential need very much. It may be that we should think of ourselves as aiding a certain type of creature (a person) and pretty much ignore past goods already had. But this objection to distributing in accord with need does not sit very well with giving different weights to different outcomes in absolute years. For if we were just concerned with not abandoning a person, his outcome should not count so much either. Therefore, if need is weak relative to outcome, it is not so via this intermediate premise of treating persons just as persons. Rather, we may simply value good outcomes and will not sacrifice too large an outcome to achieve a smaller gain to the neediest.

If neediness should not outright dominate outcome, then we must consider how important fairness is and see what sort of a difference the outcome will make for the neediest versus the non-neediest (if not how far it goes to making up the extra need of the neediest). If there is DMV of life, a year to a 20-year-old may be worth as much as five to a 50-year-old, but it will still not be as significant a gain as twenty years to a 50-year-old, and the fact that it goes to the needier may not make up for this.

More will be said on conflicts of need and outcome in the next chapters.

Perfect Tissue Typing, Outcome, and Need

Suppose need should modify our evaluation of outcomes somewhat in light of some weight to fairness. Then the requirement of perfect tissue-typing should be forgone (or at least modified); this would give the neediest a chance at a good they might otherwise be totally denied. Assuming there is a connection between perfect tissue typing and good outcome, the emphasis on perfect tissue typing reflects, at least in part, a concern with achieving the best outcome.[25] If the use of immunosuppressive drugs (such as FK506 developed by T. E. Starzl) can prevent rejection, only a form of concern for the best outcome, that is, a life closest to normal because it involves no need for drugs, would justify insisting on perfect tissue typing as a way of avoiding rejection. (Even if we accept a notion of need as urgency, favoring the better tissue typing puts an outcome factor ahead of need.)

Suppose the concern is that incorrect typing produces sensitization and, therefore, might make a person with a transplant worse off than he would have been without it. This is indeed not a concern merely to achieve the best outcome. It is an attempt to avoid the worst outcome. The fear of sensitizing someone seems misplaced, however, if his alternative is death. That is, death is usually the worst outcome. We should, therefore, worry about sensitization only when a candidate does not face death or there is only temporary scarcity, that is, a candidate passed over now will not die because another organ could be found later.

NOTES

1. I was prompted to draw these distinctions, and construct alternative procedures for distribution depending on which state we are in, by a doctor's comments at Massachusetts General Hospital in Fall 1989.

2. Chapters 1 and 2.

3. Note that for brevity's sake, I speak of an "urgent person" rather than the person with the most urgent claim. Further, by the most urgent claim I mean not necessarily the

morally most important one, but the one that needs to be met sooner or it will be too late because the person dies or lives a worse life otherwise.

4. But note that there seems to be a mistaken assumption in judging that the amount someone would be willing to pay to save his life is a good measure of its subjective value. Suppose someone did not care about other particular people, and so did not care how much money he would leave to others in his will. He would then be prepared to pay a great deal to prolong his life only for a little while, simply because money when he is dead has no value at all to him. The fact that he would pay what would otherwise be valueless to secure something does not show that he values this something highly. He might be prepared to pay most of his fortune to remain alive for one more week, even though he believes that it is hardly worth the trouble to survive for so short a time. (Derek Parfit made these points.)

5. I am indebted to Thomas Scanlon for emphasizing to me that the fairness and value-of-outcome factors should be separately emphasized.

6. I emphasize again that I am using the Report's notion of outcome, which focuses on additional length of life. This contrasts with a philosophical notion of outcome which may include within it how fair the distribution of years of life is.

7. See Norman Daniels, *Am I My Parents' Keeper?* (New York: Oxford University Press, 1990).

8. As in John Rawls's *A Theory of Justice.*

9. This way of putting the objection was raised by a member of the audience at my DeCamp lecture, "Organs for Transplantation: From Whom, To Whom," at Princeton University, November 1990.

10. See his "Contractualism and Utilitarianism" in Sen and Williams (eds.), *Utilitarianism and Beyond.* For more discussion of reasoning behind the veil see below.

11. Mark Johnston reminded me of this point in this context. It is related to the second point made above concerning the difference between DMU as I have used the term and the use of DMU in its ordinary application to money.

12. On the distinction between achievements and goods of which more is better, see Chapter 4.

13. Barring the existence of hell. On these issues see Chapters 1 through 4.

14. Notice that in saying this we would be comparing the size of the potential loss with what someone has already had in order to decide who will bear the loss. This is to indirectly abandon a Maximin (helping the worst off first) approach to distribution. The maximin policy would never impose the greater loss on someone who so far has had less good than someone else. Derek Parfit and Thomas Hurka emphasized the difference between the added utility and the value of giving it.

15. Ronald Dworkin made this point and the general objection to always favoring the younger.

16. In "Innumerate Ethics." The point his cases make is also supported by Thomas Scanlon in "Contractualism and Utilitarianism," and by Thomas Nagel in *Equality and Partiality.* (New York: Oxford University Press, 1991).

17. Thomas Scanlon writes in "Contractualism and Utilitarianism," p. 123, that "It does not follow, however, that contractualism always requires us to select the principle under which the expectations of the worse off are highest. The reasonableness of the Losers' objection to A is not established simply by the fact that they are worse off under A and no-one would be this badly off under E. The force of their complaint depends also on the fact that their position under A is, in absolute terms, very bad, and would be significantly better under E. This complaint must be weighed against those of individuals who would do worse under E. The question to be asked is, is it unreasonable for someone to refuse to put up with the Losers' situation under A in order that someone else should be able to enjoy the benefits

which he would have to give up under E? As the supposed situation of the Loser under A becomes better, or his gain under E smaller in relation to the sacrifices required to produce it, his case is weakened." Our emphasis on absolute degree of need of the worse off, how big a gain will come to the worse off, and how much will be lost to the better off incorporate the considerations Scanlon points to. We add as well *comparative* degree of need, i.e., checking to see how much (or little) better off the better off are than the worse off.

18. The latter is Kantian terminology.

19. I first presented this analysis of equality in 1984 in Ronald Dworkin's seminar in political philosophy at NYU Law School. I was reminded of its relevance to this issue by Dennis McKerlie's "Equality Between Ages," in *Philosophy & Public Affairs* 21 (Summer 1992): 275–295. My discussion bears on his discussion of "simultaneous equality."

20. Doctors do not, of course, know exactly how long each person will live if given an organ, so outcome is never certain. The judgment of outcome is made in terms of the probability that a given person will die within various time periods based on statistics of similar persons. For example, someone we expect to have a good outcome has a low probability of dying within a month and a higher probability of dying at a distant time in the future. Someone who has a poor expected outcome has a high probability of dying soon and only a low probability of being alive at a distant time in the future. If this is the best data we can hope for, we must work with it. It would complicate matters in further discussion to introduce such precise details, so I shall simplify and assume a single given predicted outcome per person.

21. For description of these tests see James Griffin's *Well Being, Its Meaning, Measurement and Moral Importance* (Oxford: Oxford University Press, 1986) and Thomas Scanlon's "Value, Desire and the Quality of Life," in M. Nussbaum and A. Sen, *Quality of Life* (Oxford: Oxford University Press, forthcoming).

22. Thomas Nagel made this point.

23. For a complete description of such a system, see Michael Walzer, *Spheres of Justice* (New York: Basic Books, 1983). We must distinguish this justification for ignoring potential achievements from the belief, common in real life, that we cannot be sure who will achieve what or cannot tell whose achievements are more worthwhile.

24. Rawls has emphasized this in his discussions of the meaning of liberal neutrality.

25. Some (e.g., Starzl) have argued that anything less than perfect antigen matches— and matching is only used for kidneys—does not produce a significant difference in outcomes and insisting on doing matches needlessly reduces the number of organs from whites available for use by blacks.

13

Distribution of Resources: Urgency and Outcome

I. URGENCY^T VERSUS OUTCOME

Conflicts of Urgency^T and Outcome

We have suggested that in situations of real scarcity, need (understood as how bad overall someone's life is by the time of death) should have some added weight relative to urgency^T. So the neediest might be treated over the more urgent, outcomes constant, in true scarcity. Also, a given degree of U^T will have more weight when it belongs to the needier. Accept for the sake of further discussion that both candidates have equivalent pasts: they are the same age and have had the same opportunities and goods of life so far. However, one is more urgent^T than the other. (Strictly, this means one is also somewhat needier than the other since one will die somewhat younger than the other.) Medical personnel emphasize a possible conflict between urgency^T and outcome since those who would die soonest usually have the worst prognosis after transplantation. Still, what is crucial is differential outcome with and without an organ, and there might not be as great a conflict between urgency^T and outcome if the differential outcome was greater for the urgent^T than the differential outcome was for the less urgent^T. Let us assume even differential outcome is worse for greater urgency^T, in order to investigate the conceptual issues. (The neediest, as we have described them, tend to be young. If the young are not as urgent^T, they tend to produce better outcomes. Still, conflicts can also arise between satisfying neediness and producing the best outcome, even when the needy are young.) The Report notes the pressure toward helping the most urgent^T and recognizes that even patients seem to prefer that the most urgent be helped first. Putting aside such preferences of other potential recipients, how should we deal with conflicts between urgency^T and outcome[1] in conditions of true scarcity?

The short answer to this question follows from our discussion in Chapter 12. There we said that, conservatively speaking, need should have some added weight relative to outcome and some added weight relative to urgency^T. Should urgency^T have less weight relative to outcome than need has? The best (even if not certain) grounds for saying this is if need totally dominates urgency^T. That is, if urgency^T is looked at as merely a slight difference in need, and so results in far less DMU of life or claim based on fairness than does greater need, then it should actually have less weight relative to outcome than need does. As a minor form of difference in need, urgency^T is not likely to yield as great differences between candidates as consideration of age. This is because differences in urgency^T are concerned with how soon in the future candidates will die rather than with how long they have lived. Therefore, if this were all there was to urgency^T, the factors by which we multiply outcomes would not be as large as those by which we multiply the outcomes of the neediest.

But if urgency^T represents some other values, for example, the pressures of the here and now, or simultaneous equality rather than overall equality and it is a factor whose import is modified but not dominated by need, then theoretically urgency^T may have as great or even greater weight relative to outcome than need has. Indeed, if urgency^T has a characteristic that fails to impress us at all when compared with greater need, it could still stand out in the comparison with outcome. Indeed, theoretically, urgency^T might have greater weight relative to outcome than need has even if need dominated urgency^T, so long as the values represented by urgency^T were not just a form of minimal need. That is, need could even totally dominate this other value, which however has greater importance relative to outcome. (This is another example of a permissible "intransitivity.")

My own sense is that great need (e.g., dying young) should have more weight relative to outcome than does great urgency^T, even if the latter represents some unique value, though only in what is definitely known to be true scarcity.

However, if urgency^T should still have some added weight relative to outcome, then we can represent this by multiplying the expected outcome of the most urgent^T person by a factor that varies with the comparative and absolute degree of urgency.^{T}

Cases

Now let us consider some hypothetical cases that involve varying outcomes in absolute numbers of years. Candidates have the same pasts, and if someone does not receive an organ now, there will be no opportunity for him to get another one.[2] (This is true scarcity.)

Modifying Maximin: Real Value versus Buffer Value

Case 1. Suppose we must choose whether to give an organ to A, who will die tomorrow if she does not receive a transplant, but will live three weeks if she does; or to B, who will die in a year if he does not receive a transplant now, but live twenty years if he does (see Table 13-1). Even someone who would ordinarily favor treating first those who would be worst off (the "maximiner") will, I believe, decline to give the organ to A. This is probably because the gain is not significant even to her, relative to her position if not treated. In Chapter 3, we argued that even short periods of life can be significant as "buffers," that is, their function is merely to put off death. If we gave great normative weight to this role of time as a buffer (granting that psychologically it has weight), we would give greater weight than I believe we should to urgency^T. Suppose we instead decide that twenty years is too big an outcome to lose for the sake of the three weeks. I suggest that this indicates,

Table 13.1

		Need	
	Age	Urgency^T	Differential Outcome
A	20	Tomorrow	3 weeks
B	20	1 year	19 years

in part, that we think we should treat the three weeks primarily in the light of their real (versus buffer) value. The real value is their urgency^T-adjusted value. This real value is not great even to the person who receives it. This does not deny the psychological pull of outcome-as-buffer, but it reduces its normative significance. Would we always consider the three weeks primarily in terms of its real rather than its buffer value? I suggest that, although we calculate the real value of the three weeks (i.e., multiply it by the f for urgency^T) independent of comparing it with what the other candidate's outcome would be, deciding whether to treat the three weeks as buffer or real value does depend on comparing the candidates' potential outcomes. That is, we consider what the opportunity cost would be to give the three weeks. If it is great, we ignore the buffer value and focus on real value. If the cost is smaller, we may allow buffer value to play a larger role.

In general, we could minimally change a strict maximin theory in the following way: Only when what would be gained by the worst off is a gain that makes a real value significant difference to him should we forgo giving the better-off person a much greater gain. (Finding that a gain is significant is not intended to decide between an objective and a purely subjective determination of what is a significant gain to a person (i.e., it allows that someone might be satisfied with what is not worth having), but it does filter out much of the buffer role. Furthermore, in keeping with the de-emphasis of structural factors, we must explicate the idea of significant additional time in some way other than by its being time in which to complete projects.) Call this the Modified Maximin Rule, or Modified Maximin.

The status, in absolute terms, of the worst off may get better and better (and be, in fact, quite high in absolute terms). Then it will take a much greater potential gain, in absolute terms, to produce a gain that would make a real value significant difference to the worst-off person. (The buffer value of time does not vary in this way.) However, suppose there is not much DMU of life. Still it may be that there is DMV in giving even significant utility. Therefore, as the absolute condition of the worst off gets better, it would take a greater potential gain, in absolute terms, to overcome the moral worth of giving a yet bigger gain to someone who already had more. As someone is better off, each additional unit is worth less morally speaking so it takes more to be a morally significant improvement. Therefore, as the status of the most urgent (and also neediest) gets better, there will be fewer instances in which it will be morally correct to give a gain to the worst off rather than a much larger gain to the better off.

We have already applied this rule implicitly, and even gone beyond it, when we discussed the possibility that a big outcome for the less needy candidate could swamp the claim of the neediest (even after we multiply the neediest's outcome by a

DMU factor and a fairness factor, reflecting his absolute and comparative neediness). That is, we considered that even a gain that was significant to the neediest person who was not absolutely well off could be swamped because of the bigger gain to the less needy. (Our earlier discussion of Sob[3] and Sob[4] in chapters 9 and 10 raised a different objection to pure maximin. There we dealt with cases where we could offer one person a *great* gain that totally ameliorated his need (i.e., saved his life), but the cost of doing so in terms of aggregated lesser losses, e.g., twenty arms or cases of paralysis was so great that even here and now we could offer proportional chances or even prevent the greater loss.)

Divisible versus Indivisible

Even if the worst off (in terms of urgency[T]) are quite well off, it may still be preferable to deal with *divisible rather than indivisible goods*. This point is directly applicable to the allocation of organs if they are divisible, e.g., rather than giving one person multiple organs at one time where this would produce a great benefit, we give him only some of what he needs, if this gives partial benefit, using an organ for someone else. That is, it may be preferable to be able to give both the better off and the worst off something, even at the expense of an overall utility loss. (By overall utility loss, I mean that the sum of what we give to the better off and worst off does not equal what we could have given had we given to the better off alone.)

In particular, suppose that, given only buffer gain to the worst off, it would not be morally required to aid the worst off at the expense of a particular larger gain to the better off. Still, if we could somehow produce a buffer gain to the worst off and still give the better off something, the small gain might be big enough to be significant *relative* to the loss that the better off would suffer to achieve it. This is because the better off would also be getting something, and the loss to him would then not be so great. Call this the *Divisibility Rule.*[3]

It is likely that the moral claim on us of the Divisibility Rule is less strong than is the claim of the Modified Maximin. This is because what is at stake with Modified Maximin is a real-value significant good to the worst off, but with the Divisibility Rule what is at stake seems to be simply a general concern with equality and nonabandonment. That is, Modified Maximin tells us not to deprive the worst off of significant value. The Divisibility Rule tells us not to deprive someone of buffer value because it is concerned to give something to everyone, even only of buffer value. Neither Modified Maximin nor the Divisibility Rule says that if a benefit has real-value significance, we should make bringing it to the worst off contingent on the cost to the better off.

Case 2. Suppose we must choose whether to give an organ to C, who will die tomorrow if she does not receive a transplant, but will live one year if she does; or to D, who will live one year if he does not receive a transplant now, but live twenty years only if he receives one now (see Table 13-2). In this case, it might be argued, taking care of the worst off first in accord with Modified Maximin could reasonably determine a solution. This is because the gain to the worst off has real significance to her—I here employ an objective evaluation of a year to her but assume she consents to the procedure—*and* because we will be seeing to it that C has at least as much time alive (an additional year) as D has before giving D more than a year.

Table 13.2

	Need		
	Age	Urgency^T	Differential Outcome
C	20	Tomorrow	1 year
D	20	1 year	19 years

The Maximin Physician

If Modified Maximin were the just way to distribute a scarce resource in this case, we might face a conflict with doctors' desires to make the most productive use of their skills. That is, maximining here will require doctors to put aside the pride they take in producing not only the longest possible life but the greatest differential outcome. Apparently some doctors enter certain specialties because they want to always have good outcomes. This was true of those who specialized in infectious diseases before the AIDS epidemic, and it is one reason why these doctors now have great psychological difficulty dealing with AIDS patients. Oncologists, by contrast, have greater tolerance for poor outcomes. But, while some doctors can tolerate poor outcomes *if* that is the only outcome they can produce, they cannot tolerate it well if they have the option of producing a better outcome.[4] The outcome orientation, furthermore, is encouraged by the fact that the government will not pay for many procedures if there is not a certain significant survival rate. A doctor who was willing to produce minimal outcomes for the neediest—the true Maximin physician—would not be reimbursed by the government.

To repeat: Our earlier discussion on the relation of need to outcome suggested that better outcomes do not have to be ignored in order always to take care of the neediest. If differential urgency^T were important only because it produced differences in overall need, then, given it produces less in this respect than do differences in past life, outcome would weigh even more relative to differential urgency^T than to differential need. (This is just another way of saying that when the difference in overall need is small, outcome plays a greater role.) However, we assume that urgency^T is important for other reasons. Even so, this does not necessarily mean that it has greater weight relative to outcome than need does (though this is not impossible). For example, one person's dying young may have greater weight relative to another person's large expected outcome than does someone's being near death.

We shall return to consider further modifications to Modified Maximin, which permit the production of better outcomes. However, first, let us consider another issue.

Modified Maximin Inegalitarian

Consider Case 3, in which, I believe, the Modified Maximin solution may conflict with more than just producing the best outcome. Suppose we must choose whether

Table 13.3

		Need	
	Age	Urgency[T]	Differential Outcome
E	20	Tomorrow	20 years
F	20	1 year	19 years

to give a scarce organ to E, who will die tomorrow if not treated now, but live twenty years if treated; or to F, who will die in one year if not treated now, but live twenty years only if treated now (see Table 13-3). (The option represented by E conflicts with the real-life truth that urgent[T] cases most often have poor outcomes.)

In this case the desire for good differential outcome is best satisfied by saving the worst off. Yet, one suggestion for this case is that we think *equality* is better served by tossing a coin between the two parties rather than maximining. (Notice that this is a very different complaint than that Modified Maximin is inegalitarian because it does *not* always take care of the worst off first.) I emphasize that tossing a coin is not an abdication of responsibility. It represents the fact that we think the candidates are entitled to equal chances, perhaps because there are no morally significant differences between them, or for some other reason. It also represents our taking seriously the fact that, from the personal point of view of each candidate, it matters whether he himself is saved. Why would we think we should toss a coin? One possibility is that E, the potentially worst-off person, will, if treated, turn out to be overall much better off than the untreated person. The difference between E's twenty years if treated, and F's one year if not treated seems to be much greater than the difference between E's dying tomorrow and F's having one year alive without treatment. That is, the one-year difference for which we are trying to compensate if we follow a maximin policy is much less than the difference we create (0:1 versus 20:1). Furthermore, we create the difference at the expense of F's chance of gaining nineteen more years for himself.

The problem presented here, when there is no way to deal with the currently worst off without making him better off in the future than others, has to my knowledge, not been considered in the literature on maximin and social policy. Yet, I believe, it is a prevalent phenomenon.[5] (Recall that in Chapter 7, it was the worry that those originally worst off might wind up best off that argued against changing from majority rule to proportional chances.)

Modified Maximin Inegalitarianism and Significant Stakes

A problem for this analysis of Case 3 is presented by Case 4. Here F' would die in a year if untreated, but survive for two years if treated now, while E's prospects remain the same as described above (see Table 13-4). In this case it is also true that helping E would create a difference between E and F' greater than the original difference between them (i.e., 0:1 versus 20:1). Yet I believe we should here treat E.

Table 13.4

	Need		
	Age	Urgency^T	Differential Outcome
E	20	Tomorrow	20 years
F'	20	1 year	1 year

Is this simply because we can thereby produce many more differential good years (twenty versus one), whereas previously, we could have produced almost as many extra good years (nineteen) for F? Or is it because what F' stands to gain if treated is not much more than he would get if not treated? Suppose F" stood to gain a total of ten years in Case 5 (see Table 13-5). Here he stands to gain much more than the year he would otherwise have, but much less than E's potential twenty. Should we still automatically help E?

At the very least it seems that when someone would have only a small percentage of the good he could potentially get (e.g., one year of a potential twenty), and he is not much better off than the worst off, going with a policy of straightforwardly helping the worst off to wind up better off is problematic.

Unavoidable Inequality

A problem for the analysis that recommends equal chances for E and F is that it will *usually* be true that the difference we create by giving someone an organ will produce more inequality than that for which we are trying to compensate. Suppose *both* people will die tomorrow unless given an organ and live twenty years if given it. When we toss a coin to decide who gets it, we create more inequality than if we had let both die (perfect equality) (i.e., 0:0 versus 20:0). Maintaining equality in actual outcome has been overridden as a value when we decide to toss the coin. However, in this case, though we should create the large inequality, we do owe the contestants equality in the form of equal chances.[6]

Indeed, consider E and F again as originally described (Case 3), where E will die tomorrow or live for twenty years and F will live one year or twenty years. We see that giving the organ to E does not, in fact, exacerbate inequality more than giving the organ to F. This is because if E receives it, he will live twenty years and someone else will live one year (20:1), whereas if E does not receive it, E will die

Table 13.5

	Need		
	Age	Urgency^T	Differential Outcome
E	20	Tomorrow	20 years
F"	20	1 year	10 years

soon and someone else will live twenty years (0:20). It seems that the second end-state contains more inequality than the first.[7] That is, it is a mistake to focus only on the great inequality produced if E gets an organ and F doesn't, and on the inequality in what will occur if neither gets the organ. We must consider also the inequality that would exist if F got the organ and E didn't.

Two additional points should be made. It is true that in Case 3 as well less inequality would exist if no one got the organ. But it seems an unacceptable price to pay for less inequality that no one get to live a much longer life. In addition, it is important to distinguish the issue of inequality from that of the formerly worst-off party winding up better off. In some situations, though perhaps *not* in the organ transplant case, a switch in who occupies the role of worst off may carry its own, separate negative weight. But the same inequality can exist whichever person occupies the worst-off position, and the switch in occupants is a separate factor. Indeed, there may be a conflict: inequality could be reduced if the person who originally had the worst prospect became the one with the better prospect, because she got fewer additional years than the other person could get.

Chances

Suppose there is *more* inequality produced if F gets the organ than if E does. It is still possible that equality is best served by a coin toss which F might win. In this case the difference in the *differential* outcomes is small (i.e., 20 for E and 1 for F versus 0 for E and 19 for F) in comparison to the absolute difference between the best and worst prospects for each individual. That is, urgency^T is only slightly different, and differential outcome is large and only slightly different. When this is so, *a greater sense* of equality is achieved with a fair coin toss. The fact that one candidate's expected outcome without the organ is somewhat worse than the other's—and even the (different) fact that he is highly urgent^T—should not immediately determine whom we favor. The difference in life that could be had independent of the organ might pale in significance, become nonsalient, given the very good differential outcomes possible for both candidates with the organ.

(But even if we could produce perfect equality without chances, it may be preferable to produce more inequality. For example, suppose we can either give each of two people 5 units, or give each a 1 in 2 chance of 20 units. And suppose each regards this 1 in 2 chance as being worth more, since his expected benefit would be sufficiently greater. If we follow the second course, as both would prefer, we give each an equal chance, but there will be inequality in the outcome. How much does the latter matter? Could it show that we ought to give each 5 units, though both would prefer the other course? If equality is at a sufficiently low level, the equal chance for a much greater benefit distributed unequally may be preferable.[8])

Proportional Chances

There is another possible alternative in Case 3. When E and F each stand to live twenty years, the correct alternative may be to give *weighted chances* that reflect the slightly greater importance to E of winning. (I am less inclined to think he is owed a greater chance just because of the slight difference in his differential outcome.) This would make the difference not irrelevant but also not determinative of an outcome. We may give E a greater chance to win by, metaphorically, putting his name on more straws in a hat than we put F's on. This is a scheme of chances proportional to urgency^T. (A similar proposal might be made for need, i.e., differences in pasts.)

As discussed in Chapter 10, some[9] have suggested that we should always use proportional chances when it is possible to do so, there is some difference in need, and we have an indivisible good to distribute. Differential need is translated into differential DMU. So, if a million dollars would do a poor man a thousand times more good than a rich man, we should give the poor man a thousand times the chance to get it that the rich man gets. This leaves it open whether the rich man will win the money. (Proportional chances has been suggested for dealing with responsibility: if there is an 80 percent chance that one company is responsible for pollution and a 20 percent chance that another company is, proportional chances could result in the company who most probably didn't cause the damage being liable for compensating the victims.)

I believe the general use of proportional chances is wrong. If we use it generally, it will often be that the wrong person has wound up with the good (or evil). When the difference in need or urgency is great, the person with greater need or urgency should receive the benefit, other things equal. And when the difference in need or urgency is very slight, the difference should be irrelevant. But proportional chance has its place, as in the case we are now discussing. In such a case, we do not believe we would have the wrong outcome just because the less urgent^T party received the benefit; we think it would be wrong to say one deserves to have it. And yet there is some difference in urgency^T which is not irrelevant, and that should have some weight in the decision making. Given that the greater proportional chance is given to the more urgent^T, it is then acceptable for the less urgent^T to win.

In any case, if we toss a coin between E and F in Case 3, we are again in conflict with the doctor's desire to make the most productive use of her technical expertise. This is because she maximizes the number of extra years produced over all (as well as years in one person) if she lets F live one year naturally and gives the organ to E.

Lending Organs

Suppose, contrary to our original assumption, that it were possible to give transplants to each of the candidates at some time in the future so long as we had an organ, and also suppose that it was possible merely to *lend* organs. Then, with E and F as originally described, we could equalize by letting E have the organ for one year and then tossing a coin between E and F for the remaining time it could provide. We would remove the organ from E and give it to F if E lost the toss. Lending organs and then removing them (if this were technically feasible) in this way does not eliminate true scarcity; it only delays it, since both parties can be satisfied for a year, but only one can be cared for after the year is over. I suspect that many would object to a doctor's removing an organ from its first recipient when that person could continue to live. Yet, I am not sure there is really any strong moral objection to achieving equality in this way. The fact that we may not take someone's organs that he did not receive from us does not mean it would always be morally wrong to take back the organs we had given him. This would be true even though he died because we did so. This would be a case of terminating lifesaving aid in order to aid someone else. It is true, however, that such a policy would diminish a person's identification with the transplanted organ as his. (A loan policy, with required removal after death, is easier to accept. Requiring recipients of an organ to donate their other organs at death in exchange for the organs they have received has already been mentioned as an acquisitions policy. Rather than give in hope of getting, one gives in return for having gotten or gets in return for a commitment to give.)

Alternatives to Modified Maximin: Chances Proportional to Outcome

In moving toward equal or proportional chances in Case 3, we are moving even further away from Maximin than when we moved to Modified Maximin. As we know, there are yet more radical moves away from Modified Maximin. Consideration of these moves arises when we return to the issue of large differences in outcomes possible for each candidate, when the worst off in terms of urgency^T would have a significant but much less good outcome. (Case 2 with candidate D first raised this issue.) Changes in Maximin are also relevant to cases like those we have dealt with in the last chapter in which the pasts of candidates differ significantly. In these cases, the needier may be the less urgent^T and also present us with worse outcomes than the less needy. In Chapter 12, an objection to serving the needier was raised. If their outcome does not do much to relieve their need and if it costs someone else who is not much better off a great deal, perhaps we should not help the neediest. This could be true even if the potential gain to the neediest is significant, that is, significant benefit may still not do much to alleviate a great need. However, we were also concerned that focusing on how much need was satisfied versus size of gain might be incorrect. Now we return to this problem of the relation between outcome and need in greater detail, including both the relation between urgency^T and outcome, and need and outcome.

Brock's Proposal

We have considered giving equal chances as a way to achieve equality, and proportional chances as a way to satisfy the worst-off without offending too much against equality when the two conflict. We considered these proposals in the unusual situation in which helping the worst off produces such a good outcome that it produces much inequality. Dan Brock[10] calls for dealing with the general conflict between what he calls equity and outcome by giving chances in proportion to (differential) outcome. Brock thinks that equity demands equal chances for all, regardless of need or outcome. He sees chances proportional to outcome as a compromise between equity and the desire for efficient use of scarce resources. This policy would give the neediest even with very low outcome some chance of gaining the organ, but their significant outcome could lose to a less needy person's better outcome.

One puzzling aspect of Brock's proposal is his view that equity demands equal chances regardless of need (and urgency^T) for an organ. Rather it seems more likely that equity sometimes demands taking care of the worst off (neediest or most urgent^T) if not all can be helped (Maximin or Modified Maximin) rather than giving everyone equal chances. However, there is at least one way to try to justify the claim that equity demands equal chances for all who have some need for a transplant, (i.e., would be in some way badly off without it) and some minimally significant outcome: If every such person had a moral right as an individual to a transplant but we could not provide everyone with one, it may seem reasonable to think that each such person has a moral right to an equal chance to obtain one. This equal chance is a substitute for the fulfillment of each one's equal right to an organ. (This could also be true if each such person had a clear conditional right to get a transplant if anyone gets one.) If this justification were correct, the conflict between equal chances and outcome should be drawn as Brock draws it.

It is possible, however, that even if everyone has a right to have something when there is no scarcity, equity does not require that each person have an equal claim under conditions of scarcity. For example, relative degree of hunger might become relevant as a selection device for scarce food, even if everyone has a right not to be hungry to any degree when there is no scarcity. (Evidence for such a right would be our having a duty to keep producing food so long as anyone was still hungry to any degree.) It is only if we think of the right to be given the thing as something like a property right, which gives someone a claim independent of need, that it seems equitable to ignore other criteria under conditions of scarcity. (In our discussions of Sobjectivity in earlier chapters, we assumed approximately equal need and argued that other utilities were irrelevant in deciding whether to give equal chances to those with rights based on equal need.)

In the case of transplants, furthermore, it is not clear that everyone does have a right to one, provided only that he has some need and some hope for a useful outcome, when there is no scarcity of organs. Suppose not everyone, but only 50 percent of the needy, would have a right to a transplant, even if there were no scarcity of organs (because of the expense of transplants, for example). Then all might still have a right on grounds of fairness to an equal chance if they were all equal (or approximately equal) in the respects that are relevant for distribution. But if there were differences in, e.g., need, fairness might no longer require equal chances.

This account leaves it open that differential outcome, not differential need, could be the factor by which we select patients, it just insists that equity calls for dealing first with the worst off (the neediest or most urgent^T).

Suppose this were so, and proportional chances according to outcome were intended as a compromise between (i) catering to need or urgency^T—rather than catering to equal chances for all—and (ii) catering to outcome. Then we should give lower outcomes a proportional chance *only if* they are accompanied by greater need or urgency^T than those which accompany better outcomes. That is, those with both worse outcomes *and* need or urgency^T less than or equal to others should *not* be given proportional chances at all. (Suppose we thought that those with equal or lesser need or urgency^T *and* lesser outcome do deserve a chance in proportion to the outcome they offer us. Then we should think that the neediest and most urgent^T are owed *more* than a chance in proportion to the outcome they offer us. After all, they present us with an additional and different sort of claim based on greater need and urgency^T.)

Multiplying Outcomes

An alternative policy already suggested is to multiply the absolute outcome of the neediest or more urgent^T by a factor that correlates with their relative and absolute need or urgency^T, representing the greater moral worth of the fact that it would be the neediest who would be helped if he got the organ. Let us repeat these points for emphasis. Multiplying the outcome of the neediest represents the greater value of giving some absolute number of years to the neediest than to the less needy. The multiplicative factor is chosen both relative to absolute degree of neediness and to how that neediness compares with the neediness of the other candidate(s). The less absolutely and comparatively needy a person is, the lower will be the multiplicative factor. Multiply the outcome further to take account of the fact that that outcome will go to a needier person, to represent the value of fairness. (If we do multiplication for DMU we are still assuming that the goodness of the outcome directly corresponds to the total sum of benefits. The DMU multiplication merely gives us a more accurate estimate of the size of these benefits. The 'fairness' multiplication tells us instead what is the moral value of these benefits. We no longer treat moral value as directly corresponding to the size of benefits.) When the less needy still have more outcome points, however, they would be given the organ, if only these two factors of need and outcome were relevant.

For differential urgency^T, we can multiply the outcome by a factor representing the absolute and relative urgency^T of the most urgent^T. (This factor does not essentially represent the DMU of life or concern for fairness, in that one party will not be so much worse off at the time they die than another. It represents the press of the "here and now" and for equality here and now. If the absolutely urgent^T are likely to have the worst differential outcomes, even multiplying their absolute outcomes may not help them much.)

How does this scheme compare with chances proportional to outcome? It will probably not allow the neediest or more urgent^T with very low outcomes ever to win against the less needy with high outcomes. However, it probably gives more likelihood of giving an organ to the neediest or most urgent^T who have reasonably high outcomes than does a system of chances proportional to outcome. I believe the scheme involving factored multiplication of outcomes, all in all, gives greater weight to need or urgency^T without allowing it to be a trump. It also gives these factors a more rational role, since chances correlate with need or urgency^T per se, even though this is done by multiplying outcome by factors related to need or urgency^T. By contrast, in chances proportional to outcome, chances correlate only with outcomes offered, even if the only lesser outcomes given chances are those attached to the needier/more urgent^T.

A third alternative is to give chances proportional to need or urgency^T, if the neediest do not also have highest outcome. This would allow the neediest with low outcomes to win sometimes when the use of a multiplicative factor would not permit this. But this scheme might not give adequate weight to outcome.

Outcome as Sole Determinant

A fourth scheme argues that distribution according to outcome (understood to be number of additional years) *is* the fair solution; it is morally correct to ignore need or urgency^T when it conflicts with better outcome. The claim is, roughly, that if we reason in one particular way from behind a veil of ignorance, this scheme would be chosen.[11] (Again, the veil is a device to ensure unbiased decision making. It denies to deciders knowledge of their actual position in the world. They are ignorant of who in particular they will be and assign no greater probability to being one person than another.) It is claimed that distribution according to outcome would be chosen since it maximizes our individual expected utility. That is, if we have no greater chance of being one person than another and will benefit more from a better outcome, we should give the better outcome the best chance of coming about.

It is, however, debatable whether highest expected utility would be chosen from behind the veil when some will be needier than others. Many think that for situations in which there are significant differences in need, Maximin is what would be chosen from behind the veil. (We shall return to consider the veil of ignorance debate further below.)

Justification for the Move from Maximin

Let us assume that Modified Maximin is to be preferred to Maximin, not only when urgency^T differs significantly for those with equal pasts, but when pasts differ and when overall need can modify the weight of the urgency^T component. How do we justify the further move from Modified Maximin to an even greater concern for outcome? For one thing, the decision to adopt Maximin or Modified Maximin from behind the veil of ignorance is usually argued for (successfully or not) when a person's whole life prospects are at stake. This means that a great deal of potential benefit is at stake for the worst-off person even if we give him the lesser outcome. It does not imply that we should use Modified Maximin when the amount of benefit at stake for the worst off is not a whole lifetime but only a few years.

The tendency not to help the neediest or most urgent^T when we can do them significant good which, however, is relatively much less than the good to others was further clarified by considering Parfit-type cases, in which we could save a finger for Joe, but we can prevent deafness in Jim.

Furthermore, recall the reasoning in Chapter 10. There it was suggested that from society's point of view it might be acceptable to institute policies that fund saving a greater number of people who each suffered significant lesser losses (e.g., broken arms) instead of instituting policies saving fewer who are worse off (e.g., facing death from a rare disease). It was suggested that the cost in terms of lesser losses might be appropriately considered in deciding whether to prevent the greater loss. If society funds expensive organ transplants, it can choose to do so only if the outcomes producible are worth the investment in this enterprise rather than in another. If some individuals offer significant outcomes that are below what would justify society's investing in the enterprise as a whole, when others at the same time offer better outcomes, then our organs should be given to the candidate who offers the "fundable" outcomes. This argument, however, will not justify selecting a far superior outcome over a significant and fundable one.

The problem is also addressed by Scanlon's understanding of contractualism, where we search amongst individuals for the strongest complaint which it is not unreasonable for someone to raise. The strongest complaint, he says, does not necessarily come from the person who will be worst off under one policy. It might come from the person who would lose out on great deal he might have had under another policy, in order to purchase only a small gain for the worst off, especially if the worst off person is not very badly off in absolute terms. In the cases before us, we are considering whether to help the less badly off get a better life in preference to helping the worst off avoid an even worse fate. That is, we help (a) someone who has not much better prospects (b) get a big period of life, (c) when the alternative is to help someone who is relatively not much worse off (d) get something (a year) that is significant. (Again, I hesitate to say, it does very little to meet his absolute need.) It is true, however, that this way of doing pairwise comparisons of individuals diminishes the straightforwardness of deciding what policy is reasonable. For we must first decide whether an objection to a policy is reasonable or unreasonable, without relying on the intuitively plausible view that it is unreasonable to ask one person to fall to a lower level under one policy than another would fall to under a second policy (though it must be admitted that even the latter seems unacceptable, if it is taken to imply that someone need not fall to a lower level to avoid harming a potential victim than his potential victim would fall to if he is harmed).

If we continue to distinguish need (how overall badly off one will be without the organ) from urgency^T, we can construct the following sets of cases. To see how outcome plays against need, we hold urgency^T constant in Case 6 (see Table 13-6).

In this case, suppose we multiply G's outcome to express the greater value of its going to the neediest where the multiplicative factor is correlated with G's need relative to H's and G's absolute need. We may still think that H should get the organ because G's outcome does little for G and costs H much.

Table 13.6

	Need		
	Past	Urgency^T	Differential Outcome
G	20 years	1 month	2 years − 1 month
H	50 years	1 month	20 years − 1 month

Table 13.7

	Need		Differential Outcome
	Past	Urgency^T	
J	20 years	1 year	20 years − 1 year
K	20 years	3 months	3 years − 3 months

To see how outcome plays against urgency^T, we hold need constant in Case 7 (see Table 13-7). We may think the less urgent^T candidate should be helped: The difference in urgency^T is not great, so the multiplicative factors do not differ by much, and the greater benefit does much more for J than the lesser benefit does for K. What may also be relevant in the analysis of this case is that the person with the less urgent^T claim will have a quite urgent^T claim if not treated. Might we turn against producing the best outcome if the "urgency" of J were as great as the outcome of K if treated, that is, three years? The desire to give K as much as J would have anyway, when K will otherwise have little, may still vary depending on how much we can give K and J. (I here ignore how much what we can give alleviates his need; even a significant amount may not do much in this regard.)

CONCLUSION

Determining the relative weight of outcome to need and urgency^T is a complex matter involving the comparison of differential outcomes with absolute and relative need and urgency^T, as well as comparison between outcome of one candidate when treated and outcome of the other without treatment.

NOTES

1. Again, I emphasize that the outcome we are concerned with is differential outcome, that is, the *difference* between the outcome expected without an organ and that expected with an organ. This means we are concerned with efficiency in distribution. (If we simply wanted to help someone live as long as possible, we might add one year to a fifty-year life rather than ten years to a thirty-year life.)

2. The last assumption focuses the discussion on the significance of *settled* outcomes. Therefore, throughout these cases, when I say someone will die in a certain length of time unless given a transplant now, I am assuming, just for the sake of argument, that no other opportunity to do a transplant will occur even if he lives several years without the organ.

3. The Divisibility Rule seems to be related to the justification for the Ideal Procedure discussed in Chapter 7. The idea is that sharing a benefit is encouraged if it buys an otherwise left-out group something at not too great expense.

4. That there is such pride was emphasized to me by Dr. Richard Weil of New York University Medical School.

5. I first described it in the "U.S. Task Force Report on Organ Transplantation: Criticism and Alternatives." (1989).

6. After I had written this, Parfit made the following comment: "This is the kind of case that may lead us to believe that we should not be Teleological Egalitarians, we should not believe that inequality is in itself bad. [For such egalitarians] would have to agree that, if the better off suffered some misfortune which made them as badly off as everyone else, that would be in one way a change for the better. We may be unable to believe that. This is the Leveling Down objection to Equality." Parfit also makes this point in his unpublished draft ("On Giving Priority to the Worse Off.") But inequality might be in itself bad, and yet be overridden by a good such as someone getting a benefit.

7. I owe this point to Richard Revesz.

8. Parfit makes this point in correspondence.

9. For example, John Broome.

10. In "Ethical Issues in Recipient Selection for Organ Transplantation," in Deborah Mathieu (ed.), *Organ Substitution Technology: Ethical, Legal, and Public Policy Issues* (Boulder, Colo.: Westview Press, 1988).

11. Dan Wikler suggests this in "Equity, Efficacy, and the Point System for Transplant Recipient Selection," *Transplantation Proceedings* 21 (1991): 3437–3439.

14

Distribution of Resources: Outcome, Waiting Time, and Money

In this chapter we continue the discussion of conceptual and substantive issues in distribution, including further discussion of the role of differential outcome and determination of who is the worst off, waiting time, and ability to pay.

Equal Need or Urgency and Different Outcomes

Suppose we return to the assumption that the pasts of our candidates are equal *and* also make urgency^T and urgency^Q equal. Accordingly, we will assume that Case 8 candidates L and M are equally needy and that both will die tomorrow if they do not receive an organ. If L receives a transplant, she will live one good year, whereas if M receives a transplant, he will live twenty good years. (Again, this is an unrealistically good outcome for current transplants.) Where there is no conflict with need and urgency, the Report would recommend going with the best outcome. Should we? (I use one year for L, but it might be useful to run through the discussion again, with five years for L. Even though this is a more significant period, I do not believe it will alter the results.)

Someone who thought we should not automatically go with the best outcome might give the following argument: To pick M automatically is to take a social point of view according to which all that matters is that somebody get to live the most number of years. But this is also a satisfactory outcome from M's personal point of view. That is, even if we don't consider the benefit to society, we are doing more good for M himself than we could do for L. Hence we do not view M as a mere means to a greater number of years; we are concerned with the greater good we can do for him. But what of L? Her failure to get an organ is not satisfactory from her personal point of view since she will die having lost out on the significant gain to her of one year.[1]

It might be suggested that, once the gain to L is significant enough so that he would not be obligated to sacrifice it to help save M from death, we as third parties should toss a coin between L and M. (This is what a position like Sob^1 or Sob^2 would recommend when applied to cases where the extra utility that one candidate offers is a major chunk, indeed, larger than the base provided by both candidates. It is not what Sob^3 would recommend.) Each person might claim to have a right that the best be done for him that we can do, once the outcome is significant to him *and* socially worthy of investing in, given scarce money. Further, it might be claimed, one's right to this is not stronger just because more good can be done for one. Our duty is to each person, not to the good per se, and we will have done as much of what we should do if we do the best we can for either candidate. These suggestions do *not* depend on the claim that L's one year is as significant to L as M's twenty years are to M. It could be argued that this is (usually) a false claim since a twenty-year gain to L would be more significant to L than the one-year gain is to her. As evidence for this, consider that L would be willing to undergo surgery that might be immediately fatal for the sake of a significant chance to increase her life span from one to twenty years. (Her preference for the surgery is compatible, however, with the subjective value of one year being greater than one-twentieth of the value of twenty years.)

Choosing the Better Outcome: Behind a Veil of Ignorance?

What are the objections to tossing a coin between such equally needy or urgent individuals who have different outcomes? Imagine that we occupied a position behind a veil of ignorance and were ignorant of both the particulars of our own future and our own present circumstances. This fiction is designed to ensure that in deciding on principles for the distribution of goods, no one will offer principles biased to favor his or her own circumstances. From this position, we could make an unbiased decision about policies. Some have suggested that from this position we would have no knowledge of our chances of being in any position and would choose a Maximin policy (helping the neediest person first). Others have suggested that when we are dealing with two equally needy or urgent individuals, we would choose a policy according to which the one standing to gain the most is aided. The latter policy, it is argued, would be chosen (very roughly) for the following reasons: One would have no more reason to think one would be in the position of one individual rather than the other, so one would assign equal chances of being in any position. (This contrasts with those who say we would have no knowledge of our chances and should assign no values.) One would also care more about getting twenty years of life than about getting one year; therefore, one would want to maximize one's chances of getting the thing one wanted most. So one should support the policy that gives the organ to the person who would live the longest if he got it. (If one assigns 50 percent probability of being in each position, then assigning anything less than 100 percent probability of getting the organ to the person who will live longest reduces one's chances of getting the longest life.)[2]

Counterobjection: Scanlon's Analysis of the Point of Reasoning behind the Veil

This argument for picking the larger outcome is based on a particular sort of understanding of decision making behind a veil of ignorance. The sort of reasoning employed in the objection is employed by those who also argue that we should choose higher expected utility rather than Maximin or even Modified Maximin from behind the veil of ignorance. That is, we not only should maximize outcome between equally needy candidates, we should not necessarily help the neediest.[3]

However, we have already mentioned (in Chapter 11) Thomas Scanlon's view that deciding in ignorance by supposing that one might turn out to be any of the persons who will be affected by a policy (whether or not one assigns definite probabilities of being in one position or another) does not correctly capture the point of contractualism. It may also not be the proper way to understand Rawls's own aims in using the veil of ignorance.[4] (An indication of this is that Rawls favors Maximin.) Scanlon argues that the point of contractualism is to find policies acceptable to all (each), i.e., policies it would be unreasonable for any to reject. We should take seriously how the policy affects each person who will be affected by it. To do this, we must consider the individuals involved as truly separate persons, not positions that one person, reasoning behind the veil of ignorance, has some probability of coming to occupy. If we do this, we will favor Maximin to highest expected utility, though, Scanlon believes, we may also favor giving bigger benefits to some rather than smaller benefits to the worst off. The version of contractualism that Scanlon develops does not imply a need for ignorance in order to arrive at policies, but he also believes that the spirit of Rawls's theory—though not the possibility of interpreting it as emphasizing what one rationally self-interested person behind the veil would choose—is really meant to force individuals to identify with every separate person who will be affected by a policy. Nagel's reinterpretation of how to reason behind the veil of ignorance specifically emphasizes this identification with each separate person.[5]

But if we insist on identification with each separate person affected by a policy, will we necessarily favor, of two equally needy persons, the one who will live longest? That is, Nagel's and Scanlon's exposition of contractualist reasoning may suggest that we should give L an equal chance with M. For if we identify with each individual, will we not try to see things from his point of view, and then will we not see that for L the loss of a year is significant enough that he would not give it up to help someone else get twenty years? This, some may think, justifies *us* in giving L and M equal chances.[6]

Yet in an earlier article,[7] Scanlon himself argued that, of two policies that would each help a different segment *of the worst-off group,* a Rawlsian should select the policy that produces the better outcome for its subgroup, given that the subgroups are equal in number. Is this consistent with identifying with each person who occupies a position as a member of the worst-off group, for those not helped may lose something significant?

How can the earlier result of Scanlon's be derived while still adhering to something close to Maximin (rather than highest expected utility)? That is, if we do not identify with each person as a separate person we do not get something like Maximin, but we do get best outcomes. If we identify with each person we seem to get something like Maximin, but not best outcomes where need is equal.

One possibility is that we have misdescribed the implications of Scanlon's recent version of contractualism. For Scanlon believes that providing a small gain to the worst off at the cost of a very big loss to the better off may sometimes be an unreasonable policy; this is why he rejects pure maximin. Could the person who would be much better off through a transplant argue that he could reasonably reject a policy that requires him to forego such a great gain just so that a comparatively small gain of one year will go to an equally badly off person? And can the truth of this be consistent with identifying with each person affected?

Another way to get both Maximin and best outcome when need is equal is to identify with the personal point of view of each person—yet not so that any who would lose something significant that they need not sacrifice to prevent another's greater loss, are treated as equal to those who would suffer the greater loss—so that the worst off is taken care of first, but allow for some substitution of equivalents when all are equally among the worst off.

Substitution of Equivalents and Scanlon's Theory

This proposal suggests that we, as third parties, should not act by giving equal weight to the personal points of view of L and M. Rather, we should take a more objective view and accept that, whoever is saved, at least one year *is* added to someone's life. This is true even though, from L's personal point of view, it is not as good if M is saved, and so L wants his equal chance to get a significant benefit. The objective view involves us in substituting equivalents: L's one year can be substituted by M's one year. Employing the analysis from Chapter 9, we will take this objective view when the additional possible gain to M is large enough that it becomes salient to an outside observer relative to the fact that L wants his chance at life. We consider the additional nineteen years of life we could save by choosing M. We ask ourselves not only whether M himself should have to sacrifice nineteen additional years so that L may have an equal chance to live, but whether we show sufficient concern for the value nineteen years has to M if we value more highly (L's) equal chance for one year.

In fact, Scanlon (and Nagel employing Scanlon's model) do allow substitution of equivalents to play a part in contractualist reasoning. When they say we must identify with the point of view of each person, they do not take this to imply (like Taurek) that we remain tied to each person who would suffer an equal (let alone unequal) loss. Rather they think we must check each person for his complaint, but may balance equivalent *types* of complaints. But still, is it reasoning of just the sort we have described that someone would offer if, on Scanlon's model, he were to explain his not unreasonable rejection of a proposal for equal chances? To repeat what we said in Chapter 11, on Scanlon's model it seems that each person must raise an objection from his own point of view. But, as our rejection of Sob[2] implied, we did not think that any loss an individual could reasonably object to *making* was one that would be salient to us as outsiders when choosing between that individual's loss and someone else's desire for an equal chance. Perhaps in the case we are considering, all that is needed is to distinguish between what, from some individual's point of view, it is not unreasonable to object to donating on one's own and what it is not unreasonable to object to third parties doing (or permitting to happen) to one.

To return to the salience test, even if we use it, we shall not always choose the individual who would receive the best outcome. This is because the difference between what he would gain and what the other person would gain may be small enough so that it is something we, as choosers, should value less than someone else's having an equal chance for a significant good. For example, if it were a choice between saving someone who will live twenty years or someone else who will live eighteen, we should still toss a coin. (What would we say about choosing between someone who will live twenty-five years and someone who will live seventeen? Perhaps we would show insufficient concern for the additional eight years of which one candidate is capable if we valued more the equal chance for the seventeen. I suspect one's rational intuitions about these cases (and more reasoning about the grounds for them) would become more firm the more exposure one had to making decisions. This may be the sort of case in which proportional chances is appropriate.)

In addition to using the outsider's saliency test, we can ask how L should feel (especially after he has had his year) knowing that his one year of life came at the expense of nineteen to M. We would, I think, expect L to understand if we decided to help M receive so much more than we can give her. That in this case M's objection to equal chances is a stronger objection than L's objection to not having a chance. This is consistent with its being true that if a scarce resource belonged to L himself, he need not give it away to help M.

Choosing the Better Outcome: Counting Numbers versus Concentrated Benefit

In another case, if the argument for numbers counting is correct (see Chapter 6), L should easily understand our abandoning him to help twenty other people each avoid immediate death and get one year of life. Then it may seem that it can only be the issue of the concentration of benefit in one person that would inhibit his understanding if we automatically save M.[8] That is, he may think, Why should one person's having the lucky opportunity to be benefited greatly deprive me of my chance for anything significant at all? Perhaps this is the issue then.

We may agree that distribution of smaller benefits over many should be preferred to concentration of benefit in one. For example, perhaps M himself should understand if we would help nineteen people each get one year rather than help him get nineteen additional years. (Even this might be a hard choice; each may get from one year very little that satisfies his need, but M gets a chance really to make a life. This, of course, involves giving weight to a structural feature of a life.) Still, when only L faces M, the apparent arbitrariness of M rather than L having the chance to gain a great deal should not make us ignore that it is a positive factor to be able to give someone a great deal, as it is to be able to give a great many smaller benefits.

A Problem: Worse Outcome versus Better Outcomes

The salience test is modeled on that presented in Chapters 9 and 10. But notice that the case to which we apply it here is different from those to which it was previously applied. We have already noted that it is applied to a case where the additional benefit is concentrated rather than spread to someone else besides another contestant. Previously, we dealt with cases in which, for example, we had to choose between saving Joe and saving Jim plus Nancy's arm. Second, the additional benefit is larger than the base utility offered to either candidate; this contrasts with the case offering a life versus a life plus an arm. Third, we are dealing here with individuals who face the same worst outcome (death) if not helped, but whose best outcomes if helped differ. The model of our previous discussion would suggest individuals whose worst outcomes differed (e.g., one faced loss of an arm, the other faced loss of both arms), but whose best outcomes were the same (i.e., cured).

The application of a salience test to cases where the best outcomes differ is I believe more problematic than its application to cases where worst outcomes differ. Treating the person who will be worse off by a significant degree may have a different moral role from producing the best outcome. Suppose Joe and Jim have equal need or urgency, but one stands to gain one year of life, the other, two years if given a scarce organ. The difference here is not sufficiently great to cause us to ignore Joe's desire for an equal chance, I believe. (Likewise, we would not expect Joe to feel badly at the thought that his one year came at a cost of two years someone else might have had.) By contrast, suppose one person stands to lose one arm while another stands to lose two arms. Here twice the loss, making one person face a worse possible outcome than the other, should understandably lead us to help the worse off.[9] Likewise, suppose one person will die in one year if not treated, and the other will die in two years. If the outcome possible for each is equal and not so great that it swamps the difference in need or urgency[T], then the needier should be treated.

This example does not refute the claim that our decisions should be sensitive to differences in *best* outcome. Nevertheless, it suggests that it will take a bigger difference in best outcomes to make a difference in how we treat equally needy or urgent[T] patients than the difference it takes in worst outcomes to make a difference in how we should treat patients.

It also suggests that the move from numbers counting to concentrated benefit counting is even more complicated than suggested above. For, if more in the way of best outcome is called for, then two years outcome in one person may not be a salient difference over one year in another, but giving one year to two persons rather than to one person is a salient difference. This again suggests we cannot move directly from the permissibility of counting numbers to the permissibility of counting a concentrated benefit. Still, this may only mean that the difference in a concentrated best outcome must be greater to make a difference.

Is One Worse Off If One Loses Out on a Bigger Benefit?

A possible response to drawing this distinction between differences in best outcomes and differences in worst outcomes, which would support helping the person who stands to gain significantly more, might come from assimilating the case of one who loses out on a better outcome to the case of one who is the victim of a worse outcome. That is, it might be claimed that one *is* worse off if one reaches the same end-state as someone else through losing out on a better outcome. Consider this argument in more detail.[10]

We would ordinarily save the person who would suffer a much greater loss. This is the person for whom the decision makes the most difference. Therefore, since losing twenty years is a greater loss than losing one year and the difference the decision makes is one year for L but twenty for M, we should help M, not L. There is a peril in using this specific argument, however. Cases where we help the person who will lose the most are typically cases where not preventing the greater loss signifies that its sufferer would be worse off by reaching a lower level than the sufferer of the lesser loss. But, in our case, L and M would, by hypothesis, be at an equally bad level (dead), though one will lose out on more in getting to that position than the other. Compare our case with one in which we can prevent a person newly one-legged from losing another leg or a two-legged person from losing two legs. More is at stake for the second person, in the sense that our decision makes more of a difference for him. Would he be worse off if he were legless than the other person would be if he were legless?

Louis Kornhauser[11] suggests that we say that, ex ante (when we are deciding), M *will* be worse off than L because he stands to lose more. Ex post (at death), L and M will be equally badly off. We make our decisions ex ante; therefore, we should help M.[12]

I agree that more is at stake for M. Suppose that ex ante he will be worse off because he will lose out on more real possibilities. This would not necessarily make him *sufficiently* worse off than L to lead us to automatically give him the organ. Ex ante, when one's goal is to avoid death, the time beyond any significant period that puts off death may have diminishing value. (This consideration is consistent with L's valuing twenty years for herself more than one year and with its being true that an ordinary person will probably choose immediately life-threatening surgery in order to increase his life prospects from one to twenty.)

The primary point, however, is that it seems odd to say that a person will be worse off, relative to another, on the basis of the fact that he has more wonderful possibilities that will not be realized. On the contrary, it seems that the fact that someone will face a truly horrible end state (death shortly, or base poverty) is more important in determining how badly off someone will be, rather than whether he has lost out on a truly magnificent alternative. It cannot be denied, however, that we say a tragic event occurred when someone is where they are because they failed a real chance to rise higher.

Let us try to sort out the issues here. We must decide whether one person is worse off than another. That is one question. Another question is whether some event (e.g., death or poverty or pain) has *made* that person worse off than another. Then we must consider *how* that event has made him worse off.

How Death Makes Someone Worse Off

Let us begin with the last factor first: *How* does death make someone worse off? First, it may make him worse off than he might have been. We have argued (in Chapters 1 through 4) that death is primarily an intrapersonal comparative evil; it is bad because it deprives someone of the possibility of significant goods of life he might have had. It is not an intrinsic evil like a painful state of existence. This means that death's happening could be worse for one person than for another because it deprives him of more of the goods of life. It makes him worse off than he might have been to a greater degree than death makes another worse off than the other might have been, compatibly with their both falling to the same low baseline (death). Suppose we work with the assumption that death itself can deprive us only of the goods we had a realistic possibility of getting. Then death is a worse event for the person who could otherwise have lived twenty years than for the one whose biology is such that he could otherwise have lived only one year.

With respect to other bad prospects (classified under urgency^Q), such as a life in pain, the evil may be intrinsic *as well as* comparative. That is, the painful life may be intrinsically equally bad for two people, and yet deprive only one of them of much he might otherwise have done. For example, only one of them might otherwise have had a profession he could have practiced had he not been in great pain.[13] When the future life would be a great intrinsic negative, this fact may swamp the fact that the event is a greater intrapersonal comparative evil for one person than it is for another.

Does a Worse Death Make One Worse Off?

Suppose that the event of death would be worse for Joe than for Jim because it threatens to deprive him of more that he might otherwise have had. This still does not mean that death results in Joe's falling to a worse baseline, nor in Joe's having had a worse life than Jim will have by death's happening to him. For another event may already have deprived Jim of the goods of life, so that the combination of what death deprives him of and what that other event deprives him of makes his life as bad as Joe's. Accordingly we might say that something terrible has happened in one person's life and not in another's if death makes the one person lose magnificent possibilities realistically open to him. On the other hand, something terrible has happened in, or is true of, another person's life if he never had such magnificent possibilities to begin with or was deprived of them by some cause other than death. Someone who never had the possibility of living twenty years if given an organ was deprived of that possibility by some event other than death (e.g., his disease having progressed too far already). But he may, nevertheless, be seen as losing out on the possibility of twenty years of life, as much as the person who loses this possibility through death alone.

Preventing the Largest Avoidable Loss

Suppose we accept this argument: The fact that death is a comparative evil and a worse event for one person than for another does not imply that one person's life has gone worse than the other's has. We must be careful here: We do not mean that one person is not worse off than the other because death is *not* a state in which a person *is* worse off than if he had lived. We mean that one person has not had a worse life than the other, because both have lost out on as many real possibilities, though one has lost it all through death and the other through death and other causes. Further suppose we agree they have both hit the same low baseline. We might still think we should help the person who will lose the most *through death* because this is a large loss we can still prevent. By contrast, thinking of the person who has been robbed *by his disease* of the possibility of more than one year of life, there is no way we can help him to regain the (possibility of the) other nineteen years.

This reasoning treats cases where need and urgency are the same, but possible outcomes differ, in the same way as we treat those in which one person may be needier than another, but less can be done for him. (Again, we are also tempted to say that what can be done for him does little to alleviate his need but it is not clear this concern with a structural feature should influence our judgment.) That is, we think of L as someone who has irrevocably lost the chance for nineteen more years of life and now stands to lose the chance for one year, and of M as someone who now stands to lose his real chance for twenty years. The lives of both candidates will have gone equally badly if they are not aided, but we can do much more for one person than we can do for the other. (The potential gains to each may be significant; but it is the comparative judgment that is carrying weight.)

Suppose (counter to what I have argued) we agree that if death is a greater comparative evil for one candidate than for another, that candidate's life will have gone worse (though he will not be in a worse state) if he dies than if the other candidate does. I still do not believe it is because we think M would have had the worse life (nor, obviously, because we think he will have hit a lower baseline) than L if we didn't select him that we should give M the organ. After all, his life must not only have gone worse but *sufficiently worse* than L's through losing out on a realistic better alternative if that difference is to determine a decision. Rather, I believe we think that we might as well shoot for the magnificent outcome, since someone will have to die through losing one year no matter whom we fail to aid, and we can prevent the great loss of nineteen years only in one case. (Of course, as I have argued, we have a *loss* of the many additional years even in the life where we cannot prevent it and both fall to the same baseline.) Alternatively put, we get one year no matter whom we aid and an additional nineteen years in one life only. (This is the substitution-of-equivalents analysis.) These facts make us ignore the other fact, that L and M are different persons and that L wants her equal chance to avoid death and get a significant good. Also, if we give the organ to L, then a year later when she must die, we will feel most intensely that that year has been purchased with nineteen additional years of life that would have been possible for someone else.[14] If we may produce the better outcome, we should still do so for the right reason: not because it is socially useful, and not because we can take greater pride in what we produce. But just because more good can be done for a particular person.

Equal Rights, Social Utility, and Outcome

If each person had a right to a transplant (given need and minimally significant outcome), but the needed transplants could not be guaranteed, then an equal chance independent of outcome might be seen as a required substitute. But this is not necessarily correct. As we noted above (in discussing the issues of urgency[T] and neediness versus outcome), it is possible that even those with rights to have their needs met might have to compete with each other on the basis of degree of need, under conditions of scarcity. Could selections be made on the basis of outcome as well? This, indeed, seems hard to justify if each has a strict right to a transplant. (An analogue here is rights to free speech, which are not protected less or more strictly—even with scarcity in protective mechanisms—depending on how much good these rights do for those who have them.) Such protection is consistent with the idea that respecting rights takes considerable precedence over producing good outcomes. This is usually claimed about negative rights; in this case, it would be claimed about positive right to be transplanted too.

However, it may not be true that everyone or anyone has a right to a transplant, at least independent of sufficiently good outcomes. For social investment in this expensive technology—which takes money away from other types of social investment—may make sense only if outcomes are greater than the minimum that is significant to individuals. It is a stronger claim, however, to say that social investment is driven by the goal of producing the best outcome when this costs us other people's adequate outcomes (let alone caring for the needier). I suggest (again), therefore, that the argument for the efficient use of social investment is not strong enough on its own to account for favoring the very best outcomes even when need and urgency are held constant. This leaves it open that whatever rights there are to transplants could be had equally by individuals with at least good outcomes. To complete the argument for favoring better outcomes against such a view based on rights, we should, I believe, look upon the additional good done by better outcomes not merely as a return on social investment, but, in accord with the analysis offered above, as an expression of concern for the good possible to individuals whose lives are at stake.

Proposal

Significant differences in outcome should count in distribution decisions.

Outcome, the Doctor's Role, and Social Policy

Taking into account such differences between outcomes may present conflicts for some doctors. It has already been noted that some doctors may find it frustrating to take care of the neediest (as distinct from the most urgent[T]) if this produces a poorer outcome than might be possible if another patient were treated. Or they may not want to distinguish, in giving a minimally significant benefit, between the neediest and the most urgent[T] because it is frustrating to stand by when one could help a life at greater risk and not do so. These problems arise because most see medicine as directed to medical benefit alone—urgently needed or as large as possible—rather than to consideration of fair distribution of life years.

Some doctors may experience another conflict. Suppose they can produce a benefit in someone such that, were resources not scarce, they would of course provide the benefit. Then some may feel they should give that benefit an equal chance to be provided even if they could produce a larger benefit elsewhere. (This is the doctor who is not inclined to favor better outcomes.)

There is reason to think that a doctor's commitment to his or her patient should, indeed, make him or her act to achieve this minimally significant outcome for the patient. This, however, may only mean that the decision between patients who present different outcomes should not be made by any patient's doctor. After all, each patient's doctor will be in competition with other patients' doctors over a scarce resource. The decision should be taken out of each doctor's hands and made by those who have no commitment to any *one* of the patients, or by a routinized selection procedure. This procedure should not reflect some doctors' refusal to distinguish between merely minimally significant and better outcomes.

Waiting Time and Line Jumping

Line jumping for reasons of urgency^T, in situations of some degree of the organ scarcity, imposes at least an additional probability of death on someone who has been waiting for an organ. If scarcity is only temporary, this is still the probability of reduced quality of life because of an extra wait. Line jumping is done in order to eliminate an even higher probability of death or poor quality of life for someone who has not been waiting as long. Suppose we knew that one of those jumped over will definitely die before another organ is found. Then the jump makes no sense, so long as the time the "jumped-over" will have had alive, beyond what the "jumper" would have had if not jumped, is not significant. In such a case, there is no real difference in urgency^T after all between the one jumped and the one jumped over.

There may, of course, be other reasons for jumping besides urgency. For example, if a needier person (as I have described "need") appears, perhaps he should jump over a less needy but more urgent person. Should length of time waiting at least count in favor of limiting the increase in probability of death or poor outcome that we may impose on someone by jumping over him for any of these reasons? Why?

Does Waiting Time Represent Commitment?

Catering to considerations of need to stay alive and of urgency both represent, in different ways, concern to avoid the worst possible outcome. Does giving weight to a place in line represent concern for something like commitment? Do we have a commitment to those already on line? If we do, it will be important to consider what reason we give for line jumping. This is because we may be justified in overriding a commitment for reasons of urgency and need to stay alive (i.e., to avoid a very bad outcome), but *not* in order to produce the best differential outcome. This is an extension of the common nonutilitarian intuition that a mere increase in utility does not justify breaking a promise, but that avoiding a disaster may well provide such a justification. Then, even if differential outcome mattered when distributing in the absence of differential commitment, it might not matter if waiting times signified commitment.

In other contexts, position in a waiting line does function like a commitment. For example, if someone arrives on a movie line even a few seconds earlier than someone else, the first arrival is (prima facie) owed a ticket first. The argument that there should be a coin toss because there is only an insignificant period of time separating two people on line for a ticket is not correct.

One reason why time waiting (in a movie line or an organ line) might be treated as a commitment factor is that it is thought to be the result of a form of random selection and so stands in for equal chances gotten by a fair toss of a coin. The idea here is that it is random who gets ill *and* who gets what place in line. (Or, alternatively, it is not influenced by improper factors, e.g., socioeconomic power.) Suppose this were true. Commitment on such grounds might still be overridden by greater need, even though commitment is not so easily overridden by better outcome.

In fact, however, who gets onto an organ line is both affected by factors unrelated to the earlier appearance of disease and is not random. For example, those with better medical care, which is in part determined by socioeconomic conditions, tend to get on lines first. Even if this were not true, the relevance of need *and* outcome to distribution would still raise questions about the appropriateness of the idea of a commitment to those on line (or ill) first.

Waiting time may not be a commitment factor at all, unless we announce it to be. Waiting time is not, typically, a commitment factor in emergency rooms, where urgency takes precedence. This is true, I believe, even if the person jumped in the emergency room will actually suffer significant damage, so long as this damage is less than that of the urgent patient. (In emergency rooms, the rule should not be take the sickest first, but take the person who will be worst off if not helped first.)

Negative Experience

Furthermore, it might be suggested, waiting time should count at all only when it involves *negative experience*. Suppose someone were totally unconscious while waiting for his organ. If waiting time is given some credit for purpose of distribution only when it is accompanied by pain or harrowing expectation and uncertainty, the unconscious person would receive no credit. But an unconscious person has been deprived of conscious time alive, and this might count. If both negative experience and lost experiences did justify counting time waiting, this would make it only a utilitarian, rather than a deontological commitment, factor and not very weighty. Should negative or lost experience of waiting play a tie-breaker role in choosing who lives and dies between otherwise equivalent candidates? That is, should someone lose something as important as an equal chance for life in a lottery for life simply because he has not had as hard or depriving a wait? This is problematic, I believe (unless difficulty or deprivation is used as a randomizing device.)

A Proposal

We might count waiting time in the following ways: (a) If place on line was really a function of time of occurrence of disease, and nothing else, then waiting time could be used as a random device to choose between candidates whose differences are morally irrelevant. (This assumes who gets a disease first is itself random; if it were related to socio-economic or racial status this would not be so.) (b) If not, we could still give an organ to someone who is otherwise approximately equal in morally relevant respects to another candidate, but who also has had a negative or depriving wait, when this choice only increases the other candidate's *risk* of not getting another organ, but does not consign the other candidate to certain death. If we follow this policy, we impose on the person who is jumped over an increased risk of dying without an organ and an increased risk of a significant reduction in good outcomes. This is because the longer one waits, the worse one's condition and one's expected outcome typically become. This proposal assumes there is only temporary scarcity or else uncertainty as to whether and when more organs will become available. It cannot be applied in situations where the candidates face true scarcity, so that one's getting an organ means the other dies. True scarcity is the context we have, for the most part, been assuming in our discussion.

Furthermore, (c) negatively experienced or depriving waiting time could count against the greater outcome or urgency^Q of the less needy or less urgent candidate. That is, concern for helping the worst off supports the idea that producing the best possible outcome is less important vis-à-vis a harrowing wait than is need or urgency^T. Still waiting time is not a total trump over better outcome or greater urgency^Q. We can go for a somewhat less good outcome in the one person with greater negatively experienced waiting time, but not an outcome that falls very far below what is possible. Alternatively, the harrowing or depriving wait can be weighed against someone else's prospects for a worse future represented by urgency^Q. Here the idea is that bad or missed adequate experiences while waiting that occur in one candidate are appropriately weighed against the expected bad or missed adequate experiences of another candidate in the future. I suggest that these proposals represent the maximum significance that waiting time should be permitted to have.

Uncertainty

One drawback to giving little significance to place in line and permitting jumping for need, outcome, and urgency is the resultant inability of patients to form stable expectations. One never knows that one won't be jumped. If more significance were given to time on line, it would be reasonable to form a more stable expectation about when one would be treated.[15] If stable expectations are a good, they support holding to a line.

Stable expectations about who will next receive a transplant have positive value. But so do expectations that fair criteria for distribution will be employed. I have here chosen to emphasize the latter factor.

Money: No Individuals Pay?

Most think that a fair distribution of organs would not result from distribution according to *ability to pay*. (Strictly speaking, this should be *actual payment*.) Some may argue for government-subsidized organ transplants for those who cannot pay or have no insurance. The Report says that distribution only to those who can pay would be "wealth discrimination." Is this an appropriate characterization, however? It seems peculiar to think that not giving things free to people who cannot pay is an invidious form of discrimination, of the same sort as race discrimination. Only when a characteristic is not relevant to what is to be distributed does invidious discrimination result. The assumption, then, is that wealth is not a relevant characteristic. The problem here is that the transplants will have to paid for somehow, and it may be morally inappropriate to expect one person to pay for another via taxes beyond a certain point. A system may tax to a certain extent and provide services without regard to income to some degree. Yet perhaps it could *also* permit individuals who can afford to pay to acquire organ transplants after available tax money is exhausted. (This is one type of two-tier system. Another type decides who gets an organ independent of ability to pay, but if the person selected can pay he does even before tax money is exhausted. If he cannot he is subsidized.)

Is there a conflict between helping the most people who most need organs or whose outcomes will be best and distributing organs on the basis of ability to pay? Consider the following case in which an organ transplant which would have been government funded goes to the highest bidder *instead:* A very rich person (R) and a very poor person (P) both need the only suitable organ now available or they will die tomorrow. Five other people are also about to die because the government does not have the money to pay for their lifesaving organ transplants. Suppose that if we sell the organ to R at a very high price, the money from the sale will be used to finance the procedures that transplant organs to the five other people. Why should we not see the choice between giving the organ to R or to P as a choice between saving P and saving six other people's lives? Might justice recommend saving as many lives as possible by distributing the organ to R? [Permitting sales only if the funds help others get care might soften the inequality of a two-tier distribution system, which permits the rich to get more. But notice that this is a third type of two-tier system, different from the two mentioned above. In the case we describe, a transplant that would have been done (on P) at government expense would be paid for instead (and done on R) because this would help more people.]

Suppose R does not in fact need the organ as much as P does. Selling it to R will still save five lives, whereas giving it to P will save only one. Why should we not analyze the situation as simply involving a fair choice between saving one versus saving more lives?

Auctions

Those who think it permissible to sell the organ to R in these cases if and only if the money is used for the five, should, I believe, be in favor of holding occasional auctions at which organs are sold to the highest bidder. Some who need the organs more than the highest bidders will not get them, but more lives will be saved over all, so long as the money is used properly.

Would occasional auctions be morally inappropriate because they involve taking money for an organ that is a gift from a donor? (The Task Force Report implies that it is the fact that organs are gifts that make payment for them inappropriate.) Why should an altruistic donor object to his organ being used to save the maximum number of lives? The auction runs, after all, on the same principle as Goodwill Industries or other charities. In these charities, a donor may give a coat to the charity at no charge. The charity does not (necessarily) give the coat to the person who needs it most. It may sell the coat to the highest bidder who is not in great need. It then uses the money to buy other things for many needy people. Furthermore, the needy person who would have got the coat had there not been an auction or sale may not be among the eventual recipients of those goods purchased with the coat money. (Ability to pay might be involved in distribution in many ways besides auctions. Requiring payment for what the procedure costs, limited to those who need the organ and will have good outcomes, is still distribution by ability to pay since those unable to pay will not get the transplant.)

The Unfairness of an Auction

If the auction is not permissible in this case, its impermissibility must have something to do with deep objections to simple consequentialist reasoning that considers only the best overall outcome. It must have something to do with its being impermissible *not* to give the organ to the person who needs it most or provides the best outcome, or to select between equally needy people by seeing them as possible means to some further end rather than as ends in themselves. At least when the organ would have been given to P had R not shown up.

Suppose R needs the organ as much as P, and the people his money can help to get organs also need our organ. It has been argued (in Chapter 7) that it is permissible to give proportional chances to one side, all of whose members need our organ, when *we* cannot help them all but someone on their side could help them by some other means besides use of our resource. In this case, R and the others should each receive a proportional chance, but giving the organ to R outright may be unfair. (The reasoning here was that with one organ available each person would have received a $\frac{1}{7}$ chance, and the five connected via R may pool their chances. An alternative view is that we should simply give the organ to R, who will then save the others. The reasoning behind this view is as follows: If we had had six organs and could only go to the left to save one or go to the right to save six, we would have gone to the right and saved six. Since we would have saved the greater number and cannot, we should help anyone who can, even if he does not save them by distributing what we had to distribute. This is because, it might be said, we have failed the six by not having more organs and should use whatever means we have to help them. But if we had only one organ and justice did not require that we have more for all six in what sense have we failed them?) Of course, even if counting numbers is unfair, considerations of unfairness may sometimes be overridden by outcome considerations.

Suppose R needs the organ much less than P, but those he can help need it as much as P. Fairness would dictate giving it to P or another one of those who need it most. If one of those whom R would help wins it in a toss with P, he may choose to give it to R. For then R would provide money for transplantation of organs into all except P (who, let us suppose, can use no other organ except the one that has already been given to R).

Those who think that holding an auction is impermissible must also distinguish that procedure from others in which an increase in good consequences would be a legitimate reason for distributing a resource in a certain way. For example, suppose the single organ itself could be used to make a serum that will save twenty lives. Then it is permissible to use the organ to save twenty people rather than one. Note, too, that auctions may be objected to even if they do not allocate organs on the basis of differences in wealth. Suppose there were no differences in purchasing power of those bidding. Nevertheless, some might bid more than others for an organ because they *cared* more about living. But life may be an item that should not be distributed on the basis of the strength of preferences for it.[16] One reason might be that it satisfies an objective interest in addition to any preference.[17] Analogously, if some people prefer candy to a balanced diet, that does not mean that we should provide them with the balanced diet only in accord with their preference.

My aim here is not fully to deal with such objections, but to make clear that we may lose a medically better outcome (more transplants performed and more lives saved) by always distributing organs without regard to money. Such distribution may, nevertheless, be morally correct because it is fair. The Report, then, fails to notice that there can be conflicts between the goals it says we should set ourselves, distributing organs fairly (repeatedly emphasized) and distributing organs "in a manner that accomplishes the greatest good for the community" (p. 77). Would contributions of organs decrease if the public became aware that some organs were distributed to the wealthy? Why should they, if it were understood that this happened only when it maximized the numbers of lives saved? Should they object because it is simply unfair? If the public objected on grounds of unfairness, should we not refrain from distributing to R simply because it is unfair, rather than because the public would object to its unfairness?

On the Governmental Obligation to Fund Organ Acquisition and Transplant Surgery

Having dismissed any distribution according to ability to pay that excludes those unable to pay, the Report provides three specific arguments for the conclusion that government should, if necessary, pay for all types of transplants. *Although the conclusion may be correct,* I wish to point out how the Report's arguments fail to prove it.

Argument 1: Assuming Responsibility for Adequate Health Care

The first argument claims that, even without proof that our government is required to provide health care for the poor, it can be shown that a government that has already assumed a responsibility for "an adequate level of health care without excessive burdens on the ill person," as ours has done, has committed itself to all new procedures fitting under that description. Therefore, it has a responsibility to support organ transplants for the poor and uninsured.

Objection

Do transplants fall under the description "adequate level of health care"? The answer is not obvious. For example, it is not clear they do if we are interested in maintaining normal species functioning and yet we propose to transplant the elderly.[18] But suppose they do. It is still possible (and seems reasonable) that the duty assumed by the government was to provide for adequate health care only within reasonable cost. If the costs would increase beyond a certain point if we added new transplant procedures, the government need not fund all such procedures. It may select among procedures in a fair way.

Argument 2: Which Services to Pay for

How could the government select among procedures? This question forms the basis of the Report's second argument for government funding. There is no relevant difference between procedures the government already funds (e.g., kidney transplants) and newer procedures. Therefore, it has no grounds for refusing funding to new procedures that would not also apply to already funded procedures (p. 104).

Objection

Suppose there is an upper limit on costs the government is obligated to bear. Then, so long as it selects fairly among procedures, it may fund some and not all. Where there are no intrinsic relevant differences selecting randomly would be fair. Alternatively, older procedures already funded may be kept, and newer ones not funded. This could be done on the combined grounds of the efficiency of keeping in place what already exists and a sort of randomness of first come, first served. (The Task Force itself recommends first come, first served when organs are scarce with respect to patients equal in need and expected outcome.) That is, whichever disease happened to get a "cure" first, gets funded. In general, given the reasonableness of the assumption that there was always an intended upper limit on required funding, one cannot generate additional governmental duties to fund *simply* by using a consistency argument. That is, the fact that there are no relevant intrinsic differences between procedures already funded and those to be funded does not make funding only some inconsistent. In general, the fact that only some procedures or only some people are being treated, not all, by itself does not obligate us to care for all. Finding fair ways to select among procedures to be funded or people to be treated can be an acceptable substitute for funding everything for everyone.

Argument 3: Not Taking Payment for Gifts

The final argument used by the Report is supposed to derive a governmental obligation to fund transplants for the needy, independent of the first two arguments. That is, independent of the government's having assumed responsibility for health care and independent of there being no relevant differences between procedures already funded and those yet to be funded. The claim is that because donors give organs as gifts, we owe it to donors both to distribute the organs *and* to distribute the organs independent of ability to pay. (This is broader than the claim that it would be wrong for doctors to profit by charging for organs when the donors get nothing. This is because the money that recipients paid for organs could go to a worthy cause, and yet the claim is this would be wrong.)

Objection

The government cannot be put under a new obligation to spend in excess of any other required level of spending simply because a donor offers to give us something that is useful for others. Could someone put you under an obligation to spend the money to build a house for the homeless by giving you the parts for such a house? Furthermore, as the analogy with Goodwill Industries was meant to suggest, we can often charge for what is donated without reimbursing the donor.

However, suppose someone has induced another person to donate a good by leading him to believe that the item will be provided free to the public. He may then be required to accept the cost of putting the item to use. Suppose the government did induce organ donations by promising to give the organs away free and to fund their use in the needy who are unable to pay. Then it may be obliged to pay costs. This suggests that if there is a spending level beyond which the government ought not go, the government should not encourage donations by promising to pay for all organ use.

Therefore, a government that justly failed to fund some transplants should not encourage endless donations of organs. It could explain to the potential donors that governmental payment for the financially needy would be unavailable beyond a certain point. However, some individuals could themselves (for example, via insurance) afford to pay for a transplantation procedure they medically need and by which they would be benefited. Further, the government would funnel the organs to such needy people with the ability to pay. Should not a potential donor under such circumstances still be willing to donate?

Finally, suppose the government had met its limited obligations to pay for transplants before using all organs. Would it be better to let the rest go unused for the sake of equality or to let those who could pay use them, though the poor would not be served? In the auction case discussed above, the organ being auctioned was imagined as being one the government would have had a duty to transplant into the poor person if someone richer had not wanted it, and the richer person might not merit it as much as the poor person on fair distribution criteria. By contrast, in the case I am here discussing, money is buying an organ the government would not have had a duty to transplant into anyone, an organ that therefore would have been wasted.

I conclude that, although there may well be arguments for the conclusion that the government should fund all transplants for the needy and uninsured, the Report has not provided them.[19] But notice that in arguing only for the government's duties with regard to the poor and uninsured, the Report can accept that selection of recipients be on the basis of criteria independent of ability to pay, and yet if the person (or his insurer) selected can pay, he should. Such a system differs from (and seems superior to) one in which we do not even think of taking payment until the government's resources are exhausted, at which point selection of recipients would be totally dependent on ability to pay.

NOTES

1. Some may think we ought to produce the greater number of years because longer life is clearly the better outcome. By contrast we should not choose to prolong one life-style over another because it is not clear what the better life style is. This is an inadequate view for several reasons. First, sometimes it is clear that one person's life-style is better than another's, and better for the person who lives it, and yet this may be irrelevant to a decision on who gets an organ. Furthermore, knowing that more years is better than fewer would certainly make a decision easy if we were choosing between two options for one person. But when two people are involved, choosing the objectively better outcome of longer life is not in the interest of the person who could be benefited by the less good outcome. This raises questions about whether we should produce the objectively better outcome.

2. This is my phrasing of an objection raised to me by Norman Daniels.

3. John Harsanyi employs the veil of ignorance in this way. Daniel Wikler also presents this sort of argument for why concern for outcome of treatment is the equitable solution, totally bypassing Maximin. (See Chapter 13.)

4. T. Scanlon, "Contractualism and Utilitarianism," in Williams and Sen, *Utilitarianism and Beyond*.

5. Thomas Nagel, "Equality," in *Mortal Questions* (Cambridge: Cambridge University Press, 1979), pp. 106–27.

6. For example, I believe it follows from John Taurek's view that numbers should not count, that we should toss a coin between K and L *when we already know who occupies which position*. However, he would not believe it is what we should do when we do *not* already know whether K or L will have the best outcome. Then he would agree that we should go with the best outcome. This is because it maximizes each individual's chance to get what he wants most, the good outcome. Taurek's reasoning, when in ignorance of one's position, seems to be based on thinking of one's chances of being in any given position; it does not stem from identifying with the person who actively occupies any position.

7. T. Scanlon, "Rawls' Theory of Justice," *University of Pennsylvania Law Review* 121 (1973): 1020–1069.

8. Notice that it is only when the extra utility above the base utility offered by each candidate is at least as great as that base utility that we can move from a salience argument to a numbers-counting argument. That is, only then will there be enough extra utility to constitute additional units equivalent to the units of at least two original candidates.

9. It is very well possible that losing both arms makes a life more than twice as bad as losing one arm. Certainly being blind is much worse than twice as bad as losing one eye.

10. We already considered it in Chapter 10, and its note 13.

11. Personal communication.

12. This is a variant of the view suggested by Nagel that one is worse off if one has come to the same end state through having lost out on more.

13. This is not intended to suggest that we should prefer a candidate for an organ who would have a profession to one who will not.

14. But we would not have given up outright nineteen years for one; by adopting the coin-tossing alternative, we retained a 50 percent chance of getting those nineteen years.

15. I owe this point to Brad Lichtenstein.

16. I owe this point to Richard Revesz.

17. A distinction drawn by Thomas Scanlon in "Preference and Urgency," *Journal of Philosophy* 72, no. 19 (Nov. 1975): 655–669.

18. See Norman Daniels, *Just Health Care* (New York: Cambridge University Press, 1985).

19. For discussion of how government commissions do and should argue for conclusions see my "The Philosopher as Insider and Outsider," *The Journal of Medicine and Philosophy* (1990): 347–374.

15

Procedures for Distribution

Having considered some conceptual and substantive issues involved in the distribution of resources, let us consider specific proposals for distribution procedures. Once again we use organ transplants with scarce human organs as an example. However, the procedures described may be applied to distributing any scarce resource. Why should we want a procedure, rather than have committees that decide? It has been argued that procedures are preferable to committees since we want to know how a committee is deciding, and a committee that is consistent in its decisions will eventually crystallize a procedure anyway while inconsistent committees are not desirable. What this argument for procedure misses is the possibility that rational choice is not reducible to a procedure and that (in accord with Aristotle's view) good judgment and sensitivity can be present even when we are unable to give a formal characterization of what constitutes such rational choice. A committee might have good judgment without having a procedure. On this view we can still investigate aspects of a problem, as we have in the previous chapters, but we should not expect to settle on a routinized procedure. Some have also argued that societies do not always want to be clearly confronted with the decision procedures they employ; for example, it can conflict with their announced belief that life must be preserved at all costs.[1]

To these two anti-procedure arguments we can counterargue as follows: (a) While giving the point about judgment its due, it may be possible to go further than it suggests in the direction of delineating a procedure that mimics sensitivity of judgment. We may legitimately hope to do more than list factors, just as we may legitimately hope to go beyond listing prima facie duties in general ethical theory, by constructing much more complex and sensitive principles that, e.g., tell us just whether and when it is permissible to break a promise for what greater goods. (b) The public may be sufficiently worried about unfairness that it would prefer a public display of reasons, even if it threatens pleasant illusions.

The question remains, why should the procedure not be the result of a democratic vote, either by society at large or by recipients of organs? Majority votes do not ensure substantive fairness of results; the democratic vote may be for an unjust distribution system. (It is only if we are dealing with a situation in which there is no independent standard for fairness of a result that pure procedural justice, i.e., generating a result—which may itself be procedure—by a morally acceptable procedure, is enough to ensure us of the moral acceptability of the result.) Furthermore, the decision as to what should be decided by reasoning and what by majority rule is not necessarily appropriately made by majority rule; we may have to reason about which questions should be decided by reasoning and which by votes. If we have some hope of reasoning to a fair procedure, whose fairness we can explain to the public, and the consequences of unfairness are sufficiently grave, it pays to try to reason our way to a procedure.

KILNER

John Kilner[2] offers the following procedure:

1. Check candidates for their capacity to be medically benefited to some significant degree and their willingness to accept an organ. One might also check for probability of getting that benefit, but differences in outcomes beyond a minimally significant one do not count.
2. Of those who satisfy (1), give the organ to those facing most imminent death.
3. If (2) does not select a unique candidate, then, of those satisfying (1), select between recipients by either (a) giving to those whose special responsibilities make others' lives (or something as important) depend upon their lives, or (b) checking to see which way more lives can be *directly* saved by use of our resource.
4. If (3) does not decide, select among the remaining candidates by lottery. This represents the right of each of the remaining candidates to an equal chance.

Criticisms: Urgency versus Need

Let us assume that condition 1 is fulfilled, and also that there is true scarcity, that is, there will not be enough organs for all those who require them. Condition 2 tells us to treat the most urgent[T] case first. But what if a less urgent[T] person is needier in the sense that he has had less opportunity for and less adequate conscious life. For example, he is 20 years old and his competitor for an organ is a significantly more urgent[T] 60-year-old with a past life full of adequate conscious experience. Because the criteria we have suggested in Chapter 11 give the needier some preference, they might pick the younger recipient. Kilner's criterion would pick the 60-year-old, leaving the younger person to die.

Recall that we argued that the person who needs an organ most to stay alive (urgent[T]) may not be the person who most needs to continue living (need). This is because what primarily makes death bad is the absence of more time alive (and the goods this time brings). The most urgent[T] person may already have lived a longer life than other candidates for organs. Even if this does not mean there is DMU of life, it can mean that fairness is in favor of giving something to those who have had less.

Therefore, we can distinguish the most urgent[T] candidate from the neediest. The former is the one who will die soonest or live the worst life from now on. The neediest is the one who will have had the worst life at the time he dies. Ordinarily we think it is worse to die younger rather than older. (This might not be so for the very young, or if the young had accomplished much and the old had not. But then we have also argued that we should emphasize length of adequate conscious life rather than successful projects.) Therefore, in general, the younger person needs to go on living more than the older person.

Special Responsibilities and Dependents

Suppose someone who satisfies Condition 1 has dependents who would lose as much as the second organ candidate if the first candidate, their provider, does not receive the organ. Kilner believes we may then give the organ to the candidate with the dependents if the second candidate is not facing more imminent death. In the light of our discussion, we can raise several questions about this.

First, the fact that we choose between people on grounds of their causal efficacy does seem unfair. So the case described above is different from one in which our resources can be distributed either to one person or to many. It is also different from a case in which one candidate for an organ but not another can help us distribute *our* resource. Therefore, according to our earlier discussion, Kilner's condition 3a is more problematic than 3b. If sufficient good is at stake, unfairness may be overridden. This suggests that in the problematic cases those dependents who stand to lose a great deal should be counted, but for less than their full weight as separate needy persons. For example, rather than two outnumbering one straightforwardly in Condition 3(a), it might take four to outnumber one, when fairness is taken into account.

Second, Kilner thinks that unless the dependents stand to lose as much as the two contestants stand to lose, they should not be considered.[3] I discussed matters bearing on this issue in detail in Chapters 8 through 10 and concluded that we might give a higher chance to save Jim's life and Nancy's arm, rather than give Joe an equal chance for life. We also should choose Jim and Nancy if she will be totally paralyzed, even though Nancy does not stand to lose as much as Joe or Jim. Perhaps Kilner's procedure would prohibit both this last decision and proportional chances. Yet these cases differ from Kilner's 3a in that they involved direct use of our resources to produce the extra utility and so involved no unfairness in relying on a causal relation. We do not want to allow the significant, but lesser losses to dependents always to count in deciding whom to save, in part because of unfairness. I have suggested in Chapter 13 that we might even deal differently with the psychological and life-style problems occasioned by the loss of a parent or spouse than with those problems brought about by the loss of an arm, in part because of causal relations, in part because of separate spheres. The former should not count even though the latter does, holding causal relations constant. So, while Kilner's reasoning about dependents who would lose less than each organ candidate seems wrong (in the way Sob[1] seemed wrong), our conclusions about what weight to assign in such dependent cases are not substantially different from his. The choice Kilner's procedure would determine in family cases seems correct.

Third, as noted, Kilner allows us to consider the fates of those who do not directly need an organ when they causally depend on someone who does. He is not disturbed by allowing the causal relation to determine whose life we save. Why then should Kilner insist that we give priority to the person who meets Condition 2? That is, why, according to Kilner's principles, may not one choose as a candidate for an organ someone less urgent^T than others, so long as those who depend on him will lose as much as the most urgent^T candidate? This is the case if a doctor who is indispensable to saving other lives needs an organ to make her function efficiently, though not to prevent her dying. If Kilner would advocate such a transplant, then there may again be a problem of fairness.

Fourth, Kilner allows us to consider the numbers of lives that can be saved by a resource only *after* we have considered urgency^T. This implies that it is correct to withhold a resource from many people, allowing them to die if they will live some minimally significant extra time beyond the most urgent^T patient, rather than allow the urgent^T patient to die immediately and save the many others. Suppose, for example, that twenty people who if treated could have lived ten years each will die a year from now, if, instead of them we save one person from death tomorrow so that he may live one year. Let us assume that Kilner intends his procedure to apply in conditions of true scarcity. Then Kilner's attention to urgency^T before numbers, as well as his commitment to ignoring differences in outcomes above a medically significant minimal benefit, would lead him to save the single urgent^T person. It would also lead him to save one urgent^T person who will die tomorrow and live three years if saved, rather than twenty people who will die in six months if not saved now but who, if saved now, would each live for three additional years only. (In this case, unlike the previous one, we hold differential outcome per person constant).

What would our discussion, as opposed to Kilner's, suggest we decide in such a case? We have suggested letting need modify the weight of urgency^T and limiting concern for both by concern for outcome. This concern for outcome should apply in a context of true scarcity where Kilner would recommend saving one urgent^T person but where we could otherwise save many people, each of whom is significantly less urgent^T. Our discussion in Chapter 10 of a case in which we must choose between saving many from paralysis and saving one life may be helpful on this point. There we suggested that society might find the cost of helping the worst off too great and allocate resources to preventing paralysis (or saving many arms). A doctor may still feel an obligation to save the worst-off individual she confronts, but a socially instituted decision procedure might constrain a doctor to distribute the organ to save the twenty less urgent^T, especially if they will otherwise die shortly too, rather than the most urgent^T.

Lottery and Outcome

After considering medically significant outcome and its probability, urgency^T, and numbers of individuals who stand to be affected as much as our original candidates, Kilner recommends equal chances for any remaining candidates. But our discussion suggests some role for differential outcome (including within it probability of any number of years) and for time waiting on line.

At what point should significant differences in good outcome enter into the decision making? If we treat the neediest before the most urgent^T, we will, in a sense, already have to consider outcome. For it was suggested that neediness not be a trump, but only given extra weight. The value of a certain absolute number of outcome years will be greater the less someone has had of life so far, both because of DMU and because of its moral value of going to the neediest. Therefore, for both these reasons an outcome *smaller* in absolute terms may have greater weight. However, suppose we are concerned with when we should give an outcome larger in absolute terms a more significant role. It seems that just as number of lives might be weighed against one person's urgency^T, so the amount of benefit we could provide someone might be weighed against neediness and urgency^T from the beginning. This is a rejection of Maximin. For example, suppose the neediest candidate could only receive one year and the less needy candidate could get ten years. Giving the one year to the needier candidate may be worth more than giving several years to the less needy. Yet even taking this into consideration it might be better to bring about ten years than to bring about one year even multiplied by a factor for the fact that it goes to the neediest. If it is a sufficiently better thing that we can do, it could swamp neediness. Ten years given to a 10-year-old (i.e., great need and a large outcome) may swamp twenty years to a 40-year-old. This is a radical conclusion since we prevent the formal good of a quite complete life to the 40-year-old without thereby giving the 10-year-old a full life. But ten years to a 20-year-old (less need) may not swamp twenty years to a 40-year-old. Again, this is a radical conclusion since it might be argued the achievements possible for a 20-year-old are more significant than for the 10-year-old. The radical results stem from ignoring various formal goods of life and focusing on adequate conscious life.

Notice that our analysis will be *very* different if we think the 20-year-old is needier than the 10-year-old. (How could we?) Or, if we agree that the ten years from twenty to thirty give more value than the years between ten and twenty and allow this to weigh. That is, even if the 10-year-old needs life more than the 20-year-old, he will get less of what he needs if he gets an additional ten years than the 20-year-old will get from his ten years. I suspect we think this is true. But we would then be considering factors other than the mere experiencing of adequate conscious life in deciding on the value of time alive for purposes of distributing an organ.

The overall point here is just that differential outcome to an individual should be considered from the beginning in our distribution decisions.

Lottery and Waiting Time

Return now to Kilner's Condition 4. Should we hold a lottery even though one person has been waiting longer than another? Not if waiting time *is* the lottery. Kilner recognizes this. On the other hand, if it is not the lottery, should the fact that someone had experienced a grueling waiting time be enough to make a straightforward substantive difference between life and death in candidates otherwise equal in morally relevant respects? It hardly seems so.

We have suggested that negatively experienced waiting time could count against a difference in outcome and urgency^Q, holding up a distribution on the basis of better outcome or worse life prospects. It could also be given weight if it only reduced another candidate's chances for an organ, as in situations of temporary scarcity.

STARZL'S POINT SYSTEM

Next, let us consider point systems for distributing organs for transplantation.

Starzl[4] describes a point system for the distribution of kidneys in which no one factor (for example, best outcome or urgency^T) has lexical priority over another, although it should be kept in mind that, in the case of kidneys, there is not much urgency^T since dialysis is an alternative. Kilner's system gives first priority to minimal medically adequate outcome and second to urgency^T (assuming consent). In Starzl's system, proper blood types and negative cytotoxic antibody status are necessary conditions for eligibility (conditions of minimally adequate outcome). Then his system assigns the following points:

1. a maximum of 10 points for waiting time in line, assigned in the following way: if there were five people waiting, the person waiting longest would receive $\frac{5}{5} \times 10 = 10$ points, a person who had the second-longest waiting time would receive $\frac{4}{5} \times 10 = 8$ points, a person who was third would receive $\frac{3}{5} \times 10 = 6$ points, etc.

2. a maximum of 12 points for antigen matching (It is believed [at least by some] that the better the antigen match, the better the outcome with an organ is likely to be. If this were true, factor 2 would be an outcome maximizing factor. It is agreed by all that a perfect [6-antigen] match increases success a good deal; it is not clear that less than this provides more than a minimal statistically significant difference. With the availability of immunosuppressive drugs, such as FK409, it is not clear that antigen matches are needed for assuring the "take" of an organ or for maximizing outcome at all.)

3. a maximum of 10 points for degree of sensitization (i.e., the degree to which someone will reject tissues, thus making it difficult to find an acceptable organ). One gets more points if one is more sensitive, because a matching organ is hard to find.

4. a maximum of 10 points for urgency, ranging from limitations on one's lifestyle to nearness to death (As noted, because there is a backup of dialysis in the case of kidneys, death is not often a prospect.)

5. a maximum of 6 points for logistic factors, such as the patient's geographic location near a donor's organ that will decay rapidly.

Factors 3 through 5 are what I would call the *Maximin* factors; taking care of them helps avoid the worst state of affairs—the death of a potential recipient before getting an organ or the decay of an organ so that no one benefits from it. Degree of sensitization is also a factor to be considered in maximizing outcome, as sensitivity reduces the chances of an organ's taking.

This system seems to give more weight to outcome factors than to patient urgency/need or waiting-time considerations, but the latter two types of factors together (can) more than equal the weight of outcome factors. We can reach this conclusion by the following calculation: 12 (antigen) + 6 (logistics) + 5 (½ of sensitivity) = 23 for outcome factors; 10 (urgency) + 5 (½ of sensitivity) = 15 for need or urgency; + 10 for waiting time = 25. (We divide sensitivity points between the outcome and urgency categories, given its two conceptual roles. Notice also that concern for logistics helps avoid the worst outcome (because it is an *organ* urgency criterion) and is not therefore a *patient* urgency criterion.)

Unlike Kilner's system, Starzl's does not count dependents or attend to numbers who could be directly benefited by the organ. Starzl's system also differs from kidney systems that check first for perfect matches, and if there are none goes with time waiting (if urgency is not at issue.)

Problems of the Point System

Despite the great benefits of this point system, I believe some problems still exist. In examining these problems, I shall consider the system as a general model for the distribution of organs, not just for kidneys, in order to highlight general issues. (In fact, Starzl's system places less emphasis on urgency[T] than nonkidney systems (as used by the United Network for Organ Sharing (UNOS)) would, and it can count antigen matches, which is not done for hearts and livers.) I shall also assume that ability to pay is not a relevant factor in distribution. For the sake of this discussion, I shall also put to one side whether the number of dependents matters and the issue of regional versus national or international distribution.

Objectivity and Quantitativeness

A general problem with the point system is that it may conceal the degree to which judgment is still required in decision making.

Starzl describes the system as "objective,[5] contrasting it with "ad hoc selection at odd hours, guided by often faulty memory . . . or by incomplete . . . information.[6] However, assigning definite maximal points to objectively verifiable criteria does not necessarily make a system ethically correct. The content of the criteria and the number of points they each deserve are crucial. Starzl provides no rationale for the system's selecting only the factors that it does select or for assigning the maximum number of points to the different factors that it does assign.

For example, Starzl himself has disputed the claim that there is a correlation between number of antigens matched and outcomes.[7] If there were no correlation, then the fact that antigen matching is a determinate and objective way to assign organs would be no more important than that counting hairs is. We must also consider the possibility that a nonquantitative system whose objectivity is not so obvious to everyone might come closer to giving an (objectively) correct answer than a quantitative system that ignores relevant but nonquantitative factors. One reason relevant factors may not be strictly quantifiable is that the points Starzl assigns to some factors do not merely signify an ordinal ranking of people with respect to that factor; they signify cardinal ranking. They imply, for example, that a person with two points has exactly twice the urgency as the person with one point. It is unlikely that we can judge in this way. Any point system that adds the figures assigned can, therefore, be misleading. It can also result in the wrong person's being chosen if someone is given twice as many points as someone else on some dimensions though he is not really twice as worthy on these dimensions.

On the other hand, in one respect the Starzl system fails to quantify enough. The way the system assigns points for time waiting has the effect of ignoring the difference in absolute times waiting. Here points are assigned by mere ordinal ranking. The result is that A can be given a two-point difference over B because he has been waiting five months longer than B while B is also given a two-point difference over C even though he has been waiting only two weeks longer than C. In the Starzl system, the difference between four points and two points does not mean that one person has been waiting twice as long as another. Hence, if waiting time should affect distribution in the way Starzl thinks—a separate issue—those waiting longer may not get as many points as they should relative to those waiting shorter times. Hence they may lose an organ they should get. It seems the system should be changed at least so that points correspond to a given absolute unit of waiting time. That is, here the system can and should be based on cardinal not ordinal rankings. Of course, it may be that overall less weight should be given to waiting time and only negative-experienced or depriving waiting time should make a difference.

Judgment and Empirical Questions

Suppose we do go the route of quantifying because despite its problems it is a useful heuristic device. Then judgment based on moral reasoning is still unavoidable in deciding which factors should matter and how many points different factors should be maximally worth. Judgment is also necessary to determine whether there should be a lexical order in which factors are considered, so that someone who is needier should be taken first despite his points on other factors. We first have to consider different types of cases, decide which factors we think morally weightier than others, construct a system that reflects these judgments, and then use it to decide other cases.

Once we have decided how weighty different factors should be and whether there is a proper order for their consideration, we could check to see whether a system directly gives them their proper weight and role. If it does not, we should also check to see to what degree, as a matter of empirical fact, there is covariation between different factors in a system. Covariation may indirectly permit the factor that should have more weight to receive it because another factor's points move in the same direction as the weightier factor itself does. For example, suppose waiting time mattered more than the ten points it is maximally assigned by Starzl. Those waiting a long time may frequently be those who have become most urgent and are most sensitized. Therefore, given that these other factors receive separate points, those with long waiting times may more frequently get organs in the Starzl system than we would be led to believe just by considering the direct points allotted to waiting time.

We must also, of course, use judgment in assigning particular points for each factor to actual individuals, keeping in mind the difficulty noted above that cardinal rather than ordinal ranking is particularly hard to do with some factors.

Applying the Starzl system as described to the distribution of organs may or may not lead to morally incorrect decisions in selecting recipients. Let us consider this issue, taking the direct weight the system gives to various factors at face value. We shall allow ourselves to repeat certain distinctions already discussed earlier.

Need versus Urgency

The system takes no account of the distinction we have been using between needing an organ most in order to stay alive or to live well (urgency) and needing most to stay alive or live well (need). One can be needier even if one is not as urgent. For example, suppose a 20-year-old will definitely die in a year if not given an organ *now*. He will then be worse off dying at 21 than a person of 50 will be if he dies tomorrow through lack of an organ. The Starzl system, however, would treat equivalently a 50-year-old person and a 20-year-old person who had the same points for his five factors. Indeed Starzl seems to equate differential treatment on the basis of age with differential treatment on the basis of sex. The analysis I have provided suggests the two are not the same: a woman may need more life as much as a man, but an older person may not need more adequate conscious life as much as a younger person.

Priority among Factors

Let us assume candidates of the same age and, hence (roughly) same need. The Starzl system does not give lexical priority to those with greater urgency. That is, it does not straightaway give the organ to the individual with higher points for urgency. (This is not necessarily wrong.) So if applied generally, it may give an organ to someone who would live for two years without it anyway and get an additional four years if given the organ now (before he gets worse), rather than to someone who will die soon without it and live two years with it. But it may be morally right to help first those who would be worst off, so long as they get some significant medical benefit, before we help those who will be better off anyway. (This is a Modified Maximin solution.) Alternatively, it may be right to give at least some greater weight, if not lexical priority, to the degree of need and urgency, over outcome. This could be done by giving more than one-half of the maximal points allotted in the system as a whole to need and urgency rather than to outcome factors.[8] (Recall the Starzl system was shown to give more points to outcome than to need factors.) Even so revised, a high outcome could still overcome greater need or urgency.

If need as described above were more important than urgency, more maximal points should be assigned to it. In addition, if the moral value of fairness is important we could represent the greater value of a differential outcome of an absolute number of years to the neediest by assigning diminishing numerical factors to ages at, let us say, ten- or twenty-year intervals. We then multiply the neediest's absolute differential outcome points (based on years times probability of achieving them) by this factor. (This is in addition to assigning more maximal points for need.) Still, all this does not imply that greater need is a trump over absolute outcome. For we may consider that even the adjusted outcome we produce for the neediest is much smaller than the absolute differential outcome we could produce for someone else.

Waiting Time

The Starzl system gives weight to time waiting. It may do this because waiting involves negative experiences, such as raised and defeated expectations or deprivations of adequate experience. It may be using waiting time as a partial lottery device or to help stabilize expectations to some degree. A significantly more urgent person could fail to get an organ simply because someone else was waiting much longer. After all, the same maximal number of points are assigned for waiting time and urgency in the Starzl system. Some might object to this equivalence on moral grounds, believing that urgency, need, and expected outcome should be placed ahead of even negatively experienced time waiting in medical settings. This would mean that comparatively fewer maximal points should be assigned to waiting time than to either outcome, need, or urgency. Even if waiting time is used as a tie breaker between otherwise relevantly equal candidates, it thereby deprives someone of an equal chance in matters of life and death. This seems too much weight for it to have, unless it is being used as a lottery device and not for its intrinsic significance.

I suggest that if waiting time were not a legitimate lottery device, its intrinsic features may be allowed to reduce another candidate's *probability* of getting an organ; this becomes relevant only if there is temporary rather than real scarcity. Negatively experienced or depriving waiting time may also be weighed against a less needy candidate's greater outcome points or his urgency^Q in true scarcity. After all, it seems reasonable that bad experience in the past (on line) should weigh against someone else's expected bad experience in the future and that time lost experiencing life while on line should diminish the value we place on another candidate's providing a better outcome. Waiting time could be a lottery device in true scarcity only if, e.g., it were not correlated with socioeconomic status, that is if it were not correlated with the rich getting on line first.

Conclusion and a Modified System

If there are moral problems, the Starzl system's reported success in eliminating waiting lists of nonsensitized blood type A and type AB recipients and reducing waits of type O and type B recipients is still not sufficient grounds for endorsing it. For it is consistent with this success that some individuals who did not receive organs should have gotten them instead of those who did get them, conceivably even at the expense of fewer total transplants performed and longer waiting lists in general. This is because the rights of a few may trump the maximizing of overall good consequences.

We can summarize the recommended alternative ways of assigning points in a Starzl-like system assuming real scarcity, as follows:

1. Need modifies urgency^T (as these concepts were differentiated above), but greater urgency^T and the outcome accompanying it may outweigh the combination of greater need and lower outcome.
2. There should be more maximal points assigned for need or urgency than for outcome, but these points should be counted only when some minimal number of outcome points accompany them.
3. Even fewer points should be assigned to waiting time than to outcome. Furthermore, waiting-time points should be counted only against another candidate's higher outcome or higher urgency^Q points.
4. A multiplicative factor by which to multiply outcomes should be assigned at *significant* age intervals.

With respect to (3): objections to jumping over someone because we cannot do as much for him as for another person are, I believe, objections not to the relative importance of waiting time and outcome, but to choosing on the basis of differences in outcome even when both candidates come at the same time. There *would* be special objections if waiting time represented a *commitment* to treat in a certain order for then (as noted above) better outcome would be a *much* weaker reason than need for jumping.

On the basis of our discussion of the conceptual issue, we can construct a modified Starzl system with four factors; need (N), urgency (U), outcome (O), and waiting time (W), with the following points: N = 20; U = 10; O = 10; WT = 5 (ratio of 4:2:2:1). (Need might be given less weight than urgency, e.g., 10 points, if it should only have less of a modifying effect.) The scale for each factor is determined independently, and then it is given a set weight in points. That is, the ratio is not meant to imply that twenty months of need is equivalent to ten months of urgency. Factors used to multiply outcomes on the basis of need should also be assigned at age intervals. In true scarcity, waiting-time points are to be added only against another candidate's higher expected outcome or his urgency^Q (worse life prospects).

AN ALTERNATIVE PROPOSAL

Priority between Factors in Real Scarcity

As previously noted, the Starzl point system does not give any factor lexical (absolute) priority over other factors. This shows up when it adds up points on all dimensions at once, rather than checking for points on some dimensions before others.[9] Yet it might be suggested that in true scarcity need should trump outcome, at least when accompanied by a minimally significant outcome. Taking care of the worse off first, before improving the lot of those already better off by producing greater outcome, might be said to have priority.

However, lexical priority may not be called for. Consider for simplicity's sake a system similar to Starzl's with four factors: Need (N), defined as how badly off the person will be when he dies, i.e., (roughly) how long he has lived; Urgency (U), defined solely as how bad or short the rest of someone's life is expected to be without an organ; Outcome (O), defined as increment in years expected with an organ over life without an organ (calculated by multiplying years times their probability) and Waiting Time (W), defined as how long someone has been waiting for an organ.

Urgency and Outcome

To give priority to some factor over others is to draw a qualitative distinction between factors. Assume to begin with that N is relatively equal between candidates. Deciding that U has some priority over O (in virtue of a desire to help the worst off first) would not necessarily imply that greater U is a trump over O. That is, we do not stop counting the O (and W points) of the less urgent person and merely give the organ to the most urgent. For example, when the O possible for the most urgent is very poor, U should not trump. But this only means that there should be a minimum O-level. U could still be considered as, in a sense, trumping O if someone with significantly lower U points and very high O points, was automatically excluded by someone with lower U and minimal O points. Furthermore, if there is only a slight difference in U between the worst-off person and the next worse off and each has high O points, it seems morally wrong for greater U to be a trump. Instead, these two candidates should be given equal chances (or proportional chances if the difference is only somewhat greater).

One suggestion for a procedure (for use between two persons) is that, where the difference between greater and lesser U is not significant and expected outcomes are approximately equal, we either ignore the difference in U or give weighted chances. That is, we give somewhat greater chance of getting the organ to the one with greater U. This still leaves open the possibility that the less urgent candidate will get it. Where there is more than a slight difference in U, and the O of the most urgent offers some minimally significant extra period of medically worthwhile life, we then stop counting and help the most urgent.

A second suggestion is that we multiply the most urgent person's O points by a certain factor when there is a significant difference between his urgency and anyone else's and he has some significant O. The factor will differ depending on absolute and comparative urgency. It represents the value of taking care of who is worst off as judged by the measure of the "here and now worst off." In this scheme, there is still a chance that the less urgent will get the organ if the less urgent has a better prospective outcome.

This alternative proposal differs from the changes suggested above to a Starzl-like system. There, we followed Starzl in assigning different maximal points to different factors. It was important to get the right interfactor comparisons represented by different maximal points. Here, we need not assign different maximal points to outcome and urgency. We can just rank—on a cardinal scale if possible—people on separate outcome and urgency scales, and then do our multiplication of absolute differential outcomes by the multiplicative factors.

Several Multiplicative Factors

The second of these proposals considers the possibility that the U of the most urgent counts for more when U is great in absolute terms, but not so much more when U is lower in absolute terms. So a small but significant improvement in life prospects may be enough when urgency is absolutely great to outweigh a better outcome in the less urgent. However, the threat of losing a better outcome in the less urgent may outweigh a small but significant gain to someone who is still comparatively more urgent but not very urgent in absolute terms. Hence, the most urgent should get more weight attached to his O points the more absolutely urgent he is. That is, more points are assigned for each month of urgency and used to multiply outcome.

To capture these complications, we might have a *continuous function* in our distribution system. The relative weight of U to O in the most urgent could vary with the absolute values of U. So, $U = O$ when U is not great, and $U = 3 O$ when urgency is absolutely greater. The greater weight of greater U can be represented by multiplying the O points accompanying different U's by different factors. That is, when the most urgent is not very urgent, his O is counted once; when he is very urgent, it is multiplied three times. (The multiplicative factors here are purely hypothetical. In reality, one would have to derive them by seeing what judgments we would make about cases, e.g., if, in true scarcity, it would take the threat of losing a ten-year outcome to a person who will die in one year if not treated now, to stop us giving one year to a person who would die tomorrow, then just less than ten is the multiplicative factor to use for an outcome in the most urgent when there is this difference in urgency.) If we use multiplicatives based on absolute figures for urgency in both candidates, this will also capture comparative urgency.

It is suggested that the justification for treating the relation between urgency and outcome in this way is that it is permissible for society to take into account the loss of a greater benefit to another individual in deciding whether to help the most urgent. The less absolutely and comparatively urgent the most urgent is, and the less he stands to gain if helped, the more we may consider the losses to the less urgent. This is a controversial position, however, and was discussed in detail in Chapter 14. If differences in outcome, above a significant minimum, should not matter, we could theoretically still take the minimal significant outcome and multiply it by factors for absolute and comparative urgency.

Urgency and Numbers of Lives

The same general relation described between urgency in one candidate and better outcome in another candidate could also hold between urgency and number of lives of the less urgent, each of whom has no better expected outcome than the most urgent. Indeed, the fact that the benefit is distributed, rather than concentrated in one less urgent competitor, is a point in its favor.

Need

Let us drop the assumption we have been making that need is equal. There is reason to think that in true scarcity, need should modify the weight of urgency. For very great need, there may even be a lexical ordering relative to urgency. But even need is not dominant over outcome. This means that a more urgent candidate with a better outcome could beat a needier candidate. The relation of need to outcome (and to number of lives that can be saved of those with lesser need) is structurally the same as the relation of urgency to these factors, for example, the outcome of those significantly needier than others is multiplied by a factor that is larger the greater the absolute (and hence comparative) need. Here the multiplicative factor represents the fact that the outcome will satisfy the neediest and hence satisfies demands of fairness. So one year to a 20-year-old may, morally speaking, be worth three to a 60-year-old. (If there were DMU of life years, for example beyond a certain point in life, an additional multiplicative factor could be used.) For purposes of simplicity (with allowances made for exceptions at very young ages), we may assign multiplication factors for absolute and comparative need at ten year intervals, with the youngest receiving the largest factor. (This would be represented by a step function.) If the outcome of the less needy is much greater, that person may still receive the organ. (Some might suggest that there is a significant complication in connection with multiplying the outcomes of the neediest by factors adjusted to their degree of absolute (and also comparative) need: It is not only greater comparative and absolute need per se that should lead us to give an organ. It is also the degree to which the organ can satisfy that need. Suppose we could agree that the younger are needier the younger they are (down to a certain age); they will be worse off if they die than anyone else. We multiply their absolute outcome to indicate that the outcome is going to the worst off. However, even then, the need-adjusted additional life we can offer may do little to make a better life for the worst off. Even when the outcome is significant, the needier someone is the less likely we are to ameliorate his need by much even with a significant outcome. Should the calculation reveal this, so that we then give the organ to the less needy? Or is the fact that we provide something significant, even if unsatisfying, enough? I have suggested that, when what someone needs is life, we focus on significant amounts of adequate conscious life, rather than how much of a need it satisfies. (I also continue to downplay other structural characteristics of time, e.g., completing a project may make an older person's time more valuable than time that is purely preparatory to achievement for the young. Yet I have suggested we err in the right direction by taking the modest perspective, and giving extra weight to more time simply experiencing adequate life.)

Negatively Experienced Time Waiting

In real scarcity situations, the intrinsic characteristics of time waiting (e.g., bad experiences or absence of experience) can enter into the comparison by giving some extra weight to one candidate in comparison to the better outcome or worse life prospects presented by the less-needy other candidate.

This completes our discussion of factors in conditions of true scarcity.

Priority between Factors in Temporary Scarcity

Suppose scarcity is only temporary and another organ can be found in a short time for anyone who needs it. Then the urgent should be taken first, in order of urgency, assuming they have some medically significant outcome. However, suppose it will take time to find another organ and during this time those waiting get sufficiently worse so that their prospects for a good outcome are diminished. Then we should help the *urgent^T* rather than the *neediest* only if this does not decrease the probability of a good outcome for the neediest by too much. Further, the permitted reduction in probability of a good outcome should be lower as the need is greater. Those with prospects for a very good outcome can tolerate a longer wait for another organ better since a reduction in their good prospects still leaves them with more. Therefore, in temporary scarcity good *outcome* should not have as much of an influence in determining who gets an organ relative to *need* or *urgency* as it has in real scarcity, since we do not forego it entirely if we first serve the needier or more urgent.

Time Waiting

Time waiting's intrinsic significance can be used as a tie breaker in situations of temporary scarcity. This is because it then just reduces the speed at which someone gets an organ, and may decrease somewhat the probability of a good outcome. Indeed, we could just go with waiting time, except for dealing with the most urgent cases, since the needy people and relatively good outcomes would be served in this way too, and it is easier to employ.

Priority between Factors in Uncertainty

What if we are not certain whether other organs will appear before those people not chosen die or suffer other very bad consequences? We should treat those most urgent who have the hope of some minimally significant outcome only if this has less of an effect on the chances of the neediest getting an organ than was permitted in conditions of temporary scarcity. This is because we are not certain the neediest will get an organ after all. This policy will probably still result in the deaths of some of the neediest. But at the time of choice, we cannot say for sure about any given needier person that it will be he or she who dies. On the other hand, the more urgent person has a much higher probability of dying. We may prefer to use our resources to stop the death we know to be certain rather than ensure an organ for the neediest. We do not want to conserve a resource we may not need because another one appears.

Outcome should count less against need in the situation of uncertainty than in real scarcity. This is because there is less probability that someone will die than in real scarcity, and we have some preference for the needier being saved. (This is why we attach a multiplicative factor for outcome to it.) In sum, the needier can be given more of an edge when the cost of doing this in terms of good outcomes is less, and the cost is less with uncertainty than with scarcity. (Since we may get quite good outcomes anyway.) But still, outcome counts for more against need in conditions of uncertainty than it does in situations of only temporary scarcity.

Time Waiting

In situations of uncertainty, should time waiting's intrinsic characteristics be used as a tie breaker between those equal in morally relevant respects, if we are not sure whether or not everyone will get an organ? This may be giving it too great a role in these circumstances, unless it can function as a lottery, since it can determine death.

A General Description of a Procedure in Real Scarcity

How would we summarize the components of the alternative conception we have been describing as a definite procedure *in true scarcity?* Essentially, the proposed system modifies the weight of urgency by need and gives added weight to each over outcome. However, the extra weights are not outright dominant and outcome is considered from the beginning. Because waiting time can be considered against outcome and urgency^Q, it too, can be counted from the beginning (or alternatively, giving it less role, at the end). There is, therefore, no lexical ordering.

For purposes of a procedure, it seems easiest to see this system as measuring all other values in terms of *outcome,* against which they are pitted. One very general description of an *outcome modification procedure* that captures the conceptual points we have made is

1. Add extra outcome points to the outcome of the person waiting longest;
2. Multiply the outcome points of each candidate by the multiplicative factors assigned cardinally in accord with a linear function (representing the moral weight of fairness) for need and urgency representing the weight of helping those worst off now.;
3. Total the outcome points. The candidate who has significantly more points wins.
4. If no one wins this way, we toss a coin.

SPECIFIC OUTCOME MODIFICATION PROCEDURES

What follows does not take into account urgency^Q separately from urgency^T; it assumes differences in outcome matter, and that waiting time is not a commitment factor.

Table 15-1 presents some sample scales that do reflect the 4:2:2:1 weighting for N, O, U, and W, but do not reflect diminishing marginal utility. (We need not be

Table 15.1

Need		Outcome		Urgency		Waiting Time	
Yrs. of Age	Pts.	Yrs. Expected	Pts.	Yrs.	Pts.	Yrs.	Pts.
100	1	20	10	5	0	5+	5
90	2	18	9	4.5	1	4	4
80	4	16	8	4	2	3	3
70	6	14	7	3.5	3	2	2
60	8	12	6	3	4	1	1
50	10	10	5	2.5	5	0.75	0.75
40	12	8	4	2	6	0.5	0.5
30	14	6	3	1.5	7	0.25	0.25
20	16	4	2	1	8	0	0
10	18	2	1	0.75	8.5		
0	20*	1	0.5	0.5	9		
		0–1	0.2	0.25	9.5		
				0	10		

*We can reject this bottom line, if we think the very young are not firmly enough established in life to be worth giving such great consideration.

wedded to these ratios. It is especially high for need.) The scale for need is constructed to reflect the view that relative neediness of candidates is measured by comparing how far they are from the length of life people should have. (Here the very generous age of 100 is the upper limit.) As noted above this is only one way to think about neediness (understood as how badly off someone will be overall at time of death). The intervals represent the idea that fairness dictates giving a higher multiplicative factor to someone the less she will have had overall if she dies. The intervals on this scale do not say that the 10-year-old is twice as needy as the 20-year-old. It indicates that the 10-year-old is ten years worse off or $1\frac{1}{8}$ times as badly off; hence he is given a factor two points higher. For shorthand, I will refer to the need points of A as A_n, and so forth. Let's say that significant need is some number represented by S_n and that a significant difference in the need of two rivals is some number represented by SD_n. The other factors will work the same way. It would be helpful if we defined, on each metric, what counted as significant, but I have not done this here.

Here are some sample procedures for scarce resources in general and applicable to organs if scarce:[10]

Outcome Modification Procedure A. Suppose there are two candidates, A and B, for a resource. Procedure A counts need, urgency, and outcome first, and then, if that is not determinate, considers waiting time. (Later, we shall consider a procedure that considers waiting time from the start and is, in this sense, closer to the general description I have recommended. It is simpler, I believe, to consider this alternative system first.) For need or urgency to count, both the need and urgency must be significant and the difference between the two rivals' need and urgency must be significant.

1. Need
   a. Is either A_N or B_N significant? (Is it the case that either $A_N \rightarrow S_N$ or $B_N \rightarrow S_N$?) If yes, proceed to step 1b. If not, go to step 2.
   b. Is $/ A_N - B_N /$ significant? (Is it the case that $/ A_N - B_N / > SD_N$?) If yes, proceed to step 1c. If not, go to step 2.
   c. Calculate $(A_N) (A_O)$ to yield what we will label A_{NO}. Perform the same operation for B: $(B_N) (B_O)$ to yield what we will label B_{NO}. Go to step 2.
2. Urgency
   a. Is A_U or B_U significant, that is, is $A_U \rightarrow S_U$ or $B_U \rightarrow S_U$? If yes, go to 2b. If not, and the answer to 1 was no, go to 4, otherwise go to step 3.
3. Need and Urgency
   a. If there are results from 1c and 2c add them and compare A and B's modified outcome points. That is, $A_{OU} + A_{NO} = A_O (A_U + A_N)$ labeled A_{OUN}, $B_{OU} + B_{NO} = B_O (B_U + B_N)$ labeled B_{OUN}. So, compare A_{OUN} to B_{OUN}. If there are only results from either 1c or 2c, then compare A_{OU} to B_{OU} or A_{NO} to B_{NO}.
   b. Simple version: Award the resource to whichever candidate has the highest score.
      Or

Significance requirement: If / $A_{OUN} - B_{OUN}$ / is not significant, do not award the resource yet. Proceed to step 5.

Or

Priority to the needy requirement: If the candidate with greater need has the greater score at this point, award the resource to her. Otherwise, go to step 5.

4. Waiting time (where need and urgency do not significantly differ)
   a. Optional: Is / $A_W - B_W$ / significant? If so, go to step 4b. If not, is / $A_O - B_O$ / significant? If it is, give to whomever has higher outcome. If not, go to step 6.
   b. Modify outcome points by adding the waiting time points to it.
      $$A_O + A_W = A_{OW}$$
      $$B_O + B_W = B_{OW}$$
      Go to step 4c.
   c. Is / $A_{OW} - B_{OW}$ / significant? If not, go to step 6. If it is, award the resource to the candidate whose outcome plus waiting time score is higher. If $A_{OW} > B_{OW} \rightarrow$ organ to A. If $B_{OW} > A_{OW} \rightarrow$ give to B, etc.
5. Waiting time (where need and urgency do count, but don't yield determinate results)
   a. Optional: Is / $A_W - B_W$ / significant? If so, go to step 5b. If not, proceed to step 6.
   b. Modify outcome points as in step 4b. Go to step 5c.
   c. Multiply
      $$A_{OW} \times (A_O + A_N) = A_{UNOW}$$
      $$B_{OW} \times (B_O + B_N) = B_{UNOW}$$
   d. Alternative schemes:
      d1. Whoever has the highest UNOW score from step 5c, gets the resource.
   Or
      d2. If the neediest has the highest UNOW score, the neediest gets the resource. (This is if we think the neediest should get more preference.) If not, go to step 6.
   Or
      d3. If the difference between the rivals' step 5c results is not great, go to step 6. If it is significant, award the resource to the highest score (or to the highest score if the most needy); otherwise, go to step 6.
6. Flip a coin.

Outcome Modification Procedure B. An alternative procedure uses waiting time, and the way it modifies, from the beginning. As such it more accurately represents my general description of a procedure. Here we shall outline the steps in vaguer terms.

1. Check to see if either has a significant waiting time and if the waiting-time differential is significant. If not, use the normal outcome points. If so, add the outcome points and the waiting-time points together. (The scales already reflect the different weights of the two measures.)

2. Check on significance of need and significance of need differential. If there isn't any, proceed to step 3. If there is some, multiply the figures from step 1 times the need score.

3. Check on the significance of urgency and the significance of urgency differential. If there isn't any, go to step 4. If there is some, multiply the figures from step 1 times the urgency scores.

4. Add the results from steps 2 and 3. If there aren't any, award the resource to whoever has the highest score from step 1. Otherwise (or optionally, if there is not much of a difference between step 1 scores), go to step 5. If there are results:

   Alternative A: Give to highest score.

   Alternative B: Give to the highest score only if it belongs to the neediest. Otherwise, step 5.

   Alternative C: Give to the highest score, only if there is a significant differential between the final scores.

   Alternative D: Significant differential and neediest requirements. Combination of C and B. Otherwise, step 5.

5. Flip a coin.

Another Scale for Need. As already noted, an alternative way to describe comparative neediness is simply on the basis of how much each candidate will have had at the time he dies, independent of how far each is from some length of life thought to be appropriate for any person. A scale representing this, to be substituted for the one in Table 15.1, is as follows:

Need	
Yrs. of Age	Pts.
100	1
90	10/9
80	5/4
70	10/7
60	5/3
50	2
40	5/2
30	10/3
20	5
10	10
5	20
0	100*

*We can reject this bottom line, if we think the very young are not firmly enough established in life to be worth giving such great consideration.

Outcome Modification Procedure C. An alternative incorporates the idea of the DMV of life and/or fairness. The modification required is the introduction of a function by which to multiply absolute years in accord with age to cope with different degrees of need. As noted, it may be there is no or only slight DMU (perhaps at large intervals, in a step function) at all stages of life. There may be significant DMU after a certain age only. Let us represent an extreme view, however. For example, suppose we thought that a 10-year-old should have twice as many points as a 20-year-old and a 30-year-old, half that of the 20-year-old, etc. In that case, the proper equation would be $N = y = C/2^x$ where C = the number of points given to the most needy case, for example, 20, and x would range over the natural numbers, in this case, 10 years = 1; 20 years = 2, etc. We get the need points in this way (rather than by using the scale we introduced in the first procedure exhibited in Table 15.1) and use them to multiply outcome points from the scale introduced in that first procedure. If we want the function to operate differently (perhaps less severely), then a different equation might be appropriate. For example, $y = C/1.3^x = N$. This is a continuous function, for we get different results for every number inserted for x. We could also have a step function representing DMU. Then we would get the same results for a certain range of values of x. For example, if $x \geq 10$ and ≤ 20, we assign the same value, 1, to x in $C = 20/2^x$.

Outcome Modification Procedure D. The previous procedures are applied to pairwise comparisons. But a significant alteration must be made if more than two people are up for a resource, as is usually the case. Attending only to significant differences between candidates, rather than absolute differences, may lead to (sorites-type) problems, since if we ignore insignificant differences between pairs of candidates, we may wind up ignoring truly significant differences between candidate 1 and candidate 20. (Analogously, two colors lying close together on a spectrum may not differ significantly, but there are still significant differences between those further apart. If we ignore insignificant differences and, hence, do not note absolute differences, we shall wind up missing the significant differences between those lying at further distances from each other on the spectrum.) Therefore, suppose twenty were in competition for an organ; we should omit in the previous procedures examination of significant differences in N, U, O, and W and carry out the steps, checking only for significant N, U, O, and W and taking account of absolute differences. When all the OWNU calculations are done for the twenty, then we may have a cut off line for number of points. We use a random decision procedure to select from among those above the line who do not differ significantly from each other.

CONCLUSION

These procedures have been described using the idea that some differentiation on the basis of age is morally permissible at every age. Suppose that, realistically, it would be impossible to institute procedures incorporating this view, even if it were morally correct, as public policy (more difficult than instituting a procedure that incorporates the idea of a point late in life when some differentiation is permissible.) Then a procedure, minus such general age differentiation, would not generally modify outcome by need and steps involving such modification should be omitted. Likewise, suppose that, realitically, it is impossible to get precise figures on expected outcome or urgency. Then the procedures will have to be modified to use more approximations. Still the remaining system would not give weight to urgency unless some significant outcome accompanied it, and in situations of true scarcity, it would not automatically treat the urgent, even when they had significant differential outcomes (e.g., one year). Higher outcome in the less urgent could lead us to treat them.

Further modifications to the system would be needed for situations of temporary scarcity, where the urgent with significant outcome would be treated first. Also for situations of uncertainty where urgency would be given greater weight, by for example increasing the multiplicative factor associated with it. (Only if hope were a virtue, or were an attitude that helped produce the state of affairs hoped for, should procedures based on temporary scarcity always be used. If they were used, that would mean, as noted above, treating first the urgent with at least some significant differential outcomes.)

MULTIPLE ORGAN TRANSPLANTS

Our discussion has focused on deciding which of two people should receive one organ, and we have briefly discussed deciding which of several people should receive one organ. We now deal with the choice of either assigning multiple organs to one person or assigning each of the multiples to other people. Our question is, from a moral point of view, is it permissible for one person to receive more than one organ for transplantation?

First, we must be clear about the context in which the question is posed, for this should affect the answer. If there is no scarcity in the supply of the requisite organ, nor scarcity of funds to transplant, and if there is some need for the organs and some expected benefit from them, then it is permissible for one person to receive more than one organ for transplantation. If we are in a situation of temporary scarcity, where this means that, while everyone who needs organs cannot now be served, everyone will eventually get one after some wait and without very bad side effects as a consequence of the wait, then it is morally permissible to give more than one organ to one recipient. If we are in a situation of true scarcity, where this means that some will either die or have other very bad outcomes because not everyone can be serviced, then the answer to our question becomes more difficult to formulate. (It will also be difficult if there is uncertainty as to which of the three situations I have described we might be in.) I shall consider our question in the context of *true scarcity*.

Types of Temporal Need: I

Next, we must consider that there are several different types of temporal need. First, one person might need more than one organ *at the same time,* e.g., organ cluster surgery. Under this class, there are again subdivisions. First, the multiple organs might be such that they can *only be used by anyone in unison.* That is, no one can use any of these organs on their own, and any recipient would have to use them together. In this case, it is morally permissible for one recipient to receive more than one organ. (I put to one side the issue of scarcity of funding for surgery and care, in case the funding is greater than that required for single organ transplants. I also assume outcomes can be good in such surgeries.) In a second type of temporal need, the organs at issue might be such that each could be given to other people if all are not given to the one recipient. *This is the sort of situation, i.e., in true scarcity, giving more than one organ to one recipient at one time, when each organ could be used by others individually,* that first raises what most people may see as *the crucial moral issue*: more lives could be saved (or other bad fates avoided in more lives) if organs were distributed to several people than if they all go to one person. For example, if two organs are involved, we might save two lives by giving each to two needy persons (B and C), rather than giving both to someone (A) who needs both.

But note that even if the greater number of lives could be saved, the assumption that the greater number should be saved is not always correct. It is most obviously correct when all relevant factors between the candidates are (approximately) equal. But they may not be. One person may have relevant factors that make taking care of him morally more important than saving a greater number of individual lives in part because the others are not as urgent, have already had more years of life and/or can be offered fewer years in the future, or have not been waiting as long.

Relevance to Multiple Transplants: Same-Time Decision

Consider the case of a same-time decision in which one person will live if multiple organs are transplanted, or two persons will live if each receives one organ. If all relevant factors are equal or nearly equal in each of the candidates, we should save the greater number of people. That is, in this situation, the *answer to our question would be no.* Furthermore, sometimes even if only one of the two people needing one organ has points equal to the one person needing multiple organs, the *answer is no.* This is so if the second person has significant urgency/need and outcome. But suppose that there is a significant difference between the morally relevant factors of the single person and each of the other two. For example, consider the following case in which two organs can go to A or one each to B and C. (For argument's sake, we always assume, unless otherwise noted, that a person can be transplanted now or never.) I list age (roughly corresponding to need as defined above), urgency, and expected outcome from time of transplant. To simplify, I omit waiting time.

Table 15.2

A	B	C
20 years old	60 years old	60 years old
1 month to live	mediocre quality of life	mediocre quality of life
10-year good quality outcome	normal quality life for 5 years	normal quality life for 5 years

In Table 15.2, A is more urgent, needier, and offers a better expected outcome than either B or C. In this case we may do a multiple.

Aggregation Versus Pairwise Comparison

One important philosophical issue in these types of cases is whether, in deciding what to do, we *aggregate or do pairwise comparison* of scores in a point system or other decision procedure. Aggregation would permit us to add the scores of B and C together. By contrast, pairwise comparison involves comparing A with B and then with C, one at a time. Since A has greater need and urgency than either person he confronts, supporters of pairwise comparison would give *a yes answer to our question;* indeed they would urge us to take care of the worst off person first. To them, it makes no sense to sum urgency or need of two less urgent people, since two less urgent or needy cases do not add up to one greater urgency. The idea that we would prevent two tragedies rather than one is not determinative because we should consider how big the tragedy is that we are preventing. But it may make some sense to consider the total number of life years we can produce overall by summing over many people. Further, the mere fact that we can help more people is a point in favor of distributing the life years produced rather than concentrating them in one person by doing a multiple, at least when the one person is not more urgent or needier.

Hence, even in a system which gives somewhat greater weight to need and/or urgency, we may require a lower total in aggregated outcome than in concentrated outcome to help overcome the greater need, urgency, or outcome of one other candidate.

Nevertheless, aggregation of the *greater* need or urgency of each of several persons makes sense, since fairness is thought to involve taking care of the worst off first and more unfairness is worse than less.

To be more specific about some of these matters, consider the four cases in Table 15.3, where "<" means "lesser", ">" means "greater", "U" stands for urgency, and "O" stands for outcome. Two organs can go to H or one each to J and K. To simplify my example, assume urgency varies with need, though it often does not. Also, assume we are working with a system in which need/urgency are given somewhat more weight than outcome. In Case 1, the system would often say *yes to*

Table 15.3

H	J	K
1. >U	<U	<U
>O	<O	<O
2. >U	<U	<U
<O	>O	>O
3. <U	>U	>U
>O	<O	<O
4. <U	>U	>U
<O	>O	>O

our question, if H's urgency and outcome are sufficiently greater than those of the other two, but *no* if not. For Case 2, the system would (less) often say *yes*, if H's urgency is much greater than the others', and *no* if not. For Case 3, the system often says *no*, but may say *yes*, if the single person's outcome is relatively very great. For Case 4, the system says *no*. As the number of individuals who join J and K increases, it will be harder to justify transplanting H instead.

Types of Temporal Need: II

But there is *a second type of temporal need* which may arise, again assuming a context of true scarcity. In this case, one patient, who has already received an organ at t(ime) (1) needs another organ later at t(2). (The interval of time between t(1) and t(2) may vary. To simplify I consider only cases with two organs.) Call this the *split-time* need situation. The need for the later organ may arise because the first organ failed, after working successfully for a significant period or after failing to work at all. (The issue of patient responsibility for organ failure (via neglecting to use anti-rejection drugs or from alcohol abuse) may arise more correctly when a transplant fails than when the original organ does. This is because a transplant is a second chance. If responsibility for failure should play a role in determining who gets an organ, this factor will be especially relevant to a *no* answer in split-time multiple transplant decisions. However, I will ignore this factor in this paper). Alternatively, the patient may need a totally different organ, one unrelated to his earlier need.

In both cases the following is true: (1) There is some prior investment in the person—call him E. (2) If the organ originally given was in short supply, then because of the choice at t(1) another person, F, either died or had a poor outcome because E received an organ. (3) There is one organ at issue at t(2), which can go to E or G. This means that only one other person would die or suffer some other bad outcome *now* if E gets his second organ, but if E's first organ was scarce, then if E gets two transplants, *two* people will have died or suffered some other bad outcome on account of saving E. (4) It is also true that he will have gotten two organs, when, let us suppose, his competitor at t(2) will not have had any, being a first time candidate. (5) In the split-time need situation, if the need does not arise because of the immediate failure of the first organ, the recipient may already have received some significant benefit from the transplant. This means that many split-time situations (in contrast to situations in which multiple organs must be given at one time) involve (what economists refer to as) "divisible benefits." That is, in one-time decisions, the recipient who needs multiple organs gets all or none of the benefit of transplantation; in split-time decisions, the benefit can be divided so that he or she gets some but another person gets the rest.

Sunk Cost and Years of Life

In split-time cases factors (1) (investment) and (2) (foregone benefit to another) raise the issue, much discussed by rational choice theorists, of "sunk cost." Not only has there been an investment in one person but there has been an opportunity cost, e.g., someone else who could have benefited from receiving an organ at t(1) was lost. Most experts in rational choice seem to think that attending to sunk cost is irrational when one must decide what to do next. For example, if we could produce just as good an outcome in G as in E, the claim is that we should ignore the fact that we have already both invested in E and lost F on account of it. The average person, however, is likely to feel a sense of failure—the degree of this feeling will vary depending on how significant a portion has already been received by E of the divisible benefit—if they "abandon" a project in which they have already invested and for the sake of which someone else has already been denied a benefit, to begin a new project. Though, of course, G will now also be lost if they remain committed to E, they may not feel they have failed with him, if they never tried to help him. (The sense of failure may even lead one to "throw good money after bad," for example, if the expected outcome in a patient who needs a second or sixth organ is likely to be worse than in one who has not previously received an organ.) In the real world of organ transplants, "commitment" (an ersatz variety) becomes important because statistics are kept on the outcomes only of people one has already made one's patient, not on those who have never been treated. Doctors may be driven to multiples by the desire to show a longer outcome in one person rather than shorter ones in several people, even if other reasons recommend spreading a divisible benefit.

In the particular case of doctors, attending to sunk cost and remaining truly committed may be less irrational than in other cases, at least for individual doctors in their personal relationship to individual patients. But this does not mean that we should not have a more detached individual or mechanism making decisions about distribution of organs.

My own view on dealing with split-time decisions is that at t(2) it is too late to save two lives instead of one; F is already beyond help (we assume). So we should forget about the fact that two will have died so that one may live. What about the fact that one person will receive two scarce organs, when someone else will not receive any? Here we must decide what scarce item we are really concerned about distributing: organs or life years. Suppose we compare the original recipient and his competition up for an organ at t(2), and see that the original recipient still has not had as many life years, is more urgent, and so will die sooner than the other candidate would if he does not get an organ, and he also offers a much better outcome than the new candidate. The reason we care about transplants, presumably, is because of their effects on life, not because they are intrinsically worth having for their own sake. Therefore, what is crucial, I believe, is whether someone has had or will have less or certain goods, not how many organs they will have had. This means we should not only reduce the role of sunk cost (which leads to retransplant) but also ignore whether one person will get several organs when another has had none, (which leads away from retransplanting) and just evaluate the different candidates at the time [t(2)], using whatever factors are relevant to distribution. From the point of view of a patient, this means that before being transplanted for the first time, he can be certain of gettng not another organ if he needs it, but he need not fear abandonment if things do not go well. Rather, he can expect to be treated as an equal in the competition for the next organ.

But suppose we had known ex ante (i.e., before any decisions had to be made) that E would need two organs, F would need only one, and G would need only one.

One way of viewing this situation, is that we would have been confronted once again with the *crucial moral issue*, i.e., whether to give no organs to E so that two lives could be saved instead of one.

Consider first a split-time decision with *no ex ante knowledge* at t(1) of the fact that L will need another organ five years into his expected ten year outcome, where a transplant can take place only at t(1) for L or M, and only at t(2) for L or N, (see Table 15.4). If we give the organ to L at t(1), we must consider whether L is worthy of the organ at t(2). One of the reasons *the answer here may be yes* is that it makes no sense to aggregate the need and expected outcome of M and N, as we can no longer help M if we do not help L at t(2).

If we had ex ante knowledge that the recipient of an organ would need another one later, i.e., if we know ex ante what his first outcome would really be, we should use the model for one-time decisions for split-time decisions, if we have data on the other two candidates. Then we would more often get a *no answer*—though not necessarily for the data in Table 15.4—because we could aggregate points for the two single-organ candidates, even while adding the two separate outcomes for the multiple organ recipient. Note the following modification, however: With ex ante knowledge of L's degree of need at t(2), if the data had warranted it, we might have decided to "divide the goods," giving only one organ to the potential multiple organ recipient and aiding someone else at t(2). (The point is that only five years of L's potential 10-year outcome is going to a 20-year old, his second five years is going to a 25-year-old. Hence the figure for L's need is not constant. If need were a morally relevant factor, this would matter when comparing his neediness with the neediness of the other candidates.)

Related to this, a split-time model involving ex ante knowledge should be applied to cases in which multiple organs are needed at one time *if they are not needed for an all-or-nothing outcome,* but because they enhance the outcome in terms of length of life. For example, if one organ would give five years and two organs would give ten years, this is analogous to giving an organ at t(1) for a five year outcome and a second organ at t(2) to get a second five year outcome. One could instead choose to divide the benefit, and give only one organ at the one time.[11]

Table 15.4

t(1)	t(2)
L	L
20 years old	25 years old
1 year to live	1 year to live
10-year expected outcome	5-year expected outcome
M	N
20 years old	60 years old
2 years to live	2 years to live
3-year expected outcome	3-year expected outcome

NOTES

1. It is sometimes said that in England no one over fifty-five was, for a time, eligible for dialysis. But doctors did not tell this to their patients. Rather, they told those older patients who could have been helped by dialysis that their cases were such that they could not be helped, eliding the distinction between a social decision not to help and the physical impossibility of helping. Similarly, George Annas (in "The Prostitute, the Playboy, and the Poet") claims that one can avoid the embarrassment of people dying on line while waiting for scarce organs by reminding potential transplant applicants of the side effects of the procedure and so discouraging them from applying. This will give the appearance that not many of those who need organs are dying without them. By contrast, some schemes (such as that proposed by Nicholas Rescher in "The Distribution of Exotic Life-Saving") divide the selection procedure into two steps, first finding all those who need the scarce resource at all and could be helped by it, and second, selecting from that pool. Such schemes (courageously) make it obvious that some who could be helped (if only to a small degree) will not be.

2. *Who Lives, Who Dies* (New Haven: Yale University Press, 1990).

3. In reaching this conclusion, he refers to my own earlier work, "The Choice Between People, Commonsense Morality, and Doctors," though this does not, in fact, accurately represent the final position of that article.

4. T. Starzl et al., "A Multifactorial System for Equitable Selection of Cadaver Kidney Recipients," *JAMA* 257 (1987): 3073–3075.

5. Starzl et al., "A Multifactorial System for Equitable Selection of Cadaver Kidney Recipients," p. 3073.

6. Starzl et al., "A Multifactorial System for Equitable Selection of Cadaver Kidney Recipients," p. 3075.

7. Starzl is opposed to giving weight to the antigens for other reasons as well. He argues that it can lead to fewer blacks getting organs (since their matches are poorer) and unfairly ignoring time waiting. He also argues it may result in fewer organs gathered since perfectly matched organs are sent outside a region and regional use seems to be an incentive for the harvesting of organs. His giving points to anything but a perfect match seems to be a concession to the "real world" of transplants.

8. While I have suggested that we use multiplicative factors to represent greater need, I here speak of greater maximal points in order to see how greater need could be represented in a system closely modeled on Starzl's.

9. However, it has been pointed out to me by Seana Shiffrin that it could provide lexical ordering by assigning more points to a factor than the maximum total of all the rest.

10. The working out of these procedures that embody my suggestions for the significance of different factors is totally due to Seana Shiffrin. She should not be thought to agree with my ideas, but she receives all credit for laying them out in the form of a procedure.

11. Seana Shiffrin reminded me of the enhancement case.

Bibliography

Adams, Robert M. "Existence, Self-Interest and the Problem of Evil." *Nous* 13 (March 1979): 53–65.

Anscombe, G. E. M. "Who Is Wronged?" *The Oxford Review*, no. 5 (1967), pp. 16–17.

Annas, George. "The Prostitute, the Playboy, and the Poet: Rationing Schemes for Organ Transplantation," in John Arras and Nancy Rhoden (eds.), *Ethical Issues in Modern Medicine*, 3d ed. pp. 553–557. Mountain View, Calif.: Mayfield Publishing Co., 1989.

Brock, Daniel. "Ethical Issues in Recipient Selection for Organ Transplantation," in Deborah Mathieu (ed.), *Organ Substitution Technology: Ethical, Legal, and Public Policy Issues*. Boulder, Colo.: Westview Press, 1988.

Broome, John. "Selecting People Randomly." *Ethics* 95 (October 1984): 38–55.

Bruckner, A. and Fischer, J. "Why Is Death Bad?" *Philosophical Studies* 50 (1986): 213–221.

Childress, James. "Who Shall Live When Not All Can Live?" in Ronald Munson (ed.), *Intervention and Reflection*, 3d ed., pp. 503–511. Belmont, Calif.: Wadsworth Publishing Co., 1988.

Daniels, Norman. *Am I My Parents' Keeper?* New York: Oxford University Press, 1990.

———. *Just Health Care*. New York: Cambridge University Press, 1985.

Dillard, Annie. "Teaching A Stone to Talk." In *Teaching A Stone To Talk*, pp. 67–76. New York: Harper & Row, 1982.

Dinello, Daniel. "On Killing and Letting Die." *Analysis* 31 (1971). Reprinted in Bonnie Steinbock (ed.), *Killing and Letting Die*, pp. 128–131. Englewood Cliffs, N.J.: Prentice-Hall, 1980.

Dukeminier, J. "Supplying Organs for Transplantation," 68 *Michigan Law Review* 811 (1970).

Dworkin, Ronald. *Taking Rights Seriously*. Cambridge: Harvard University Press, 1977.

Epicurus. "Letter to Menoeceus," in *Letters, Principal Doctrines & Vatican Sayings*, Greer Russell, tr. New York: Macmillan, 1964.

Feldman, Fred. "F. M. Kamm and the Mirror of Time." *Pacific Philosophical Quarterly* 71, no. 1 (March 1990): 23–27.

Foot, Philippa. "The Problem of Abortion and the Doctrine of Double Effect." In *Virtues and Vices*, pp. 19–32, Oxford: Basil Blackwell, 1978.

———. "Utilitarianism and the Virtues." *American Philosophical Association, Proceedings and Addresses* 57 (November 1983): 273–283.

Glover, Jonathan. "It Makes No Difference Whether or Not I Do It." *Proceedings of the Aristotelian Society*, Suppl. Vol. 49, 1975.

Griffin, James. *Well Being, Its Meaning, Measurement and Moral Importance*. Oxford: Oxford University Press, 1986.

Harris, John. "The Survival Lottery." *Philosophy* 50, no. 191 (January 1975): 81–87.

The Hastings Center. *Ethical, Legal and Policy Issues Pertaining to Solid Organ Procurement* (October 1985). Hastings, New York: The Hastings Center.

Kagan, Shelly. "The Additive Fallacy," reprinted in John Martin Fischer and Mark Ravizza (eds.) *Ethics: Problems & Principles*. Fort Worth, Texas: Harcourt Brace Jovanovich, 1992.

————. *The Limits of Morality*. Oxford: Oxford University Press, 1989.

Kamm, F. M. "The Choice Between People, Commonsense Morality, and Doctors." *Bioethics* (Summer 1987): 255–271.

————. *Creation and Abortion*. New York: Oxford University Press, 1992.

————. "The Doctrine of Double Effect: Theoretical and Practical Issues." *The Journal of Medicine and Philosophy* 16 (October 1991): 571–585.

————. "Equal Treatment and Equal Chances." *Philosophy and Public Affairs* (Spring 1985): 177–194.

————. "Ethics, Applied Ethics, and Applying Applied Ethics," in D. Rosenthal and F. Shehadi (eds.), *Applied Ethics and Ethical Theory*, pp. 162–187. Salt Lake City: University of Utah Press.

————. "Harming Some to Save Others." *Philosophical Studies* 57 (1989): 227–260.

————. "Killing and Letting Die: Methodology and Substance." *Pacific Philosophical Quarterly* 64 (Winter 1983): 297–312.

————. *Morality, Mortality*, Vol. II. New York: Oxford University Press, forthcoming.

————. "Non-Consequentialism, The Person-as-an-End-In-Itself, and the Significance of Status." *Philosophy and Public Affairs*, Fall 1992: 354–389.

————. "Organs for Transplantation: From Whom, To Whom." Lecture presented at the DeCamp Lecture Series, Princeton University, November 1990.

————. "The Philosopher as Insider and Outsider," *The Journal of Medicine and Philosophy* (1990): 347–374.

————. "The Report of the U.S. Task Force on Organ Transplantation: Criticisms and Alternatives." *Mt. Sinai Journal of Medicine* (June 1989): 207–220.

————. "Supererogation and Obligation." *Journal of Philosophy* 82 (March 1985): 118–38.

————. "Why Is Death Bad and Worse Than Pre-Natal Non-Existence?" *The Pacific Philosophical Quarterly* 69 (June 1988): 161–164.

Keillor, G. "The Lowliest Bush a Purple Sage Would Be." In *Happy To Be Here*, pp. 224–227. New York: Penguin Books, 1983.

Kilner, John. *Who Lives, Who Dies*. New Haven: Yale University Press, 1990.

Kornhauser, Lewis, and Lawrence Sager. "Just Lotteries." *Social Science Information* 27 (1988): 483.

Larkin, Philip. "The Old Fools." *High Windows*. London: Faber & Faber, 1974.

Lewis, C. S. *The Problem of Pain*. London: Collins, 1957.

Lucretius. *De Rerum Natura*, 2nd ed. Cyril Bailey, ed. Oxford: Oxford University Press, 1922.

McKerlie, Dennis. "Equality Between Age-Groups," *Philosophy & Public Affairs* 21, no. 3 (Summer 1993): 275–295.

Mothersill, Mary. "Death." In J. Rachels (ed.), *Moral Problems*, 1st ed., pp. 371–383, New York: Harper & Row, 1971.

Nagel, Thomas. "Death." In *Mortal Questions*, pp. 1–10. Cambridge: Cambridge University Press, 1979.

————. "Equality." In *Mortal Questions*, pp. 106–127. Cambridge: Cambridge University Press, 1979.

————. *Equality and Partiality*. New York: Oxford University Press, 1992.

————. "The Fragmentation of Value," In *Mortal Questions*, pp. 128–141. Cambridge University Press, 1979.

————. *The View from Nowhere*. New York: Oxford University Press, 1986.

————. "What Is It Like to Be a Bat?" In *Mortal Questions,* pp. 165–180. Cambridge: Cambridge University Press, 1979.

Nozick, Robert. *Anarchy, State and Utopia*. New York: Basic Books, 1974.

Otsuka, Michael. "The Paradox of Group Beneficence." *Philosophy & Public Affairs* 20, no. 2 (Spring 1991): 132–149.

Parfit, Derek. "Innumerate Ethics." *Philosophy & Public Affairs* 7, no. 4 (Summer 1978): 285–301.

————. "On Giving Priority to the Worse Off." (unpublished manuscript, 1992).

————. *Reasons and Persons*. Oxford: Oxford University Press, 1985.

Rawls, John. *A Theory of Justice*. Cambridge, Mass.: Harvard University Press, 1971.

Rescher, Nicholas. "The Distribution of Exotic Medical Lifesaving Therapy," in John Arras and Nancy Rhoden (eds.), *Ethical Issues in Modern Medicine*, 3d. ed. pp. 542–553. Mountain View, Calif.: Mayfield Publishing Co., 1989.

Sadler, M., and B. Sadler. "Transplantation and the Law: The Need for Organized Sensitivity." 57 *Georgetown Law Journal* 57 (1968–69): 5–54.

Scanlon, Thomas. "Contractualism and Utilitarianism." In A. Sen and B. Williams (eds.), *Utilitarianism and Beyond,* pp. 103–128. Cambridge: Cambridge University Press, 1982.

————. "Preference and Urgency." *Journal of Philosophy* 72, (1975): 655–669.

————. "Rawls' Theory of Justice." University of Pennsylvania Law Review 121 (1973): 1020–1069.

————. "Value, Desire and the Quality of Life." In M. Nussbaum and A. Sen (eds.), *Quality of Life*. Oxford: Oxford University Press, forthcoming.

Sen, A. "Agency and Rights," *Philosophy & Public Affairs* (Winter 1982): 3–39.

Silverstein, Harry. "The Evil of Death." *The Journal of Philosophy* 77 (July 1980): 401–423.

Singer, D. A., et al. "Ethics of Liver Transplantations with Living Donors." *New England Journal of Medicine* 321, no. 9 (1989): 620–621.

Starzl, T. E., et al. "A Multifactorial System for Equitable Selection of Cadaver Kidney Recipients." *JAMA* 257 (1987): 3073–3075.

Taurek, John. "Should the Numbers Count?" *Philosophy & Public Affairs* 6, no. 4 (Summer 1977): 293–316.

Thomson, Judith. "Some Ruminations on Rights." *Arizona Law Review* 19 (1977): 45–60.

————. *The Realm of Rights*. Cambridge, Mass.: Harvard University Press, 1990.

————. "The Trolley Problem." *Yale Law Journal* 94 (1985).

Unger, Peter. "Causing and Preventing Serious Harm," *Philosophical Studies,* 65 (1992): 227–255.

The Uniform Anatomical Gift Act. 57 *Georgia Law Journal* 5 (1968–1969), sec. 3, no. 4.

U.S. Task Force on Organ Transplantation. *Organ Transplantation: Issues and Recommendations*. U.S. Dept. of Health and Human Services, Public Health Service, Health Resources and Services Administration, Office of Organ Transplantation, Washington D.C., 1986.

Veatch, Robert. "Whole Brain, Neocortical, and Higher Brain Related Concepts of Death." In John Arras and Nancy Rhoden (eds.), *Ethical Issues in Modern Medicine*, 3d ed. pp. 148–157. Mountain View, Calif.: Mayfield Publishing Co., 1989.

Walzer, Michael. *Spheres of Justice*. New York: Basic Books, 1983.

Weller, T. *The Book of Stupid Questions*. New York: Warner Books, 1988.

Wikler, Daniel. "Equity, Efficacy, and the Point System for Transplant Recipient Selection." *Transplantation Proceedings* 21 (1991): 3437–3439.

Williams, Bernard. "The Makroupolus Case, or the Tedium of Immortality." In J. Rachels (ed.), *Moral Problems,* 1st ed. New York: Harper & Row, 1971.

Index

ACN-4536   1/17/94

R
726
K35
1993
—
V.1